THE FEDERAL BUDGET
Politics, Policy, Process

THE FEDERAL BUDGET
Politics, Policy, Process

THIRD EDITION

by Allen Schick

BROOKINGS INSTITUTION PRESS
Washington, D.C.

ABOUT BROOKINGS

The Brookings Institution is a private nonprofit organization devoted to research, education, and publication on important issues of domestic and foreign policy. Its principal purpose is to bring the highest quality independent research and analysis to bear on current and emerging policy problems. Interpretations or conclusions in Brookings publications should be understood to be solely those of the authors.

Library of Congress Cataloging-in-Publication data

Schick, Allen.
    The Federal budget : politics, policy, process / by Allen Schick.— 3rd ed.
        p.   cm.
    Summary: "Updates and expands the assessment of the long-term budgetary outlook, addressing such issues as the collapse of the congressional budgetary process and the threat posed by the termination of discretionary spending caps. Concludes with a look at how the nation's deficit will affect America now and in the future"—Provided by publisher.
    Includes bibliographical references and index.
    ISBN-13: 978-0-8157-7735-9 (pbk. : alk. paper)
    ISBN-10: 0-8157-7735-3 (pbk. : alk. paper)
    1. Budget—United States. 2. Budget process—United States. I. Title.
    HJ2051.S3424   2007
    352.4'80973—dc22   2007027758

9 8 7 6 5 4 3 2 1

The paper used in this publication meets minimum requirements of the American National Standard for Information Sciences—Permanence of Paper for Printed Library Materials: ANSI Z39.48-1992.

Typeset in Adobe Garamond

Composition by Cynthia Stock

Printed by R. R. Donnelley
Harrisonburg, Virginia

Contents

6

The Congressional Budget Process 118

7

Revenue Legislation 162

8

Authorizing Legislation 191

9

The Appropriations Process 214

10

Managing Federal Expenditures 275

11

Budgeting for the Long Term 304

BOXES

FIGURES

TABLES

EXHIBITS

Preface

When the first edition of this book was published in 1995, the federal government had just completed twenty-five consecutive years of budget deficits. To many observers, the budget predicament was hopeless. The nation's leaders and institutions seemed to lack the political will and fiscal tools to rein in spending and produce sufficient revenue to balance the books. The country's economic future was at risk—if the budget could not be balanced when the elderly were a small, stable portion of the population, how would the government meet its commitments in the twenty-first century, when an aging society would greatly add to its financial burdens?

By the time the second edition of this book was published in 2000, the federal government had begun accumulating record surpluses that, according to official projections made at the time, would enable it to pay off the public debt by the time the baby-boom generation flooded the retirement ranks. Like any other projection, those that foresaw a rosy future were likely to be wide of the mark. Projections are predicated on assumptions about future economic performance and political actions. Variances from the expected economic course affect future budget outcomes, as do decisions by Congress and the president. Only one thing is constant in federal budgeting, and that is change.

After four years of surpluses, deficits returned in fiscal year 2002, reaching a record in nominal terms of $413 billion in fiscal year 2004.

Although deficits declined in the ensuing years, they are expected to surge dramatically in a decade or so from now due to underlying demographic factors.

What accounted for the wide swings in the deficit in such a short period of time? Budgetary change is an amalgam of politics, policy, and process; all three contributed to the turnaround in the budget's fortunes and its subsequent setback. During the late twentieth century, divided political control of government tempered demands for higher spending and impeded efforts to cut taxes. Policy changes—in particular, tax increases enacted during the George H. W. Bush and Clinton presidencies—boosted federal revenue. Budget rules and procedures were reengineered in the 1990s to strengthen fiscal discipline. During the George W. Bush presidency, the enactment of large tax cuts, a significant boost in defense and homeland security spending following the 9/11 terrorist attacks, a mild recession in 2001, and other factors led to a return of the deficit. Notwithstanding the economic growth that America has experienced, without these political, policy, and procedural changes there would have been no surplus; similarly, changes in policy and political direction, coupled with diminished interest in budget discipline, allowed the surplus to disappear.

Much of the debate regarding the upcoming 2008 election season revolves around future budget policies. The budget's political importance is partly a matter of size, for the federal government collects almost $3 trillion annually—equal to approximately one-fifth of the nation's gross domestic product. The budget is also important because it is one of the principal means by which the government establishes priorities and defines programs.

Another side of the budget is less well known but no less significant. Budgeting entails complex rules and procedures that influence government policies and financial outcomes. Some rules deal with substantive policy, others with the manner in which the budget is compiled in the executive branch and voted on in Congress. This book describes how budgeting works at each stage of executive and legislative action—from preparation of the president's budget through the appropriation and expenditure of funds—and assesses the impact of budget rules on policy decisions. It explains how the budget was transformed from deficit to surplus and back to deficit, and discusses various proposals to change the rules.

The author wishes to thank Robert Keith of the Congressional Research Service and Edward Davis of the Congressional Budget Office for explaining some of the recent innovations in budgetary practice and furnishing other assistance in this new edition. On the editorial side, Starr Belsky edited the manuscript, Inge Lockwood proofread the pages, and Enid Zafran prepared the index.

ALLEN SCHICK
July 2007
Washington, D.C.

THE FEDERAL BUDGET
Politics, Policy, Process

1

Conflict and Resolution in Federal Budgeting

This book is about the politics and processes of federal budgeting and the policies that emerge from them. No discussion of budgeting can be complete unless it takes all three aspects into account. Many governmental activities combine process and politics, but budgeting differs because certain basic tasks must be completed each year. No matter how difficult the choices or how uncertain the outlook, the president must submit a budget and Congress must make appropriations. If the president or Congress decides that the time is not right to change tax policy or to act on a particular legislative proposal, either can defer action until an agreement is reached. But they cannot default on their responsibility to decide the budget. When they do, federal programs and agencies shut down for lack of funding, and the work of government comes to a halt. Yet even when shutdowns occur, most recently in 1995–96, there ultimately is an agreement between the president and Congress.

In budgeting, then, there is conflict and resolution. Politics and process have a dual role in igniting conflict and in prodding the protagonists to set aside their differences. How the conflict unfolds and how it is resolved varies from year to year, but one can distinguish two broad patterns in federal budgeting. In one, the procedures of budgeting predominate; in the other, political factors hold sway. Much of this book details the procedures by which budgetary decisions are made.

1

This world of budgeting is one of regularity and predictability, in which players know what is expected of them and behave accordingly, conflict is muted, budget decisions are made at the margins, and the status quo predominates.

There is, however, another world of budgeting that is not so strongly bound by procedure and is unpredictable and turbulent. It is a world where substantial policy changes occur, or at least big changes are sought—a world in which Democrats and Republicans, sometimes members within each party as well, war not only over incremental issues but over past decisions and commitments. It is a world clouded by threat of breakdown, and resolution often comes through summit negotiations between the president and congressional leaders. Here, the combatants write the rules and script as they go along. But like the world of budgetary order and calm, it is also a world in which there ultimately is resolution.

CONFLICT

The federal budget is an enormously complex undertaking. It entails the active participation of the president, key advisers, and many members of Congress; the efforts of thousands of staff in the executive and legislative branches; and the attention of numerous interest groups. It consists of thousands of big and small decisions, complicated rules and procedures, and debate over the composition and amount of public revenue and spending. The process is often tense and contentious because so much is at stake and so many institutions and interests are affected when budget decisions are made. The government takes in and spends about $3 trillion annually—an amount equal to approximately one-fifth of the nation's gross domestic product. The federal government is the largest source of income for millions of American households and the largest investor in physical and human capital. Managing the federal debt makes the federal government the largest participant in capital markets.

However, the budget is much more than a matter of dollars. It finances federal programs and agencies and is a vital means of establishing and pursuing national priorities. In a fundamental sense, the federal government is what it spends. Through the budget, the government assists millions of families in meeting basic expenses and provides a financial safety net for the sick, elderly, and other dependent persons. The budget invests in the country's future by paying for roads and other physical assets, as well as for education and other human improvements. It signals to allies and adversaries the role of the United States in the world, and it is a key instrument of steering economic policy and stabilizing household income.

With so much at stake, it is not surprising that budgeting is often a difficult, conflict-laden process. As big as the budget is, there is never enough money to satisfy all demands. To budget is to fight over money and the things that money buys. The conflict sprawls between the Democratic and Republican parties (and frequently within them as well) and between the legislative and executive branches. Budgeting creates strife between Congress's authorizing committees, which have jurisdiction over federal programs, and its appropriations committees, which control a large portion of federal spending, and between the committees responsible for tax legislation and those responsible for spending decisions.

As the budget has grown and become more prominent in U.S. political and economic life, the scope for conflict has expanded. Thousands of budget makers and influencers work in Washington, many on the staffs of congressional committees and executive agencies. Many others representing national corporations, trade associations, states and localities, foreign governments, and other interests mobilize to protect or expand their share of the budget's largess. The news media closely cover budget fights and issues, reporting developments in both executive suites and legislative chambers. In some years, the budget is the centerpiece of the president's agenda as well as the vehicle for enacting much of Congress's legislative output. In national politics, it is now the age of budgeting.

But as the budget has grown in size and scope, it has become less supple and more constraining. A new-millennium president who inherits a $3 trillion budget may have fewer genuine choices than did predecessors who worked with budgets that were less than $100 billion. A generation ago, in 1970, this writer collaborated on a Brookings Institution project, *Setting National Priorities,* that analyzed and explained the president's budget options and choices. The title and tone of that publication optimistically intimated that by means of the budget, the government could set priorities and policies that would make significant differences in the well-being of the United States and its citizens. In those not-so-distant years, the budget was still regarded as a malleable, empowering process; it enhanced the capacity of the government to govern. Through sound decisions, the budget could bolster economic conditions, buy cost-effective defense, humanely and efficiently allocate costs and benefits, and create a more bountiful future. Nowadays, the budget often appears to be a limiting process, imprisoned in old commitments that narrow the options available to the government. A twenty-first-century president has fewer options for Social Security than President Franklin Roosevelt had when the program was established in 1935, and fewer options for health care than President Lyndon Johnson had when Medicare and Medicaid

were enacted in 1965. In some years, the budget appears to crowd out genuine choice and forces tomorrow's opportunities to give way to yesterday's decisions.

How can this be? How can the budget be both bigger but weaker? How can it have more resources but less choice, more programs but fewer options? A full consideration of these questions would require an inquiry into the condition of American democracy in the early twenty-first century. Budgeting is not the only process that has suffered a loss in capacity—as measured by the volume of public laws, legislating by Congress has also come upon hard times. Both have been weakened by attrition in public trust and confidence, an imbalance between what Americans want from government and what they are willing to give it in political and financial support, protracted conflict over the role of government, social ills that seem irremediable through federal action, and more. Budgeting cannot be confident and efficacious when government is not.

To argue that the federal government and the machinery of budgeting are weaker than they once were is not to conclude that initiative and change are impossible. Ronald Reagan, in 1981, and Bill Clinton, in 1993, demonstrated that presidential leadership and budgetary resources are potent forces for redirecting national policies, changing tax laws, and reallocating federal money. They showed that the budget can be an instrument for change, that it need not be locked into old policies and priorities, that the opportunity to govern can be enlarged, and that the machinery of government can be deployed in pursuit of new political objectives. Both presidents exploited the rules and procedures of budgeting to alter established policies, even though the easier course would have been to accept the status quo. Each invested an enormous amount of scarce political capital in his first budget, and each stirred up vast amounts of budgetary conflict. In the end, each trimmed his objectives to get what he could, leaving other matters for future budget battles.

In budgeting, change and conflict go hand in hand. Without the latter, there would not likely be much of the former. Because 1981 and 1993 were inaugural years in which a president from one party succeeded a president from the other party, it is not surprising that change was the order of the day. In recent times, however, there have been quite a few other conflict-laden years: 1995–96, when a new Republican majority in Congress sought to revamp national priorities; 1997, when Congress and the president warred over and finally agreed on a measure to liquidate the deficit; and 1998 and 1999, when the president and Congress clashed over appropriations bills. Conflict also escalated during President George W. Bush's first term (2001–04), as the president sought and won enactment of major tax cuts, and in his second term, as the costs of military activities in Iraq and Afghanistan mounted and the expiration date of the earlier tax cuts loomed closer.

RESOLUTION

Regarding intense conflict as inevitable would miss the many years—rarer in recent times than in previous decades—when budget issues were resolved quietly, with little fanfare and with little effort to significantly alter the course of government policy. The absence and mitigation of conflict are as indigenous to budgeting as are the flare-up and enlargement of conflict. Three of the ten years during the 1990s (1991, 1992, and 1994) had calm budget seasons in which the president called for, and Congress considered, few policy changes.

Budgeting has two inherent features—one that broadens the scope of conflict and that narrows it. Conflict is expanded by friction over who should pay and who should benefit, over how the tax burden should be distributed, and over which programs should grow and which should shrink. Budgeting is an allocative process in which there never is enough money to allocate. It is also a redistributive process in which some gain and others lose—some get back more from government than they pay in taxes and others get less. It is a process of choosing among the many claims on public resources, which even in good times do not suffice to cover all demands. It is a rationing process in which the budget is resolved by excluding some claimants from its bounty. It is a process in which, expressly or indirectly, the government decides on its role and sets priorities. All these characteristics broaden the potential for conflict, not only on the large stage of American politics—between Republicans and Democrats and between the president and Congress—but also on thousands of back stages, in the bowels of government agencies when initial budgets are drawn up, in interest groups and lobbying firms where plans are made to seize a larger share of the pie, and in state and local governments, which see the federal Treasury as a vast pool of money from which they are entitled to their just share.

But there is another feature of budgeting that pulls it in the opposite direction, one that contains conflict and constrains ambition. This arises out of the characteristic mentioned in the opening paragraph, that budgets must be resolved. Containing conflict begins in the earliest stages of the process, when claimants ask for less than they want, and continues to the last stages, when combatants set aside remaining differences in order to reach agreement. Budgeting rarely is all-out war, for if it were, even the best efforts of the disputants would not bring closure.

It is not only self-denial that enables budgeting to achieve resolution. The process itself brings order and routine to budgetary demands and decisions. Budgetary procedures regulate conflict by parceling out tasks and roles, establishing expectations and deadlines for action, and limiting the scope of issues that are considered. Conflict is dampened by the routines of budgeting, the repetitive tasks that are completed with little or no change year after year, and by the patterned behavior of participants. Budget makers normally display a willingness to compromise that is often lacking when other matters are in dispute. When this accommodating disposition is lacking, as it was in 1995–96, routines break down and the process collapses.

THE TWO WORLDS OF BUDGETING

It would be facile to conclude that there are two worlds of budgeting—the political world in which conflict is pervasive and policy change is substantial and ambitious, and the procedural world in which order prevails and is tempered and incremental. In reality, politics is as much a part of the world of budget resolution as it is of budget dispute. Similarly, rules and procedures inhabit the world of budgetary conflict as well as the world of budgetary peace. Incrementalism, which is the premier strategy for containing conflict, is as much an aspect of the politics of budgeting as are the conflagrations that engulfed budgeting in the 1990s. And when there is vast conflict, the various parties must rely on the machinery of budgeting to reach agreement.

As box 1-1 details, there are indeed two worlds of budgeting—one of big ambitions and large conflict, the other of modest ambition and minor flare-ups. The first is the world of change, the other the world of status quo. In most years, there is a bit of each in federal budgeting; budgeting without incremental routines would be chaotic, and budgeting without change would be unacceptable.

▼

BOX 1-1
Conflict and Calm in Budgeting: 1993 versus 1994

In 1993 President Clinton proposed major tax and spending changes, and the Democrat-controlled Congress reluctantly went along. The following year both sides opted for a status quo budget, as health care reform dominated the agenda. The budget resolution contained reconciliation instructions in 1993 but not in 1994. Continuing resolutions were necessary in 1993 to keep the government running, but in 1994 all regular appropriations cleared by the start of the fiscal year.

1993	1994
President Clinton's budget	
Inaugural budget, released on April 8, proposed major tax increases, changes in discretionary spending, and $500 billion in net deficit reduction over five years	Status quo budget sought only minor adjustments in discretionary spending; Clinton's proposal to restructure the health care system occupied most of the congressional session
Congressional budget resolution	
Contained reconciliation instructions and was adopted before the statutory deadline for the first time since 1976	Made only minor adjustments to the president's request; adopted by the House on May 5 and by the Senate one week later
Reconciliation bill	**Health care reform**
Conference report passed the House, 218-216, on August 5; Senate passed it the following day 51-50 by Vice President Al Gore's tie-breaking vote; signed by Clinton August 10	No reconciliation bill; Senate Majority Leader George Mitchell (D-Maine) announced on September 26 that health care reform was dead for the year
Appropriations	
Only 2 of 13 regular appropriations bills completed by the start of the fiscal year; last one cleared the Senate November 10	All regular appropriations bills cleared Congress by October 1, the start of the fiscal year

In the 1992 election, Clinton talked about jobs, college education, the ability to own a home, affordable health care, and retirement with economic security. But when attention shifted to deficit reduction, Clinton, against the advice of close political advisers, altered his agenda and offered a massive package of tax increases, some spending cuts, and stimulus investments. He proposed $700 billion in gross deficit reduction over five years, slashing defense spending, making some cuts in domestic spending, imposing tax increases on high-income taxpayers and corporations, and seeking $200 billion in new spending and targeted tax relief. In the end, Clinton got most of what he asked for, but he was forced to alter his energy tax and abandon his stimulus program.

continued

▼

BOX 1-1
Continued

In 1994 Clinton's budget sought little more than to rearrange a small amount of discretionary spending. OMB Director Leon Panetta said, "The real purpose of this budget is to stay on track with what was done last year." Many in Congress shared similar sentiments. Senator Kent Conrad (D-N.Dak.) said, "The fact is [that] we had a significant package of deficit reduction last year. That tells me we ought to stay the course [this year]." A fuller explanation is that Clinton's 1993 plan barely survived, and he expended much of his political capital to get a modified version enacted. By 1994 he was weaker and did not want to engage in another round of budgetary conflict with members of his own party.

Furthermore, the budget receded to the periphery as attention centered on health care reform. Despite the pressures to release the health proposal at the beginning of his administration, Clinton waited until the 1993 reconciliation bill was enacted before unveiling the mammoth, 1,342-page overhaul. The House and Senate were fixated on health care reform throughout the 1994 session, although neither chamber voted on the plan. As did the budget in 1993, Clinton's health care plan crowded out other initiatives; not a single piece of substantive legislation was enacted before the mid-term election, which cost Democrats control of Congress.

When Congress debated the reconciliation package in 1993, Republicans, opposed to the tax increases and defense cutbacks, united against it. Clinton had to shop among his own party members to find enough votes for this major piece of legislation. While no Democrat wanted, as Senator Bob Kerrey (D-Neb.) said, "to cast the vote that brings down [Clinton's] presidency," liberals wanted additional spending for social programs, and conservatives sought smaller tax increases and more spending cuts. It took the all-out personal lobbying efforts of Clinton, Vice President Al Gore, and other administration officials to secure a bare House majority; 41 Democrats and all Republicans voted against the package. In the Senate, Mitch McConnell (R-Ky.) argued that "the only promise Bill Clinton has fulfilled is his promise of change—he has changed all of the policies that got him elected while making the middle class pay more." Six Democrats sided with all of the Republicans voting against the measure, but Vice President Gore's tie-breaking vote secured its passage.

During the 1993 appropriations process, Congress delivered on the deficit-cutting promise, but conflict delayed the bills. Eleven of the thirteen regular appropriations were unfinished by the start of the fiscal year. Three continuing resolutions later and for the first time in twenty years, Congress held discretionary spending to roughly the same level as the previous year. At the same time, Democrats reallocated spending to fund most of Clinton's earlier-reduced investment programs.

The following year, Congress cleared all of the annual appropriations bills before the start of the fiscal year—at the time, only the third such occurrence since 1948. There were numerous pressures to wrap up the bills quickly—most notably, the appropriations chairs' determination to finish on time and Clinton's desire for action on health care reform before the session ended.

2

The Evolution of Federal Budgeting

From Surplus to Deficit to Surplus

The process and politics of budgeting revolve around two main institutions of government power: the presidency and Congress. The evolution of federal budgeting has been a long contest between these two political branches for control of the purse. Their weapons have been the rules and procedures of budgeting; each has sought to impose its policies and priorities on the other by leveraging public resources to dictate how big the government should be and how the money should be spent. For more than two hundred years these institutions have vied for political power, sometimes cooperating and sometimes confronting one another. Sometimes Congress has held the advantage; other times the president has. Rarely have the two sides enjoyed budgetary parity. Instead, the dominance of one has corresponded with the weakness of the other. The struggle has led each branch to establish its own budget process, each with its own budget staff and operating rules.

The evolution has not only resulted in distinct budgetary roles for the president and Congress—it has also given the federal government two very different ways of spending public funds: one centered on annual appropriations, the other on mandatory legislation. While appropriations are the form of congressional control envisioned by the Constitution, during the second half of the twentieth century Congress and the president increasingly relied on authorizing legislation to entitle Americans to payments from the Treasury. Appropriations and entitlements take different paths through Congress and are subject to different budget rules and constraints. However, they are merged in both the presidential and congressional budgets to show total federal spending.

The rise of entitlements has been associated with another important budgetary development—prolonged deficit spending. Chronic deficits have been a recent phenomenon fueled in large part by the requirement that the government pay for entitlements regardless of its financial condition. It took a long time for Congress and the president to adjust to the fiscal realities of the "entitlement state." It was not until near the close of the twentieth century that they managed to do so, producing balanced budgets after decades of uninterrupted deficits. However, these surpluses vanished in less than a handful of years, and deficits again became the norm early in the new century.

This chapter tells the story of federal budgeting from the three vantage points mentioned thus far: the contest between the president and Congress for budgetary power, the changing composition of federal spending, and the vacillation between surpluses and deficits. The chronicle is broken into three periods, which are delineated by important milestones in federal budgeting. The first period was from 1789, when the First Congress met, until 1921. It was characterized by congressional dominance, small government, and frequent surpluses. The second period was initiated by the Budget and Accounting Act of 1921 and continued until the Congressional Budget and Impoundment Control Act of 1974. It was characterized by presidential dominance, the growth of government, the enactment of major entitlement legislation,

and frequent deficits. The most recent period, from 1974 to the present, is one in which deficits ballooned, disappeared, and then reappeared; federal spending and entitlements continued to rise; and the president and Congress repeatedly fought over budget policies. Inasmuch as the focus of this book is on current budget process, politics, and policies, the description of the first two periods is brief, while that of the current period is longer and more detailed. In discussing the contemporary period, the book is particularly concerned with why large deficits emerged in the 1980s, how they were liquidated by the end of the 1990s, why they returned early in the twenty-first century, and how budgeting has adjusted to the permanence of the entitlement state and to protracted conflict between the president and Congress.

In budgeting, the final chapter is never written. The next fiscal year is no more than 12 months away, and with it come changes in the budget's numbers and new twists and turns in the relationships of those involved with budgeting. From afar, the process may appear to repeat itself year after year, but for those locked in combat, each year brings fresh opportunities and issues. In 2001 the newly won budget surplus seemed secure; official projections showed rising surpluses through the first decade of the twenty-first century. Three years later, the government faced record deficits that exceeded $400 billion and were projected to total several trillion dollars over the next decade. The history of budgeting does not consist of promises and projections but of outcomes and experiences. Moreover, actual budgetary results rarely conform to expectations. Budgeting is full of shocks and surprises, which will forge a budgetary future that will be politically and financially different from the outlook at the start of the millennium.

LEGISLATIVE DOMINANCE: 1789–1921

The Constitution grants Congress the power to levy taxes and provides that money may be spent only pursuant to appropriations made by law. It does not specify how these powers are to be exercised, nor does it provide for a federal budget or for the president to have a significant role in the nation's financial matters (other than that of signing or vetoing bills passed by Congress). In fact, the practice of budgeting was unknown when the Constitution was written. Modern budgeting emerged in Europe during the nineteenth century and was imported into the United States early in the twentieth century.

But if budgeting was unknown, the role of Congress in deciding revenues and spending was well established. Centuries of struggle in England between Parliament and the Crown over the power of the purse culminated in the principle that the government's authority to tax and spend must be conferred by legislation. It took centuries to implant this principle in England, but by the time the American colonies were waging war for their independence, its acceptance on this side of the Atlantic was a basic tenet of limited, democratic government.

Congress's power of the purse was designed to constrain executive authority. The Constitution bars the president and federal agencies from spending money unless they have prior authorization from Congress. But it was not just the totals that Congress constrained; it also ruled over individual items of expenditure by making detailed appropriations. Exhibit 2-1, drawn from the 1799 appropriation for the Treasury Department, shows a typical line-item appropriation. Each line was a separate limitation on the specific amount permitted for a particular purpose. In some years, Congress gave spending agencies limited discretion to transfer funds among items; in others it insisted that the funds be spent exactly as appropriated.

In the early years of American government, the House Ways and Means and the Senate Finance Committees handled revenue and spending legislation, as well as other financial matters. Although the government was small, the practices devised during the formative years set precedents for congressional action during the next two centuries. From the start, the House took the initiative on both revenue (as stated in the Constitution) and spending bills; the Senate acted only after the House had completed its work. Appropriations were made one year at a time, in bills whose sole purpose was to supply money to federal agencies. Legislation was handled in separate measures; it was taken for granted that appropriations and legislation should not be combined in the same bill. Thus the First Congress passed one law creating the War Department and another law appropriating money to it. Although subsequent Congresses made appropriations in a number of separate bills, the First Congress folded all appropriations into a single bill.

While the Constitution does not prescribe any particular budgetary outcome, it was accepted that each year's spending should not exceed that year's revenues. As figure 2-1 shows, the balanced budget norm was adhered to in two-thirds of the years from 1789 through 1916. Most of the exceptions were during wartime, when a surge in federal spending led to deficits. But the deficits were small and short-lived; when the war ended, budgetary balance was restored. Deficits were also occasioned by adverse economic conditions; these, too, tended to disappear when the economy recovered.

The balanced budget norm coexisted with the notion that government should be small and limited. It was also accepted that the size

▶ EXHIBIT 2-1
Line-Item Appropriations: Eighteenth-Century Style

For compensation to the Treasurer, clerks, and persons employed in his office, five thousand eight hundred and fifty dollars.

For expenses of firewood, stationery, printing, rent, and all other contingencies in the treasurer's office, six hundred dollars. . . .

For the payment of rent for the several houses employed in the Treasury department (except the treasurer's office) two thousand seven hundred and thirty dollars and sixty-six cents.

For the expense of firewood and candles in the several offices of the Treasury department, (except the treasurer's office,) three thousand five hundred dollars.

For defraying the expense incident to the stating and printing the public accounts for the year one thousand seven hundred and ninety-nine, (including an increase of two hundred dollars in consequence of an extension of the revenue and expenditures,) one thousand two hundred dollars.

For defraying the expense incident to the removal of books and records of the Treasury department from Philadelphia to Trenton, during part of the summer of the year one thousand seven hundred and ninety-eight, including the extra expenses of the several officers, clerks and messengers in each office, four thousand four hundred dollars. . . .

For the wages of persons employed at the different branches of melting, refining, coining, carpenters, millwrights, and smiths' work, including the sum of eight hundred dollars per annum, allowed to an assistant coiner and die forger, who also oversees the execution of the iron work, seven thousand.

For the purchase of ironmongery, lead, wool, coals, stationery, office furniture, and for all other contingencies of the establishment of the mint, six thousand three hundred dollars.

Source: *United States Statutes at Large*, 5th Cong., 3d sess., March 2, 1799, chapter 25, p. 717.

(a) Line-item appropriations were common up to the twentieth century, but the degree of itemization varied from year to year. Some were even more detailed than the appropriation exhibited here.

(b) With line-item appropriations, a perennial issue facing Congress was the extent to which it should authorize spending agencies to transfer funds among the items. Inasmuch as each line is a legal limit on expenditure, these transfers could be made only with Congress's approval.

(c) As government grew, the individual items receded in importance, and Congress was impelled to lump them into broad categories. Nowadays most federal agencies have a single appropriation covering all their operating expenses.

FIGURE 2-1
Deficits and Surpluses, Fiscal Years 1789–1916

Millions of dollars

Source: *Historical Statistics of the United States: Colonial Times to 1970*, 93d Cong., 1st sess., H. Doc. 78, part 2, Y 335–38.

of government should not vary significantly from year to year and that the amounts spent during the previous year should, with only small adjustments, determine the amount appropriated for the next. In contrast to contemporary government, in which compiling the annual budget often centers on the quest for money to expand federal programs, during much of the nineteenth century the process normally involved estimating the next year's cost of activities already under way. Increases were modest and were more a reflection of territorial expansion and population growth than the drive to enlarge government. Nevertheless, federal spending was significantly higher in 1900 ($521 million) than it had been in 1800 ($11 million).

In nominal terms, federal spending quadrupled during the War of 1812, doubled during the Mexican War, and increased twentyfold

TABLE 2-1
Impact of War on Federal Spending, Selected Fiscal Years, 1811–1974

Millions of dollars

War	Prewar			Wartime peak			Postwar		
	Outlays	Fiscal year	Surplus or deficit	Outlays	Fiscal year	Surplus or deficit	Outlays	Fiscal year	Surplus or deficit
War of 1812	8	1811	6	35	1814	–24	22	1817	11
Mexican War	23	1845	7	57	1847	–31	45	1849	–14
Civil War	63	1860	–7	1,298	1865	–964	358	1867	133
Spanish-American War	366	1897	–18	605	1899	–89	521	1900	46
World War I	713	1916	48	18,493	1919	–13,363	6,358	1920	291
World War II	13,653	1941	–4,941	92,712	1945	–47,553	34,496	1947	4,018
Korean War	38,835	1949	580	76,101	1953	–6,493	68,444	1955	–2,993
Vietnam War	118,528	1964	–5,915	183,640	1969	3,242	269,359	1974	–6,135

Sources: *Historical Statistics of the United States: Colonial Times to 1970*, 93d Cong., 1st sess., H. Doc. 78, part 2, Y 335–38; and *Budget of the United States, Historical Tables, Fiscal Year 2000*, table 1.1, pp. 19–20.

during the Civil War (table 2-1). Spending receded after each war (except for Vietnam) but always remained well above prewar levels. Between wars, while its composition changed, total spending remained stable. For example, the federal government spent $358 million in fiscal 1867 (the first full fiscal year after the Civil War) and only $366 million in fiscal 1897 (the last full fiscal year before the Spanish-American War). The government typically accumulated debt during wartime, was burdened by interest payments after the war ended, and gradually undertook new spending as debt was paid off and interest charges declined. In the last decades of the nineteenth century, paydown of the public debt was financed by revenues that sufficed to cover total peacetime expenditures. With federal budgets consistently at or near balance, the public debt receded from $2.8 billion in 1866 to $1.3 billion in 1900.

Financial stability was maintained despite the lack of a presidential budget system to coordinate revenues and expenditures. As long as the government was small and its financial needs modest, a national budget was not necessary for producing acceptable outcomes. Congress managed to coordinate federal revenues and spending decisions by acting on the various bills affecting federal finances. Two related developments, however, brought this comfortable situation—coordinated outcomes without coordinated control—to a close. One was increased fragmentation in Congress; the other was the growth of federal spending and the emergence of peacetime deficits.

The first step toward fragmenting congressional action occurred as a byproduct of the Civil War, which greatly added to the cost of government and to Congress's workload. To ease the burden on the House Ways and Means and Senate Finance Committees, the House in 1865 and the Senate in 1867 separated revenue and spending jurisdictions by establishing new appropriations committees. The second step, which began in the 1870s in the House and then spread to the Senate, was the legislative committees' seizure of control over half of the appropriations bills. These committees wanted spending jurisdiction because they were dissatisfied with the tight constraints imposed by the new appropriations committees. This fragmentation of spending power led, some scholars have argued, to higher federal expenditures.

Legislative fragmentation was mirrored by decentralization in the executive branch. The president had a limited role in overseeing federal finances. Many agencies submitted spending requests directly to congressional committees, without prior review by the president. The various requests were compiled by the Treasury in an annual *Book of Estimates,* but little effort was made to coordinate spending by individual agencies or to ensure that they totaled to an acceptable amount and were in accord with national policy.

Fragmentation and the progressive rise in federal spending (which doubled in nominal terms between 1894 and 1915) led to persistent peacetime deficits. Spending exceeded revenues in 11 of the 17 years from 1894 to 1910. To battle these deficits, the government introduced a national income tax and created an executive budget process. While the income tax amendment was ratified in 1913, the budget proposal (promoted by a national commission headed by former president William Howard Taft) provoked considerable controversy. World War I erupted before Congress created an executive budget process. As a consequence of the war, federal spending soared from $726 million in 1914 to $19 billion five years later. The public debt followed a similar trend in those five years, escalating from $1 billion to $26 billion. Shortly after the war, Congress conceded that it needed strong presidential leadership to control spending. It passed the Budget and Accounting Act of 1921, which established the presidential budget system that has operated for more than 80 years. Box 2-1 lists this and other landmarks in federal budgeting.

PRESIDENTIAL DOMINANCE: 1921–74

The 1921 act did not expressly alter the manner in which Congress makes revenue and spending decisions, though the House and Senate amended their rules to return jurisdiction over all spending bills to the appropriations committees. The main change was to give the president a formal role in budgeting before Congress acts on the appropriations bills. The 1921 law requires the president to submit an annual budget to Congress and bars agencies from giving their requests directly to Congress.

The act also created the Bureau of the Budget (renamed the Office of Management and Budget [OMB] in 1970) to help the president decide the amounts to be requested. His annual budget sets forth revenue and spending recommendations that influence Congress, although it is not bound to follow them. For each element in the budget, Congress may appropriate more or less than the president requests. Similarly, it may diverge from the president's preferences on revenue legislation.

The 1921 act does not require a balanced budget, but it was predicated on the strong expectation that presidential coordination would restrain federal spending. In effect, the Budget and Accounting Act made the president an agent of congressional budget control. It was expected that because Congress would consider the president's proposals before making its own decisions, it would act in a more disciplined and coordinated manner than it had when agencies directly lobbied for additional money. With the White House holding agencies on a tight spending leash, Congress would appropriate less, thereby enabling the government to balance its books.

These expectations were borne out during the early years of presidential budgeting. The new process had immediate success in regulating federal finance. In the 1920s, taxes were

BOX 2-1
Milestones in Federal Budgeting, 1789–2006

1789 Constitution
Gives Congress the power to lay and collect taxes and to borrow money; requires appropriations by Congress before funds can be drawn from the Treasury

1802–67 Congressional Committees
House Ways and Means Committee established as standing committee in 1802; Senate Finance Committee established in 1816; House Appropriations Committee established in 1865; Senate Appropriations Committee established in 1867

1837, 1850 House and Senate Rules
House and Senate bar unauthorized appropriations

1870, 1905–06 Antideficiency Act
Requires apportionment of funds to prevent overexpenditure

1921 Budget and Accounting Act
Provides for an executive budget; establishes the Bureau of the Budget in the Treasury Department and the General Accounting Office

1939 Reorganization Plan No. 1
Transfers the Bureau of the Budget to the new Executive Office of the President and expands the bureau's role

1967 President's Commission on Budget Concepts
Adoption of the unified budget, including trust funds

1974 Congressional Budget and Impoundment Control Act
Establishes the congressional budget process, procedures for legislative review of impoundments, House and Senate Budget Committees, and the Congressional Budget Office

1980 Omnibus Reconciliation Process
Reconciliation used for the first time in the congressional budget process

1985, 1987 Gramm-Rudman-Hollings Acts
Set deficit reduction targets and created sequestration procedures

1990 Budget Enforcement Act
Establishes caps on discretionary spending, pay-as-you-go (PAYGO) rules for revenue and direct spending, and new budget rules for direct and guaranteed loans

1990 Chief Financial Officers Act
Provides for a chief financial officer in all major agencies to oversee financial management and integrate accounting and budgeting

2002–06 Expiration of BEA Rules and Return to Deficit
BEA rules expire and, after four years of surpluses (1998–2001), the deficit returns and reaches record levels in nominal terms, peaking at $413 billion in fiscal year 2004. For more than a decade, the Senate has had internal rules on PAYGO and discretionary spending caps. In 2007 the House adopted its own PAYGO rule and the Senate revised its existing PAYGO rule in a manner consistent with the House version.

FIGURE 2-2
Deficits and Surpluses, Fiscal Years 1917–74

Billions of dollars

Source: *Budget of the United States Government, Fiscal Year 2008, Historical Tables,* table 1.1, pp. 21–22.

reduced, and both expenditures and the public debt declined. These outcomes may have been partly due to the conservative mood of postwar America, but the single-minded fiscal discipline imposed by the new system was also an important factor. Throughout the 1920s, the president's eager budget controllers maintained a tight grip on agency spending, demanded efficiency, and insisted that agencies make do with either less or no more than they had the previous year.

Then came the Depression and in its wake the New Deal—a vast, permanent expansion in the scope, scale, and cost of government. At the eve of the Depression in 1929, federal spending totaled approximately 3 percent of GDP; a decade later, at the eve of World War II, it was 10 percent. Although expenditures tripled during the 1930s, revenues failed to keep pace, and the government incurred substantial deficits throughout the decade (Figure 2-2). However, World War II brought a massive inflow of revenue, as Congress converted the individual income tax into a mass tax, imposed very high rates (reaching to 91 percent of taxable income), and established a new system for withholding taxes from paychecks. These and other provisions produced a surge in revenues, which were seven times higher in 1945 than they had been five years earlier.

Following the pattern set after previous wars, Congress lowered taxes in peacetime but retained most of the additional revenue raised during the war to finance a permanent expansion of government. Congress maintained the broad-based, high-rate individual income tax, as well as the withholding system. Big government was here to stay, thanks in part to the taxes that were made politically palatable by war. Federal outlays averaged 17 percent of GDP during the 1950s, more than triple the 1930s level. The upsurge in revenue enabled the president and Congress to produce budgets that were at or near balance.

The new money transformed the president's budget role from spending controller to program planner. During the 1950s and 1960s, it became customary for the president to prepare a legislative program in tandem with the annual budget. The president used the budget to propose spending initiatives, which shaped Congress's agenda and media coverage. There was no opprobrium and little political cost for the president to ask for more, provided that his proposals were paid for out of existing revenues and not by borrowing or new taxes. Congress followed suit by authorizing and appropriating more—sometimes resisting or trimming presidential initiatives, other times providing even more than the president requested.

This was the age of the "imperial presidency," a term coined by scholars to characterize the extent to which the president dominated national policy. The budget was one of his chief tools, enabling him to formulate programs, promote spending initiatives, and preside over a new burst of governmental expansion that culminated in the Great Society legislation enacted in 1964 and 1965.

With the rise in revenue and spending as a proportion of GDP, the president increasingly used the budget to fine-tune the economy—keeping it on a high-employment, low-inflation course—by adjusting the budget to stimulate or dampen aggregate demand. The notion that the budget should balance the economy superseded the balanced budget norm. Deficits were acceptable to spur the economy to operate at full potential and to reduce unemployment. As long as the economy was booming, small deficits were seen as a prudent means of promoting national well-being.

But the Vietnam War and the growth in entitlements brought this idyllic period in national politics to an end. The war challenged presidential leadership; the growth in entitlements called into question the adequacy of existing budgetary instruments. Because the war was unpopular, Congress was reluctant to pay for it with tax increases. It did enact a small surtax in 1968, more than a year after President Lyndon Johnson had requested it and at only about half the rate he wanted. While the surtax and continued economic growth generated a small surplus in fiscal 1969, it was the last surplus the government achieved for nearly three decades.

Widespread distaste for the Vietnam War tainted attitudes toward budget deficits. Rather than considering deficit spending an appropriate means of financing military operations, many Americans regarded it as evidence of fiscal irresponsibility and of the destabilization and policy distortions brought about by the war. To make matters worse, when the war ended, federal spending did not recede as it had after previous wars, and the budget did not return to balance. In fact, there was no post–Vietnam War year in which federal spending fell below the fiscal 1966 level—there was no peace dividend.

The post-Vietnam budgetary situation differed from the pattern set in previous wars because the composition of federal spending had changed. Figure 2-3 compares the shares of federal spending accounted for by payments

FIGURE 2-3
Composition of Federal Outlays, as Percentages of Total, Fiscal Years 1940, 1960, 1980, 2000ª

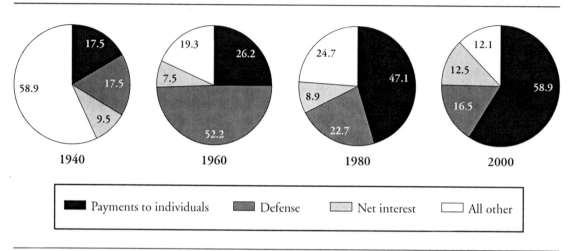

Source: *Budget of the United States Government, Historical Tables, Fiscal Year 2008,* table 6.1, pp. 118–25.
   a. Totals add to more than 100 percent because "undistributed offsetting receipts" are not included.

to individuals and other categories at 20-year intervals from 1940 to 2000. During this period there was a fundamental reversal in the ratio of mandatory to discretionary spending. Payments to individuals (mostly entitlements) were 18 percent of total spending in 1940. In 1960 the government spent almost three dollars on discretionary defense and domestic programs for every dollar of individual payments; today it spends almost two mandatory dollars for every discretionary one. There was no peace dividend after Vietnam because the increase in mandatory payments exceeded the decrease in defense spending. Between 1969 and 1973, defense expenditures declined $6 billion, but payments to individuals soared almost $50 billion. Consequently, the budget was hobbled by large, persistent deficits (see figure 2-2).

The increased share of the budget determined by eligibility rules and payment formulas weakened the president's budget capacity. As table 2-2 indicates, federal payments to individuals have continued to escalate as a pro-

portion of total outlays. In some years the president's budget has been more a means of estimating next year's cost of past commitments than of recommending the program and financial policies of government. Vietnam and Watergate, which undermined confidence in presidential leadership and soured relations with Congress, also weakened the president's budget power.

CONGRESS VERSUS THE PRESIDENT: 1974–2005

Things came to a head in the early 1970s, when President Richard Nixon warred with Congress over budget priorities and refused to spend billions of appropriated dollars. Spurred by concern that the budget was out of control and rejecting presidential leadership, Congress sought to bolster its role by creating a new legislative budget process.

Congress's quest for budgetary independence culminated in the Congressional Budget and Impoundment Control Act of 1974,

TABLE 2-2
Federal Payments to Individuals, by Selected Programs, by Decade, 1960–2000, 2005, and 2010

Program	1960	1970	1980	1990	2000	2005	2010[a]
Payments to individuals							
Total (billions of dollars)	24	65	279	586	1,055	1,490	1,950
Total constant (2000) dollars (billions)	117	249	545	733	1,055	1,340	1,532
Percent of total outlays	26	33	47	47	59	60	64
Percent of GDP	5	6	10	10	11	12	12
Outlays for selected programs (billions of dollars)							
Social Security (OASDI)[b]	11	30	117	246	406	518	677
Medicare (HI)	0	7	34	107	215	334	513
Medicaid and SCHIP	0	3	14	41	118	182	233
Food stamps	0	1	9	16	18	33	39
Family support (AFDC/TANF)[c]	2	4	7	12	18	21	21
Civil service and military retirement	2	6	27	53	78	94	118
Supplemental Security Income	0	0	6	11	30	35	42
Veterans assistance[d]	5	9	21	29	46	62	82
Recipients (millions)							
Social Security (OASDI)	15	26	36	40	45	48	53
Medicare (HI)	0	20	25	31	39	42	46
Medicaid and SCHIP	0	15	22	25	36	53	55
Food stamps	0	4	21	20	17	26	26

Sources: *Budget of the United States Government, Historical Tables, Fiscal Year 2008*, tables 11.1–11.3, pp. 194–229; *Budget of the United States Government, Analytical Perspectives, Fiscal Year 2008*, table 25.5, p. 375; *Budget of the United States Government, Analytical Perspectives, Fiscal Year 2002*, table 14.3; *Social Security Bulletin, Annual Statistical Supplement, 1998*, tables 5A4, 8E1, and 9H1.

a. Estimated.

b. Abbreviations: OASDI, Old-Age, Survivors, and Disability Insurance; HI, hospital insurance; SCHIP, State Children's Health Insurance Program; AFDC, Aid to Families with Dependent Children; TANF, Temporary Assistance for Needy Families.

c. AFDC was replaced by TANF in 1997.

d. Includes all activities covered by the Veterans Benefits and Services (700) functional category of the budget.

which Nixon signed into law less than one month before Watergate drove him from office. This measure provides for Congress to adopt an annual budget resolution that sets revenue, spending, the surplus or deficit, and debt totals, and allocates spending among 20 functional categories.

In expanding Congress's budget responsibilities, the 1974 act did not alter the formal role of the president. As before, the president submits a budget each year, and Congress has the option of accepting or rejecting his recom-mendations. But now Congress has its own budget blueprint, economic assumptions, program analyses, spending priorities, and its own ideas on how revenues and spending should be changed.

To a degree that may have been unforeseen when the 1974 act was formulated, the new system institutionalized and expanded budgetary conflict. The president and Congress have their own budgets, and neither has a formal say in what the other does. Congress has its own Congressional Budget Office (CBO)

TABLE 2-3
Era of Divided Government, 1969–2008

	White House	House	Senate
1969–76	Republican	Democrat	Democrat
1977–80	Democrat	Democrat	Democrat
1981–86	Republican	Democrat	Republican
1987–92	Republican	Democrat	Democrat
1993–94	Democrat	Democrat	Democrat
1995–2000	Democrat	Republican	Republican
2001	Republican	Republican	Republican
2001–02	Republican	Republican	Democrat
2003–06	Republican	Republican	Republican
2007–08	Republican	Democrat	Democrat

and no longer has to rely on the administration's economic projections and program estimates. Of course, the two branches have to resolve differences to make appropriations and legislate changes in revenue and entitlement laws. But first, they fight. Moreover, rather than fighting over the details, as was once common, they now fight over big policy matters—the size of government, defense versus domestic programs, how much total spending and revenues should rise from one year to the next, whether to cut the deficit by trimming expenditures or by boosting taxes, and so on.

If the new congressional budget process opened the door to conflict, a long spell of divided government and weak economic performance kept the door open for an extended period. Table 2-3 shows that in all but 11 of the years between 1969 and 2008, the White House was controlled by one party and at least one house of Congress was controlled by the other party. Not only was government divided, but Republicans and Democrats repeatedly clashed on budget policy—in particular, on the steps that should be taken to deal with chronic deficits.

The congressional budget process had the misfortune of being launched about the time the nation's economic performance deterio-

rated. The postwar economic boom, which brought large, steady gains in productivity, national income, and other measures of economic well-being, ended abruptly in 1973–74 with the first oil shock. Inflation, unemployment, and interest rates soared, productivity stagnated, and real disposable income dropped. New terms, such as stagflation and the misery index, entered economic language to describe the adverse conditions. A weak economy took its inextricable toll on the federal budget, and deficits, which had been relatively small before the establishment of the congressional budget process, became much larger.

The 1974 Budget Act did not ordain that the budget be balanced, nor did it bar Congress from adopting budget resolutions with big deficits. But the new process was enacted on the expectation that deficits would be smaller because Congress has to expressly vote on them. This expectation was thwarted by economic distress: the deficit averaged $111 billion a year (3.6 percent of GDP) during the first decade of the new process (fiscal years 1976–85) compared with $16 billion (1.4 percent of GDP) during the previous decade (fiscal years 1966–75).

Divided government and chronic deficits locked both ends of Pennsylvania Avenue in

FIGURE 2-4
Deficits and Surpluses, Fiscal Years 1975–2006ᵃ

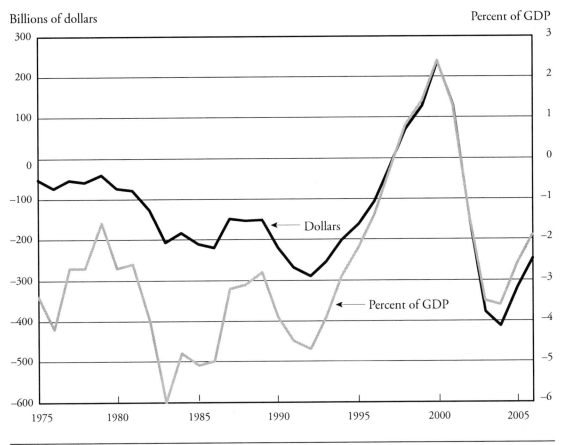

Source: *Budget of the United States Government, Historical Tables, Fiscal Year 2008,* table 1.1, pp. 21–22, and table 1.2, pp. 23–24.
 a. The transition quarter is evenly distributed between 1976 and 1977.

prolonged budgetary conflict. The president had his budget; Congress had its budget resolution. Each branch acted unilaterally, but in some manner or another, there also had to be a meeting of the minds each year. Although there was budgetary conflict, there also was budgetary resolution.

During the 1980s budgetary conflict was resolved in ways that added to the deficit. Figure 2-4 shows a striking descent into deficits during the 1980s. Before fiscal 1982 the peak

deficit was $79 billion (in fiscal 1981); in the dozen years after fiscal 1982, the smallest deficit was $150 billion (in fiscal 1987). One does not have to search far for the root causes of the deficit explosion. It resulted from policy mistakes and political impasse during the Reagan presidency. Within months after he took office in 1981, Reagan got Congress to adopt a far-reaching economic program that slashed tax rates, boosted defense spending, but only modestly cut domestic programs. Individual income tax rates were cut by 25 percent, dozens of tax breaks were added to the revenue code, and future tax rates were automatically indexed to inflation. Official estimates made at the time projected a $749 billion revenue loss over the next five years. Through the appropriations process, Congress added more than $100 billion to annual defense spending, and although it made significant cuts in domestic spending, many cutbacks were subsequently reversed.

Reagan's budget program was vigorously promoted by "supply-siders" who argued that tax cuts would stimulate the economy and thereby generate higher revenues in the future. Things did not work out this way. A recession in 1982 and budgetary stalemate between the president and Congress led to annual deficits of $200 billion—in the famous words of Reagan's budget director, David Stockman, "as far ahead as the eye can see." Congress responded to the deficit crisis by passing the Balanced Budget and Emergency Deficit Control Act of 1985, commonly referred to as Gramm-Rudman-Hollings (GRH), after the bill's principal sponsors. The act called for the progressive reduction in the deficit in each fiscal year from 1986 through 1990 and for a balanced budget in fiscal 1991. This objective was to be enforced by an automatic cancellation of budget resources if the projected deficit exceeded the target for a fiscal year by more than $10 billion. After the Supreme Court declared the original GRH law unconstitutional, Congress passed a revised version, which postponed the target year for a balanced budget to fiscal 1993.

Despite the threat of sequestration—withholding funds when deficit targets are exceeded—the actual deficit exceeded the GRH level in each fiscal year the law was in effect. Although it may have had a slight dampening effect on deficits, GRH was seriously defective. It did not require the actual deficit to be within the target, but only that the deficit projected at the start of each fiscal year be within that year's allowed level. Any increase in the deficit during the fiscal year, whether because of estimation errors, changes in economic conditions, or new policies, did not require congressional or presidential action to offset the increase. Reliance on projected rather than actual deficits led to manipulation of budget estimates, bookkeeping tricks instead of genuine savings, and much higher annual deficits than had been projected. In fact, the budget deficit was higher in GRH's last year (1990) than it had been in 1984, the year before the enactment of GRH.

Although GRH was a fiscal failure, it left an enduring imprint on budget practice. Figure 2-5 shows GRH and other legislation designed to control the deficit. In an age of divided government, it pioneered the notion that politicians should be restricted by budget rules when making revenue and spending decisions. Both the Budget and Accounting Act of 1921 and the Congressional Budget Act of 1974 authorized the president and Congress to take any budget action they deemed appropriate. In contrast, the premise of GRH was that politicians require prefixed rules barring them from making certain budget choices because they cannot be trusted to do the right thing on their own, and they certainly cannot make the hard decisions needed to discipline federal revenue and spending.

Budget Enforcement Rules

Congress and the president were beset by an impending budget crisis in 1990. The GRH target allowed a deficit of only $64 billion for fiscal 1991, but budget projections made in July 1990 indicated a deficit in excess of $230 billion—far more than could be sequestered

FIGURE 2-5
The Battle of the Budget, 1981–2006

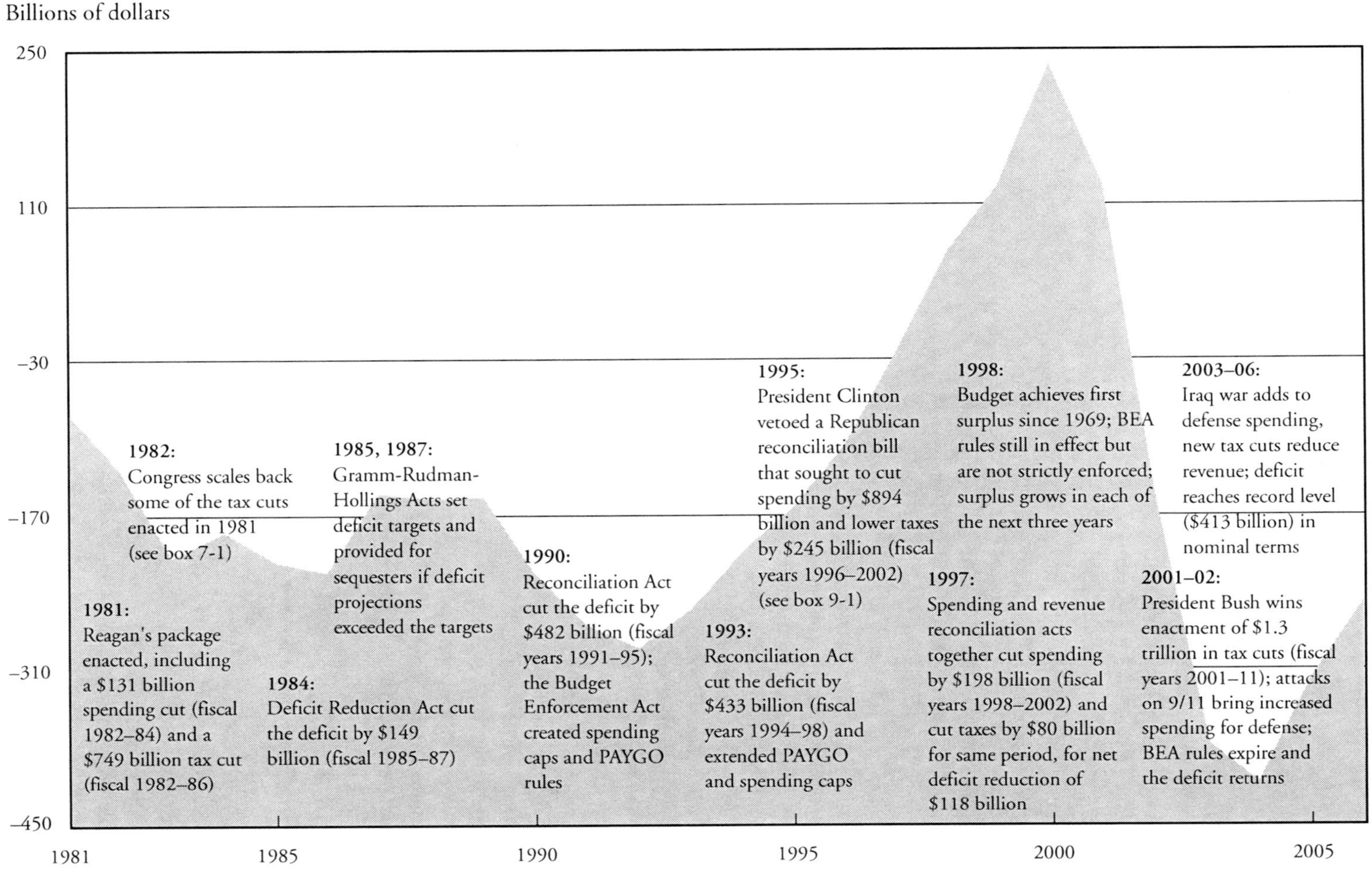

Billions of dollars
250
110
–30
–170
–310
–450
1981
1985
1990
1995
2000
2005
1981: Reagan's package enacted, including a $131 billion spending cut (fiscal 1982–84) and a $749 billion tax cut (fiscal 1982–86)
1982: Congress scales back some of the tax cuts enacted in 1981 (see box 7-1)
1984: Deficit Reduction Act cut the deficit by $149 billion (fiscal 1985–87)
1985, 1987: Gramm-Rudman-Hollings Acts set deficit targets and provided for sequesters if deficit projections exceeded the targets
1990: Reconciliation Act cut the deficit by $482 billion (fiscal years 1991–95); the Budget Enforcement Act created spending caps and PAYGO rules
1993: Reconciliation Act cut the deficit by $433 billion (fiscal years 1994–98) and extended PAYGO and spending caps
1995: President Clinton vetoed a Republican reconciliation bill that sought to cut spending by $894 billion and lower taxes by $245 billion (fiscal years 1996–2002) (see box 9-1)
1997: Spending and revenue reconciliation acts together cut spending by $198 billion (fiscal years 1998–2002) and cut taxes by $80 billion for same period, for net deficit reduction of $118 billion
1998: Budget achieves first surplus since 1969; BEA rules still in effect but are not strictly enforced; surplus grows in each of the next three years
2001–02: President Bush wins enactment of $1.3 trillion in tax cuts (fiscal years 2001–11); attacks on 9/11 bring increased spending for defense; BEA rules expire and the deficit returns
2003–06: Iraq war adds to defense spending, new tax cuts reduce revenue; deficit reaches record level ($413 billion) in nominal terms

Sources: *Congressional Quarterly Almanac, 2004;* and *Budget of the United States Government, Historical Tables, Fiscal Year 2008,* table 1.1, pp. 21–22.

BOX 2-2
Starting Down the Road to Liquidate the Deficit: The 1990 Budget Summit

The Gramm-Rudman-Hollings Act, which promised to balance the budget and calm budgetary strife between the Democrat-controlled Congress and the Republican White House, provoked renewed conflict between the warring branches in 1990. In January President George H. W. Bush insisted that he would veto any tax increase; in November he signed a big tax hike into law. When Congress convened, GRH threatened to sequester funds if statutory deficit targets were exceeded; by the end of the session, a new set of rules replaced GRH. The year started with Congress and the president taking opposite positions on virtually every budgetary issue; it ended with them making budgetary peace through tense summit negotiations that produced the Omnibus Budget Reconciliation Act of 1990

June 26
Bush announces that tax increases are necessary.

September 30
Agreement on budget summit package reached; first continuing resolution (CR) passed.

October 5
House rejects the budget resolution that would have codified the summit agreement; Congress passes second CR.

October 6
Bush vetoes the CR; partial federal government shutdown lasts three days.

October 26
The House, 228-200, and the Senate, 54-45, adopt the conference report on the budget reconciliation bill.

November 5
Bush signs the reconciliation bill.

(OBRA-90), the first and arguably most important step in turning massive deficits into surpluses.

Bush's fiscal 1991 budget relied on rosy economic assumptions to meet the GRH deficit target. But Democrats were reluctant to take the lead in proposing tax increases or additional spending cuts to realistically meet the target. As fiscal 1991 neared, revised projections estimated the deficit to be on a steep rise—$166 billion more than the figure released in Bush's budget six months earlier. With signs that the economy was slowing, Bush reluctantly agreed to negotiate with "no preconditions" concerning taxes and other budget issues. These talks initially failed to produce an agreement on how to avoid a GRH-triggered $100 billion cut in government programs. Unable to devise a tenable alternative, Bush admitted that "tax revenue increases" were necessary. This reversal handed Democrats two political victories—the president took the initiative on tax increases, and it split the Republican Party. Rank-and-file

continued

(withheld) without doing serious damage to national defense, social programs, and payments to needy households. Difficult negotiations produced an omnibus package of tax increases, some spending cuts, and new budget enforcement rules (box 2-2). The revenue and spending changes were estimated to slash $482 billion from deficits over the following

five years. But because the nation plunged into recession in 1990, about the time the final touches were being put on the package deal, the deficit continued to rise, peaking at $290 billion in fiscal 1992 (see figure 2-5).

Despite this rise in the deficit, the new rules laid out in the Budget Enforcement Act of 1990 (BEA) did not require sequestration or

▼

BOX 2-2
Continued

Republicans openly criticized Bush, calling his proposal unacceptable. Bush replied that "getting this deficit down, continuing economic expansion and employment" were more important than campaign promises.

But an agreement still had to be reached on the mix of tax increases, spending cuts, and a new deficit target. Bush and Republican members of Congress advocated a cut in the capital gains tax; Democrats insisted on an accompanying increase in the income tax rate for high-income earners. Senate Minority Leader Robert Dole (R-Kans.) reminded the factions, "If we don't get a budget agreement, we're in real trouble. I mean everybody—Congress, the president. We just have to get it done." On the eve of the new fiscal year—the most important deadline in federal budgeting—negotiators announced that a deal had been struck.

When a budget resolution adopting the summit agreement was brought before the House, conservative Republicans and liberal Democrats who had been, as Representative Tom DeLay (R-Tex.) quipped, locked out of the "fourth branch of government—the summit," joined to defeat it 179–254. To avoid a government shutdown, Congress passed a continuing resolution. An outraged Bush vetoed the measure to "put pressure on Congress." The president's veto tactics were effective—government offices closed and Congress was forced to act.

After passing a budget resolution, Congress cleared, and Bush signed, a reconciliation bill in three weeks—a task that usually consumes months. An examination of the roll call shows how far the bill had moved toward the Democratic position. In the House only 47 Republicans supported the package while 126 voted against it; 181 Democrats voted for it while 74 voted against. At the signing, Bush called it "a compromise that merits enactment." The centerpiece of OBRA-90 was a combination of revenue and spending changes projected to reduce the deficit by an unprecedented $482 billion over five years. The reconciliation act also set five-year discretionary spending caps and established PAYGO rules but allowed the deficit to grow as long as Congress did not explicitly increase it. Yet this new process tightened the purse strings and set the budget on a path that led to a surplus eight years later.

The road to OBRA took a political toll. Bush suffered the most: in a single year he had abandoned his campaign promises of "no new taxes" and lower capital gains taxes, alienated the conservative wing in his party, and scarred relations with Democrats. In the end Bush paid the ultimate political price: two years after signing OBRA, he was defeated for reelection.

any other response if the deficit exceeded targeted levels. One of the lessons Congress and the president derived from the failure of GRH was that it is futile to set fixed annual deficit limits that cannot be adjusted for changes in economic conditions or for reestimates of program expenditures. Fixed limits can be overtaken and rendered unworkable by unforeseen developments, such as the 1990–91 recession. Political leaders came to understand that they must control the revenue raised and the money spent in order to contain the deficit. In line with this reasoning, BEA established a new deficit control process that distinguishes between discretionary spending, controlled by annual appropriations, and direct spending, controlled by substantive legislation. The BEA rules were initially effective only for fiscal years 1991 through 1995, but they were subsequently extended through fiscal 1998 and then again through fiscal 2002, when they expired. In view of the political attractiveness of these statutory controls, they may be reestablished; internal congressional rules that augmented the BEA rules also have been renewed from time to time, most recently when the Democrats regained control of Congress in 2007.

The BEA rules were not complicated, but implementing them entailed complex budget calculations and procedures. BEA had three basic rules: adjustable deficit/surplus targets, discretionary spending caps, and pay-as-you-go (PAYGO) rules for revenues and direct spending. Although BEA was devised to deal with deficits, the rules also pertained to years in which the budget has a surplus. These rules are assessed in chapter 4.

Budgeting during the Clinton Era

Bill Clinton campaigned for president in 1992 by emphasizing the need to rebuild the economy and remedy social problems. Nevertheless, shortly after taking office, Clinton put deficit reduction at the top of his agenda, giving it priority over health care reform, one of his main campaign promises. The package of tax increases and spending cuts that Clinton signed in August 1993 had short-term political costs but brought the president longer-term political gains. It enabled Clinton to wrest budget leadership from congressional Republicans and to preside over a truly extraordinary turnaround in the condition of the federal budget. In fact, Clinton had little to do with some of the main factors that transformed the budget from deficit to surplus, but one cannot fault him for taking credit for the

budgetary improvement that occurred on his watch. After all, he would have been blamed if the nation's fiscal condition had deteriorated while he was in office.

Clinton's initial budget moves did not bring immediate political gains because the deficit remained high from 1993 through 1995 (though it was lower than it had been) and because the president shifted political attention to his controversial universal health insurance plan. That plan preoccupied Washington from the time it was introduced in the fall of 1993 until its final death throes in the summer of 1994; its failure set the stage for the Republican capture of both the House and Senate in the 1994 midterm elections. Republicans controlled Congress for the first time in four decades and confronted Clinton by passing a budget measure that would have slashed taxes and benefit programs. When Clinton vetoed that bill, Republicans confronted him on annual appropriations, setting the stage for two partial shutdowns of the federal government that revitalized the Clinton presidency and profoundly affected recent budget history.

Historians will debate who was to blame for the shutdown—Clinton, who vetoed a measure that would have kept government offices open, or congressional Republicans, who wanted to force major budget changes on a recalcitrant president. But there can be no doubt that Republicans were blamed in the court of public opinion. Clinton's poll ratings soared and stayed high through subsequent budget battles, while Republicans lost House seats in both the 1996 and 1998 elections and Speaker Newt Gingrich (R-Ga.), the architect of the Republican takeover of the House and of their budget war with Clinton, resigned from Congress.

As Clinton's political fortunes soared and those of congressional Republicans foundered, there were annual budget battles between the president and Congress. The 1996 battle ended with Clinton stealing one of the Republicans' favorite campaign issues by leading the charge for welfare reform. In 1997 it ended by Clinton taking away the Republican claim that they were the only party that could balance the budget by negotiating an agreement that projected an end to deficits in 2002. In both 1996 and 1997, Clinton forced Congress to appropriate billions of dollars more for his priorities than Republican leaders wanted. Much the same occurred weeks before the midterm elections in 1998, when he got Republicans to agree to an omnibus appropriations bill that added billions for his programs. In this case, Republicans obtained more money for their priorities, but they were blamed for overspending on pork while Clinton got accolades for addressing the country's social needs. To top off his triumphs, the budget was balanced in 1998, four years earlier than had been projected in the 1997 budget deal, giving Clinton bragging rights on an extraordinary feat.

Clinton scored yet another achievement in 1999 when he ignored the discretionary spending caps and forced congressional Republicans to appropriate approximately $30 billion more than the caps allowed. Clinton once again got credit for spending on national priorities, such as education, while Republicans were blamed for an assortment of budget tricks that they had to use to fit the spending under the caps. What enabled Clinton to achieve victory was not only his political skills but a cooperative economy, which allowed him to spend more while maintaining a budget surplus. What also helped Clinton's cause was that he got away with vetoing a Republican-passed tax cut, despite receipts being at an all-time high relative to gross domestic product.

HOW THE BUDGET WAS BALANCED AND UNBALANCED

Liquidating the deficit ranks as one of the supreme budgetary accomplishments in American history. The return of deficits, only four years after they had vanished, also ranks as one of the great turnarounds in American budgetary history.

In explaining how the deficit was liquidated and why it returned, one must examine the performance of the economy, changes in tax laws, trends in defense spending, and the extent to which politicians have been constrained by budget rules. These are the key drivers of contemporary aggregate budget outcomes. As table 2-4 shows, all four of these drivers contributed to liquidation of the deficit in the 1990s and its reappearance in the next decade. The fact that all four factors reversed direction at the same time accounts for the extraordinarily wide swings in budget outcomes. Each of these is reviewed in the paragraphs that follow.

Economic Conditions

Every budget is hostage to economic performance. Congress and the president cannot balance the budget when national output is declining and unemployment is soaring. Budget receipts are highly sensitive to changes in economic conditions; spending is less sensitive, but even a small shortfall in economic performance can have a big budgetary impact. CBO has estimated that if the annual real growth rate over the next decade were just one-tenth of a percentage point less than it has assumed, the fiscal 2016 budget deficit would be $60 billion greater than current projections.

When the deficit peaked in 1992, the United States was emerging from the recession that occurred at the start of the decade. When

TABLE 2-4
Main Drivers of Aggregate Outcomes in Budgeting during the Clinton Presidency and George W. Bush Presidency (First Term)

Driver	Clinton presidency: 1993–2000	Bush presidency (first term): 2001–04
Economic conditions	Real GDP grew each year of the Clinton presidency; when he left office, it was more than one-third higher than when he entered. However, the economy weakened in the final months of his term.	Growth was sluggish early in the George W. Bush presidency, and the economy went through a brief recession (three quarters of negative growth in 2001) but recovered in subsequent years.
Tax policy	Clinton began his presidency with a tax increase; budget revenues also were boosted by the 1990 tax increase signed by the first President Bush.	Bush began his term with large tax cuts. Additional large tax cuts were enacted in 2003.
National defense	The 1990s began with the fall of the Berlin Wall and the end of the Cold War. Defense spending was stable in nominal terms; real defense spending declined.	The twenty-first century began with the 9/11 terrorist attacks and the wars in Iraq and Afghanistan. Real defense spending rose significantly.
Budget discipline	The 1990s began with the enactment of budget enforcement rules that constrained spending. Compliance with these rules weakened late in the Clinton presidency, as the arrival of budget surpluses spurred Congress to boost spending.	Budget enforcement rules generally were set aside and were allowed to expire in 2002. All categories of spending (defense, nondefense discretionary, and mandatory) rose significantly.

the budget was balanced in 1998, the economy was completing the seventh consecutive year of growth, during which 13 million jobs were added and inflation averaged less than 3 percent. The budget benefited from this economic success: revenues escalated as corporate profits and personal incomes rose, spending dropped as welfare rolls declined, the crisis in the banking sector was resolved, and inflation in the health care sector moderated.

But economic good times alone do not account for the budget's unexpected turnaround. Measured in terms of growth rates, the eight consecutive years of expansion during the 1980s (from the end of the Reagan-era recession in 1982 to the onset of the Bush-era recession in 1990) outperformed the boom of

the 1990s, as table 2-5 shows. Real growth averaged 4.0 percent a year during the 1980s' expansion but only 3.7 percent during the 1990s' boom. The two expansions were structured differently, which may partly explain their different revenue impacts. The 1980s' growth began at a high rate and then tapered off; the 1990s' expansion began with low growth that accelerated as the expansion continued. More civilian jobs were added in the 1990s, and the unemployment rate was lower. A fair comparison of the two decades would have to take into account the fact that the boom of the 1980s followed a decade of "stagflation," while the 1990s' expansion followed a long period of growth that was briefly interrupted by the 1990–91 recession.

TABLE 2-5
Comparison of Economic Performance, 1983–90 and 1992–99,
by Selected Indicators

Economic indicator	1983–90	1992–99
Average real GDP growth rate[a]	4.0	3.6
Average annual civilian unemployment rate[b]	6.7	5.6
Total civilian jobs added (millions)	18.0	15.0
Cumulative percentage increase in real per capita disposable income[a]	20.5	14.5
Average annual consumer price index[b,c]	3.9	2.6
Average ten-year Treasury note rate[b]	9.5	6.3
Cumulative percentage increase in productivity[d]	12.5	13.9

Sources: *Economic Report of the President,* February 2000; Bureau of Economic Analysis; Bureau of Labor Statistics.
    a. Based on chained 1996 dollars.
    b. Calendar year average.
    c. For all urban consumers.
    d. Output per hour of all persons in business sector.

Revenue Policies

Although the surplus would not have emerged in the 1990s without a cooperative economy, it also would not have occurred if budget makers had repeated the policy mistakes of the 1980s. Deficits did reemerge after 2000 because of policy changes, not just because of adverse economic conditions. Differences between the revenue and spending paths taken during the two decades led to very different budgetary outcomes.

The sharpest contrast between the two decades was in revenue policies. In the 1990s, Congress passed and the president signed two major tax increases; in the next decade, the president and Congress produced two major tax cuts. The 1990s began with a deficit reduction package that combined an estimated $180 billion in revenue increases (over the 1991–95 period) with about $300 billion in spending cutbacks (including lower interest payments). This was followed by another deficit reduction package in 1993, during the first year of the Clinton presidency, that was projected to boost federal revenues by approx-

imately $240 billion over five years. It is important to note that these amounts were projections made at the time the deficit reduction packages were enacted, and that they were derived from the baseline methodology described in chapter 4. Actual revenue and spending changes certainly deviated from these projections.

George W. Bush launched his presidency in 2001 with a $1.3 trillion tax cut (over 11 years) and obtained an additional $350 billion tax cut (also over 11 years) in 2003. The actual size of these revenue losses was probably understated because of "sunset" provisions that made some tax cuts appear to be temporary. (See chapter 7 for a discussion of sunset provisions in tax legislation.) There is no doubt, however, that the marked shifts in tax policy first tilted the budget to surplus and then back to deficit.

The changes in revenue policy were accentuated by the swings in economic conditions. The tax increases of the 1990s were followed by an economic boom that enriched federal revenues; the tax cuts of the new century

FIGURE 2-6
Year-to-Year Change in Federal Revenues, Fiscal Years 1993–2006

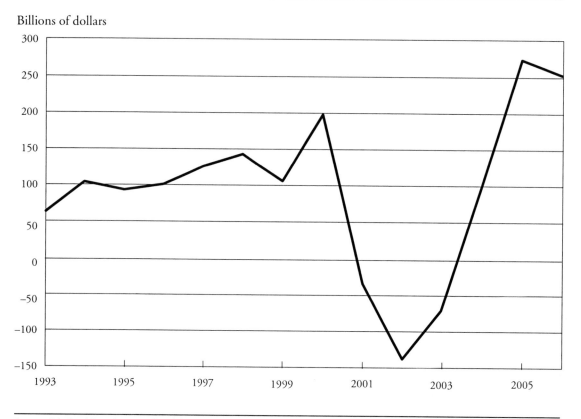

Billions of dollars

Sources: Calculated from data in *Budget of the United States Government, Historical Tables, Fiscal Year 2008*, table 1.1, pp. 21–22.

occurred during a time when revenues were adversely affected by economic weakness. During the Clinton years, total revenues climbed from 18 percent of GDP to more than 20 percent. By 2004, however, they had receded to a little more than 16 percent of GDP. While these shifts may not appear to be large, they are truly gargantuan, for in today's economy, every percentage point change relative to GDP amounts to more than $100 billion. Figure 2-6 depicts the combined economic and policy impact in terms of the year-to-year change in federal revenues. The annual revenue gains during the 1993–2000

period were remarkable; so too were the annual revenue declines that followed.

Defense Spending
The 1990s began with the collapse of the Soviet empire and the end of the Cold War; the next decade began with the September 11 terrorist attacks on the United States and the war in Iraq. Through most of the 1990s, defense spending, which had leveled off during the second half of the 1980s, receded both in real terms and as a proportion of total budget outlays. Figure 2-7 shows that real defense

FIGURE 2-7
Trends in Real Defense and Nondefense Discretionary Spending, Fiscal Years 1989–2006

Billions of constant FY2000 dollars

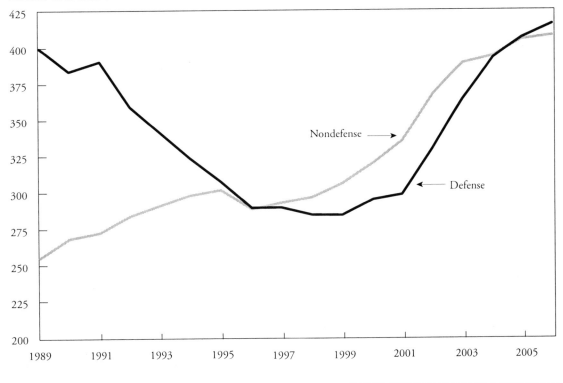

Sources: *Budget of the United States Government, Historical Tables, Fiscal Year 2008,* table 8.2, p. 134.

outlays peaked at almost $400 billion in 1989, but were less than $285 billion a decade later. Real defense outlays then reversed course and exceeded $400 billion in fiscal 2005. Defense's share of total outlays dropped from 28 percent (1987) to 16 percent (1999) and subsequently regained some of its lost budget share, rising to 20 percent of total outlays in 2005.

Perhaps the most extraordinary feature of the ups and downs in defense spending is that they were not in synch with shifts in tax policy. Until the 1990s, changes in income taxes generally corresponded to trends in defense spending. Income tax rates were boosted in

wartime and lowered after the war. If this pattern had prevailed in recent times, income tax rates would have declined in the 1990s and increased in the next decade. In fact, the highest tax rate on individual income was 28 percent in 1990, 39.6 percent at the end of the decade, and 35 percent in 2004. The most plausible explanation of this anomaly is that the record deficits in the early 1990s heightened concern about the government's financial condition, while the rapidly escalating surpluses in 1998-2001 desensitized public opinion to deficit spending. There is a lag between the emergence of a large deficit and the response in public opinion. In the early 1990s, respondents in public opinion polls rated the deficit among the country's leading problems, and politicians responded by increasing taxes despite the fact that the threat to the national economy had abated. The situation was exactly the opposite early in the twenty-first century, as public anxiety about the deficit waned, and the president pushed tax cuts through Congress despite the new threat to national security. This explanation suggests that if high deficits persist in the years ahead, tax rates will move upward.

Budget Discipline

Shifts in public opinion impact the budget by weakening or strengthening fiscal discipline in the White House and Congress. The 1990s began with the Budget Enforcement Act (BEA), which set annual limits on discretionary spending and established a PAYGO rule requiring legislated changes in entitlement or revenue laws that increase the deficit to be offset by cuts in other mandatory spending or by revenue increases. It is highly probable that even in the absence of BEA rules, big deficits would have deterred Congress and the president from establishing new entitlements and impelled them to seek savings in old ones. Yet BEA did make a difference in some years by fortifying politicians who wanted to constrain the incessant rise in federal spending with rules and resolve to resist new demands on the budget.

BEA (which is reviewed in chapter 4) was in effect during fiscal years 1991 through 2002. Its impact on discretionary spending varied during this 12-year period. It did not constrain domestic spending at the outset because the appropriations committees obtained a large, upfront increase in exchange for accepting the caps. It was quite effective through most of the

Clinton presidency, for as Figure 2-7 shows, real discretionary domestic spending was lower in 1998 than it had been in 1994. By 2003, however, it was 30 percent higher, as the arrival of large surpluses undermined budget discipline and unleashed spending demands in the White House and Congress. Most of this increase occurred during George W. Bush's first term, demonstrating that a conservative Republican can outspend a liberal Democrat when budget sentiments change. In sum, the budget rules worked, but only after the caps had been set at a high level and before the surpluses loosened budgetary discipline.

The impact of the four drivers discussed in this section is summarized in table 2-6, which draws on CBO data to show how the $5.6 trillion surplus projected for the next 10 years in 2001 was transformed into a multitrillion dollar deficit projection just a few years later. Some observers regard this extraordinary swing as evidence that budget projections are unreliable; a more important lesson is that the budget is affected by external conditions and policy choices. The economy took a toll, but most of the evaporation of the surplus was due to decisions by the president and Congress.

IS SELF-CORRECTION ENOUGH?

The shift from large deficits to large surpluses and back to large deficits suggests that budgeting is inherently a self-correcting process in which political pressure, either to avoid blame for unsatisfactory outcomes or to do the right thing, restores equilibrium. Self-correction involves not only policy changes in revenue and spending but also legislative and procedural changes, such as the Budget Enforcement Act, to rebalance fiscal outcomes. The self-correction hypothesis leads one to be wary of fundamental changes in budgeting that would strip elected majorities of power to

TABLE 2-6
What Happened to the Projected Budget Surplus?[a]

Billions of dollars

Factors	2002	2003	2004	2005	2006	2007	2008	2009	2010	2011	2002–2011
CBO projected surplus (January 2001)	313	369	397	433	505	573	635	710	796	889	5,609
Lower projected revenue											
Enacted tax cuts	−75	−179	−265	−212	−178	−166	−167	−166	−180	−110	−1,698
Revenue reestimates	−308	−381	−308	−301	−299	−292	−280	−279	−285	−276	−3,009
Higher projected outlays											
Higher appropriations	50	120	171	188	151	138	137	140	144	148	1,388
Enacted increases in mandatory spending	21	51	49	49	69	73	79	84	86	87	649
Outlay reestimates	25	15	−3	−10	−20	−25	−40	−50	−64	−58	−230
Net interest	−9	−10	19	61	103	189	247	299	354	406	2,679
Total impact on surplus	−471	−737	−809	−801	−800	−834	−870	−918	−986	−967	−8,193
CBO projected deficit (January 2005)	−158	−378	−412	−368	−295	−261	−235	−207	−189	−80	−2,583

Source: Congressional Budget Office (unpublished database).

a. Negative revenue figures and positive outlay figures reduce the surplus projections.

work their political will. Nevertheless, it must also be acknowledged that self-correction is flawed and costly and that modifications to various features of budgeting may improve outcomes or reduce political friction.

At times budgeting seems to be anything but regulated and self-correcting. Such was the case throughout the 1980s and the early 1990s, when federal spending annually exceeded revenues by hundreds of billions of dollars. The deficit appeared to be so intractable that virtually all observers (this author included) saw little prospect that the budget could be brought back into balance. But it was, and when the previous edition of this book was completed, Washington politicians were fighting over surpluses that were projected to exceed $3 trillion during the first decade of the new millennium. Policy mistakes that spawned high deficits were followed by policy corrections that restored budgetary

balance and then by new policy mistakes that produced record deficits early in the new millennium. These will not be the final shifts in the budget's fortunes. In budgeting, self-correction works in both directions, liquidating both big deficits and big surpluses. Politicians act when the deficit is perceived to be too high and spend more or tax less when the surplus seems too large.

These adjustments are neither automatic nor painless. They do not follow a set course, and changes in policy or in economic conditions can slow or accelerate them. The path to self-correction is lined with tricky turns, and neither the timing of the adjustment nor the manner in which it is accomplished can be foretold. Consider the 1990s, a decade that began and ended with divided government. Early in the decade, when the deficit approached $300 billion, budget pundits blamed divided government for the sorry outcome. Democrats and Republicans, the explanation ran, prefer to point the finger of blame at one another rather than make the hard choices to stanch the red ink. But at the decade's end, when surpluses emerged, experts credited divided government for the turn-around, explaining that it blocked both Republicans' attempts to trim taxes and Democrats' proposals to boost spending.

By all accounts, divisions between the two political parties have been a critical feature of recent American political history, but the political incentives that drive elected officials to abhor both oversized deficits and burgeoning surpluses ultimately prevail, regardless of the party lineup in Washington. Federal taxes were raised in 1990 with a Republican in the White House and the Democrats in control of Congress; they were raised again in 1993 when Democrats ran both political branches. Why were taxes raised? The answers differ slightly for the two presidents who signed the revenue increases into law. Congressional Democrats and budget aides pressured George Bush, who knew that taxes had to be raised to avoid sequestration. Clinton took the initiative in proposing tax increases; he perceived that without action to reduce the deficit, chronic deficits would hobble his presidency. Though their motives differed, both presidents put the budget on a self-correcting course.

Self-correction does not mean that revenues and spending are stable in real or nominal terms or relative to the gross domestic product. These aggregates escalated steeply during the past sixty years; it is highly unlikely that they will ever recede to pre–New Deal or pre–World War II levels, or even to the levels experienced during the 1950s. The size of government reflects political judgments on the programs Americans want and are willing to pay for. Self-correction refers to the balance between revenue and spending, not to the absolute or relative size of government. The size of government is a political question decided by democratically elected leaders, not by preset limits on revenues or expenditures.

Some observers argue that the steep rise in revenue and spending is due to a built-in bias in democratic politics and that the size of government has expanded because the benefits of spending are concentrated among a relatively small number of recipients while the costs are dispersed among the taxpaying population. Beneficiaries therefore have a much stronger incentive to campaign for higher spending than taxpayers have to mobilize against higher taxes. But if budgeting is so markedly skewed in favor of higher spending, why is federal spending a significantly smaller share of the U.S. economy in the first decade of the twenty-first century than it was two decades earlier? And why is total government spending a much smaller share of GDP in the United States than in virtually all other developed countries? It is a mistake to assume there are no political counterpressures against government spending and taxation. If there were none, politicians would easily disable or evade constitutional or statutory restrictions on their power to tax and spend.

In budgeting, rules are important because they make it easier or harder for politicians to take corrective action. Most of the rule changes made in the congressional budget process since it was inaugurated in 1975 have encouraged self-correction. These include lengthening the time frame of budget resolutions, the reconciliation process, discretionary spending caps, PAYGO limits on revenue and direct spending legislation, and the use of baselines to score budget actions. But not all reforms have succeeded; the abortive Gramm-Rudman-Hollings Act provides ample evidence that politicians sometimes substitute bookkeeping tricks for genuine adjustment.

Self-correction can be painful, especially when it is necessitated by policy mistakes that have destabilized the budget. The turnaround from deficit to surplus in the 1990s took two decades and countless budget battles between the president and Congress, as well as within the legislative branch. Looking back at this protracted struggle leads one to wonder whether changes in the machinery of budgeting and the behavior of participants might ease the process, block serious policy mistakes, reduce friction and pain, and accelerate correction. Correcting from deficit to surplus is a fractious process that leaves few combatants unbloodied. Political trust and capacity take a beating, as does the budget process itself. Why go through years of deficits and conflict that could be averted by preventing the emergence of big deficits in the first place? More to the point, why not implement stronger budget controls and thereby forestall the accumulation of trillions of dollars in public debt?

There are other signs of the toll the budget battles have taken. Since the early 1980s, legislative debate and program policies have been decided predominantly in terms of budgetary impact rather than substance. Budgetary friction has disabled much of the authorizations process in Congress, leading it to cram major legislative actions into omnibus budget reconciliation and appropriations bills. In recent decades, budgeting has become a game of political brinksmanship, with key disputes resolved in last-minute summit negotiations between the president and congressional leaders. Such negotiations have undermined the normal committee process in Congress. Provisions have frequently been enacted in omnibus bills without prior legislative consideration. The finger pointing by the parties and the lies and gimmicks sometimes used to make budgetary peace have taken a heavy toll, such as diminished public trust and confidence in national political institutions. The scars that decades of budgetary warfare have left tempt one to conclude that there must be a better way.

BALANCED BUDGET AMENDMENT

Budgeting is an adaptive process that reinvents itself in response to changes in financial and political conditions. But the adjustment process is fractious and painful. This section examines proposals to require a balanced budget.

During the high-deficit era in the 1980s and 1990s, repeated demands were made for a constitutional amendment requiring a balanced budget. In 1995 the House approved a balanced budget amendment by 300-132, but the Senate fell one vote short of the two-thirds majority that is needed for constitutional amendments. (The text of that amendment is shown in exhibit 2-2). When the budget was balanced, demands for constitutional change abated, but efforts to amend the Constitution reemerged when deficits returned. Yet the best time to act on a balanced budget amendment may be when the budget has a surplus and dire measures are not needed rather than when deficits are rampant and balance appears to be unattainable.

Balanced budget amendments come in several forms. Some would merely require a planned balance at the time budget decisions were made; others would go further and require an actual balance. Most versions would waive the balance requirement during wartime or by a supermajority (such as a three-fifths) vote in the House and Senate. Rather than consider textual differences, the discussion here focuses on two overriding questions: Do inadequacies in self-correction justify a constitutional restriction? What would be the likely impact of a balanced budget rule on budget procedures and outcomes?

▶ **EXHIBIT 2-2**
Proposed Constitutional Amendment to Require a Balanced Budget

SECTION 1. Total outlays for any fiscal year shall not exceed total receipts for that fiscal year, unless three-fifths of the whole number of each House of Congress shall provide by law for a specific excess of outlays over receipts by a rollcall vote.

SECTION 2. The limit on the debt of the United States held by the public shall not be increased, unless three-fifths of the whole number of each House shall provide by law for such an increase by a rollcall vote.

SECTION 3. Prior to each fiscal year, the President shall transmit to the Congress a proposed budget for the United States Government for that fiscal year in which total outlays do not exceed total receipts.

SECTION 4. No bill to increase revenue shall become law unless approved by a majority of the whole number of each House by a rollcall vote.

SECTION 5. The Congress may waive the provisions of this article for any fiscal year in which a declaration of war is in effect.

The provisions of this article may be waived for any fiscal year in which the United States is engaged in military conflict which causes imminent and serious military threat to national security and is so declared by a joint resolution, adopted by a majority of the whole number of each House, which becomes law.

SECTION 6. The Congress shall enforce and implement this article by appropriate legislation, which may rely on estimates of outlays and receipts.

SECTION 7. Total receipts shall include all receipts of the United States Government except those derived from borrowing. Total outlays shall include all outlays of the United States Government except for those for repayment of debt principal.

SECTION 8. This article shall take effect beginning with fiscal year 2002 or with the second fiscal year beginning after its ratification, whichever is later.

Source: *Balanced Budget Amendment*, H.J. Res. 1, 104th Cong., 1st sess., 1995.

The case for amending the Constitution rests on the conviction that all deficits are irresponsible, regardless of their size or cause, and that statutory remedies do not work. A constitutional rule would not distinguish between big deficits and small ones, nor between deficits that result from cyclical weakness in the economy and those embedded in a structural imbalance between revenues and outlays.

Throughout American history, the prevailing sentiment has been that deficits are injurious to the well-being of the country. The main concern has been that by spending beyond its income, the government burdens future generations, which have no voice in making the decision and do not directly benefit from it. At times the argument is couched in moral terms, as if it were utterly wrong for government to finance operations with borrowed funds. This moral stance has been relaxed during wartime, when supporting military forces has been deemed more important than making ends meet. And it has been overtaken by events during recession, when the drop-off in revenues has compelled the government to borrow.

Reformers should be wary of imposing constitutional restrictions on democratic majorities. Statutory remedies have enormous advantages, as the successful implementation of budget enforcement rules in the 1990s indicates. Statutory rules can more readily distinguish between big deficits and small ones, those stemming from cyclical disturbances and those caused by structural problems, those that are temporary and those that persist, and between those based on willful miscalculation and those due to circumstances that the president and Congress could not foresee when they made the budget. Statutory requirements can be fine-tuned as experience accumulates and as politicians learn what works and what does not.

Even if a balanced budget amendment were inscribed in the Constitution, its implementation would depend on legislation that defines the scope of the budget; establishes accounting rules for receipts, outlays, and other transactions; and specifies what is to be done in case of unplanned deficits. Implementing legislation would have to take account of faulty estimates, changing economic conditions, emergencies, and other occurrences not foreseen when the budget was approved. It would have to prescribe rules for determining which entities are federal and included in the budget and which are not. And it would have to deal with the budgetary treatment of capital investments, loans, asset sales, and several other types of transactions.

In many years, the economy has the final say as to whether the budget is balanced. The odds are overwhelming that in periods of moderate to severe economic weakness, the Constitution would have to retreat in the face of economic realities. In fact, most versions of the balanced budget rule permit Congress to waive the requirement in time of emergency. But waiver would not be automatic; it would have to be supported by a congressional majority (or supermajority), leaving open the possibility that a waiver would not be approved and that balance would not be achieved. If a balanced budget amendment may be suspended for economic necessity, it will also be overridden for political expedience.

Perhaps the most troubling aspect of a constitutional amendment is that it might induce governmental paralysis. The rule could open the door to situations in which Congress lacks both a majority to pass a balanced budget and a supermajority to permit deficit spending. A balanced budget amendment infringes on the fundamental democratic principle that elected officials should make policy. In my view, if the political process spawns unwanted deficits, correction should be sought through statutory remedies.

CONCLUSION

The history of budgeting shows periodic swings in relations between the president and Congress. At some points one branch of government dominates; at others the situation is reversed. The Constitution granted the power of the purse to Congress to constrain executive authority. Yet early in the twentieth century, Congress enlarged the role of the president to restrict federal spending. When many felt that the president was overly dominating the process, changes in the rules of the game reestablished Congress's role. While there will never be a permanent balance of power, each branch will continue to reposition itself to increase its leverage.

At one time the federal budget did little more than finance public works projects, national defense, and agency operations. Although not mandated, the norm was for the budget to be at or near balance. This was possible when government was small and had few costly obligations. Now the majority of federal spending is for payments to individuals. With these payments and interest charges mushrooming to absorb two-thirds of the budget, it seemed impossible to escape persistent peacetime deficits. There was continual conflict over what actions should be taken to put the nation's fiscal house back in order.

The additional layers of rules and laws added in the 1980s and 1990s to guide the politics, processes, and practices of budgeting centered on one premise—politicians need to be restricted in the financial choices they make. At times politicians have made some tough decisions on their own—for example, increasing taxes on upper-income earners and capping discretionary spending—to help steer the budget to surplus. Within a surprisingly short period, the deficit was liquidated, but this turnaround did not last, nor did it end budgetary warfare. At this writing, multitrillion dollar deficits have been forecast for the first decades of the new century. The only thing certain about these projections is that they will be wide of the mark. Perhaps the government will maintain a deficit for many years to come. If it does, the never-ending budget battle between the president and Congress will enter a new phase.

3

The Budget's Shifting Boundaries

An essential step in using or interpreting any budget is to understand what the numbers mean. In federal budgeting, not every dollar taken in is counted as a receipt, nor is every dollar paid out counted as an outlay. To say that the government collects or spends about $3 trillion a year means that these are the official totals reported according to the budget rules currently in effect. But several types of numbers coexist in the federal budget. The next chapter explains the political arithmetic and rules of budgeting. This chapter explains the technical numbers, which are based on accounting rules as to how various transactions are counted and recorded, and maps out the boundaries of budgeting, describing which transactions are included or excluded from the budget.

RECEIPTS, BUDGETARY RESOURCES, AND OUTLAYS

The federal government has various accounting rules and conventions for computing receipts and expenditures. These practices affect the amounts recorded in the budget as well as the behavior of participants and the outcomes they produce. The key concepts are receipts, budget authority and other budgetary resources, and outlays. The term *receipts* is synonymous with the term *revenues,* with the former preferred by the executive branch and the latter by Congress.

Receipts

Most of the money the government receives is recorded as revenue; some is not. The basic rule is that money the government collects in the exercise of its sovereign power (such as the power to tax or to regulate) is counted as a budget receipt; money the government receives in the conduct of business-type operations is counted as an offsetting collection. Borrowed funds are not included in receipts, and repayment of debt principal is not counted as an outlay. The roughly $3 trillion in annual revenues comes mostly from income and social insurance taxes, but customs duties, fines, and compulsory user charges also are included. Business-type revenue, such as asset sales and certain user charges, does not appear on the revenue side of the budget but is netted against outlays, usually of the agency or account that collects the money. These offsetting collections reduce total budget outlays but do not increase revenues. The income of government-sponsored enterprises is netted against their expenses, and the net amount is recorded as income or outlay.

Budget Authority and Outlays

The federal government has an obligations-based budget system. The key points of decision and control pertain to the obligations authorized or incurred, not to the outlays disbursed during the year. When Congress appropriates money, it gives agencies *budget authority* to enter into obligations. Congress may also provide budget authority in legislation that enables an agency to incur obligations. *Obligations* are incurred when an agency enters into a contract, executes a purchase order, or takes any action that commits the government to make payment. Some obligations, such as those ensuing from loan guarantees (discussed later in this chapter), are con-

tingent on default or some other event. By law, contingent liabilities are excluded from budget authority, but an exception is made for guaranteed loans. In these cases the estimated subsidy cost of the loans is included in the computation of budget authority.

Money that first becomes available for obligation in a particular fiscal year is counted as *new budget authority* in that year's budget. Under this rule, when Congress makes an *advance appropriation* for a future fiscal year, the new budget authority is charged to the year in which the money first becomes available for obligation. For example, if Congress makes a $1 billion advance appropriation for fiscal year 2009 in an appropriations act for fiscal year 2008, the money is not counted as part of fiscal year 2008 budget authority. This rule, discussed in chapter 4, has enabled Congress to appropriate more while staying within spending limits.

Some programs, particularly those financed by trust funds, have *permanent budget authority* that becomes available each year without congressional action. By law, all money in the Social Security fund (and most other trust funds) is available for obligation, but only the amount obligated in a fiscal year is counted as new budget authority.

Executive and congressional budget documents sometimes refer to *budgetary resources,* a term that includes, in addition to new budget authority, all other money available for obligation in a fund or account. These resources may derive from transfers, user fees deposited in the account, unobligated balances carried over from the previous years, or other sources.

Outlays occur when money is disbursed by check, electronic transfer, or cash. The budget surplus or deficit is calculated as the difference between cash receipts and outlays. (A small portion of outlays, associated with direct and guaranteed loans and certain other transactions, is not accounted for on a cash basis.) Although outlays generally receive more public attention than budget authority does, the latter is more important in managing the government's finances. Congress does not directly control total outlays or those of federal agencies; rather, it regulates outlays indirectly by providing budget authority. Each year's outlays derive principally from new budget authority, but a portion also derives from budget authority carried over from previous years. For example, the fiscal year 2008 budget estimated that outlays would total $2.902 trillion for that year. More than three-quarters of this amount ($2.313 trillion) was estimated to come from new budget authority; the remainder ($589 billion), from unspent budget authority enacted in prior years.

To clarify the relationship of budget authority and outlays, it may be useful to think of them as akin to deposits and withdrawals. When Congress provides budget authority, it deposits financial resources in an agency's account. When the agency incurs obligations, it encumbers these resources, and they are no longer available for any other purpose. Finally, when the agency pays its obligations, it withdraws resources from the account.

The relationship of budget authority and outlays varies among federal programs and depends on the rate at which budget resources are disbursed. In programs with high spendout rates, most new budget authority is disbursed during the year for which the funds were provided. Budget authority provided for salaries and other operating expenses typically has a high spendout rate; resources provided for construction or procurement have relatively low rates. For example, more than 95 percent of the new budget authority appropriated for military pay is spent during the year, but less than 5 percent of the new money allocated for shipbuilding is disbursed in the year for which

it was provided. Spendout rates are used in enforcing discretionary caps (discussed in chapter 4), which limit both new budget authority and outlays.

In estimating the amount of outlays to be derived from appropriations, CBO uses spendout rates (based on historical trends) to calculate the percentage of the new money that will be disbursed during the year. Because they are based on spendout rates, the outlays specified in the budget for the current or future fiscal years are (with only a few exceptions) merely estimates of the amounts to be disbursed. Actual outlays are known only after the fiscal year has ended.

In some programs the numerical relationship between budget authority and outlays provides a useful clue to financial trends. When new budget authority is rising faster than outlays, more resources are being added than are being used; hence future program activity is likely to expand. However, when new budget authority is flat or declining but outlays are increasing, future program activity is likely to decline because resources are being used faster than they are being replenished. (This pattern does not apply to trust funds or to programs that spend almost all of their budgetary resources on salaries and other operating expenditures.) Figure 3-1 charts trends in defense spending from 1977 through 2006. Note that at the start of this period, budget authority and outlays grew at approximately the same pace. During the Reagan defense buildup in the early 1980s, however, budget authority rose steeply, and the gap between it and outlays widened. The reverse occurred during the second half of the decade: defense budget authority leveled off, but outlays rose, narrowing the gap between them. During the 1990s, defense budget authority and outlays were stable in nominal terms, and the gap between them was small. However, the gap

FIGURE 3-1
Defense Budget Authority and Outlays, Fiscal Years 1977–2006

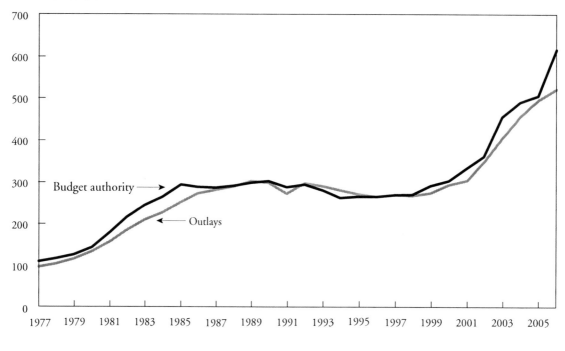

Billions of dollars

Source: *Budget of the United States Government, Historical Tables, Fiscal Year 2008,* table 3.1, pp. 46–54, and table 5.1, pp. 85–99.

again widened after the 9/11 terrorist attacks, as new budget authority increased for military operations in Iraq and Afghanistan.

SCOPE OF THE BUDGET

The president's budget for fiscal year 2008 estimated that the federal government would spend $2.902 trillion for that year; it also estimated that the government would spend only $2.439 trillion for that year—$463 billion less. Both estimates were accurate. The inclusion of two different estimates of outlays for the same year was not a mistake. The first was calculated on a unified basis; the second counted only on-budget outlays. How much

the budget takes in and spends depends on what is included and excluded. By some measures the totals are much higher than those reported in the unified budget.

In 1968 the government adopted the principle of a unified budget that accounts for all receipts and expenditures of federal entities. This principle, enunciated by the President's Commission on Budget Concepts, replaced an older method that excluded trust funds from the budget. The commission successfully argued that the unified budget provides a fuller picture of financial transactions, facilitates use of the budget as an instrument of economic policy, and enables the government to establish priorities among programs financed by different sources. The unified budget includes general funds and trust funds, current and capital expenditures, the transactions of government-owned enterprises, and loans issued or guaranteed by the government. But despite its broad scope, the budget does not provide a truly comprehensive account of federal revenues and expenditures. Certain funds and transactions, such as government-sponsored enterprises and the future costs of various federal insurance programs, are excluded. Yet some argue that the budget is too inclusive—that self-financing trust funds, such as Social Security and the Highway Trust Fund, should be walled off from the budget.

The scope of the budget is not merely a matter of how revenues and spending are classified. It affects the reported size of the budget surplus or deficit and involves conflict over the budgetary treatment of Social Security and other trust funds. Some have argued that budget accounting rules have discouraged the government from investing in capital improvements because it treats these investments the same as spending on current operations; others have argued that the rules fail to recognize the future costs of current budget commitments, such as the obligation to pay pensions to federal employees when they retire.

Funds in the Budget

The budget consists of four main types of funds: general, special, trust, and revolving. General funds are not earmarked by law for specific purposes; accordingly, there is no direct link between taxes paid and services provided. Almost all individual and corporate income taxes, and certain excise taxes and user charges, are deposited into the general fund. National defense, interest on the public debt, the operating expenses of most federal agencies, many grants to state and local govern-ments, and some entitlements are paid for out of the general fund. It accounts for approximately two-thirds of federal revenues and outlays.

In contrast to the general fund, trust funds are designated by law for particular purposes. But inasmuch as Congress established these funds, it can abolish them, change the amounts paid in or out, and also change the purposes for which the fund's assets are used. For example, the revenue-sharing trust fund (financed by general revenues) was terminated during the 1980s. Some Highway Trust Fund money has been diverted to mass transit. In some years a portion of the federal gasoline tax has been paid to the general fund, while in other years all gasoline tax receipts have gone to the Highway Trust Fund. The federal government does not have a fiduciary obligation to manage trust funds for the benefit of those who pay into the fund or receive money from it. The only major exceptions are trust funds owned by Indian tribes, which the federal government manages on their behalf. In recognition of the unique status of Indian tribe trust funds, OMB removed them from the budget beginning with fiscal year 2000.

If the federal government can unilaterally dispose of trust funds, why does it establish them? What difference is there between money held in the general fund or in a trust fund? The answer to these questions lies more in the realm of politics than law. Politicians may prefer trust funds for several reasons: it may be easier to raise taxes when the money is earmarked for a particular purpose, trust funds may have an advantage in competing for scarce budget resources, and having a trust fund may offer some assurance that the money will be used for intended purposes. Trust funds are somewhat less than a contractual commitment but much more than an empty gesture. Although trust funds are sometimes raided, in almost all cases, the money is used for the stated purpose.

Although trust funds are not inviolable, earmarking revenues to them does influence budget decisions. These funds generate strong expectations, bordering on entitlements in some cases, that the money will only be used for prescribed purposes. Moreover, when revenues are set aside in a trust fund, intended beneficiaries can more easily monitor government spending and thereby oppose diversion of the money to other uses. But a trust fund is only as secure as its beneficiaries are powerful. When beneficiaries are strong, the government may be unwilling to risk the political costs of raiding the trust fund. When they are weak, there may be little risk. With 50 million Americans receiving monthly payments from Social Security and more than 100 million workers expecting benefits in the future, Social Security is politically sensitive. It is off-budget, has its own budget enforcement rules, and is not subject to the reconciliation process. In contrast, the revenue-sharing trust fund lacked its own revenue source and made payments to state and local governments rather than to individuals or households. Its advocates were too weak to deter Congress from abolishing the fund when it wanted the money for other programs.

Trust funds have been a recurring source of budgetary controversy. One issue is whether these funds should be included in the budget; another is whether trust funds should be required to lend their balances to the federal government.

The unified budget combines all funds in a comprehensive set of accounts. However, Social Security's off-budget status excludes it from the computation of budget totals. Despite this, most official and media reports on the budget continue to include the Social Security trust funds, as well as other off-budget entities such as the Postal Service.

Some critics argue that by including Social Security and other trust funds in the overall budget, the federal government uses the balances in trust funds to finance its general operations. The long-standing practice has been for the government to borrow all trust fund balances and to pay the prevailing rate of interest on Treasury bonds of comparable maturity. Trust funds have no choice in the matter; they must lend their balances to the government. At one time these balances were relatively small, but since the 1980s, they have spiraled from $200 billion to more than $3 trillion, largely because of the buildup in Social Security reserves. In fiscal year 2006, the government paid approximately $170 billion in interest to various trust funds.

Some regard this as merely a bookkeeping arrangement that enables the trust funds to earn interest on retained balances. Others believe there should be an arm's-length relationship between the budget and the trust funds. They argue that the trust funds should be managed to achieve a market rate of return—which is likely to be higher than is earned on Treasuries—and that combining trust and general funds masks the true condition of the federal budget. Resolution of this issue is likely to be linked to decisions on the future of Social Security. (This issue is briefly discussed later in this chapter in connection with measurement of budget surpluses and deficits, and also in the concluding chapter.)

Special funds share characteristics of both the general fund and trust funds. Most special funds, such as the Land and Water Conservation Fund and the National Wildlife Refuge Fund, are financed by user fees and other earmarked revenues. Although they are accounted for separately, special funds are grouped together with general funds under the label "federal funds." Diversion of money is more common in special funds than in trust funds.

The final category consists of revolving funds, most of which carry out businesslike activities, selling goods and services and using the income to finance their operations. Revolving funds are recorded in the budget on a net basis—income minus outlays. Thus, if a revolving fund has $1 billion in income and $1.2 billion in outlays, the unified budget records $200 million in outlays.

Government-Owned and Government-Sponsored Enterprises

The federal government owns and operates various businesses, including the U.S. Postal Service, the Government National Mortgage Association, and the Pension Benefit Guaranty Corporation. All corporations owned in whole or in part by the government are included in the budget on a net basis—expenses are subtracted from income to show the net budgetary impact. For example, the Bonneville Power Administration, which produces and sells hydroelectric power in the Pacific Northwest, had $2.4 billion in expenses for fiscal year 2006, all of which was offset by income.

The budget contains special statements for most government-owned corporations, including a statement of income and expense, and a balance sheet. Because these statements are based on commercial accounting standards, they differ from the financial data provided for federal agencies, and they cannot be combined with regular budget schedules.

In contrast to government-owned corporations, enterprises established but not owned by the government are excluded from the budget because they are deemed to be private entities. The government does not have any equity in these government-sponsored enterprises (GSEs), most of which obtain financing from private sources. The biggest GSEs, such as the Federal National Mortgage Association (Fannie Mae) and the Federal Home Loan Mortgage Corporation (Freddie Mac), engage in credit activities that finance agriculture, home ownership, student loans, and other activities.

Although GSEs serve public objectives and benefit from governmental sponsorship—they borrow at highly favorable interest rates and some enjoy special tax breaks—neither the president nor Congress reviews their finances. The aggregate assets and liabilities of GSEs run into trillions of dollars, and their annual lending exceeds $1 trillion. Although GSEs are self-financed, a few have a standby line of credit at the Treasury, and most have obligations that the government implicitly guarantees. Financial schedules of GSEs are published in the budget appendix but are not included in the totals.

The schedules included in the fiscal year 2008 budget for several of the largest GSEs are blank; they do not include any financial data because the affected entities have engaged in accounting irregularities that make it necessary for them to restate their financial activities for previous years. The financial misstatements have run into the billions of dollars, triggering alarm in Washington about the management of some GSEs. Pressure is building to strengthen federal oversight and limit the volume of transactions that certain GSEs can engage in. There is concern that the federal government may have substantial financial exposure if some GSEs encounter difficulty, as well as concern that sectors that are heavily dependent on ready access to capital (principally housing) may be adversely affected by mismanaged GSEs.

Direct and Guaranteed Loans

The government participates in two types of loan transactions: it directly lends to borrowers, and it guarantees loans made by others.

The Federal Credit Reform Act of 1990 changed the budgetary treatment of both types of loans from a cash basis, in which disbursements were recorded as outlays, to a new system that shows the estimated subsidy cost of these loans as outlays.

This system requires that funds be budgeted and appropriated to finance the estimated subsidy cost of loans. The subsidy cost is defined in the 1990 act as "the estimated long-term cost to the government of a direct loan or a loan guarantee, calculated on a net present value basis, excluding administrative costs." The net present value is calculated by discounting estimated future cash flows (disbursements by the government and repayments to it) of each loan program using a discount rate equal to the interest paid by the Treasury on borrowings of comparable maturity. In general, loans may be obligated or guaranteed only to the extent that Congress has appropriated funds to cover the subsidy cost.

Estimating this cost is a complex undertaking that is done annually for each credit account. The process differentiates between the subsidized portion of loans (the cost to the government) and the unsubsidized portion (the amount that will be repaid, recovered, or not defaulted). In the case of direct loans, the subsidy cost may be due either to default by borrowers or to below-market rates of interest. In the case of guaranteed loans, the subsidy cost may be due to default.

Budgeting for these loans entails three types of accounts: *program accounts* receive appropriations for the subsidy cost of loans and for associated administrative expenses, *financing accounts* handle all cash flows for direct and guaranteed loans, and *liquidating accounts* manage cash flows deriving from loans made before 1992. Table 3-1 explains the purpose and budgetary status of these accounts.

Although the rules of the 1990 act are complicated and involve assumptions about the volume and timing of defaults, recoveries, and payments, there also is a political dimension to the credit budgeting system. In shifting from a cash basis to subsidy cost, credit reform made direct loans less expensive to budget makers and guaranteed loans more expensive. In the past the entire amount paid out for direct loans was budgeted as an outlay. Now only the subsidized portion appears in the budget as an outlay. For guaranteed loans the old system did not record outlays until a default occurred and the government made good on its obligation. Now estimated payments for default are budgeted as outlays. In fiscal year 2006, the federal government obligated $58 billion in direct loans and committed $281 billion in new loan guarantees. To cover the subsidy cost of these transactions, Congress appropriated $8 billion for direct loans and $24 billion for loan guarantees. These amounts are low because of the federal government's generally favorable experience with its loan portfolio. In fiscal year 2006, the government wrote off just over 1 percent of its direct loans, and terminated just over 1 percent of loan guarantees, because of defaults.

MEASURING THE BUDGET

The fact that some items are included and others are excluded from the budget raises questions as to how revenue and spending totals are measured. The reported surplus or deficit is not the only valid measure, nor is it always the one that the media discuss. The surplus or deficit is commonly defined as the difference between the total the government takes in and the total it spends. But this is not the way transactions are measured in the federal budget. The official surplus or deficit is the difference between the receipts and outlays recorded

TABLE 3-1
Accounting for Direct and Guaranteed Loans

Description	Program account	Financing account	Liquidating account
Purpose of account	Receives appropriation for the subsidy cost of loans and associated administrative expenses	Handles all cash flows for loans and guarantees	Handles all loans made before fiscal 1992
Budget status	Subsidy cost included in budget authority and outlays	Means of financing; not included in receipts or outlays	Cash receipts and payments included in the budget
Cash flows	Transfers subsidy cost appropriations to financing account	Receives subsidy payment from program account; Borrows unsubsidized part of loans from Treasury; Collects repayments, fees, and interest from borrowers; Disburses new loans, makes payments on defaulted loan guarantees, repays the Treasury with interest	Collects repayments, interest, and fees on old loans; Pays defaults and interest subsidies on old loans

in the budget. Consequently, the scope of the budget affects the reported budget outcome. To the extent that receipts and outlays are not budgeted on a cash basis, neither is the surplus or deficit. To the extent certain items are excluded from the budget, they also are excluded from its totals. The actual totals may vary by tens of billions of dollars, depending on what is included or excluded. The alternative measures shown in figure 3-2 are used for various budget purposes.

The Unified Budget

The unified budget is the broadest measure, though it does not include all payments for which the government may be liable. It includes the off-budget entities, trust funds, and both capital and operating accounts, but it does not include government-sponsored enterprises or (with the exception of loans) the future costs of current budget commitments. It does not cover contingent liabilities (except guaranteed loans), such as those the government incurs in insuring bank deposits and private pensions, nor does it recognize the future outlays that will result from the obligation to pay Social Security, Medicare, and other entitlements. The amounts involved in future claims on the federal Treasury are truly gargantuan. By some estimates the government's exposure to various insurance schemes exceeds $5 trillion. We return to this issue in chapter 10 in discussing a balance sheet approach to federal finances.

On-Budget Totals

On-budget totals differ from the unified budget in their exclusion of Social Security and the Postal Service. The off-budget status of these entities is designed to protect them from spending constraints in the rest of the budget.

FIGURE 3-2
Alternative Measures of the Deficit and Surplus, 10-Year Intervals, Fiscal Years 1980–2005[a]

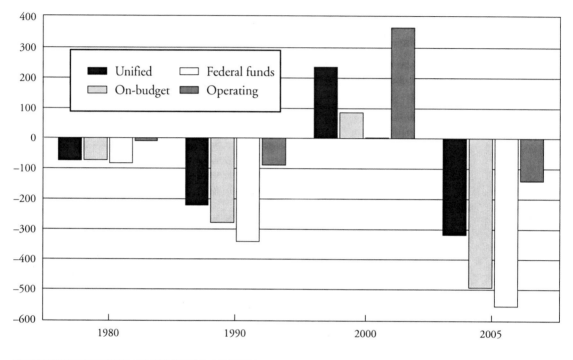

Billions of dollars

Source: *Budget of the United States Government, Historical Tables, Fiscal Year 2008,* table 1.1, pp. 21–22, table 1.4, pp. 27–28, and table 9.2, pp. 165–67.
   a. Operating budget amount is not adjusted for depreciation or other write-offs.

By itself off-budget status makes little difference. However, Social Security's protected status is reinforced by its exemption from reconciliation and sequestration, two of the government's tools for cutting expenditures. Because Social Security is so large, excluding it from budget totals would impair the government's ability to measure the fiscal impact of its budget decisions. In fact, Social Security is almost always included in governmental and media reports on the budget.

Since 1983, when Social Security was last overhauled, the on-budget totals have been less favorable than those reported on a unified basis. In fiscal 2006, for example, the unified deficit was $248 billion, but the on-budget deficit was $434 billion. The difference between the two sets of numbers is due almost entirely to the buildup of surpluses in Social Security funds in preparation for the upsurge in the retired population in the twenty-first century. Under current policy, when Social Security draws down its accumulated balances, the unified budget will have a smaller surplus or a bigger deficit than the on-budget totals. However, there is a strong probability that both Social Security and its budgetary status will be significantly altered by the time most baby boomers begin entering the retirement stream.

The Federal Funds Budget

The federal funds budget excludes all trust funds. As noted earlier, it consists of the general fund and special funds. The federal funds deficit amounted to $555 billion in fiscal year 2005, more than $200 billion higher than the unified budget deficit for that year.

Large federal funds deficits are troubling harbingers of future fiscal stress. Almost all non–trust fund payments are made from this source, including interest on the public debt, the operating costs of government agencies, national defense spending, and most grants to state and local governments. Most federal fund receipts derive from individual and corporate income taxes. The deficit indicates a fundamental mismatch between the resources available to government and demands placed on it. The huge federal funds shortfall also indicates an unwillingness of Americans, or their leaders, to pay for all the general services they receive from government. They appear more willing to be taxed when the money is earmarked for particular purposes, such as Social Security and Medicare, than when it is deposited into the general fund, where there is no explicit link between taxes paid and benefits received.

In 2005 general fund receipts covered barely two-thirds of general fund expenditures. For every dollar received from government programs, taxpayers paid less than 70 cents. This bargain cannot last forever, however, and the federal funds deficit points to the strong possibility that income tax rates will be boosted in the future.

The Capital and Operating Budgets

In contrast to the practice of state and local governments, the federal budget does not segregate capital and operating expenses. Both expenditures for current operations and for the acquisition of buildings, roads, and other

TABLE 3-2
Federal Investment Outlays, Fiscal Year 2006

Billions of dollars

Description	Amount
Physical assets	
Defense	97
Nondefense	29
Grants	64
Research and development	
Defense	73
Nondefense	50
Education and training	
Direct federal	61
Grants	56

Source: *Budget of the United States Government, Historical Tables, Fiscal Year 2008,* table 9.2, pp. 166–67, table 9.7, p. 181, and table 9.9, pp. 189–91.

fixed assets are budgeted as outlays. From time to time, proposals have been made to separate the two types of expenditures, but none have been adopted. However, the budget provides supplementary information on capital investments. One measure shown in figure 3-2 uses a restrictive definition of such outlays that includes spending on physical assets but excludes research and development as well as investment in human capital through education and training. A broader definition in table 3-2 includes investment in research and development as well as spending on education and training. In fiscal year 2006, the federal government spent $190 billion on the acquisition of physical assets, half of which were for defense purposes. Of that total, $64 billion went to finance assets acquired by state and local governments. It spent $123 billion on research and development, mostly for military weapons, and another $117 billion on education and training.

Clearly, having a separate investment budget would paint the government's fiscal position in a more favorable light than the unified budget shows. But subtracting the gross amount invested in physical or human capital from the operating budget would misstate the government's financial condition. If a separate capital budget were introduced, it would be appropriate to charge the operating budget for depreciation and write-offs of capital assets. If these adjustments were made, the operating surplus or deficit would differ from that reported on a unified basis only to the extent that there was a net change in the government's stock of physical or human assets.

The main rationale for combining current and capital investment expenditures is to show the budget's aggregate impact on economic activity. Some have argued, however, that having a single budget hinders planning and financing of capital improvements, shortens the time horizon of budget makers, and leads politicians to cut investment spending when the budget is tight. But a number of difficult questions would arise if a capital budget were seriously considered. Should the capital budget be confined to investment in fixed assets or should it be expanded to include investment in human capital? Would a broad definition of investment weaken budget control by enabling politicians to shift spending from the operating budget to the capital budget? How should the federal government budget for roads and other facilities that it finances but that states or other governments own? Would the federal government be required to charge the operating budget for depreciation, for the loss of military weapons, and for other costs that are written off under generally accepted accounting rules?

Interest in a capital budget tends to peak when the federal government is running a large budget deficit. Some argue that segregating investment expenditure would enable the government to reduce the reported size of the deficit. When the government has a surplus, interest in a separate capital budget wanes, but a surplus may provide the most propitious opportunity to change the budget treatment of investment expenditure. When there is no deficit to hide, the government can base its decision on prudent accounting rules rather than on efforts to weaken budget control.

CONCLUSION

After two centuries of adaptation, the budget is still in a state of flux. Its boundaries are uncertain, and there are several alternative ways of measuring the government's financial flows and condition. How the surplus or deficit is measured depends on how the budget is defined. This problem cannot be resolved, however, by replacing one measure of the budget with another. The budget has multiple measures because it has multiple uses. Each measure tells a different story; none provides a snapshot of the budget from all appropriate vantage points. A budget constructed on the basis of cash flows provides essential information on the financing needs of government and is cast in a form that politicians can understand and deal with. But a cash flow budget discloses little about the future financial claims on the government. For this purpose a balance sheet might be more useful, especially if it is refined to prudently evaluate the risks associated with insurance programs and other contingent liabilities. For other purposes a budget segregated by funds or between capital and operating expenditures might be more appropriate.

Although there are many ways to tell the budget's story, there can be only one basis for deciding the budget. Congress cannot review the budget one day and make allocations on the basis of cash flows, return the next day and independently decide how much should be invested in capital improvements, and then take a fresh look on another day and determine what should be done to each budgetary fund. More than a generation ago, the government decided that the unified budget provides the most comprehensive basis for making and reporting budget decisions. However, the short-term Social Security surplus and the long-term Social Security deficit have called into question the adequacy of the unified budget. On the one hand, it has enabled the government to borrow the surplus for other uses; on the other hand, it has masked the approaching problem of paying for an aging population.

Congress has responded to these pressures by trying to wall off Social Security from the budget. In the future it may also exclude other trust funds or establish a separate investment budget. But these possible developments will not put an end to debate on the appropriate boundaries of the budget. As long as there is a federal budget, questions will be raised as to whether particular transactions should be in or out. What is put in at one time might be taken out at another. This has been budgeting's history; it will also be its future.

4

The Political Rules and Arithmetic of Budgeting

Every budget is a compilation of numbers on the revenues, financial resources, obligations, outlays, borrowing, and deficit or surplus of the government. The federal budget has millions of these numbers, computed and reported on the basis of rules and practices that have accumulated over the years. The rules do not always conform to the way businesses or other governments account for their finances. Some are derived from laws, such as the Congressional Budget Act of 1974 (CBA) and the Budget Enforcement Act of 1990 (BEA); many are not recognized in law or in accounting principles but nevertheless determine how financial transactions are recorded in the budget. But different rules produce different numbers. An increase does not always mean more money is being raised or spent than in the previous year, and a decrease does not necessarily mean that less money is being raised or spent. Changes in revenue and spending are measured in terms of assumptions and projections that are distinctive to federal budgeting. This chapter explains the main rules for calculating the budget impact of revenue and spending actions. It begins with a brief overview of federal budgeting and then compares two types of spending, discretionary and direct, and describes the different processes for each. Next, it focuses on baseline projections and assumptions, and the complex world of scoring—measuring the budgetary impact of legislation and other actions that affect the budget. Since the budget is hostage to the performance of the economy, the chapter also includes an assessment of the role of economics in budgeting.

OVERVIEW OF THE ANNUAL BUDGET CYCLE

Two centuries of evolution have produced a complex budget process, with many players and stages, defined rules and roles, and layers of procedure. Each reform has deposited its distinctive requirements; some have faded away, and others have been incorporated into the ongoing activities of budgeting. The various requirements revolve around an annual cycle that begins with formulation of the president's budget in the executive branch, involves four separate sets of congressional action, then moves to agencies, which implement their approved budgets, and concludes with the review and audit of expenditures. Table 4-1 lists the major actions taken during the fiscal year 2008 budget cycle. While the timetable is constructed on the assumption that each action is completed on schedule, it has become common for Congress and the president to miss certain deadlines. Nevertheless, the basic steps are repeated year after year with little change, though particular procedures may vary with the president's style and relationship with Congress or in response to changes in economic or political conditions.

Table 4-1 indicates that the federal government has an annual budget process that sprawls over several years. This extended cycle means that at any given date, the federal government is typically juggling three fiscal years: the year in progress (the "current year"), the year Congress is considering (the "budget year"), and the year after that for which agencies are preparing budget requests (the first "outyear"). The overlap of several fiscal years

has made budgeting an arduous, year-round activity that allows little time for pause and reflection and little opportunity for thinking strategically about the purposes and direction of federal programs.

In budgeting, the calendar is king, telling participants what they are supposed to do and when. Even when deadlines are missed, the calendar shapes actions and expectations, and patterns the roles and behavior of those who make budgets and spend money. The most important date on the budget calendar is October 1, the day the new fiscal year begins. Agencies begin compiling their budgets with this date in mind, the president sends his budget to Congress mindful of the time required for legislative action, Congress organizes much of its work around this date, and agencies open and close their books on the basis of the October 1 starting point.

The President's Budget

Preparation of the president's budget generally begins in a decentralized manner, with each agency using its own procedures and guidelines for assembling its request. Formulation usually takes 8 to 10 months—longer in large agencies, shorter in very small ones. Because of the long lead times, agencies must make budget decisions with great uncertainty about the conditions that will prevail when the funds are actually spent.

Agency budget preparation is concentrated during the spring and summer of the calendar year preceding submission to Congress. OMB reviews agency requests in the fall, after which it recommends program and spending amounts. Agencies have a brief period to appeal for more funding than OMB recommended. Once all the issues have been resolved, the budget is printed and distributed to Congress and the interested public.

TABLE 4-1
Timetable of the Fiscal 2008 Budget Cycle

Calendar[a]	Activities
2006	
March–June	Budget guidelines and preliminary policies are developed; agency budget offices issue call for estimates to operating units.
July–September	Agencies formulate detailed requests, which are submitted to OMB.
October–December	OMB reviews agencies' requests and issues passbacks; agencies appeal to OMB and/or the president; final decisions are made.
2007	
January	CBO releases *Budget and Economic Outlook* for fiscal years 2008–17.
February	President submits his fiscal year 2008 budget to Congress no later than the first Monday in February.
March 15	Congressional committees submit views and estimates on the budget to budget committees.
April 15	Budget rules provide for Congress to adopt the fiscal year 2008 budget resolution by this date.
May 15	If budget resolution has not yet been adopted, appropriations may be considered in the House.
June–August	House and Senate act on regular appropriation bills for fiscal 2008; OMB and CBO release new revenue and expenditure projections for fiscal year 2008.
September	Conference reports and enactment of regular appropriations.
October 1	Fiscal 2008 starts; continuing resolution(s) passed if regular appropriations acts have not been enacted into law.
October 2007– September 2008	Agencies spend resources and carry out activities as authorized by Congress; Congress may enact supplemental appropriations acts for fiscal year 2008.
2008	
February	New revenue and expenditure projections for fiscal year 2008 are included in the fiscal year 2009 budget.
September 30	Fiscal year 2008 ends.
October–December	Agencies, Treasury, and OMB close the books on fiscal year 2008.
2009	
January–December and beyond	Agencies prepare financial statements; postaudits and evaluations are conducted.
February	Actual revenue and expenditure data for fiscal year 2008 are included in the fiscal year 2010 budget.

a. The deadlines listed here represent a standard timetable. However, over the past 30-plus years, certain targets have slipped more often than they have been met.

The Congressional Budget Resolution

Congressional budget action involves the four sets of committees whose functions are set forth in table 4-2. A set of House and Senate committees has custody over one of the four types of budget actions: the annual budget resolution, revenue measures, authorizing legislation, and appropriations bills. The three legislative staff agencies listed in table 4-3—the Congressional Budget Office (CBO), the Government Accountability Office (GAO), and the Congressional

TABLE 4-2
Budget Functions of Congressional Committees

Budget	Authorizing	Appropriations	Revenue
Report budget resolution	Report authorizing and direct spending legislation	Report regular and supplemental appropriations bills	Report revenue legislation
Draft reconciliation instructions and compile reconciliation bill	Oversee executive agencies	Review proposed rescissions and deferrals	Report legislation on Social Security and certain other entitlements
Allocate new budget authority, outlays, and other aggregates to committees	Submit views and estimates to budget committees on matters in their jurisdiction	Submit views and estimates to budget committees	Submit views and estimates to budget committees
Monitor budget and advise Congress on budget impact of legislation	Recommend changes in laws pursuant to reconciliation instructions	Subdivide budget authority and outlays among their subcommittees	Recommend changes in laws pursuant to reconciliation instructions
	Include CBO cost estimates in reports on their legislation	Establish account structure for federal agencies and rules for reprogramming	Report legislation adjusting the statutory limit on the public debt
		Provide guidance to agencies on expenditure of funds	

TABLE 4-3
Budget Functions of Congressional Support Agencies

Congressional Budget Office (CBO)	Government Accountability Office (GAO)	Congressional Research Service (CRS)
Issues reports with ten-year projections on the budget and the economy	Issues accounting guidelines and reviews agency accounting systems	Analyzes legislative issues and proposals affecting agencies and programs
Estimates 5- and 10-year cost of reported bills; prepares baseline budget projections and maintains database for scorekeeping	Audits operations of certain federal agencies; evaluates programs and recommends improvements	Assists committees and members by providing data and analyses relevant to their legislative responsibilities
Assists the budget, tax, appropriations, and other committees	Issues legal opinions concerning the use of funds	Compiles legislative histories of particular legislation and programs
Issues reports on options for changing federal revenue and spending policies	Reviews deferrals and rescissions to determine whether they have been properly reported and funds released as required	Issues reports on the status of legislation
Reviews the president's budget and other proposals	Investigates expenditures and agency operations as requested by congressional committees	Analyzes proposals to change federal budget practices
	Settles certain claims and debt collection issues or disputes	

Research Service (CRS)—aid Congress in performing these tasks.

Each year the House and Senate budget committees prepare a resolution, covering the next 5 (or more) years, that specifies budget totals (total revenue, budget authority, outlays, surplus or deficit, and public debt) and allocates spending among 20 functional categories, including national defense, agriculture, and health. Additionally, the budget resolution often contains reconciliation instructions directing specified House and Senate committees to report legislation that changes revenue or spending laws in accord with the policies set in the resolution. Legislation developed by committees pursuant to these instructions is packaged in an omnibus reconciliation bill that is considered by the House and Senate under special rules that expedite its passage.

The budget resolution is not a statute and does not have legal effect. Nor does it detail how federal funds are to be raised or spent. Rather, the resolution establishes the framework within which Congress considers revenue and spending measures. As a blueprint, the status of the budget resolution varies from year to year. In some years it strongly influences budgetary decisions; in others, it has little impact.

Revenue Legislation

Although Congress takes some action affecting revenues just about every year, it has no regular schedule for doing so. In some years, it hardly does anything; in a few, it makes truly significant changes in tax laws.

Revenue legislation is in the jurisdiction of the House Ways and Means Committee and the Senate Finance Committee, two of the oldest and most powerful committees in Congress. The Ways and Means Committee usu-

ally acts first because the Constitution stipulates that revenue measures shall originate in the House. Although the Senate takes up these measures after the House, it often makes major changes, setting the stage for the conference committee.

Authorizations

Under House and Senate rules, before either chamber appropriates funds, the program or agency that is to receive the money must be authorized in law. That is, Congress must first pass a law setting up the program and specifying how it operates before it appropriates funds for that purpose. There are, however, many variations in this sequence, as discussed in chapter 8.

Most congressional committees are authorizing committees. They consider legislation establishing or changing federal programs and agencies, prescribing the terms and conditions under which these operate, and overseeing their performance. Some authorizing committees are active; others go through one or more sessions without reporting major legislation. There is no standard structure or style to authorizing legislation; each committee with jurisdiction over federal programs or agencies goes about the task in its own way.

Appropriations

Annual appropriations are provided in regular appropriations bills, each of which is in the jurisdiction of parallel House and Senate subcommittees. The number of regular appropriations bills was fixed at 13 for many years, but subcommittee realignments in the 109th Congress reduced the number to 10 in the House and 12 in the Senate, and eliminated some of the subcommittee parallelism. In the 110th Congress, the new Democratic majorities realigned the subcommittees again, resulting in 12 parallel subcommittees.

Shortly after the president submits his budget to Congress, the various appropriations subcommittees conduct hearings at which agency officials justify the amounts requested. Although the subcommittees are independent of one another, all are limited by discretionary spending caps or amounts set under the annual budget resolution. To ensure that these limits are adhered to, the House and Senate appropriations committees divide the total discretionary spending among their subcommittees. When the House or Senate considers an appropriations bill, the spending provided in the bill is compared with the amount allocated to the relevant subcommittee. In some circumstances the House or Senate may be barred from considering an appropriations bill that would cause the subcommittee allocation to be exceeded. This rarely occurs, however, because appropriations subcommittees usually stay within their allocations. When they exceed the caps, they may resort to the bookkeeping tactics discussed later in this chapter.

Budget Implementation

Agencies cannot spend appropriations until OMB apportions the funds among periods or projects. Most federal agencies also have an allotment process that distributes available funds among their administrative units. With some exceptions, agencies are not permitted to obligate funds in excess of the appropriated or apportioned amounts.

Although agencies must spend funds according to the terms and conditions set by Congress, they sometimes reprogram funds by shifting them from one purpose to another in the same account. Deviations from authorized spending levels also occur when the president or other executive officials impound funds, either by delaying expenditures or by seeking to rescind the original appropriation. Special procedures, described in chapter 10, regulate impoundments.

Review and audit constitutes the final phase of the budget cycle. Because of the size of the federal government, financial management is decentralized, with each agency having responsibility for the propriety and efficiency of its expenditures and for maintaining complete, accurate financial records.

DISCRETIONARY AND DIRECT SPENDING

In effect, the federal government has two distinct budget processes, each with its own path and players. One involves discretionary spending, controlled by the appropriations process; the other involves direct spending and revenues, controlled by authorizing and tax legislation. Discretionary spending covers the approximately one-third of federal expenditures that is annually appropriated and includes virtually all defense expenditures, the operating costs of most federal agencies, and dozens of grant programs. During the period from fiscal year 1991 through fiscal year 2002, discretionary spending was limited by statutory caps on appropriations. In recent years, appropriations caps have been included in annual budget resolutions for purposes of enforcement in the Senate, but not the House. These caps, which are discussed later in the chapter, pertain both to budget authority and outlays. Direct spending is not controlled by annual appropriations but by the legislation that establishes eligibility criteria and payment formulas, or otherwise obligates the government. It consists mostly of entitlement programs but also includes other budgetary resources provided by authorizing legislation. Most entitlement spending is provided automatically by permanent appropriations included in the law establishing the entitlement program. Some entitlement laws, such as for Medicaid, do not contain a funding mechanism, so the necessary amounts must be provided in annual appropriations acts. When Congress appropriates for such entitlements, it must provide sufficient funds to cover the government's obligations. For these programs, the appropriations committees do not have discretion to provide less money than the government is obligated to pay.

Beginning in the 1990s, both statutory and rules-based pay-as-you-go (PAYGO) procedures have been used to enforce decisions on direct spending and revenue legislation. Major features of the statutory and rules-based PAYGO procedures are compared in table 4-4. The statutory PAYGO procedures effectively were terminated at the end of 2002, but rules-based PAYGO procedures currently are in effect in both the House and Senate. While statutory PAYGO placed certain duties on the president and the OMB director, the House and Senate PAYGO rules are completely internal to each chamber.

The statutory PAYGO procedure, in effect from 1991 to 2002, mandated that new legislation increasing direct spending or reducing revenues be fully offset so that the deficit was not increased or the surplus diminished. The remedy for a PAYGO violation was a sequester, in which the president would issue an order for across-the-board cuts in direct spending programs, based on a sequestration report prepared by the OMB director; many direct spending programs were exempt from a sequester. PAYGO did not require any offsetting action when the change in spending or revenue occurred pursuant to existing law. Thus a rise in spending because of inflation in health costs or a fall in revenues because of a weak economy would not have triggered

PAYGO. Furthermore, PAYGO did not bar Congress from passing one or more revenue or spending measures that added to the deficit or cut the surplus. Rather, it required that the net impact for a fiscal year of all such measures enacted be deficit neutral, otherwise certain funds would be sequestered (canceled automatically) to achieve the goal. OMB was the official scorekeeper for the statutory PAYGO procedure, publishing estimates of the budget impact of direct spending and revenue legislation on a multiyear PAYGO scorecard. CBO (with input on revenue legislation from the Joint Committee on Taxation) prepared PAYGO estimates and maintained a PAYGO scorecard as well, but only on an advisory basis. Until the late 1990s, revenue and direct spending legislation generally conformed to the statutory PAYGO rule, but with the budget in surplus during fiscal years 1998 through 2001, and the change in budget policy to favor large tax cuts, the rule was sometimes sidestepped by means of directed scorekeeping (which instructed the OMB director not to count certain PAYGO effects of legislation) and other techniques.

The House and Senate have adopted their own internal PAYGO rules that operate differently than did the statutory PAYGO rule. Among the key differences is that the congressional PAYGO rules apply to individual measures as they are considered and cover a longer time frame (10 years, not counting the current year). The House adopted its PAYGO rule in 2007, at the beginning of the 110th Congress. The Senate has had a PAYGO rule since 1993 and has changed it several times. In 2007 the Senate revised its PAYGO rule in a manner consistent with the House version. Enforcement of the House and Senate PAYGO rules relies on cost estimates prepared by CBO and the Joint Committee on Taxation.

TABLE 4-4
Statutory versus Rules-Based PAYGO

Feature	Statutory PAYGO	Rules-based PAYGO
Legislative basis	Budget Enforcement Act (BEA) of 1990[a]	Rule XXI, clause 10 (House); sections in annual budget resolutions (Senate)
PAYGO requirement	Net effect of all direct spending and revenue bills enacted during a session must not incur a cost on the PAYGO scorecard	Individual bills containing direct spending or revenue changes must be deficit neutral
Period of applicability	Budget year (and any carryover from the current year)	Six-year and 11-year periods, including the current year (House); budget year, first 5 years, and following 5 years (Senate)
Timing of enforcement	Within 15 days of the end of a congressional session	When direct spending or revenue legislation is considered
Means of enforcement	Presidential sequestration order implementing across-the-board spending cuts, based on OMB director's sequestration report	Point of order
Means of suspension	Designation of provisions as emergency requirements (under BEA); directed scorekeeping provisions (ad hoc)[b]	Special rule reported by Rules Committee (House; requires simple majority vote); waiver motion (Senate; requires 60 votes)
Period of effectiveness	Fiscal years 1992–2003[c]	Fiscal years 1994–2017 (Senate); fiscal years 2007–09 during 110th Congress (House)

a. The PAYGO provision in the BEA of 1990 took the form of an amendment to the Balanced Budget and Emergency Deficit Control Act of 1985, incorporating a revised section 252 into that act. The section was extended and revised by the BEA of 1997 and other laws.

b. Generally, a directed scorekeeping provision instructs the OMB director to reduce the balances on the PAYGO scorecard for one or more fiscal years by specified amounts or to reduce them to zero. In the early years of PAYGO, directed scorekeeping provisions removed savings from the scorecard; in later years, they removed costs.

c. Statutory PAYGO covered the effects through fiscal year 2006 of legislation enacted through September 30, 2002. P.L. 107-312, signed into law on December 2, 2002, effectively terminated statutory PAYGO by reducing the remaining balances on the PAYGO scorecard to zero, as noted in OMB's final sequestration report, issued on December 6, 2002.

Budgeting for discretionary spending is different from budgeting for direct spending. In discretionary spending, the basic task is to decide future spending levels; in mandatory spending, it is to estimate the cost of past decisions. While the two processes converge at various points, such as the president's budget and the congressional budget resolution, they differ along a number of key institutional and financial dimensions. Although there are some exceptions to the distinctions drawn in table 4-5, the generalizations provide a useful

TABLE 4-5
Comparison of Discretionary and Direct Spending

Feature	Discretionary spending	Direct spending
Budgetary impact of authorizing legislation	Authorizes consideration of appropriations measures	Provides budget resources
Role of the appropriations committees	Provides budget resources	Little or no control over budget resources
Frequency of action	Annual	Irregular, no fixed schedule
Enforcing budget decisions	Section 302(b) allocations to subcommittees	Reconciliation procedures
Basis of calculating budget impacts	Amount appropriated compared with current year's level and president's request for next year	Baseline projections and estimated effects of policy changes
Economic sensitivity	Low, indirect	Direct, often automatic
Political sensitivity	Variable: high for some programs, low for others	Often very high
Correspondence of budgeted and actual spending	Usually very high for budget authority, less for outlays	Sometimes low

comparison of two different budget conditions. The paragraphs below correspond to the entries in the table.

Budgetary Impact of Authorizing Legislation

An authorization of discretionary spending is only a license (required by House and Senate rules) to consider an appropriation. The amount authorized may be spent only to the extent that funds are appropriated. In contrast, an authorization of direct spending (such as entitlement legislation) either provides funds or effectively mandates the appropriation of budget resources. Spending control tends to be weaker when authorizing committees rather than appropriators dictate the amount to be spent because these committees often function

as advocates for the programs under their jurisdiction. For example, the political role of the agriculture committees is to look after the interests of farmers. Unlike the appropriations committees, they do not have to consider other demands on the budget when they reauthorize farm programs.

Role of the Appropriations Committees

The appropriations committees have effective jurisdiction over all discretionary spending; the amounts available are specified in appropriations acts. However, these committees do not control mandatory spending. Some mandatory programs are funded by permanent appropriations and bypass the annual appropriations process. Many are funded by annual appropriations, but because the spending is mandated by law, the appropriations committees do not control the amounts they provide.

Frequency of Congressional Action

With few exceptions, discretionary appropriations are voted annually for the next (or current) fiscal year. Direct spending, however, is typically enacted in permanent law that continues in effect unless it is terminated or revised by subsequent legislation. The fact that many entitlements are financed by annual appropriations does not diminish the permanence of the laws governing the amounts spent. Some entitlements, such as Medicare, have been subject to frequent legislative action; others, such as Social Security, have gone years without new legislation.

Enforcing Budget Decisions

Congress expresses its budget policy, including the changes it seeks in existing revenue or spending laws, in an annual resolution. Because this resolution is not a statute, Congress must implement its budget policies in other measures. For discretionary spending, it does so in annual appropriations; for direct spending and taxes, it passes new legislation. In both cases, Congress needs a mechanism for ensuring that these actions are in accord with its budget policy. A procedure known as section 302 allocations links annual appropriations to the congressional budget resolution. By means of this procedure, the House and Senate appropriations committees are given their share of the spending amounts in the budget resolution (under section 302(a) of the 1974 Congressional Budget Act); each then allocates its spending among its subcommittees (under section 302(b) of the act). In most cases, total spending in each appropriations bill must be within the amounts allocated to the relevant subcommittee. In recent years, caps on total discretionary spending have been included in budget resolutions, enforceable in the Senate (but not in the House) by a point of order.

In the case of direct spending and revenues, Congress relies on reconciliation procedures to implement its budget decisions; it does not apply reconciliation to discretionary spending. Although it can be a potent instrument, reconciliation is used only in those years when Congress wants to change existing revenue or direct spending laws; it is not applied in years when Congress accepts the budget outcomes that ensue from existing law. The House and Senate also enforce decisions regarding direct spending legislation as part of their internal PAYGO rules.

Basis of Calculating Budget Impacts

Virtually all discretionary appropriations are for definite amounts. In making and reporting their decisions, the appropriations committees often compare the amounts recommended to the previous year's appropriation and to the amounts the president has requested. Thus, if an account had an appropriation of $100 million in the previous year, and the president requested $120 million for the next year but the appropriations bill provided $110 million, this action would be counted as both a $10 million increase and a $10 million reduction. Direct spending legislation, however, is scored against baseline estimates of the amount that would be spent if current law continues in effect without change. Moreover, inasmuch as most mandatory spending is open-ended—the law establishing entitlements usually does not specify or limit the amount to be spent—calculations of budgetary impact are based on assumed rather than actual spending levels.

Economic Sensitivity

Budget decisions are sensitive to changes in economic conditions, but the response may be weaker in discretionary programs than in mandatory ones. Discretionary spending is not automatically adjusted for economic changes. When prices rise, Congress may appropriate more funds, or it may require agencies to absorb the inflation with the same resources they had for the previous year. But in direct spending, there often is an automatic adjustment. Rising prices trigger cost-of-living adjustments in Social Security and other transfer payments; rising unemployment boosts the number of people receiving unemployment benefits and certain other payments. In being more sensitive to the performance of the economy, direct spending may be less responsive to the condition of the budget.

Political Sensitivity

Political considerations influence all budgets. Both discretionary and direct spending programs have constituents who benefit from federal dollars and actively guard their interests. But political interest in discretionary programs is highly variable. Some programs have powerful political constituencies that lobby for additional funds; others hardly attract any attention. Direct spending is inherently sensitive because it affects the financial well-being of so many Americans. For the 50 million Americans receiving monthly Social Security payments and the 44 million enrolled in Medicare, the flow of money from Washington is a key determinant of their living stan-

dard. Cutting these and other entitlements has just about the same impact on household finances as cutting the pay of workers. It is just as visible, direct, and immediate, and as likely to provoke strong protest. It is not only their size that augments the political prominence of mandatory programs. When Congress establishes an entitlement, it gives recipients a legal right to the money, and when it indexes these payments to price increases, it entitles beneficiaries to protection against inflation. These legal rights have political value; they strengthen claims on the budget. If Congress cuts payments, it not only takes money from recipients but also infringes on their perceived rights.

Correspondence of Budgeted and Actual Spending

The final distinction in table 4-5 pertains to the amounts actually spent. Discretionary spending usually conforms closely to appropriated levels, but mandatory spending often varies significantly from budgeted amounts. Variances may be due to estimation errors, unanticipated changes in economic conditions, or policy changes. When spending veers sharply off course, it is most likely because of changes in external conditions that were not known when the budget estimates were made.

THE POLITICS OF BUDGETARY ARITHMETIC

The arithmetic of budgeting is political arithmetic—it influences budgetary policies and outcomes, and it is influenced in turn by the president, Congress, and others with a stake in budget decisions. Even when the numbers are compiled strictly in accord with technical rules and established practices, as is usually the case, they have political consequences. The numbers influence public perceptions about the budget, such as the size of the surplus or deficit. They may influence the behavior of politicians by making some types of transactions more or less expensive than others and may facilitate or impede the passage of legislation by increasing or reducing the estimated budgetary impact of a particular measure. Although the rules for recording revenues and outlays have always been important, the appropriations caps and PAYGO rules gave them added prominence. How legislation is scored may determine whether a measure under consideration (or passed by Congress) is in compliance with current budget rules.

Enforcing these rules is rarely straightforward, for much depends on assumptions about the behavior of firms and individuals affected by existing or new policies. For example, every budget specifies the amounts to be spent during the next year (or beyond) on Medicare, unemployment insurance, and other benefit programs. These figures are not firm; they are based on assumptions about future economic conditions, participation rates, and the payments those eligible will receive. In most cases, these assumptions are wrong, sometimes by small amounts, but occasionally they are wide of the mark. Even when they are wrong, however, budget decisions are based on them as if they were certain.

Budgeting pertains to the future, and since the future is unknown, it can only be assumed. Small changes in the underlying assumptions can yield quite large differences in budget entries. Yet the budget says more about its numbers than about its assumptions. The assumptions are where political opportunism and manipulation thrive. The budget staffs in the executive (OMB) and legislative (CBO)

branches manage these rules and assumptions. Each staff has a strong interest in upholding the integrity of the budget process, but neither can avoid some entanglement in the politics of budgeting. As the president's largest staff agency, OMB has the lead role in preparing and defending his budget; it cannot openly take positions contrary to White House policies. Both OMB's political operatives and career staff devise bookkeeping ploys that add up the budget to the numbers the president wants. As a congressional agency beholden to both Democrats and Republicans, CBO vigilantly guards its independence, but as the scoring of legislation has gained prominence in enforcing budget rules, it has become part of the battle between the two parties and between the president and Congress (see box 4-1). On many routine matters of budgetary arithmetic, CBO and OMB coordinate their work and produce the same numbers, but major disagreements occasionally explode into the open.

One such clash occurred over President Clinton's health care reforms, and it indicates how outcomes can be swayed by budgetary arithmetic. When Clinton sent his health proposal to Congress in 1994, he estimated that the reforms would reduce projected deficits by almost $60 billion over the next seven years. Reviewing the same proposal, however, CBO informed Congress that they would add $70 billion to the deficit. The wide discrepancy between the two estimates derived principally from differing assumptions about future health care costs.

Both OMB and CBO claimed that their estimates were free of political influence. Surely, however, it was no accident that OMB's numbers supported the president's position while CBO's challenged it. OMB's buoyant estimate helped Clinton reconcile his

▼

BOX 4-1
CBO Independence: Challenge and Defense

CBO's role in developing baseline projections and scoring the budgetary impact of legislation some-times places it into conflict with members of Congress. Members often try to influence CBO's esti-mates behind the scenes, but it is rare that disputes break out into the open. However, in 1998, as this exchange of letters indicates, House Speaker Newt Gingrich (R-Ga.) and CBO Director June O'Neill clashed on the accuracy of CBO's revenue projections. At stake were Republican claims that a projec-tion of higher revenues (and therefore a bigger surplus) would strengthen their case for tax cuts. Although CBO had increased its original revenue projection for fiscal year 1999 by $72 billion, the Republican leadership argued that this estimate should have been raised by a greater amount.

The first salvo was fired by House Republican leaders in a letter to Representative James Walsh (R-N.Y.), who chaired the House Legislative Branch Appropriations Subcommittee. Implied in this was the threat that if CBO was not more accommodating in revenue estimates, its appropriations would be cut:

> "We are deeply concerned about the increasing evidence that the Congressional Budget Office (CBO) is utterly unable to predict consistent and accurate future revenues or even the fiscal implications of changes in budget policy. Because of these failures, I urge you to direct the CBO to address these shortcomings immediately.
>
> While forecasting is an inexact science and there is some logic to being cautious, the CBO's low estimates have been consistently wrong—and wrong by a country mile. Currently, the CBO is estimating that real GDP growth will be a slow 2.1 percent over the long-term. Yet over the past 16 years the average GDP growth has been 3.0 percent, in line with the entire post World War II period. In the past, this understatement of GDP growth by 1 percent per year on average resulted in dramatic overestimates of the budget deficit and underestimates of the growing sur-plus. Comparing the CBO's 1998 deficit estimate from May 1996 to that of May 1998 shows a massive difference of $275 billion—from a $222 billion *deficit* to a $53 billion *surplus*.

continued

twin objectives of health care reform and deficit reduction; CBO's skeptical numbers gave doubting congressional committees more reasons for thwarting the president's initiative.

With so much riding on the numbers and underlying assumptions, it matters whose cal-culations have greater credence. When BEA was in effect, OMB officially measured the budgetary impact of legislation and deter-mined whether congressional action complied with the statutory budget rules. Following the expiration of BEA, however, CBO often has the upper hand when its estimates diverge

from OMB's. The reason is that Congress gen-erally relies on CBO's judgment while it is considering legislation; OMB's score is rele-vant only after a measure has passed both chambers and the president must decide whether to approve or veto it.

Having two scorekeepers is not just a mat-ter of getting a second opinion. This arrange-ment is rooted in the constitutional separa-tion of powers. In most cases, Congress wants to maintain its independence on budgetary matters; this was its principal objective in establishing CBO. But it is in the president's

▼

BOX 4-1
Continued

These forecasts are the foundation upon which Congress crafts legislation. Congress should not be put in a position of relying upon incorrect information. The CBO must address this problem. If it does not, I believe we must review the structure and funding for the CBO in this appropriations cycle."

CBO Director June O'Neill responded two weeks later, upholding CBO's objectivity and independence in budget work:

"It is important that we understand your concerns so that we can respond to them. We at CBO take our obligation to the Congress and to the country very seriously. We understand how important it is to produce state-of-the-art and unbiased estimates, projections, and studies with the highest degree of accuracy possible. CBO staff—a well-trained group of professionals—work hard to do so. . . .

Estimating errors, even large ones, can never be eliminated given the complexity of the federal government's budget, which is greatly affected by the economy here and abroad and by numerous other factors that are difficult, if not impossible, to predict exactly. With total revenues and outlays each approaching $1.7 trillion, even very small percentage deviations from CBO's projected amounts can easily swing budgetary outcomes by tens of billions of dollars. . . .

We have particularly emphasized the uncertainty involved in economic and budget forecasting in our twice-yearly reports to the Congress on the economic and budget outlook. We have also taken steps to provide the Congress with an early-warning mechanism that will signal when actual receipts and outlays are deviating from our estimates for the current fiscal year. . . ."

Sources: Letter from Republican leaders to chair of the House Legislative Branch Appropriations Subcommittee, James Walsh (R-N.Y.), Washington, June 9, 1998; excerpts from a letter to Speaker Newt Gingrich (R-Ga.) from CBO Director June O'Neill, Washington, June 23, 1998.

interest to use estimates and assumptions prepared by OMB that are responsive to his legislative objectives. When Clinton became president, he expected that there would be no need for separate projections because Democrats controlled both branches. In his February 1993 budget speech to Congress, Clinton promised to rely on CBO economic estimates. "Let's at least argue about the same set of numbers," Clinton urged, "so the American people will think we're shooting straight with them." Within a few months, however, the administration was insisting on its own budget and economic assumptions when they differed from those CBO issued.

There are two situations under which one branch may base its budgetary action on the other's numbers. One is when congressional leaders and the president rely on summit negotiations to resolve a budgetary impasse; the other is when Congress finds it advantageous to use OMB data rather than its own. When they go to the summit, the two sides cannot make much headway unless they agree on what the numbers mean. They must have the same starting points, assumptions, and scoring rules. If they do not, any agreement would quickly evaporate.

In arithmetic disputes between the two branches, CBO often takes the more cautious position, estimating somewhat lower economic growth and higher outlays. Consequently, Congress sometimes finds itself at a disadvantage using CBO numbers. On occasion, therefore, Congress has directed CBO to use OMB assumptions in scoring legislation. This practice, known as directed scoring, is discussed later in the chapter.

Scoring, like much else in budgeting, is an amalgam of procedures and politics. To conclude that the numbers are manipulated to serve political interests would ignore the extent to which numerical entries in the budget are determined by technical rules. But to assume that the numbers are churned out by a politics-free process would miss the extent to which budget makers bend the numbers to their liking. The balance between technical and political factors varies with different facets of budgeting. When the numbers represent actual transactions, such as the amount appropriated, technical rules predominate. When they represent assumptions about future conditions, such as the rate of inflation, there is greater scope for political influence. Because the budget is increasingly driven by assumptions, political arithmetic has become more important than it was a generation ago.

BASELINE PROJECTIONS

To enforce its budget rules during consideration of revenue or spending legislation, Congress must measure the budgetary impact of its actions. This task is relatively easy for programs funded in annual appropriations; Congress compares the amounts provided to the previous year's appropriation or to the presi-

dent's request. But the task can be difficult when Congress acts on revenue or entitlement legislation. In these cases, it must take account of factors that influence the amount taken in or spent, including the performance of the economy, price changes, participation rates, and the behavior of those affected by federal policy. The revenue yield of tax legislation depends primarily on future economic conditions and on the responses of taxpayers to changes in tax laws. The cost of entitlement legislation depends on economic variables, demographic trends, and the extent to which those who are eligible avail themselves of the benefits. Each program has its own factors that drive budgetary responses to legislative changes. Medicaid depends, among other things, on the actions of states in enrolling beneficiaries and setting benefits; the food stamps program, on income trends; Medicare, on the age structure of the population; and the State Child Health Insurance Program (SCHIP) is sensitive to poverty rates, family structure, and grassroots initiatives to enroll eligible children. A complex program such as Medicare is sensitive to dozens of variables; each has to be analyzed in estimating future program expenditures.

In budget making, the future is assumed. Assumptions are used to estimate spending and revenue under existing laws and to decide on changes in these laws. When Congress legislates, the estimated budgetary impact of its actions depends on assumptions about (1) the amounts that would be raised or spent without new legislation and (2) the amounts by which the legislation would change projected future revenue or spending. In contemporary budgeting, the first set of numbers is known as the baseline; the second set is the score. Both sets of numbers appear in table 4-6, which provides a hypothetical illustration of baseline projections and legislative scoring.

TABLE 4-6
Hypothetical Baseline Projection and Policy Changes, Fiscal Years 2008–12

Millions of dollars

	2008	2009	2010	2011	2012
Previous year's baseline	100.00	107.12	114.74	122.91	131.66
Assumptions					
4 percent inflation	+4.00	+4.28	+4.59	+4.92	+5.27
3 percent workload increase	+3.12	+3.34	+3.58	+3.83	+4.11
Baseline projection	107.12	114.74	122.91	131.66	141.04
Policy changes					
Cap inflation increases at 2 percent	−2.00	−4.20	−6.63	−9.30	−12.23
Slow workload increase to 2 percent	−1.08	−2.30	−3.67	−5.20	−6.92
Projected spending	104.04	108.24	112.61	117.16	121.89
Total policy changes (score)	−3.08	−6.50	−10.30	−14.50	−19.15

Both OMB and CBO prepare baseline estimates of budget aggregates (total revenue, total budget authority, and so on), particular categories of the budget (for example, national defense, income support), and for particular programs or accounts. OMB's estimates, called current services estimates, cover the next 5 years; CBO's estimates, called baseline budget projections, span 10 years. They assume that current policy will continue in effect and that spending levels will be fully adjusted for inflation. In the case of mandatory programs, the baseline is adjusted for estimated changes in workload, such as increases in the number of people receiving Social Security checks or Medicare services.

Once a baseline has been constructed, any variance from it due to legislation is measured as a policy change. In other words, legislation is scored and its budgetary impact is measured in terms of changes from the baseline. In the hypothetical case (table 4-6), baseline spending is projected to increase from $100 million in the current year to $141 million five years later. The $41 million increase, like all other baseline projections, is assumed; it will mate-

rialize only if the assumptions underlying the baseline—4 percent annual inflation and 3 percent annual workload increase—also materialize.

In this hypothetical case, legislated policy changes result in new projections below the baseline—$104 million in the first year compared with the $107 million baseline, growing to $122 million in the fifth year versus the $141 million baseline. Although these new projections show nominal spending increases, they are scored as cuts—a reduction of $3 million in the first year, rising to a $19 million reduction in the fifth year. The usual practice is to compute the score as the cumulative budgetary changes over the full period covered by the baseline. In this case, the score would be a $54 million spending reduction. If the baseline were extended to 10 years, the score would be much higher because estimated policy changes would be compounded for twice as many years.

This feature of baselines influences public perceptions of budgetary legislation. In 1999 Congress passed and Clinton vetoed a tax cut that was estimated to reduce federal revenues by $792 billion over a 10-year period. This seems to be an enormous reduction, but if the measure had been scored for only 5 years, the estimated revenue loss would have been less than one-quarter of that amount. In fact, the proposed tax cut would have amounted to less than 3 percent of the revenue expected to be collected over the 10 years.

The hypothetical example reveals another interesting feature of scoring policy changes against baselines. Legislation often results in spending that is higher than the current level but below the baseline. This pattern enables politicians to portray their actions as both a spending cut and a spending increase. They can use the baseline to make the case that spending has been reduced, and they can point to current spending levels to show that programs have been protected. Making the case both ways is no small political feat; it enables cross-pressured politicians to satisfy the conflicting demands that they cut the size of government and increase the size of programs.

The 1993 deficit reduction package President Clinton pushed through Congress illustrates how sizable savings can be enacted while program cutbacks are minimized. According to CBO estimates made when the package was enacted, Medicare was to be cut by $56 billion over five years. On its face, this cutback violated Clinton's pledge to Congress on February 17, 1993, when he launched his deficit reduction drive. "Let me be clear. There also will be no new cuts in Medicare. . . . Let me repeat this because I know it matters to a lot of you on both sides of the aisle. This plan does not make a recommendation for new cuts in Medicare benefits for any beneficiary."

How did the president and Congress manage to pare so much without cutting benefits? The Medicare program shows that the task is not as difficult as one might think. About $50 billion came from reductions in baseline payments to providers, some of which would not be counted as cuts if more stringent criteria had been used. For example, fees for surgical services were increased by 8.6 percent, far above general inflation and even above inflation in the health sector. Nevertheless, this increase was scored as a multibillion dollar cut because the baseline assumed a 12.2 percent inflation adjustment. Payments to hospitals were reduced by 7.4 percent, a smaller reduction than was provided by the law it replaced. Nevertheless, CBO scored this as savings because the new spending level was below the baseline. Several billion dollars more were saved by extending the existing requirement that Medicare Part B premiums cover 25 percent of program costs. The reported spending cuts produced by these and other maneuvers enabled Congress to enact a smattering of Medicare enhancements in the deficit reduction measure.

Like other features of budgeting, the baseline was developed for technical reasons—to give Congress a neutral starting point not tainted by the president's budget recommendations—but it also serves political ends. The baseline strongly influences public perceptions about the budget, gives budget makers incentives to structure tax and spending legislation in certain ways rather than others, and protects some programs against inflation. In discretionary spending, it strengthens arguments that appropriations should be increased to compensate agencies for inflation; in entitlements, it often transforms decisions facing the president and Congress from how much should be spent to how much should be cut.

Because the baseline hinges on assumptions, it provides ample scope for politicians to save programs by assuming savings will occur. They can meet savings targets by making some provisions temporary and taking credit for additional savings each time the provisions are

FIGURE 4-1
Alternative Projections of Medicare Spending, Fiscal Years 1996–2002

Billions of dollars

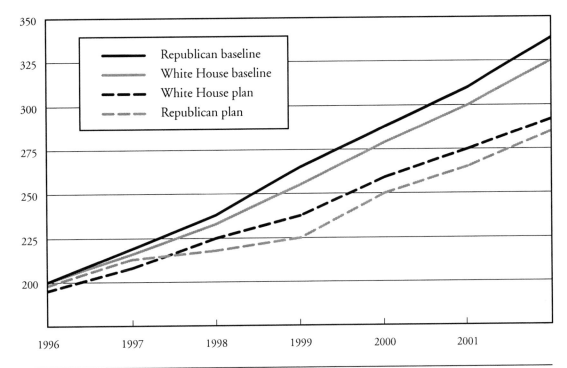

Source: Adapted from a graph in the *New York Times*, December 11, 1995, p. A1, based on Congressional Budget Office and White House estimates.

extended. They can manipulate the score by enacting legislation that is effective at different periods covered by the baseline.

Inasmuch as Congress and the president sometimes rely on different baseline assumptions, policy differences between them are distorted. This problem occurred in 1995, enabling Clinton to gain a political victory that scarred congressional Republicans through the remainder of his presidency. In 1995 OMB and CBO drew seven-year baselines that showed Medicare spending rising steeply over the period (figure 4-1). OMB assumed less health care inflation than CBO, and it therefore projected smaller spending

increases in Medicare. OMB estimated that over the seven years, Medicare spending would total $1.624 trillion; CBO's baseline totaled $1.692 trillion, $68 billion higher. Given the uncertainties in estimating future health care costs, the difference was quite small—only 4 percent of total spending. But this gap made an enormous difference in how the proposed Medicare cutbacks appeared. Because Congress used the CBO baseline, Republicans showed much deeper cuts than Clinton proposed. In fact, congressional Republicans reported $146 billion more in cuts than Clinton recommended, yet 47 percent of the variance was due to different baselines, not to policy differences. If Republicans had used Clinton's baseline, the size of their cut in 2002 would have been approximately $40 billion rather than $55 billion. If Clinton had used the Republican baseline, his cut in that year would have been about $50 billion instead of $35 billion. In terms of spending, the two plans differed by approximately $10 billion in 2002.

The moral of this story is that politicians have to be careful in choosing the baselines they use. In a dispute between the president and Congress, the side using the more cautious assumptions (for example, lower economic growth, higher inflation) exposes itself to blame for reducing spending, raising taxes, or doing other unwelcome things to the budget.

ECONOMIC ARITHMETIC

Assumptions about the future performance of the economy are among the main variables in constructing budget baselines. The relationship of the budget and the economy is reciprocal: budget policy influences economic performance, and economic conditions influence budget outcomes. The size of the budget surplus or deficit, the structure and amount of taxes, the pattern of expenditure, and the volume of debt financing affect economic growth, employment levels, price changes, interest rates, and other variables. In making budget decisions, the president and Congress must be mindful of the potential impacts on the economy. They must also take into account the impact of current and projected economic conditions. They make assumptions about nominal and real growth, inflation and employment trends, and interest rates. The president's budget usually forecasts economic performance for the current and next five calendar years; Congress relies on CBO's projections, which typically vary slightly from the president's.

Because the budget, like the baseline, is predicated on assumptions, the extent to which revenue and spending expectations are achieved depends significantly on whether assumed economic conditions materialize. Variances between assumed and actual conditions may translate into significant discrepancies between expected and actual budget results. Table 4-7 shows the budget's high sensitivity to swings in economic conditions. Much of the budget's adjustment to economic change is automatic; it occurs without presidential or congressional action and whether it is welcome or not. Outlays are sensitive to interest rates and inflation. Revenues are particularly sensitive to growth rates: a shortfall in economic performance invariably means lower-than-projected receipts. Even a minor shortfall can take a big bite out of federal revenues.

A temporary deviation from the expected economic course has lingering effects. According to OMB estimates (from which table 4-7 is drawn), if actual growth were one percentage point less than forecast in 2007 but achieved expected levels in each of the next five years, the fiscal 2012 deficit would be $54 billion higher than the amount projected five years earlier. Approximately 70 percent of the shortfall would be in revenues.

The most recent recession (as of this writing) occurred in 2001. By standard measures, it was brief and shallow, lasting only three-quarters of a year and causing real GDP to grow at only 0.5 percent for the full year. Although the recession was a blip in a long-term growth trend, it subtracted tens of billions of dollars from revenues and contributed to the shift from surplus to deficit. The recession left an imprint on the budget for the next

TABLE 4-7
Budget Sensitivity to Variances from Economic Projections, Fiscal Years 2007–12[a]

Billions of dollars

Assumption	2007	2008	2009	2010	2011	2012
Real GDP growth: 1 percent lower than projected in 2007; growth as projected in later years[b]						
Receipts	–13	–28	–31	–34	–36	–38
Outlays	3	8	10	12	14	16
Deficit increase (–)	–16	–36	–42	–46	–50	–54
Real GDP growth: 1 percent lower than projected each year, 2007–12[c]						
Receipts	–14	–44	–80	–123	–168	–216
Outlays	0	1	4	8	13	19
Deficit increase (–)	–14	–45	–84	–131	–181	–235
Inflation: 1 percent higher than assumed each year, 2007–12						
Receipts	13	43	78	118	161	209
Outlays	4	12	22	34	46	59
Deficit decrease (+)	10	31	56	85	115	150

Source: *Budget of the United States Government, Analytical Perspectives, Fiscal Year 2008*, table 12-5, p. 173.
   a. Numbers may not add up to totals due to rounding.
   b. Assumes a 0.5 percentage point rise in the unemployment rate per 1.0 percent shortfall in the level of real GDP.
   c. Assumes no change in the unemployment rate.

five years, for though the deficit declined, it remained much higher than it would have been if economic growth had not been interrupted at the start of the decade.

The longer the economy veers off course, the greater the impact on the budget. If economic growth were one percentage point lower each year from 2007 through 2012, the deficit in the sixth year would be $235 billion above original projections. The variance from budgeted levels widens each year the economy stagnates. One percentage point lower growth would subtract an estimated $14 billion from federal revenues in the first year and $216 billion in the sixth year; a one percentage point rise in inflation would add $4 billion to federal outlays in the first year and $59 billion in the sixth year.

Scoring the Economic Effects of Policy Changes

When CBO and OMB score legislation, they generally estimate the behavioral changes that would ensue from policy changes. For example, when Congress increased the earned income tax credit for the working poor, budget scorers estimated the costs that would result from giving more people an incentive to apply for this benefit. As a general rule, however, scorers do not consider possible changes in overall economic activity due to new legislation. For example, when the capital gains tax rate was lowered, the score did not include estimates of whether increased savings and investment might make the economy more productive and thereby boost federal revenues. But it did include an estimate of the additional capital gains that would be cashed in through the sale of stock and other assets.

The question of which economic impacts should be measured is often framed in terms of static versus dynamic scoring. Static scoring takes account of behavioral responses that can be reliably estimated; it does not measure changes in aggregate economic performance. Dynamic scoring includes macroeconomic effects such as changes in national output, employment levels, and investment. Differences between the two approaches can be significant: static scoring generally estimates that a lower capital gains rate will lose revenue; dynamic scoring concludes it will generate higher revenue. (This issue is discussed further in chapter 7.)

Legislation is often promoted on the grounds that it will improve economic performance. If this is so, why is the feedback from the economy to the budget not included in the score? Why not incorporate dynamic models of economic impact? Those who oppose dynamic scoring offer two main justifications for excluding macroeconomic impacts: first, these effects are exceedingly difficult to measure; second, including them would open the door to opportunistic scoring that could damage the credibility of the budget. Taken to the extreme, dynamic scoring might generate perverse conclusions that the federal government raises more money when it taxes less, and spends less when it increases expenditures. These are the kinds of justifications that condemned the federal government to high deficits after steep tax cuts in 1981 and 2001.

THE POLITICS OF SCORING

Scoring is not a static exercise in which budget experts wait until legislation has been proposed or enacted before measuring budgetary impact. As scoring has become more important, it has moved from the end of the process to the beginning. Legislation is framed so as to affect the score, and scorekeepers estimate the cost of alternatives before they are introduced. As legislative ideas are bounced around, there is a lot of behind-the-scenes interaction between budget scorers and politicians. Lobbyists and federal agencies sometimes get into the act, trying to persuade budget specialists to score matters their way.

The arcane world of scoring has rules and precedents, some of which have been published (exhibit 4-1), but there also are ad hoc accommodations in special cases. The "fingerprints rule" (rule 3 in the exhibit) is applied by OMB and CBO to classify spending as discretionary or direct. This rule specifies that legislated changes are scored to the committee reporting the measure—if an appropriations committee reports the bill, the ensuing spending is discretionary; if any other committee produces the bill, the spending is direct. The purpose of this rule is to deter evasion of budget controls, but it can produce some strange scoring outcomes. In 1999, for example, a legislative committee proposed that an automatic continuing resolution take effect whenever the fiscal year starts without enactment of all regular appropriations. Although the measure would pertain only to appropriations, CBO scored it as a $500 billion increase in direct spending because it was reported by an authorizing committee; the CBO score helped kill the proposal.

From time to time, Congress suspends the fingerprints rule when it enacts budget deals. One such case occurred in 1998 with respect to the omnibus appropriations act for fiscal year 1999 (see box 5-4), which packed eight

▶ **EXHIBIT 4-1**
Scorekeeping Guidelines

3. Direct Spending Programs: Substantive changes to or restrictions on entitlement law or other mandatory spending law in appropriations laws will be scored against the Appropriations Committee section 302(b) allocations in the House and the Senate. For the purpose of CBA scoring, direct spending savings that are included in both an appropriation bill and a reconciliation bill will be scored to the reconciliation bill and not to the appropriation bill. . . .

6. Reappropriations: Reappropriations of expiring balances of budget authority will be scored as new budget authority in the fiscal year in which the balances become newly available.

7. Advance Appropriations: Advance appropriations of budget authority will be scored as new budget authority in the fiscal year in which the funds become newly available for obligation, not when the appropriations are enacted.

8. Rescissions of Unobligated Balances: Rescissions of unobligated balances will be scored as reductions in current budget authority and outlays in the year the money is rescinded. . . .

9. Delay of Obligations: Appropriation acts specify a date when funds will become available for obligation. It is this date that determines the year for which new budget authority is scored. In the absence of such a date, the act is assumed to be effective upon enactment.

 If the new appropriation provides that a portion of the budget authority shall not be available for obligation until a future fiscal year, that portion shall be treated as an advance appropriation of budget authority. . . .

15. Asset Sales: : If the net financial cost to the government of an asset sale is zero or negative (a savings), the amount scored shall be the estimated change in receipts and mandatory outlays in each fiscal year on a cash basis. If the cost to the government is positive (a loss), the proceeds from the sale shall not be scored for the purposes of the CBA or GRH.

Source: Office of Management and Budget, "Appendix A: Scorekeeping Guidelines," in *Circular A-11*, June 2006 (www.whitehouse.gov/omb/circulars/a11/current_year/app_a.pdf).

 (a) The House and Senate Budget Committees, CBO, and OMB use these scorekeeping guidelines in measuring compliance with the Congressional Budget Act (CBA) of 1974, as amended; they also were used for measuring compliance with the Balanced Budget and Emergency Deficit Control Act (BBA) of 1985, as amended.

 (b) The purpose of the guidelines is to ensure that scorekeepers measure the budgetary effects of legislation with established conventions and with the specific requirements in the CBA and, previously, the BBA regarding discretionary spending, direct spending, and receipts.

 (c) All of the scorekeepers must agree before any of the rules are changed. New accounts or activities are classified only after consultation among the scorekeepers. Accounts and activities shall not be reclassified unless all of the scorekeepers agree.

appropriations acts and numerous authorizing laws in a single measure that was worked out in summit negotiations with the White House. A strict application of the fingerprints rule would have required that the legislative provisions be scored as discretionary spending, but Congress directed CBO to score them as direct spending.

Scorekeeping rules are sometimes changed to accommodate political interests. In the 1980s, when scoring rules were initially formalized, revenue from the sale of assets was not scored as a receipt; the additional revenue was disregarded in measuring budget impact. This rule recognized that the government's financial condition is not changed by the sale of an asset, as it is merely exchanging one type of asset (such as real estate or a promissory note) for another type (cash). In the 1990s, however, the rules were changed to score savings but not losses from asset sales.

When an interest group lobbies Congress for a tax cut or spending increase, it no longer suffices that the proposal be palatable to members of Congress; it is also necessary that the proposal get a favorable score. Some former budget and appropriations committees' staff members now provide expert advice on how to structure legislative proposals to influence the score. This game is played by both parties and in both the legislative and executive branches. Some tactics apply only to direct or discretionary spending, others to both. Although there are many variations, the tactics fall into two categories: one is to make the money (a spending increase or a tax cut) disappear; the other is to change the timing of the transaction. The discussion below deals with spending, but similar tactics are deployed in structuring revenue legislation.

Discretionary Appropriations

The spending caps have spurred Congress to rearrange appropriations in ways that enable it to spend more while professing to stay within the caps. The tighter the caps, the greater the incentive to evade them. The following paragraphs explain some of the tactics devised to lower the discretionary spending score. Congress and the president employed many of the tactics discussed here in 1999 (for fiscal 2000 appropriations) because the gap between the discretionary caps and spending pressures was extraordinarily wide in that year.

Emergency Spending

This simple and effective approach has become a significant loophole in the budget enforcement rules. When the president and Congress want to spend more than the caps allow, they have a strong incentive to designate the excess spending as an emergency because its budget authority and related outlays are outside the caps. No criteria or assessments are required to ensure that the additional spending is for true emergencies such as natural disaster relief. As detailed in box 4-2 and box 5-4, $21 billion of emergency spending was crammed into the fiscal 1999 omnibus appropriations act to resolve a preelection impasse, and an additional $15 billion was provided in that year's supplemental appropriation. The ploy was used again in fiscal 2000 appropriations because the caps did not provide sufficient room for maintaining existing programs and fully funding priorities; Congress and the president designated $20 billion, including funds for the decennial census required by the Constitution, as emergency spending.

Led by Clinton, Democrats came out ahead in the emergency spending contests in the 1990s; they got credit for fiscal prudence while securing more money for popular programs. At times, congressional Republicans have taken the position that emergency spending should be offset by cuts in other discretionary programs, but they have not consistently followed this policy. Often outmaneuvered, they reluctantly approved the increases, sometimes after getting billions more for defense.

Offsets

A second way of making money "disappear" is to offset some spending increases by rescinding previous appropriations or by increasing offsetting collections from user fees or other sources. This is one reason that the volume of rescissions Congress initiated rose during the 1990s (see chapter 10). In 1999, for example, some Republicans proposed to rescind billions of unspent welfare dollars previously appropriated to the states to offset above-cap appropriations sought by Congress. Although state protests thwarted the proposed rescission, this example illustrates how the offsets game operates.

Under BEA rules, appropriations offsets were supposed to come only from discretionary accounts; any other offsets were to be scored in the PAYGO budget. Nevertheless, Congress and the president sometimes raided PAYGO accounts to boost discretionary spending. For fiscal years 1992 through 1998, there were about one hundred instances in which reductions in mandatory spending were scored as offsets to increase discretionary spending. One such instance occurred in the 1997 balanced budget deal, which diverted to the discretionary part of the budget $3 billion in income from the sale of radio frequencies. Another instance occurred a year earlier, when $1 billion from mortgage insurance reforms was used as offsets. Clinton disregarded the firewall in his fiscal 2000 budget, which proposed appropriations that were many billions of dollars above the discretionary caps but would have been offset with increased tobacco taxes. Clinton's démarche put congressional Republicans in a difficult position—either vote for tax increases or against education. Republicans tried to wriggle out of this

predicament by designating routine expenditures as emergencies.

Directed Scoring

Money can be made to disappear by instructing CBO scorers to use OMB assumptions rather than its own. It was noted earlier that CBO tends to use more cautious assumptions than OMB; when this occurs, Congress appears to be spending more than it would if OMB's estimates were used. At times, therefore, the budget committees direct CBO to score certain appropriations with OMB's assumptions. A related tactic is for Congress to make unilateral scoring adjustments, such as a slower spendout rate or quicker revenue flow, that have the effect of reducing total budget authority and outlays. In some cases, Congress picks and chooses between OMB and CBO assumptions, taking from each those that score its appropriations as less costly.

The forgoing tactics are intended to make appropriations disappear; the ones that follow are designed to defer their appearance in the score until a later fiscal year.

Advance Appropriations

Scorekeeping rule 7 (see exhibit 4-1) provides that advance appropriations are scored as new budget authority in the fiscal year in which the funds become available. This rule enables Congress to make appropriations in one year but have the money scored against the caps for a later year. This tactic is attractive in grant programs because the federal fiscal year does not coincide with that of state and local governments. The federal fiscal year runs from October through September, whereas that of many states runs from July through June.

Congress resorted extensively to advance appropriations in fiscal 1999 and even more so in subsequent years. In evading one year's caps, advance appropriations can make it more

BOX 4-2
Evading the Spending Caps: Emergency Spending in 1999

A bill that started out in 1999 as an ordinary emergency supplemental appropriation for hurricane disaster relief ended up as a vehicle for blowing a $15 billion hole in the discretionary spending cap. Evading the caps is not a particularly difficult task because BEA does not define "emergency"; an emergency is whatever the president and Congress deem it to be. There are political land mines, however; the White House and Capitol Hill have to share in the joys of emergency spending, legislative voices calling for the additional spending to be offset by cuts in other areas have to be silenced, and Congress has to minimize legislative riders that might provoke a presidential veto.

When the 1999 legislative session opened, the two branches had a recent precedent to guide them through the budget maze. Just months earlier, Congress ended the 1998 session by negotiating an omnibus appropriations act with the president that included $21 billion in emergency supplemental spending (see box 5-4). Enacted in October 1998, a mere three weeks into the new fiscal year, that measure started with President Clinton asking for $9 billion in emergency spending; Republicans then added their own list of priority items at a cost of $5 billion, and congressional Democrats anted up another $6 billion.

But that spending frenzy did not sate political appetites. In politics, emergency spending begets more emergency spending. The pressure to spend escalated: Clinton was seeking another $3 billion in emergency funds, revenues were surging into the Treasury, the budget surplus was growing, farmers were clamoring for additional aid, hurricanes ravaged Central American countries, and the United States promised to bankroll Israeli-Arab peace agreements.

Congressional Republicans, tarnished by their avid participation in the previous year's spending spree, opened legislative consideration of the supplemental by demanding that the additional spending be offset by cuts in other programs. Senate Appropriations Committee Chair Ted Stevens (R-Alaska) argued that "only defense funds [should be] rescinded to offset defense spending and only nondefense amounts to balance the nondefense spending." Clinton maintained, however, that the additional spending was "urgent, unanticipated, and essential"; hence, it should "be funded quickly, fully, and without requiring offsets that could force unanticipated reductions in important programs." He also urged Congress "not to add extraneous authorizations to the bill, particularly narrow, objectionable riders that would serve only to generate controversy, unnecessarily delaying the urgent needed assistance contained in this bill."

The House and Senate disregarded Clinton's demands, but the two chambers passed very different bills. The House bill cost about half as much as the Senate's and targeted different items for rescissions. The House applied the emergency designation to some spending while the Senate proposed across-the-board cuts in the omnibus appropriations enacted in the previous session. Clinton criticized both bills and threatened a veto if the offsets were retained.

Before House-Senate differences could be worked out in conference, the United States began military operations in the Balkans, leading the president to request another $6 billion in emer-

continued

BOX 4-2
Continued

gency spending. With the supplemental at a level that ruled out legitimate offsets, the House Appropriations Committee entered into a bidding war to boost defense spending. Adding money for dozens of projects the Pentagon had not requested, the committee reported a $13 billion emergency supplemental. Speaker Dennis Hastert (R-Ill.) defended the committee's action, claiming that the armed forces had been "hollowed out" by six years of Clinton-imposed budget cuts. For his part, the president again asked Congress to "resist the temptation to add unrelated expenditures." Despite this urging, more than half of the House Democrats joined with Republicans to pass the bill by a lopsided margin.

The Senate did not bother to take up the military supplemental. Instead, it opted to get what it wanted in the conference. The first thing that the House-Senate conference did was to package the military supplemental into the hurricane relief bill, in effect giving Clinton the message that the price for getting the latter would be to accept the former.

In conference, Democratic and Republican senators vied for the most costly add-ons to the bill. Senator Pete Domenici (R-N. Mex.) wanted a $500 million loan program for oil and gas companies. Not to be outdone, Senator Robert Byrd (D-W.Va.) demanded $1 billion in guaranteed loans for steel companies. In a burst of Sunbelt cooperation, Senators Bob Graham (D-Fla.) and Kay Bailey Hutchinson (R-Texas) insisted on a provision allowing states unrestricted use of $246 billion in tobacco settlement money. And in a display of corn and wheat state harmony, Democratic senators Tom Harkin (Iowa) and Byron Dorgan (N. Dak.) lobbied for $5 billion in emergency aid for farmers. In addition to these spending items, a slew of legislative riders dealing with (among other things) fishing rights in Alaska, dumping waste on federal lands, and the endangered silvery minnow and Alabama sturgeon were proposed in conference.

Not surprisingly, some in Congress who were not fortunate enough to have a front seat at the conference were upset by what had happened. Representative James Leach (R-Iowa) pleaded that "emergency supplementals should never be a vehicle for passage of measures that under ordinary conditions would be viewed with utmost skepticism." But Senator Pat Roberts (R-Kans.) explained why the riders were placed in the supplemental; it "was the only vehicle we had at the time."

For the first time, an appropriations conference was televised, giving the public an unusual glimpse of the give-and-take by which compromises are forged and legislation is passed. Representative Randy Cunningham (R-Calif.) said, "Most of us who watched . . . were appalled. It made the term 'good government' an oxymoron." Many of the controversial riders and some of the additional spending were dropped in conference, but the final tally was $15 billion. Senator Stevens used the fig leaf of "emergency" to assure his colleagues that "this additional money will remain safely in the U.S. Treasury and will only be used if the President determines emergencies exist that require the expenditure of these funds." Clinton thanked Congress for the supplemental and for ensuring that the government "will continue to be there for [American families] throughout their time of need."

difficult to comply with the next year's limit. If, for example, Congress provides $10 billion in advance appropriations, the effect is to reduce the amount available within the next year's caps by an equivalent amount. Underlying the use of advance appropriations is the hope that sooner or later Congress will raise the caps to accommodate more spending. In recent years, the House and Senate have included in the annual budget resolution a cap on the amount of advance appropriations and have specified the individual accounts for which such appropriations may be provided.

Clinton's fiscal 2001 budget contained yet another way of hiding the budgetary impact of advance appropriations. He proposed that $14 billion of advance appropriations made the previous year be shifted back to fiscal 2000. Under this guise, the $14 billion was not charged to the fiscal 2000 caps when they were enacted nor to the fiscal 2001 caps when the money was spent. The government got $14 billion more to spend, and both the president and Congress declared with straight faces that they were living within the caps.

Delayed Obligations
In this scheme, which was applied in fiscal 2000 appropriations to the National Institutes of Health and other agencies, a portion of the appropriation is withheld from obligation by law until the last days of the fiscal year. Although the new budget authority is scored in the year for which appropriations are made, the outlays are deferred to the next year. This approach has been used when the cap on outlays is tighter than that on budget authority.

Delayed Payment
A related practice is to declare in an appropriations act that some payments are to be delayed until the next fiscal year. The effect is to reduce the estimated spendout rate and the amount of outlays scored against the appropriation. In 2000 some government workers and military personnel had their payday, which fell on the last Saturday in September, delayed until the next fiscal year. By delaying the payment for one day, over $4 billion in spending was shifted to fiscal 2001.

Effectiveness of the Caps

In constant dollars, discretionary nondefense spending (which includes domestic and international activities) fared better under the caps in the 1990s than it did in the previous decade when there were no caps. These programs declined 9 percent in the 1980s but increased 19 percent during the next decade. As figure 4-2 indicates, real discretionary nondefense spending was significantly higher in fiscal year 2005 ($405 billion) than it was just before Ronald Reagan launched his campaign to roll back social programs ($295 billion in fiscal year 1980). But despite the dollar increases in this part of the budget, it did not recover as a share of GDP; discretionary nondefense spending was 5.2 percent of GDP in 1980 but only 3.9 percent 25 years later.

Most of the increases for nondefense programs came at the expense of the other major component of discretionary spending—national defense. Adjusted for inflation, defense outlays were $89 billion less in 2000 than they had been a decade earlier. Steep cutbacks in defense forces mirrored this drop. During the 1990s, the Army lost 8 of its 18 active divisions, the Air Force disbanded almost half of its active tactical air wings, the Navy deactivated more than 40 percent of the fleet, and the Pentagon shed one-third (nearly one million) of its civilian and active duty military personnel. The end of the Cold War

FIGURE 4-2
Discretionary Outlays, Five-Year Intervals, Fiscal Years 1980–2005[a]

Billions of constant (fiscal 2000) dollars

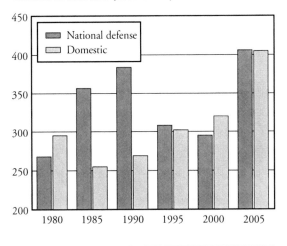

Source: *Budget of the United States Government, Historical Tables, Fiscal Year 2008,* table 8.2, p. 134.

a. Nondefense includes international programs.

evidently had a greater impact on discretionary nondefense spending than did the caps. Regardless of the caps, if the Cold War were still raging, there probably would have been no surplus in 1998 or subsequent years.

Through most of the 1990s, the president and Congress managed to live with the discretionary spending caps, but the constraint could not withstand the good times of a revenue surge and expanding economy. Clinton prodded Congress to vote for marginal increases in discretionary appropriations while claiming a commitment to controlling the budget and reducing the size of government. Although the amounts were large in dollar terms—discretionary outlays rose from $549 billion in 1997 to approximately $618 billion three years later—the amounts were too small to derail the march to a balanced budget. A

year after the deficit was liquidated, Clinton and Congress resorted to a slew of mechanisms to spend $49 billion more than the caps allowed (table 4-8). The following year, in his fiscal 2001 budget, Clinton designated this amount as "spending funded by alternative mechanisms" and proposed to shift $14 billion in advance appropriations and certain other funds back to fiscal 2000.

The caps did not work perfectly, as the heightened reliance on loopholes shows, but politicians have a strong incentive to restore them because the caps foster an appearance of fiscal discipline. As of this writing, President Bush has proposed to extend the caps for five years (through fiscal year 2012). While final decisions have yet to be made, there is a good chance that the caps will be extended annually in the budget resolution or for a period of years in law. The extent to which future caps are effective depends on the state of the budget. If the budget tightens, the caps will play a prominent role in constraining federal spending. If the budget is awash in revenue, it is inevitable that a portion of the bounty will be spent on expanding federal programs.

Direct Spending

Most of the tactics described below can be applied to both discretionary and direct spending. The following paragraphs elaborate how some methods have been used to influence the scoring of the latter.

Backloaded Spending Increases
The easiest way to remove a spending increase from the score is to schedule it to take effect beyond the period covered by the baseline. This tactic facilitated major expansions in Medicaid enacted in the late 1980s and early 1990s. The expansions were phased in over

TABLE 4-8
Spending Outside the Caps: Fiscal Year 2000 Appropriations[a]

Billions of dollars

Tactic	Budget authority	Outlays
Designated as emergency spending		
Defense Department operations and maintenance	7.2	5.4
Decennial census	4.5	3.8
Defense Department pay raise	1.8	1.8
Head Start	1.7	0.9
Other	8.5	2.6
Subtotal emergency spending	23.7	14.3
Offsets		
Federal Reserve balance transfer	3.8	3.8
Acceleration of spectrum auction receipts	2.6	2.6
Other	2.4	2.5
Subtotal offsets	8.7	8.8
Delayed obligations and delayed payments		
Pay delay	. . .	3.6
Defense progress payments	. . .	1.3
National Institutes of Health	. . .	0.9
Other	. . .	0.8
Subtotal delayed obligations and delayed payments	. . .	6.5
Fiscal 2001 advance appropriations		
Housing certificate fund	4.2	. . .
Special education	3.7	. . .
Training and employment services	2.5	. . .
School improvement programs	1.5	. . .
Administration for children and families	1.4	. . .
Other	1.1	. . .
Subtotal advance appropriations	14.4	. . .
Total	49.3	29.8

Source: Office of Management and Budget, *Final Sequestration Report,* January 25, 2000, table 2, pp. 4–6.
a. Amounts may not add to subtotals due to rounding.

more than a decade, with the result that they were never scored as spending increases. When enacted, the first year of expansion was beyond the baseline period; when that year finally was incorporated into the baseline, the expansion already was authorized by current law. With the lengthening of baselines to 10 years, it is harder to make new spending disappear. How-ever, Congress can still reduce the score by scheduling a portion of the spending increase to take effect late in the baseline period.

Offsets
The fingerprints rule dictates that offsets to direct spending increases come from revenue

or substantive legislation, not from measures in the jurisdiction of the appropriations committees. At times Congress exploits differences between Medicare and Medicaid to generate more spending in the latter by making small cuts in the former. Because it shares Medicaid responsibility with the states, the federal government pays less than 60 percent of the program's cost. However, it pays all of Medicare's expenses. This means that a $1 cut in Medicare makes room in the budget for almost $2 in Medicaid increases. The typical Medicare cuts involve reductions in payments to providers below baseline levels and an increase or extension in premiums; it rarely entails cuts in covered services.

Assessing the Impact of PAYGO

In addition to considering the scoring rules and the tactics used to lower the score, one must assess the budgetary and political contexts in which PAYGO, both statutory and rules-based, has operated in order to evaluate its impact. Inasmuch as direct spending changes are calculated in reference to the baseline, Congress and the president can make room for spending cuts that do not impair program activity by using assumptions that raise the baseline. This game has been played repeatedly with Medicare, generating hundreds of billions of dollars in scored cuts without significantly cutting benefits. Although some of the claimed savings from publicized cutbacks have been illusory and usually had a small net effect on federal spending, they have been applied to offset the cost of benefits enhancements.

PAYGO also has significantly affected congressional behavior. Although it has not halted the enactment of new spending and revenue legislation, it has changed the types of measures Congress produces. Welfare, in the form

of Aid to Families with Dependent Children (AFDC), was converted from an open-ended entitlement to a fixed block grant, and important changes were made in eligibility rules and program benefits to move recipients from welfare to work. When these reforms were enacted in 1996, official estimates projected a six-year savings of $54 billion. But because of the steep, larger-than-expected decline in welfare rolls—6.5 million fewer recipients in 1998 than in 1993—welfare reform boosted spending (above what it might have been if the old program had been continued). Agricultural price supports also have been overhauled, but the projected savings never were realized. Whenever the farm sector ran into trouble, Congress and the president poured in billions of dollars of emergency money.

PAYGO contributed to the liquidation of budget deficits by hampering enactment of new direct spending legislation and making it easier for the government to hold on to its revenue dividend (PAYGO's impact on revenue legislation is discussed in chapter 7). During the revenue surge in the 1990s, Clinton adroitly used PAYGO to thwart Republican demands for slashing tax rates, despite the emergence of a surplus and a steep rise in federal revenue as a share of the gross domestic product (GDP). However, without Clinton's strong opposition, PAYGO would not have sufficed to block the proposed across-the-board tax relief, as demonstrated by the large tax cuts signed into law by George W. Bush, Clinton's successor.

WHEN POLITICS MEETS ECONOMICS

The president and Congress are hostage to the performance of the economy. Because the future economy is uncertain when the budget is prepared, there are errors in revenue and spending projections. But because budget plans are based on assumed conditions, there may be an incentive to construct rosier economic scenarios than are warranted. This bias occurred in the early 1980s when the Reagan administration projected that a booming economy would finance tax cuts and defense spending increases, and again later in the decade when the Gramm-Rudman-Hollings process threatened the automatic cancellation of budgetary resources if the projected deficit exceeded the targets set in law. Reagan won more tax cuts by pretending that the economic outlook was better than it was, and Congress and the president avoided sequestration by projecting a more favorable economic future than the facts indicated.

Even when there is no effort to manipulate economic forecasts for political advantage, it is extremely difficult to foretell when a recession will arrive, how deep or lasting it will be, and how long its impact on the budget will linger. In nearly 50 years of budget watching, this writer can recall no instance in which a budget predicted a future recession or the worsening of an ongoing one.

The missteps of the 1980s had a chastening effect on politicians in the 1990s. During the long economic expansion that began in 1991 and continued until the end of the century, both the president and CBO repeatedly underestimated the rate of growth and resulting revenue. Part of the underestimate was due to the surprising strength of the economy, part to prudential budgeting. Regardless of the reason, the fact that the economy outperformed budget projections had much to do with the liquidation of the deficit.

The economy has the last word on the budget. There is a strong correlation between the rate of economic growth and the budget outcome. Fast, sustained growth is associated with small deficits or surpluses, slow growth with big, long-lasting deficits. The lesson of recent budget history is that cutting expenditures and raising taxes does not suffice to close the deficit when the economy is weak. The budget can grow out of a deficit only when the economy is sufficiently vigorous to produce incremental revenues that rise faster than the escalation in expenditures.

But this is not the only lesson. The evidence presented in chapter 2 clearly indicates that policy matters; budget decisions also influence the performance of the economy and therefore the size of the deficit or surplus. Stabilizing the budget requires realistic economic assumptions and realistic fiscal policies. Neither was present in the 1980s, both were in the 1990s, and the latter was absent early in the new century. It is not inevitable that when politics and economics meet, the former corrupts the latter. It sometimes happens that good sense about the economy spurs politicians to do the right thing. But when it doesn't, the fiscal position of the government deteriorates.

CONCLUSION

As budget enforcement has become more formalized, fiscal rules have been elaborated, and what once was left to negotiation is now often codified. Some numbers are political and are compiled based on the preferences of those who make or implement budgets. Other numbers are economic or programmatic; they pertain to external factors that impinge on the budget. Many entries in the budget are composites of all three types. When the budget states that a certain amount of outlays will be incurred in the food stamps program, the estimate is based on technical rules concerning the timing and recognition of transactions, political influences on projections of the number of food stamp recipients, and programmatic requirements concerning the benefits participants are entitled to receive.

In the cloistered worlds of budgeting, where many of the numbers are compiled, technical considerations often prevail. But in the public arenas, political forces are on display, with politicians tweaking the budget at the margins to obtain more spending or tax cuts than a strict application of the technical rules would allow. Although only a few percentage points (or less) of the totals, the margins are the political battlegrounds in budgeting. They represent the incremental changes from one year to the next, differences between Democrats and Republicans, and elusive accommodations between the president and Congress. In the budgetary battle, each side is armed with numbers that make its case; the numbers disagree because the political combatants disagree. In the end, however, there can be budgetary peace only if presidential and congressional political arithmetic add up to the same numbers.

5

The President's Budget

The Constitution does not require the president to prepare a budget recommending the revenues and expenditures of the government. Nevertheless, the budget has become one of the president's recurring obligations as well as one of his most important policy tools to set legislative and program objectives while charting the nation's fiscal course. Early in each legislative session, normally the first Monday in February, the president submits an annual budget to Congress. The executive budget estimates spending, revenues, and other financial amounts for the next five or more fiscal years, contains policy and legislative recommendations consistent with those estimates, presents data on the actual and projected performance of the economy, and provides detailed information on the finances of federal agencies and programs.

As detailed in chapter 2, the Budget and Accounting Act of 1921 provides the legal basis for the presidential budget system. Before that law was enacted, the federal government did not have a comprehensive budget system. Agencies submitted financial schedules to the secretary of the treasury, who compiled them in an annual *Book of Estimates*. The president was not formally involved in the process, although sometimes the White House intervened to influence Congress's revenue and spending decisions. The 1921 act made the president responsible for the national budget by requiring him to prepare and submit revenue and spending estimates to Congress annually. The act established the Bureau of the Budget, now the Office of Management and Budget (OMB), to assist him in formulating and implementing the executive budget. Although amended many times, this statute is still the principal legal source of the president's budget power. It prescribes some of the budget's form and content and also defines the responsibilities of the president and spending agencies in the process.

The president's budget is only a request to Congress; federal agencies can neither spend money nor initiate programs based on the president's recommendations. Congress is not required to adopt the recommendations, and it typically makes hundreds of changes in the course of appropriating funds and acting on legislation. Still, the president's proposals are often the starting point for congressional revenue and spending actions. The extent of presidential influence varies from year to year, however, and is dependent upon political and economic conditions.

PRESIDENTIAL ROLES AND STYLES

The formal role assigned to the president by the Budget and Accounting Act does not tell the full story of presidential involvement in the budget process. Each president brings to the office personal characteristics, along with political skills and weaknesses. Some are interested in financial matters and welcome the opportunity to make revenue and expenditure policy; others distance themselves from the budget and its myriad decisions and details. Some have robust program ambitions that can be realized only by shaping the budget to their liking; others have limited agendas that can be served with status quo budgets. Some seek to avoid friction in the annual budget and appropriations cycle; others see conflict as a necessary means of promoting their program objectives.

A comparison of Bill Clinton and other recent presidents reveals significant differences in their budgetary styles and roles (box 5-1). Clinton did not run for president to serve as the chief budget officer of the United States. During his first election campaign in 1992, he concentrated on domestic issues: jobs, the economy, education, and health care. But once elected, he made the budget his highest legislative priority for 1993. Later in his presidency, Clinton again gave top billing to budgetary matters. In 1995 he opposed efforts by a new Republican majority in Congress to make significant cutbacks in various domestic programs, and in 1997 he negotiated an agreement with the Republicans that included modest spending increases and some tax cuts and allowed him to take credit for balancing the budget. Clinton's level of involvement—sending Congress change-oriented budgets and actively wielding his veto pen when Congress proposed bills that ran counter to his budgetary preferences—welled out of personal temperament and political calculation.

George H. W. Bush, Clinton's predecessor, was largely disengaged from the budget process. Bush left the task of formulating and negotiating major budget policies to Richard Darman, his wily OMB director. In fact, Bush alone among post–World War II presidents submitted budgets without a presidential message setting forth his major policies. Instead, Darman signed the policy statement printed in the budget. Bush was also on the sidelines when the economy went into a mild recession in 1990–91 and was maneuvered into signing a 1990 tax increase that was sharply at variance with his oft-stated "no new taxes" pledge (see box 5-1). But the president paid a political price for distancing himself from the budget. He was defeated for reelection in 1992 and never got political credit for taking strong steps to curtail the budget deficit.

▼

BOX 5-1
The Age of Negotiated Budgets

Reagan Presidency: Unofficial Negotiations That Led to Tax Increases and Spending Cuts in 1982:
"The Gang [White House aides and members of Congress] conducted its meetings at Blair House, at Jim Baker's home, at the residence of Vice President Bush, and at other unusual locations to conceal the meetings from the press, and also from others in the administration and Congress. By the time the package was finally presented to President [Ronald Reagan], it was treated virtually as a *fait accompli*—something to which 'the process' had committed us. The President, along with cabinet members and senior advisors not in the Gang, was briefed on the TEFRA [Tax Equity and Fiscal Responsibility Act of 1982] proposal and participated in decision meetings with congressional leaders; but the legislative package was rolling ahead with such momentum—in the news media and among both parties in Congress—that it would have been virtually impossible to stop or even modify it."

George H. W. Bush Presidency: Formal Negotiations That Produced the Reconciliation Act in 1990:
"President [George Bush] met for 1 hour and 40 minutes this afternoon with congressional budget negotiators to consider a federal budget that would reduce the deficit substantially on a multiyear basis, allow the economy to continue to grow, strengthen the budget process, and avoid the adverse economic and programmatic effects of a stalemate that otherwise might ensue. The President and the negotiators agreed that it was important to reach an agreement as soon as possible. The President discussed the reasons for these summit meetings. . . . The President concluded his opening remarks by saying, 'The American people are tired of seeing the budget process seem to fail year after year. They would welcome our doing the job right and our fixing the process at the same time.'

The congressional leadership gave opening remarks concerning their interest in achieving a successful agreement, and all indicated a shared responsibility by both branches of the Government to reach agreement."

Clinton Presidency: Breakdown in Negotiations That Shut Down Part of the Government in 1995–96:
"President [Bill Clinton] has been working since the very good meeting on Saturday with a cross-section of Democratic members of the House and the Senate to see if we can't frame some of these budget issues in a way that will break this impasse and move the balanced budget discussions forward. We've had good conversations. There are some different approaches within the Democratic caucus, but the President is working with all points of view within the Democratic

continued

His son, who became president in 2001, carved a budget path that differed from both of his immediate predecessors. In contrast to his father, George W. Bush was engaged in budget issues, principally on the revenue side of the ledger; in contrast to Bill Clinton, early in his presidency, he showed little interest in expenditure matters and rarely negotiated with

▼

BOX 5-1
Continued

caucus to see if we can't have a more unified approach. And we're encouraged by the discussions that we've been having.

He's been doing a lot of work on this personally. He had a long meeting on Saturday, as you know, with Democratic members. And we believe it's important and vital to move forward with the balanced budget discussions and achieve the result the American people want. . . .

He's got specific ideas that he will be willing to entertain. But this has got to be a negotiation in which both sides show flexibility. And certainly, there's no one who would dispute the notion that the President has been flexible, has been willing to address the concerns of the Republican majority in Congress, has been willing to adopt their timetable for consideration of a balanced budget. What we've failed to see thus far is any sign of flexibility on their part that would acknowledge the importance of the President's priorities."

George W. Bush Presidency: Campaign That Resulted in the Enactment of Large Tax Reductions in 2001:
"The President will be traveling to Chicago, Illinois, tomorrow, where he'll be talking, making the case for his budget and tax plan, talking about the importance of economic growth, talking about how we are all in this economy together. And one of the interesting phenomenons that have happened in the American economy in the last decade or so is this growing investor class, the surge of middle income Americans, who now invest in markets, have mutual funds, who have other investments.

It's another reminder how we all are in this together. And the markets often are leading indicators, suggesting which direction the economy will grow, or go. And the President believes that he has an economic plan that can help strengthen the economy, and he will talk about that generally at the Exchange tomorrow in Chicago.

The President is going to continue to meet with members of Congress, discuss his plans with members of Congress. And we're looking forward to Thursday's vote in the House of Representatives. We expect that this will be a singular moment, a very important day for getting tax relief to the American people. And we're pleased to be working with such a do-something Congress."

Sources: Edwin Meese III, *With Reagan: The Inside Story* (Washington, D.C.: Regnery Gateway, 1992), p. 145; Office of the Press Secretary, White House, "Statement by Press Secretary Fitzwater on the Federal Budget Negotiations," May 15, 1990; Office of the Press Secretary, White House, "Press Briefing by Press Secretary Mike McCurry," December 18, 1995; Office of the Press Secretary, White House, "Press Briefing by Press Secretary Ari Fleischer," March 5, 2001.

department heads or congressional leaders on spending issues. His unbalanced budget focus led, many observers believe, to unbalanced budget outcomes. Bowing to strong presiden-

tial pressure, Congress cut federal taxes in 2001 and 2003; however, Bush let Congress enact steep increases in federal spending. George W. Bush's main expenditure interest during his first term was to expand Medicare to cover prescription drugs. His legislative success demonstrated the president's budgetary influence when he is willing to use the advantages of his office to change revenue or spending policy.

During his second term, however, chronically high deficits, fissures in his own party, and the 2006 congressional elections impelled Bush to take a harder line on spending increases. But rather than dealing with program or spending details, Bush generally only set limits on total appropriations or on the amount of additional resources to be provided in supplemental appropriations.

In budgeting, as in other areas of national policy and presidential activity, Clinton and the two Bush presidents were each very different chief executives. Each budget bore Clinton's imprint: he actively participated in making budget policy, was well informed on matters in dispute, and was familiar with salient details of federal programs (box 5-2). He made decisions concerning the size and direction of government, the composition of tax legislation, and the shape of policy initiatives. He invested time in mastering the details of the budget, meeting with department heads to discuss their budgets and resolve issues that remained after OMB completed its review.

Clinton was not the first president who shaped the budget to his will. Ronald Reagan put his stamp on the budget in 1981 (his first year in office) when he won enactment of major revenue and spending changes. Like Clinton, Reagan had to fight to get his budget through Congress. But in policy preferences, the two presidents moved in opposite directions. Reagan lowered taxes; Clinton raised them. Reagan boosted defense spending and slashed social programs; Clinton trimmed real defense spending while adding to social expen-

ditures. Yet these ideologically different presidents took similar approaches to the budget. Both understood that political success depends on changing budget policies, acted to reshape budget policy almost immediately after taking office, and got Congress to pass much of what they wanted. Both invested time and political resources in the budget, and both fought to obtain the votes that gave them a slim margin of victory.

One triumph does not make a presidency, nor does it ensure that an early success will last. Every year is a new budgetary battle for the president—a fresh opportunity to get Congress to do his bidding. Reagan's first eight months of budgetary blitzkrieg and legislative accomplishment were followed by more than seven years of political conflict and budgetary stalemate. In 1994, the year after his great budget victory, Clinton suffered the greatest legislative defeat of his presidency—the failure of Congress to reform the health care system. Clinton and Congress ended the 1995 budget cycle with a protracted impasse that shut down parts of the government. The conflict resumed in subsequent years, but the two sides managed to patch up differences without surrendering their most important objectives.

Many presidents have entered office viewing the budget as a powerful opportunity to advance their agendas; quite a few have left regarding the budget as an impediment to sweeping policy change. As they age in office, presidents perceive the budget more as an accumulation of past decisions than as a forum for making new ones. Thus recent presidents have characteristically demanded more budget change during their first years in office than they have in later years. As the cost of meeting past commitments escalates and their political capital dwindles, presidents trim their ambitions and settle for status quo or incremental budgets.

▼

BOX 5-2
Role of President Clinton in Fiscal Year 1995 Budget Formulation

Remarks by OMB Director Leon Panetta:

"The President yesterday, as [Chief of Staff Mack] McLarty pointed out, completed the final decision-making process for the fiscal year 1995 budget. . . . We had, initially, a two-hour overview meeting with the President on November 29. And then, after that, spent almost 15 hours meeting with every one of the Cabinet secretaries, as well as the key agency heads to discuss their budgets. He met with 21 departments and agency heads during that process. The meetings began on December 2 [and] concluded last Friday, December 17. . . .

The meetings with department heads by a President were really unprecedented. Normally what has happened in the past is that Presidents only saw fit to meet with Cabinet members after some of the decisions had been made and only on appeals. President Clinton, however, felt it was essential that each department have the ability to present their case for their budget and then discuss the key issues with him before, not after, any final decisions were made. . . .

I would make a presentation at the beginning of the meeting that summarized the budget for that department and then addressed the major issues that demanded presidential attention. [T]he secretary was then allowed the opportunity to speak to the budget and to those issues. There was usually a question period that followed and a discussion period that followed. [T]he meetings themselves were attended by White House staff, as well as some of the NEC—National Economic Council—representatives.

The President spent a total of about six hours, then, this week [December 20 and 21] to go over the final issues [raised during the department meetings] and then made the final decisions yesterday. OMB basically went over the broad and specific issues with him on both specific departments as well as government-wide issues. And so the formal part of this process involved about 23 hours of meetings with the President.

The process now is basically a technical one because the numbers now are basically presented back to the departments and agencies. They, in turn, translate these decisions into what are literally hundreds of thousands of numbers that feed into our budget. And then [we at OMB] ultimately scrub those numbers to make sure they all fit together when we present the final budget on February 7."

Source: Office of the Press Secretary, White House, "Remarks by OMB Director Leon Panetta," December 22, 1993.

Even when the president has early budget successes, follow-up victories may be difficult to achieve. Presidents use up political goodwill when they prod members of Congress to vote for spending cuts, as occurred in 1981, or for tax increases, as occurred a dozen years later. They cannot repeatedly demand allegiance from members who put their political careers at risk by supporting the president's budget preferences. Barely one month after winning enactment of far-reaching budget changes in the summer of 1981, Ronald Reagan was stymied when he sought another round of budget cuts. And less than one year after

Congress approved his deficit reduction plan, Bill Clinton could not get Congress to reform the health care system.

Yet it is not always the case that the president's best budgetary days are behind him. Clinton recovered his political footing in 1995 and 1996 to block the efforts of congressional Republicans to restructure federal budget priorities. Clinton also had a strong role in the 1997 balanced budget agreement, which cut taxes and modestly increased domestic spending, as well as in annual appropriations enacted during the final years of his presidency. Clinton's continuing budgetary activism and influence was the result of many factors: he had public opinion on his side, congressional Republicans badly misread public preferences and were blamed for shutting down the government, Clinton proved to be a skillful negotiator who picked fights that he could win, and he was helped by an improving economy and an emerging budget surplus. Clinton also effectively used the veto power to impose his own preferences on a recalcitrant Congress.

This edition was written about halfway through the second term of George W. Bush's presidency. While tax reduction was the signature budget accomplishment of his first term, Bush promoted Social Security reform as the main budgetary objective of his second term. Like other two-term presidents, he has striven to use his remaining political capital to escape lame-duck status. At this writing, it is too early to know whether he will succeed, but one should not be surprised if his best budget years are already behind him, as pressure to deal with the budget deficit preempts costly policy initiatives and adds to the frictions of the budget process.

CHANGES IN PRESIDENTIAL BUDGETING

Whatever his disposition, no president can ignore the budget. Submitting the budget to Congress is one of the few tasks a president must complete each year, no matter how difficult the choices or uncertain the outlook. The president must be attentive to how the budget is faring in Congress, and he must be prepared to intervene when salient issues are at stake. When the budget is released, the president's political standing is on the line; the media label it the Bush budget or the Clinton budget. The president's capacity to move legislation through Congress depends in some measure on how well his budget is received. "Dead on arrival" is the pundit's verdict that the president's budget carries little weight and will likely be ignored by Congress when it makes budget decisions. Through the budget, the president takes on responsibility for the performance of the economy and for policies that affect disposable income, prices, growth, and other key indicators. He cannot ignore budgetary responsibilities, even when the problems are not of his own making and the solutions are not readily at hand.

Even though all presidents must engage in budgeting, over the course of a generation there has been a fundamental change in the political status of the budget. This transformation has coincided with other developments that have weakened the chief executive's capacity to get what he wants from Congress. This weakening has its roots in Watergate and Vietnam—two failures that have been blamed on the misuse of presidential power. During the heyday of presidential budgeting (in the decades after World War II), the annual budget served as a platform for the president's legislative program and as an authoritative statement of national policy. Every step of the way, when it appropriated money and considered tax legislation, Congress took into account what the president had requested. Although it made many changes, these tended to be small, so that the budget that came out of Congress looked pretty much like the budget sent to it. In some recent years, by contrast, the president's recommendations have been little more than opening bids in a bargaining process. Rather than revealing his true preferences at the outset, the president often submits unrealistic proposals that have no chance of adoption and whose main function is to position him for the tough negotiations at the end of the process.

This shift has resulted from changes in federal budgeting such as the rising share of the budget spent on entitlements that constrain presidential initiative, greater congressional independence arising out of a long spell of divided government, increased activity by the many interest groups that monitor all stages of budgeting and offer detailed alternatives, and critical assessments of the president's budget by the Congressional Budget Office (CBO), the media, and others.

One of the most telling indicators of the changed status of the president's budget comes from the extensive use of baselines in making and scoring congressional budget actions. Before Congress used baselines, it typically made budget decisions by comparing its actions to the president's recommendations. The appropriations committees still operate in this manner, but nowadays all other congressional budget decisions are made in reference to CBO baseline projections. The baseline is completely unaffected by the president's budget. As a projection of revenue and spending, it assumes no change in policy; the baseline does not move up or down a single dollar if the president asks for more or less. The baseline is used by the budget committees in marking up the budget resolution, by authorizing committees in developing legislation and responding to reconciliation instructions, by congressional scorekeepers in measuring the budget impact of pending or approved legislation, and in

enforcing budget rules. Interest groups use the baseline to calculate whether their programs are being protected against inflation and to build a case for increased funding. It is no overstatement to assert that baselines have stolen much of the attention once accorded to the president's budget.

A president can compensate for institutional weakness by investing political resources in defense of his budget. With the Democrats controlling both the legislative and executive branches, the fate of Clinton's budget in 1993 rested in their hands. Yet he had to bargain with members of his own party to secure the votes needed for passage. He fought hard for his budget that year, and despite a series of cliffhanger votes and compromises, the final version was close in its main lines to his original proposal. When the Republicans took control of Congress in 1995, Clinton was forced to negotiate with political adversaries whose budget priorities differed sharply from his own. Clinton won the 1995–96 battle of the budget by thwarting Republican efforts to cut back major social programs such as Medicare and Medicaid and winning additional spending for education and several other presidential priorities. Moreover, he had a strong role in shaping new tax legislation, and he succeeded in pinning blame on the Republicans for the temporary shutdown of some federal agencies. At the start of the battle, Clinton had a low favorability rating in public opinion polls. By the end, a majority of Americans viewed his performance favorably. But the Republicans did not come away empty-handed, for they got Clinton to accept key portions of their budgetary agenda: a balanced budget, welfare reform, and tax cuts. Because each side could claim victory while protecting important budgetary objectives, each had a strong incentive to reach agreement despite the wide differences in budget policy.

The budgetary balance of power is affected by external events, such as the national security status of the United States, and by the relative standing of the president and Congress in public opinion. George W. Bush exploited both to his advantage in the aftermath of the 9/11 terrorist attacks, getting Congress to accede to most of his demands in expanding the federal government's role in education policy and homeland security. Bush's biggest budget triumph occurred in 2003, when he pressured a sufficient number of skeptical Republican members of Congress to pass legislation extending Medicare coverage to prescription drugs. Overall, Bush's presidential style was to avoid most conflicts, picking fights with Congress only when he perceived that the prerogatives of his office were threatened. Bush won large increases in defense spending, including vast amounts to finance military operations in Iraq and Afghanistan. But when public opinion turned against the war in Iraq and the Republicans lost majorities in the House and Senate, Bush no longer could prevail through gentle arm-twisting or by getting Republican Party leaders to whip rank-and-file members into line. As Bush's remaining time in office dwindled, so too did his capacity to dictate congressional action on his budget proposals and other priorities.

Who wins these interbranch disputes depends on the relative political strength and bargaining skills of the two sides. Judging from Reagan's, Clinton's, and George W. Bush's successes in budget conflicts, it appears that the president wins when he has a small number of attainable demands, does not allow the give-and-take of negotiations to dislodge him from key objectives, does a good job reading public opinion, and threatens vetoes to deter congressional actions that undermine his political standing. The president need not be familiar with the details of the negotiations—

Reagan generally was not, Clinton was—but it is important that the president neither attempts to achieve too many objectives nor allows the other side to redefine his objectives.

FORMULATING THE PRESIDENT'S BUDGET

Table 5-1 lists the principal responsibilities of the three sets of participants involved in preparing the executive budget: federal agencies, which request funds and carry out authorized programs; the Office of Management and Budget (OMB), which reviews agency requests, compiles the budget, and monitors congressional action and agency implementation; and the president, who has the final say on the policies set forth in the budget he submits to Congress.

Preparation of the budget typically begins in spring (or earlier) each year—at least 9 months before the president transmits it to Congress, about 18 months before the start of the fiscal year to which it pertains, and about 30 months before the close of that fiscal year (see table 5-2). When agencies begin work on a future budget, they are also implementing the budget for the fiscal year in progress and awaiting appropriations and other legislative decisions for the following year. In the spring of 2007, for example, most federal agencies were preparing their fiscal year 2009 requests, months before they had the final results for fiscal year 2007 or appropriations for fiscal year 2008.

The long lead times and the fact that appropriations have not yet been made for the next fiscal year mean that agency budgets are prepared with a great deal of uncertainty about economic conditions, presidential policies, and congressional actions. Agencies cope with uncertainty by keeping options open until late in the process, basing future budgets on past ones, and asking for more than they

TABLE 5-1
Budget Functions of Executive Institutions

President	Office of Management and Budget (OMB)	Federal agencies
Establishes executive budget policy and submits annual budget to Congress	Operates executive budget system and advises the president on financial and other issues	Submit budget requests to OMB; appeal to the president for more funds
Submits supplemental requests, budget amendments, and updates to Congress	Issues procedural and policy guidelines to agencies	Justify president's budget recommendations before congressional committees
Signs or vetoes revenue, appropriations, and other budget-related measures passed by Congress	Issues passbacks to agencies and recommends budget levels to the president	Allot funds among subunits
Notifies Congress of proposed rescissions and deferrals	Compiles annual budget submitted to Congress	Maintain accounting systems and systems of internal control
Appoints the director of OMB and other executive officials	Reviews proposed legislation and testimony, and monitors congressional action on appropriations and other measures	Obligate funds and preaudit expenditures
	Apportions funds and oversees implementation of the budget	Carry out activities for which funds were provided
	Scores revenue and spending legislation	Prepare annual financial statements in accord with accounting standards
	Oversees management of activities to assess agency performance and program results	Measure performance and develop performance-based budgets

expect to get. Despite the lead times, few agencies do systematic, long-term budget planning because the same staffs that are preparing the next budget also are working on the current one. Budget preparation is a busy, deadline-driven activity, with many levels of review, enormous demands for data, and a compelling need to resolve intra- and inter-agency conflicts.

The length of the budget preparation cycle and the difficulty of using it as a means of establishing objectives and priorities are largely due to the bottom-up structure of budgeting. Departmental budgets usually are assembled in a decentralized manner, beginning at the lowest level of the organization capable of formulating its own request and progressing through successively higher echelons until all requests have been consolidated into a departmental budget. However, some agencies provide policy guidance to operating units before getting into the details; most wait until requests have been assembled before making policy decisions. In most federal agencies, the divisions, branches, offices, and other administrative units prepare detailed estimates of expenditures for personnel, travel, supplies, equipment, and other items at each stage of the process. These details are reviewed, and usually revised, as the budget moves up the

TABLE 5-2
Major Steps in Budget Formulation

When	What happens?
Spring	OMB issues spring planning guidance to executive branch agencies for the upcoming budget. The OMB director issues a letter to the head of each agency providing policy guidance for the agency's budget request. Absent more specific guidance, the outyear estimates included in the previous budget serve as a starting point for the next budget. This begins the process of formulating the budget the president will submit the following February.
Spring and summer	OMB and the executive branch agencies discuss budget issues and options. OMB works with the agencies to (1) identify major issues for the upcoming budget, (2) develop and analyze options for the upcoming fall review, and (3) plan for the analysis of issues that will need decisions in the future.
July	OMB issues *Circular A-11* to all federal agencies. This circular provides detailed instructions for submitting budget data and materials.
September	Executive branch agencies (except those not subject to executive branch review) make budget submissions to OMB.
October–November	OMB conducts its fall review. OMB staff analyze agency budget proposals in light of presidential priorities, program performance, and budget constraints. They raise issues and present options to the director and other OMB policy officials for their decisions.
Late November	OMB briefs the president and senior advisers on proposed budget policies. The OMB director recommends a complete set of budget proposals to the president after OMB has reviewed all agency requests and considered overall budget policies. Passback. OMB usually informs all executive branch agencies simultaneously about the decisions on their budget requests.
Late November to early January	All agencies, including legislative and judicial branch agencies, enter computer data and submit print materials and additional data. This process begins immediately after passback and continues until OMB must "lock" agencies out of the database in order to meet the printing deadline.
December	Executive branch agencies may appeal to OMB and the president.[a] An agency head may ask OMB to reverse or modify certain decisions. In most cases, OMB and the agency head resolve such issues and, if not, work together to present them to the president for a decision.
January	OMB reviews congressional budget justification materials. Agencies prepare the budget justification materials they need to explain their budget requests to the responsible congressional subcommittees.

Source: Adapted from Office of Management and Budget, *Circular A-11*, section 10, p. 4.
a. OMB provides specific deadlines for this activity.

hierarchy. The result is that budget preparation is time-consuming and burdensome. Furthermore, budget preparation diverts managerial attention from other departmental concerns.

The bottom-up process, some argue, diminishes the use of budgeting as a means of establishing government policies and priorities. Nevertheless, since the 1960s a number of initiatives have been launched to give budgeting a more strategic and less incremental orientation. One of the most prominent was the planning-programming-budgeting system (PPBS) first introduced in the Defense Department in 1961 by Robert McNamara and prescribed for all federal agencies by President Lyndon Johnson in 1965. The most recent initiatives have been under the Government Performance and Results Act of 1993 (GPRA), which directs agencies to prepare strategic and performance plans to act as guides during budget preparation, and the Program Assessment Rating Tool (PART), introduced by OMB in 2002. While PPBS, GPRA, and PART have numerous differences, all seek a more top-down, output-oriented process. GPRA and PART are more fully discussed in chapter 10.

Incremental Budgeting

What GPRA has not yet accomplished, and what PPBS and zero-based budgeting could not do a generation ago, is to wean federal budgeting away from the tendency toward incremental decisionmaking. Over the years, most federal departments have budgeted on the expectation that virtually all activities funded in the current budget will be continued in the next and that program initiatives will be financed from incremental resources, not from cutbacks in existing programs. Agencies have therefore concentrated on how much more to seek for new or expanded programs and on how to respond to changes in government priorities. Agencies often propose modest savings in ongoing programs to show that they have lean, efficient operations, but this tactic is usually employed to get more money than they received for the current year.

Increments come in many sizes. The size appropriate for an ambitious agency that seeks

to grow may not suit an agency that has modest budget objectives. The increases sought when a program rates high in public esteem or when increments are bountiful may be inappropriate for a low-priority program or when resources are tight. Agencies and programs do not grow uniformly, nor do they grow without interruption. Many go through periods in which funding is relatively stable, followed by growth spurts and then a return to stability. The spurts may be due to the entrepreneurial verve of agency officials, opportunities opened up by new legislation, shifts in public opinion, or a crisis. One of the vital skills of budgeting is to identify and exploit these opportunities by preparing budgets that suit the times.

What an agency (or one of its units) asks for influences what it gets. An agency that requests negligible increases will not get big increases but also might go through the process without OMB or Congress making significant changes. One that seeks substantial growth may get more, but at the risk of having its budget closely reviewed and revised.

Incremental budgeting requires incremental resources supplied by either a growing economy, as was the case in the 1950s and 1960s, or by deficit financing, as occurred in the 1980s and in the current decade. As long as the economy is growing or the government is willing to borrow, it is possible to concentrate on the increment—the extent to which next year's allocations should vary from this year's—and to spend little time reexamining past commitments and ongoing programs. When neither of these conditions suffices to cover the future cost of existing programs, incremental behavior may not be sustainable. For example, during the 1990s, incrementalism became untenable in the defense budget because of a steep decline in the real resources spent on military forces. Due to the end of the Cold War and efforts to curtail federal deficits, real defense outlays dropped by one-third between 1989 and 1998, forcing the Pentagon to shed forces and close many facilities. Some critics argue that even in downsizing, the Defense Department held on to its incremental mind-set, for the military did not sufficiently reconfigure its budget in response to the change in international conditions facing the United States in the post–Cold War era.

The President's Role

Where does the president fit into the agency-centered budget process? Does he have any significant input during the early stages, when agencies prepare their estimates, or is his influence concentrated at the end when the final decisions are made? In a formal sense, the answer is that the president can intervene throughout the process to communicate his priorities, give direction to agency submissions, and set limits on the amounts and things they ask for. In fact, shortly after one year's budget is sent to Congress, OMB gives each department an allowance letter that specifies the base for the next budget cycle. Nevertheless, in a bottom-up process, it is inevitable that the president's main input comes in the final stages, after agencies have submitted their requests.

The extent to which the president is involved in the earliest stages has changed over the years. During the boom years of economic and program expansion, especially during the 1960s and early 1970s, OMB had a formal process, known as spring preview, in which it developed and communicated to federal agencies presidential guidelines for the next fiscal year. OMB gave each agency dollar targets (relatively fixed in some years, elastic in others), as well as guidance on issues to be considered in that year's budget cycle. During the 1980s, this process withered away, probably because of OMB and White House preoccupation with congressional budget actions and also because they did not want premature leaks of the president's budget decisions. Without the preview, agencies often commence budget work before the president's policies have been formally transmitted to them. Some presidents, such as Clinton, have issued policy directives early in the process to guide agencies in compiling their budgets; others, such as George W. Bush, have not entered the process until agencies assembled their requests.

The lack of robust increments and limited presidential participation in early budget preparation have the potential to weaken the president's influence. When increments are plentiful, the president could intervene late in the process by allocating some or all of the additional resources to his priorities. When his principal objective is to cut spending, the president could intervene late and impose cutbacks. The former pattern generally characterized budgeting in the Kennedy-Johnson years; the latter predominated during the Reagan administration. When the president lacks increments but still seeks major program initiatives, he may find his options limited if he waits until the last minute to put his stamp on the budget.

Whatever the advantages of early presidential involvement, it is naive to assume that all matters thought to have been settled by presidential guidelines at the start will remain settled through the give-and-take of budget negotiations. There always is some trimming needed at the end because there is always some presidential idea that needs to be accommodated in the budget. Dozens of decisions are made in the home stretch, when all the numbers have been tallied and the deadline nears for sending the budget to the printer. Defense spending typically is one of the last decisions, kept open until the final stages because the amounts are so large and billions can be quickly added or subtracted by decisions on big-ticket purchases and the size of the armed forces.

The Details of Budgeting

To budget is to compile, review, and decide many thousands of details pertaining to the operations of federal agencies, program levels, and payments to recipients of federal dollars. Even an active president, such as Bill Clinton, cannot master all of the details. Every president must focus on the relatively small number of issues that matter most to him and leave the rest to the affected agencies or OMB staff. Executive budgeting proceeds, in effect, on two tracks: one is agency-centered; the other deals with matters of interest to the president. The agency-centered process focuses on operational details: activities and projects; salaries, equipment, supplies, and other items; and the costs of programs, such as grants and transfer payments. The presidential process concentrates on proposed changes in program levels, the legislative initiatives to be included in the budget, and other policy decisions. The agency-centered process is much more detailed than the presidential one. The latter may entail several hundred decisions; the former requires thousands. The two processes overlap—some agency concerns are also of interest to the president. Nevertheless, it is useful to distinguish between the two processes because they point to an important evolution in the preparation of the executive budget. Over the years the White House has withdrawn from many details of budgeting, leaving them to the agencies or intervening only when it sees an advantage in doing so. This conserves the president's time and political resources, enabling him to defer serious review of agency requests until late in the cycle, typically in November or December (as the schedule in table 5-2 indi-

cates). Late intervention reduces premature leaks of presidential decisions and enables the White House to control the spin on budget news.

Many budget issues that matter a great deal to the affected agency are of little concern to the White House. But some agency matters are inherently of ongoing interest to the president. One such matter is the total cost of operations; another is the number of employees. When discretionary spending caps are tight, presidents squeeze operating expenses in order to make room for program expenditures. Staffing levels attract presidential interest because the number of employees is a popular indicator of whether the government is growing or shrinking.

The agency-centered process is time-consuming because an enormous number of details have to be addressed at each step. In 1993 the National Performance Review (NPR)—the "reinventing government" campaign led by Vice President Al Gore—proposed shortening the budget preparation cycle to make it more relevant to presidential concerns. NPR proposed that the president have a prominent role at the start by establishing policies and priorities that would guide the agencies in compiling their requests. But the president would have a more limited role in reviewing agencies' requests during the final stages. NPR assumed that if agencies draft their budgets in accord with presidential instructions, there would be less need to review them at the end. Moreover, NPR recommended that agencies draw up detailed estimates after policy decisions have been made rather than before. In this way, agencies would focus on presidential objectives and program performance, not on the detailed items of expenditure.

Yet the details persist in agency budgeting. One reason is that the details are important to the agencies. Managers want to know how much they will have to spend on operations, the amount that will be available for staff resources, and whether the budget will cover cost increases. Detailed budgeting is reinforced by the demands of congressional committees, especially the appropriations committees, which require extensive documentation of agency requests. The justification material submitted to these committees (discussed in chapter 9) typically contains line-item explanations of the amounts requested for salaries, supplies, and other items. Eliminating the details would diminish the influence of the appropriations committees and Congress in controlling federal expenditures. The issue is an old one—Congress's power of the purse. It is not simply a matter of the amount of time spent on preparing the budget or of the relationship between the president and federal agencies. Agencies care about the details because they expect congressional committees to care about them.

THE OFFICE OF MANAGEMENT AND BUDGET

Most of the president's budget work is entrusted to political and career staff in the Office of Management and Budget, a 500-person agency situated in the Executive Office of the President. OMB handles almost all the paperwork, makes most presidential budget decisions, and puts together the budget submitted to Congress. In addition, OMB leverages its budgetary power to prod federal agencies to improve their managerial practices.

OMB's predecessor, the Bureau of the Budget, was established in the same 1921 law that created the executive budget process. Over the past eight decades, the evolution of OMB has paralleled changes in the organization and role of the presidency. At the start, the Bureau of the Budget was placed in the Treasury Depart-

ment. A modern, well-staffed presidential office had not yet emerged, and the bureau's principal task was to constrain federal spending. The bureau's staff was small, but it single-mindedly and successfully kept spending low. Then came the Depression and the New Deal, as well as a reorientation and enlargement of the president's staff. In 1939 the bureau moved into the newly established Executive Office of the President, where it was assigned overall responsibility for federal management. It also took the lead in developing the president's legislative program and in reviewing legislation to determine whether proposed measures, or ones passed by Congress, accorded with the president's priorities. After World War II, it became customary for the president to prepare a legislative program in tandem with the budget. In the 1960s, the bureau further expanded its portfolio of presidential responsibilities, using the budget as an instrument of economic policy and making tax and spending decisions in light of intended impacts on growth, prices, and employment.

In 1970 Richard Nixon reorganized the Bureau of the Budget into the Office of Management and Budget. While the ostensible aim was to strengthen OMB's role in coordinating government activities, the main impact was to make OMB more responsive to the president's political interests. Before the reorganization, the agency (which then numbered 600) had fewer than half a dozen political appointees; after the reorganization, the political staff grew to as many as two dozen. Direct interaction between career staff and the White House diminished. Political appointees, who come with one president and depart with the next, now handle major policy chores.

This arrangement has persisted since the 1970s, but each president has tinkered with it to suit his style. Through it all, OMB has managed to give the president expert advice while carrying out his policy agenda. Balancing the two is not easy, especially now that OMB's judgments often are second-guessed by CBO, which has earned a reputation in Washington as being less partisan and more credible. When the two institutions disagree, media and seasoned observers generally rely on CBO's numbers, not because they have been proved more accurate but because they have not been tainted by presidential bias (box 5-3).

Growing congressional independence in budgetary and legislative matters has affected OMB. As recently as the 1970s, OMB career staff did not closely monitor congressional action on the president's budget. After submission of the budget, OMB examiners often spent considerable time with the agencies they oversaw, reviewing programs and assessing managerial strengths and weaknesses. As their work schedules allow, OMB staff members still engage in these activities, but they now spend much of the time when Congress is in session monitoring the progress of appropriations bills and other measures through committees and the House and the Senate. Even as it serves the president, OMB must be attuned to what is happening in Congress. This reorientation has crowded out much in-depth policy analysis and managerial review, and has reinforced the perception that the agency is partisan.

OMB Review of Agency Requests

No matter how attentive it is to congressional actions, OMB must devote much of its staff resources to preparing the president's budget. This involves ongoing relationships with the agencies and White House aides.

As agencies formulate their budgets, they maintain contact with the OMB examiners assigned to them. These contacts provide agencies with procedural and policy guidance in preparing their requests and inform the examiners of agency priorities and concerns. On an interpersonal level, the relationship usually is harmonious, but the two sides know they are budgetary adversaries. Agencies want more than OMB gives them, and their priorities and program assessments often differ from OMB's. But the two also are interdependent—agencies have information OMB wants, and OMB controls money the agencies need.

The formal side of budget preparation is based on OMB's Circular A-11, which contains detailed instructions and schedules for the estimates and other material agencies submit. The technical data are too detailed to be the basis for presidential decisions, but they are used in preparing many of the schedules printed in the budget.

Agencies submit their requests to OMB in early fall. Then OMB staff and, on important issues, presidential aides review the requests. The review typically has several distinct stages: *staff review,* during which OMB examiners review the requests, consult with agency officials, and prepare recommendations; *director's review,* at which major issues are discussed, OMB examiners defend their recommendations, and the OMB director makes budget decisions; *passback,* at which agencies are notified of these decisions and have an opportunity to appeal for reconsideration; *appeals,* which are first taken to OMB, but if agreement is not reached, may be considered by the president or certain aides; and *final decisions,* which are made up to the point that the budget documents are printed. Once they are informed of the final decisions, agencies revise their budgets to bring them in line with the president's.

The Budget and Accounting Act of 1921 bars agencies from submitting budget requests directly to Congress. This prohibition is backed by an OMB regulation (*Circular A-11,* part 1, section 22) that requires confidentiality

---

BOX 5-3
OMB's Conflicting Roles: Neutral Competence versus Political Advice

The contemporary OMB pursues two conflicting mandates—one is to provide professional assistance to the president in preparing his budget and overseeing its implementation; the other is to articulate and promote the president's views in negotiations with Congress. The first role has been part of OMB's repertoire since its predecessor, the Bureau of the Budget, was established in 1921. The second role has emerged more recently and is a by-product of divided government, widespread conflict on budgetary matters, and the use of budget summits to resolve impasses between the White House and Capitol Hill. The first requires neutral competence—the ability to advise the president on the merits, independent of political considerations; the second plunges OMB into the maelstrom of partisan politics. The first orients OMB to the activities and finances of federal agencies; the second impels it to focus on the actions and interests of Congress.

Neutral competence requires a career staff with a long institutional memory, which carries over as one president departs and another is sworn in. The staff provides in-depth, objective assessments of federal programs, options for the president's consideration, and detailed knowledge of the organization and operations of federal agencies. OMB directors must be politically savvy, but they do not slant advice just to satisfy political interests. This professional OMB operates largely behind the scenes, leaving the job of building support for the president's programs to the spending departments.

The political role requires that a large cohort of political appointees (which did not even exist under the traditional role) depart when a new president arrives. In this role, the OMB director must actively and openly build public and congressional support for the president's policies. Political realities intrude during budget preparation. This new orientation has pulled OMB away from agencies and more toward developing substantive and procedural knowledge of Congress. Nowadays, OMB—especially its director and other OMB political appointees—has to maintain ongoing contacts with congressional leaders and rank-and-file members. The politicization is further complicated because OMB leaders must publicly advocate on the president's behalf for positions they may have recently argued against within the administration. The OMB director now has a political face, appearing on television and using the media to battle Congress on pending budget matters. In some cases, OMB directors have become public figures almost apart from the presidents they serve. David Stockman, Ronald Reagan's first budget director, best personified this role, but he was not the last director to build his own power base.

Source: Portions adapted from Shelley Lynne Tomkin, *Inside OMB: Politics and Process in the President's Budget Office* (Armonk, N.Y.: M. E. Sharpe, 1998), pp. 27–29.

---

in all budget requests and recommendations before the president transmits his budget to Congress. Nevertheless, internal budget documents and decisions are often leaked, sometimes by the president, who thereby controls the prerelease news. These days it is hard to keep secrets in Washington, and there are some years in which virtually all important budget decisions have been divulged in advance of the budget's release.

The format and content of the budget are partly determined by law, but the 1921 act authorizes the president to set forth the budget "in such form and detail" as he may determine. Over the past 30 years, there has been a marked increase in the political content of the budget. Not very long ago, most of the budget and its supporting documents were devoted to financial schedules and descriptive information; the president's policies were highlighted in a budget message that introduced the technical details. Nowadays, the budget sometimes reads like a campaign document extolling the president's policies. This politicization of the budget mirrors the penetration of partisan politics into every corner of federal activity. Arguably, if the budget is the president's, it should put the best face on his policies and make a strong case for Congress to adopt them. However, the budget is also an account to the American people of the government's revenues and expenditures. Turning the budget into a political statement has diminished this facet of budgeting. The practice began in the 1970s, but it was greatly extended by Presidents Clinton and George W. Bush, who both ran the White House as if it were a continuing campaign.

The budget is not the president's last word on government finance, for he is required to submit a midsession update by July 15 (reflecting changes in economic conditions, congressional actions, and other developments). Moreover, the president may revise his budget any time during the year. Changes submitted before Congress has acted on the original request are treated as amendments; requests for additional funds that are made after Congress has acted on the affected appropriations bill are submitted as supplementals.

INFORMATION IN THE PRESIDENT'S BUDGET

As a political statement, the budget is molded to fit each president's style and policies. During George H. W. Bush's presidency, the budget was consolidated into a single volume that highlighted the future liabilities and fiscal risks facing the federal government. The Clinton administration split the budget into four volumes, and this structure has been retained by George W. Bush: (1) the *Budget of the United States Government,* which presents the president's key proposals and revenue and spending estimates; (2) the *Appendix,* which has program and financial information for each budget account; (3) *Analytical Perspectives,* which has special cross-cutting schedules and information for budget categories such as trust funds, user charges, tax expenditures, and aid to state and local governments; and (4) *Historical Tables,* which presents annual data (back to 1940 in some cases) on revenue and spending trends.

These documents include useful budget information, as well as vast amounts of "budget spin" designed to show what the president already has accomplished or promises to achieve. The budget contains the president's budget message, which highlights major policy recommendations and changes and presents expenditure data by functions, agencies, and accounts. For each annually appropriated account, it provides the text of the current appropriation with proposed changes (exhibit 5-1); a brief description of the account's programs and performance (exhibit 5-2); a program and financing schedule that classifies the account into its various programs (exhibit 5-3) and specifies its financing details (exhibit 5-4); a schedule of each account's objects of expenditure (exhibit 5-5); and an employment summary (exhibit 5-6). The budget also has special schedules for direct and guaranteed loans and for various business-type operations carried out by federal departments and corporations.

Although the president's budget is the most comprehensive source of information on

Text continues on page 108.

▶ **EXHIBIT 5-1**
Appropriations Language

Immigration and Customs Enforcement
Salaries and Expenses

For necessary expenses for enforcement of immigration and customs laws, detention and removals, and investigations; and purchase and lease of up to 3,790 (2,350 for replacement only) police-type vehicles; [$3,887,000,000] *$4,162,000,000,* of which not to exceed $7,500,000 shall be available until expended for conducting special operations under section 3131 of the Customs Enforcement Act of 1986 (19 U.S.C. 2081); of which not to exceed $15,000 shall be for official reception and representation expenses; of which not to exceed $1,000,000 shall be for awards of compensation to informants, to be accounted for solely under the certificate of the Secretary of Homeland Security; of which not less than $102,000 shall be for promotion of public awareness of the child pornography tipline; of which not less than $203,000 shall be for Project Alert; of which not less than $5,400,000 may be used to facilitate agreements consistent with section 287(g) of the Immigration and Nationality Act (8 U.S.C. 1357(g)); and of which not to exceed $11,216,000 shall be available to fund or reimburse other Federal agencies for the costs associated with the care, maintenance, and repatriation of smuggled illegal aliens: *Provided,* That none of the funds made available under this heading shall be available to compensate any employee for overtime in an annual amount in excess of $35,000, except that the Secretary of Homeland Security, or the designee of the Secretary, may waive that amount as necessary for national security purposes and in cases of immigration emergencies: *Provided further,* That of the total amount provided, $15,770,000 shall be for activities to enforce laws against forced child labor in fiscal year [2007] 2008, of which not to exceed $6,000,000 shall remain available until expended. (*Department of Homeland Security Appropriations Act, 2007.*)

Source: *Budget of the United States Government, Appendix, Fiscal Year 2008,* p. 458.

(a) This and the next four exhibits pertain to the "salaries and expenses" account for Immigration and Customs Enforcement in the Department of Homeland Security. For each appropriation account, the budget shows proposed appropriations language, a program and financing schedule, an object classification table, and descriptive information.

(b) The appropriations language contains the text of the current appropriation and the text proposed for the next year. The material in brackets is proposed to be deleted; the material in italics is proposed to be added.

(c) This is the entire text for a proposed appropria-

tion of $4.162 billion. In this and most appropriations, details on how the funds are to be spent appear in the appropriations committees reports, not in the text of the appropriations act. Note, however, the limitation of $15,000 for reception and representation expenses.

(d) Although this appropriation is for fiscal year 2008, the text proposes that up to $6 million to enforce laws against forced child labor be available for obligation beyond that fiscal year, "until expended." If the text did not mention any time period, the funds would be available only for a single fiscal year.

(e) The final part of the text indicates (in parentheses) the appropriations act in which the account appears.

► **EXHIBIT 5-2**
Program Description

As the largest investigative arm of the Department of Homeland Security, Immigration and Customs Enforcement (ICE) brings a unified and coordinated focus to the enforcement of Federal immigration and customs laws. ICE works to protect the United States and its people by deterring, interdicting, and investigating threats arising from the movement of people and goods into and out of the United States; and by protecting Federal Government facilities across the Nation. Major programs funded by the Salaries and Expenses appropriation include:

Investigations.—Responsible for investigating a range of issues, including human smuggling; narcotics, weapons and all other contraband smuggling; export enforcement, such as investigating illegal arms exports . . .; and human rights violations. ICE participates in the Organized Crime Drug Enforcement Task Force program for multi-agency drug investigations.

Intelligence.—Responsible for the collection, analysis, and dissemination of strategic and tactical intelligence data for use by the operational elements of ICE and DHS.

Detention and Removal.—Responsible for promoting the public safety and national security by ensuring the departure from the United States of all removable aliens through the fair enforcement of the nation's immigration laws.

The 2008 Budget supports the Administration's plan to improve border security and the enforcement of our Nation's immigration laws through the Secure Border Initiative. The Budget provides funding for increased interior enforcement activities, including six new Border Enforcement Security Task Forces and 22 new Criminal Alien Program teams. The Budget funds all components of immigration enforcement, including $31 million for new detention beds; $10.8 million for enhanced removal operations; $26.4 million to increase the collaboration with State and local law enforcement agencies through an expansion of the 287(g) program; $5 million to enhance ICE's gang enforcement efforts; and $5 million to achieve compliance with immigration laws and increase worksite enforcement.

Source: *Budget of the United States Government, Appendix, Fiscal Year 2008*, p. 459.

(a) The *Budget Appendix* describes the activities proposed to be undertaken in each account. In some cases, it provides workload and other performance data; but in most cases, the description is general, and unlike in the example shown here, activities are not expressly linked to requested funds. For programs that have presidential priority, the *Budget* volume (which in recent times has been transformed into a political document) lists presidential goals and objectives and provides performance data.

(b) OMB instructions issued pursuant to the Government Performance and Results Act require departments and agencies to prepare annual performance plans as well as annual performance reports comparing targeted and actual results. Only a small portion of this information is published in the budget. Some performance material is available on departmental websites.

(c) More detailed program descriptions and performance information are included in the justification material prepared by federal agencies for the appropriations committees. This material is published as part of the appropriations hearings.

(d) OMB has launched PART (Program Assessment Rating Tool) to assess all federal programs over a five-year period according to standard questionnaires. PART scores are available to the public on a governmental website (www.whitehouse.gov/omb/expectmore).

▶ EXHIBIT 5-3
Program and Financing Schedule: Programs and Resources

Identification code 70-0540-0-1-751	2006 actual	2007 est.	2008 est.
Obligations by program activity:	(in millions of dollars)		
00.01 Enforcement activities	3,529	4,155	4,155
09.01 Reimbursable program	253	297	297
10.00 Total new obligations	5,655	5,655	5,711
Budgetary resources available for obligation:			
21.40 Unobligated balance carried forward, start of year	251	401	389
22.00 New budget authority (gross)	3,849	4,440	4,720
22.10 Resources available from recoveries of prior year obligations	85	. . .	. . .
22.30 Expired unobligated balance transfer to unexpired account	15	. . .	. . .
23.90 Total budgetary resources available for obligation	4,200	4,841	5,109
23.95 Total new obligations	-3,782	-4,452	-4,452
23.98 Unobligated balance expiring or withdrawn	-17	. . .	. . .
24.40 Unobligated balance carried forward, end of year	401	389	657
New budget authority (gross), detail:			
Discretionary:			
40.00 Appropriation	3,436	3,887	4,162
40.00 Appropriation (Katrina)	13	. . .	. . .
40.35 Appropriation permanently reduced	-31	. . .	. . .
41.00 Transferred to other accounts	-26	. . .	. . .
42.00 Transferred from other accounts	13	. . .	. . .
43.00 Appropriation (total discretionary)	3,405	3,887	4,162
Spending authority from offsetting collections:			
58.90 Spending authority from offsetting collections (total discretionary)	215	297	297
Mandatory:			
60.20 Appropriation (student exchange and visitor fee)	53	54	56
60.20 Appropriation (breached bond)	73	90	92
60.20 Appropriation (immigration user fee)	103	108	113
62.00 Transferred from other accounts	. . .	4	. . .
62.50 Appropriation (total mandatory)	229	256	261
70.00 Total new budget authority (gross)	3,849	4,440	4,720

Source: *Budget of the United States Government, Appendix, Fiscal Year 2008*, p. 459.

(a) A program and financing schedule accompanies each budget account. The first three parts of the schedule (exhibited here) list major activities and the budget resources available in the account; the final four parts (in the next exhibit) provide financial detail.

(b) Each account has an 11-digit identification code.

(c) Budget schedules generally have three columns. The first reports on the last completed fiscal year, the middle column pertains to the year in progress, and the third column shows the amounts requested for the next fiscal year.

(d) This account (like most others) finances multiple activities. The text of the appropriation does not allocate funds among activities but provides an amount for all activities in the account. However, justification material and appropriations committee reports provide detailed activity breakdowns.

(e) In this account, most of the funds for fiscal year 2008 are expected to come from a single discretionary appropriation ($4.162 billion), but additional amounts are expected to be derived from reimbursements or amounts transferred from other accounts, offsetting collections (for example, user fees), and mandatory appropriations, yielding a total requested funding of $4.720 billion.

▶ **EXHIBIT 5-4**
Program and Financing Schedule: Financing Details

Identification code 70–0540–0–1–751	2006 actual	2007 est.	2008 est.
	(in millions of dollars)		
Change in unpaid obligations:			
72.40 Obligated balance, start of year	773	1,078	1,046
73.10 Total new obligations	3,782	4,452	4,452
73.20 Total outlays (gross)	–3,411	–4,484	–4,668
73.40 Adjustments in expired accounts (net)	–15	. . .	. . .
73.45 Recoveries of prior year obligations	–85	. . .	. . .
74.00 Change in uncollected customer payments from Federal sources (unexpired)	–72	. . .	. . .
74.10 Change in uncollected customer payments from Federal sources (expired)	106	. . .	. . .
74.40 Obligated balance, end of year	1,078	1,046	830
Outlays (gross), detail:			
86.90 Outlays from new discretionary authority	2,745	3,384	3,603
86.93 Outlays from discretionary balances	424	846	801
86.97 Outlays from new mandatory authority	191	206	214
86.98 Outlays from mandatory balances	51	48	50
87.00 Total outlays (gross)	3,411	4,484	4,668
Offsets:			
Against gross budget authority and outlays:			
Offsetting collections (cash) from:			
88.00 Federal sources	–240	–297	–297
88.40 Nonfederal sources	–12	. . .	. . .
88.90 Total, offsetting collections (cash)	–252	–297	–297
Against gross budget authority only:			
88.95 Change in uncollected customer payments from Federal sources (unexpired)	–72	. . .	. . .
88.96 Portion of offsetting collections (cash) credited to expired accounts	109	. . .	. . .
Net budget authority and outlays:			
89.00 Budget authority	3,634	4,143	4,423

Source: *Budget of the United States Government, Appendix, Fiscal Year 2008*, p. 459.

(a) The remaining sections of the program and financing schedule show various accounting details. "Change in obligated balances" relates obligations to outlays. Outlays are the difference between unpaid obligations at the start of the year plus new obligations incurred during the year minus actual or estimated unpaid obligations at the end of the year.

(b) "Outlays" indicates the outlays derived from current and permanent budget authority and from balances carried over from prior years.

(c) "Offsets" and "Net budget authority" show offsetting collections and certain accounting adjustments. The difference between net budget authority and outlays shown here and the gross amounts shown earlier is due to offsetting collections.

(d) The four-digit line numbers (including two decimal places) at the left correspond to definitions and information on budgetary treatment provided in OMB *Circular A-11.*

EXHIBIT 5-5
Object Classification

Identification code 70–0540–0–1–751	2006 actual	2007 est.	2008 est.
Direct obligations:	(in millions of dollars)		
11.1 Full-time permanent	894	1,057	1,057
11.3 Other than full-time permanent	44	73	73
11.5 Other personnel compensation	215	245	245
11.8 Special personal services payments	1	. . .	. . .
11.9 Total personnel compensation	1,154	1,375	1,375
12.1 Civilian personnel benefits	433	473	473
21.0 Travel and transportation of persons	43	166	166
22.0 Transportation of things	26	7	7
23.1 Rental payments to GSA	178	223	223
23.2 Rental payments to others	1	1	1
23.3 Communications, utilities, and miscellaneous charges	45	46	46
25.1 Advisory and assistance services	133	176	176
25.2 Other services	551	768	768
25.3 Other purchases of goods and services from government accounts	57	85	85
25.4 Operation and maintenance of facilities	463	334	334
25.6 Medical care	74	. . .	. . .
25.7 Operation and maintenance of equipment	33	48	48
25.8 Subsistence and support of persons	120	286	286
26.0 Supplies and materials	62	67	67
31.0 Equipment	149	86	86
32.0 Land and structures	2	10	10
42.0 Insurance claims and indemnities	3	2	2
91.0 Unvouchered	2	2	2
99.0 Direct obligations	3,529	4,155	4,155
99.0 Reimbursable obligations	250	294	294
99.5 Below reporting threshold	3	3	3
99.9 Total new obligations	3,782	4,452	4,452

Source: *Budget of the United States Government, Appendix, Fiscal Year 2008*, pp. 459–60.

(a) This schedule, which accompanies every appropriation account, classifies the budgetary resources available for obligation by the major objects of expenditure. The same object classification is used by all federal agencies. The object code numbers are printed in the left margin of the schedule.

(b) Five categories of objects are used in this schedule: personnel compensation and benefits (10), contractual services and supplies (20), acquisition of assets (30), grants and fixed charges (40), and other (90). The object code numbers associated with each category appear in the left margin of the schedule and are explained in OMB *Circular A-11.*

(c) Reimbursable obligations, which stem from offsetting collections received in return for goods and services, are separated from direct obligations, which encompass all other spending.

► **EXHIBIT 5-6**
Employment Summary

Identification code 70–0540–0–1–751	2006 actual	2007 est.	2008 est.
Direct:	(in millions of dollars)		
1001 Civilian full-time equivalent employment	12,901	15,543	16,497
Reimbursable:			
2001 Civilian full-time equivalent employment	340	340	340

Source: *Budget of the United States Government, Appendix, Fiscal Year 2008,* p. 460.

(a) For each account with personnel compensation, the budget presents summary data on the number of full-time equivalent (FTE) work years.

(b) Most agencies have some flexibility in shifting funds among object classes (see exhibit 5-5). However, most have ceilings on the number of FTEs and are expected by their appropriations subcommittees to implement their budgets, to the extent practicable, in accord with these ceilings and the object schedules. In view of the long lead time from budget preparation to implementation, deviations from these schedules frequently occur, sometimes through the reprogramming process discussed in chapter 10, but most commonly through unilateral action by the spending agency.

(c) As with the object classification schedule, the employment summary distinguishes between direct and reimbursable activities.

federal finances, it may lack sufficient detail for those interested in particular programs or agencies. Additional information may be obtained from the following documents prepared by federal departments and agencies:

—Briefing material distributed by agencies to the media shortly after the president transmits his budget to Congress. Many federal agencies hold press briefings, usually on the day the budget is released or the next day, at which they provide detailed information on their programs and finances.

—Every federal agency prepares justification material for its appropriations hearings. This material (discussed in chapter 9) usually is published a few months after the hearings are held but may be obtained earlier from the agency or from Internet sources for congressional activity.

—Most agencies prepare internal budgets (sometimes computer printouts) for their own use, but these are not normally made available to the public. Internal budgets are updated throughout the year to reflect recent developments, such as congressional actions and the obligation of funds.

THE PRESIDENT'S BUDGET IN CONGRESS

As noted earlier, contemporary presidents must deal with a Congress that has become increasingly independent on the budget and other policy matters. Recent presidents and their staffs have had to invest substantial time in monitoring legislative action and wooing members.

OMB tracks the progress of the president's budget through Congress, but its formal role in congressional budgeting is limited. OMB officials and the president's economic advisers appear before congressional committees to discuss overall policy and economic issues, but they generally leave discussion of particular

programs to the affected agencies. Agency officials have the primary responsibility for defending the president's recommendations at appropriations hearings and other congressional forums. In the hearings, agency officials justify the president's budget, even when it diverges from their real preferences. Toward this end, OMB maintains an elaborate legislative clearance process to ensure that budget justifications, testimony, and legislative proposals are consistent with presidential policy. But the appropriations process is fragmented, and agencies have informal avenues for staking out their own position on particular matters (see chapter 9).

To get his way, the president and his staff must navigate through budget resolutions, reconciliation bills, authorization legislation, annual appropriations, tax legislation, and more. His staff must be well versed in congressional budget rules. They must be smart budget counters, mindful of how legislation is scored and of how scores can be altered through budgetary sleight of hand. They also must be good vote counters in Congress and willing to twist arms to get a winning coalition. Sometimes the president negotiates with members of Congress; at other times, he goes over their heads and appeals for public support. He must know when to keep a safe distance and when to intervene, when to threaten a veto (or carry out the threat) and when to concede. He must know when to delegate to others the task of reaching agreement and when to act as his own budget director. The tough decisions and important details must be his call.

Political and Legislative Resources

The White House is a budget pulpit; from the Oval Office, the president usually has the capacity to define the terms of the budget debate. He decides which issues will be on the table, whether to seek changes in revenues and entitlements, and whether to demand program initiatives. His budget is the trigger for congressional action on these and other matters. Even when the budget is reputed to be dead on arrival, the president sets the agenda for the bargaining and legislative actions that follow. The media give the president's budget extensive coverage when it is released, policy analysts and interest groups scour its pages, and the budget, appropriations, and tax committees spring into action.

Not only does the president usually have the initiative, he can be confident that Congress will act on some of his budget proposals. Congress does not have the option of doing nothing on appropriations, and it is likely to take action pursuant to revenue proposals. But having the initiative does not ensure that the president gets his way. Every budget puts the president at risk of Congress charting its own course. To nudge legislative outcomes closer to his budget, the president must cajole a sufficient number of fence-sitting members to snatch victory from defeat. His first task is to nail down support within his own party. If, as has sometimes been the case, he lacks a majority in one or both houses, he must reach out to swing members of the other party. The votes will not be there if they are not solicited, since members of Congress have budgetary interests that diverge from those of the president. Reagan in 1981 and Clinton a dozen years later met one-on-one with many members, mostly middle-of-the-road and conservative Democrats, whose support gave them a slim margin of victory. In both cases, journalists made much of the deals that had been cut to buy votes. In fact, presidents usually offer relatively little in exchange for votes, especially during the afterglow of their elections. During the postelection honeymoon and when his public rating is favorable, a president's most valuable

resource is the predisposition of fence-sitting members to vote his way when he asks for their support. A member who meets the president before an important vote usually enters predisposed to support the president and leaves promising to vote his way.

Some presidents have been reluctant to go one-on-one in pursuit of votes. Jimmy Carter was discomfited by this aspect of congressional-presidential relations. George H. W. Bush (who had served in the House) had a comfortable relationship with many members of Congress, but on budget matters, he often stood above the fray and did not effectively exploit the advantages of his office when votes were needed. His son, by contrast, has enjoyed this part of his job. Rather than regarding telephone calls to members as a chore, George W. Bush relishes the opportunity to tell them he needs their votes and appreciates their support.

This message wears thin with repetition, which is one reason no president builds every budgetary (or legislative) disagreement with Congress into a cause célèbre. It explains why presidents tend to take their boldest budget steps early in their term and why they progressively demand and get less from Congress.

In addition to lobbying members of Congress, the president can rally support through adroit use of the media. Although few viewers or listeners are likely to be interested in the details of the latest budget battle, the media give the president an opportunity to paint Congress as recalcitrant and to demand action. Ronald Reagan used prime-time television with considerable effectiveness during his early years in office. He also broadcast weekend radio talks that were widely disseminated by the media on days when there normally was little solid news.

Clinton varied his budget tactics with changes in the political lineup. In 1993, when his party still controlled Congress, Clinton's task was to persuade fellow Democrats to vote for a deficit reduction package that included tax increases and spending cuts. To get the necessary majority, he had to provide political coverage to some Democrats who were troubled by his proposals. Clinton made two back-to-back television appearances in February 1993: the first was a brief speech that field-tested his message and primed viewers for the tax increases he proposed a few days later; the second was a vigorous presentation of the budget plan he gave Congress. This concentrated television exposure was risky, but Clinton's gamble paid off—Congress enacted the main features of his plan. Of course, the president cannot go to the country every time a budget is pending in Congress. Presidents typically limit their television appearances to important occasions.

Presidential style makes a difference in using the budget as a pulpit. It helps if the president is comfortable in the role and an effective communicator. It also helps if the president has an upbeat disposition that enables him to bounce back from bad news and if he has the staying power to keep vital objectives in focus. For all presidents, budgeting is a grind. Before one budget is resolved, another is on the way. Few issues are fully or finally resolved. Even when they appear to be, unexpected developments often intrude, derailing budget plans and complicating negotiations. It is important, therefore, for presidents to take what they can get in each year's budget cycle and to label half a loaf as a complete victory. Few presidents have excelled more at this political art than Bill Clinton. Box 5-4 describes how he built minor concessions from Republicans in the 1998 budget battle into a political triumph.

The Whole and the Parts

Presidential influence is not spread uniformly across all facets of budgeting. The president sometimes has a stronger influence on the totals than on particular programs. His revenue proposals have a strong bearing on whether Congress will consider major changes in the tax laws; his projected budget surplus or deficit often becomes the fiscal parameter within which Congress operates. In most years since 1981, Congress's budget resolution has provided for a deficit less than (or a surplus more than) or about the same as the amount budgeted by the president. The president's budget does not legitimize deficits, but it does make it politically costly for Congress to set a higher amount. For this reason, if the president comes in with an unrealistically low deficit projection, so too will Congress.

The president's influence on the budgeted—in contrast to the actual—deficit discomfited Congress during the Reagan years. Reagan's budget was often based on unrealistically buoyant economic assumptions and on "dead on arrival" proposals to cut deeply into domestic programs. Rather than manifesting presidential impotence, Reagan's budgets skillfully positioned him for negotiations with Congress. In these negotiations and in other actions, Congress saved most of the programs the president targeted for termination, but it did so within the deficit totals he dictated. Within these totals, Congress made significant shifts in priorities, taking funds from programs Reagan wanted to expand (principally defense) and giving them to programs he wanted to shrink.

Congress also restored proposed cuts by adding to the spending totals. During the 1980s, the congressional budget resolution usually allowed more total budget authority and outlays than the president had requested. In most of these years, Congress made room for the additional spending by budgeting higher revenues.

Reagan legitimized unrealistic budgeting as a tool of presidential power. Although Congress

▼

BOX 5-4
How Bill Clinton Turned Small Disputes into a Big Victory in 1998

When the Republican-controlled Congress convened in January 1998, the leadership hoped for a calm, relatively brief session in which they and the White House would agree on appropriations, cut some taxes, and make a few changes in entitlement programs. Nine months later, the two sides were locked in budgetary combat. They finally patched up differences in a 900-page omnibus appropriations bill that gave each side some of the things it wanted. It also gave Republicans another loss and Bill Clinton a big political triumph.

The year began with conditions favorable for budgetary harmony. Just months earlier, Clinton and Republicans hammered out a "balanced budget" agreement that purported

February 2
Clinton's fiscal 1999 budget is released.

April 2
Senate passes budget resolution 57-41.

June 5
House passes budget resolution 216-204.

October 1
Fiscal year 1998 ends with a projected surplus of $70 billion.

October 7
Clinton vetoes Agriculture appropriations bill.

October 21
Clinton signs the omnibus appropriations bill into law.

November 3
Democrats gain five House seats in the midterm elections.

to set budget policy in place through fiscal 2002. Moreover, as the session wore on, budgetary conditions turned out to be much more favorable than anticipated. Clinton's budget had projected a $10 billion deficit for fiscal 1998, but by the time the year ended, the government had racked up a $70 billion surplus.

Why, despite these conditions, did the White House and Congress lock horns? In addition, how and why did Clinton win? The answers come in two parts—Republican miscalculation and Clinton's brinksmanship. House Republicans moved slowly on the appropriations bills, miscalculating that as the elections approached, they would gain strength. They reasoned that the president's party had gained House seats in midterm elections only twice since the Civil War. The Republicans also assumed that as the surplus grew, so would congressional support for tax cuts. They took it for granted that taxpayers preferred to keep more of their earnings.

But Clinton figured that with the economy booming, most Americans were not concerned about taxes. Instead, they were worried about whether the Social Security system would have enough money to pay for their retirement and whether schools had enough money to do a good job of educating their children. Throughout the session, Clinton parried Republican demands with two main messages: use the surplus to strengthen Social Security and boost education spending. Clinton had other budget priorities, but his political rhetoric was concentrated on these two popular objectives.

As the new fiscal year began and midterm elections approached, Clinton vetoed the Agriculture appropriations bill, signaling that he would be willing to shut down the government once again if Congress refused his budget demands. Republicans grew increasingly anxious that they

continued

BOX 5-4
Continued

would be blamed again for a shutdown. They therefore were willing to negotiate a package deal that would resolve the outstanding budget disputes and allow Congress to adjourn.

The negotiations culminated in an omnibus appropriations bill that was fattened with budgetary goodies for both sides. Clinton got a little more for education but much less than he demanded; Republicans got more for defense and antidrug efforts. Both sides pretended that the spending increase was within the budget limits since the additional money was labeled "emergency." Clinton got Republicans to remove various riders to which he objected, including prohibiting federal funds to test or approve abortion-inducing drugs, an authorization of new roads through Alaskan wildlife sanctuaries, and a provision preventing permanent U.S. residency for 50,000 Haitian refugees. The bill was also stuffed with numerous earmarked projects and dozens of provisions that had nothing to do with the budget but everything to do with the fact that the omnibus bill was the last opportunity to pass legislation before Congress adjourned.

Clinton proclaimed the bill a victory and looked like a winner on television. Speaker Newt Gingrich (R-Ga.) and other Republican leaders also claimed victory, but they were hard put to say what they came away with. Four years earlier, the Republicans had gained control of Congress on the pledge of cutting the budget; this year they ended up voting for spending increases. When the votes were counted on election day, two weeks after Clinton signed the omnibus bill, the president's party had gained five House seats—the first time that had happened in over 50 years. Clinton's standing in the polls was near the peak of his presidency; he had transformed relatively modest program expansions into a political triumph.

---

made many changes in his budget, the revenue and spending outcomes were closer to his preferences than they would have been had he sent up a realistic budget. But the president's tactical gains came at a high cost: they made the budget into more of a bargaining chip and undermined its status as an authoritative guide to national policy.

Both George H. W. Bush and Clinton followed in Reagan's path. Year after year, Bush proposed cuts that had no chance of enactment. In fact, if a cutback was proposed in one Bush budget, there was a high probability it also was in the following one and in the one after that. Clinton used more defensible economic assumptions than his predecessors, but his budgets recommended program expan-

sions that could be accommodated within the spending caps only by playing fast and loose with the rules. In the negotiated endgames that characterized budgeting in the Clinton years, the president often got some of what he wanted. If his original budget had been realistic, he might have gotten less.

THE VETO POWER

When the two branches' priorities diverge, even a shrewd and persuasive president may have difficulty getting his revenue and spending preferences approved. This is most likely to be the case when control of government is divided and the two parties are centered at opposite poles in the political spectrum. When this occurs, Congress may disregard the president's budget and stuff appropriations bills and other budget-related matters with a slew of provisions that are contrary to his expressed policies. Over the years, many presidents have complained that they are at a disadvantage because they are compelled to sign or veto the entire bill; they cannot pick and choose from among its provisions. This disadvantage is especially pronounced when spending bills are presented to them after the fiscal year has started and failure to sign the measure risks shutting down the government. To make matters worse, Congress further debilitates the veto power when it wraps multiple appropriations bills, along with substantive legislation, into an omnibus measure. To redress this imbalance of power, presidents since the Civil War have demanded line-item veto authority, which would enable them to reject offensive provisions while signing the bill into law. In 1996 Congress gave the president a form of line-item veto, but in 1998 the Supreme Court ruled that the version adopted violated the Constitution.

In political relationships between the president and Congress, things are not always what they seem. The conventional all-or-nothing veto power is not inherently weak, Clinton's line-item veto power was not a genuine veto since it was not provided by a constitutional amendment, and enactment of omnibus legislation has more to do with the emergence of negotiated budgets than with congressional efforts to hoodwink or outmaneuver the president.

Presidents have a big advantage when they veto legislation; they win whenever members of their own party in Congress support them on the override vote. Although his party lacked a majority in Congress, George H. W. Bush had a sterling veto record, winning more than 30 consecutive override fights before los-

ing one near the end of his presidency. Bill Clinton backed congressional Republicans into a political corner during the 1995–99 budget wars by vetoing some bills and threatening to veto others. Why then have recent presidents complained about the feebleness of the all-or-nothing veto that the Constitution prescribes? Part of the answer is that Congress earmarks money for projects and inserts other provisions that may offend the president but often do not justify a veto of the entire bill. But a big part of the answer is that few recent presidents have used their veto power effectively. In the 1980s, Ronald Reagan signed omnibus appropriations bills that were chock full of provisions he did not like because he was apprehensive about shutting down the government. In any confrontation, the side that signals it is unwilling to fight loses. Clinton won because he vetoed offending bills; Reagan lost because he did not.

In many conflicts, the president need not actually veto a bill; threatening to do so suffices. In contrast to other recent presidents who merely suggested they would consider vetoing particular measures, Clinton often declared outright that he would veto pending measures if certain provisions were not removed; in these cases, Congress typically revised the bill to gain his approval. It helped that Clinton often had public opinion on his side, but the important thing is that he won. Every budget victory made him stronger for the next confrontation because he had a credible veto threat.

George W. Bush took the opposite tack during his first six years in office. He rarely threatened vetoes and did sign into law every spending bill passed by Congress. He did, of course, use Statements of Administration Policy (SAPs) and other channels to inform Congress of objections to pending appropriations bills, and he often was successful in persuading

Congress to revise spending amounts or other provisions. His unwillingness to exercise the veto power may have stemmed from the fact that Republicans controlled both the House and Senate during almost all of that period, or from an acceptance of rising spending levels. Whatever the explanation, Bush sharply reversed course in 2007 when the Democrats gained majorities in the House and Senate. By then, however, a lame-duck president, weakened by an unpopular war, had difficulty stemming spending pressures in Congress.

A line-item veto would strengthen the president's hand with respect to minor details but would not make much difference on major budget issues. When Clinton signed the line-item veto into law in 1996, he claimed that it would "prevent Congress from enacting special interest provisions under the cloak of a 500- or 1,000-page bill." Clinton exercised the line-item veto several times before the Supreme Court ruled it unconstitutional. Inasmuch as Congress established the new power by legislation rather than constitutional amendment, it was not a genuine line-item veto. Rather, the procedures (spelled out in box 5-5) would have enabled the president to cancel portions of bills passed by Congress and signed into law. The so-called line-item procedure applied to three types of legislation: appropriations bills, new direct spending, and revenue measures providing preferences to one hundred or fewer taxpayers. During the brief period that he had this power, Clinton used it on all three types of measures. He canceled a total of 82 items: 79 appropriations items, 2 targeted tax benefits, and 1 new direct spending provision. All told, the White House estimated $2 billion in savings from this exercise of the line-item veto. But in June 1998, the Supreme Court held that by canceling portions of a law that had been passed by Congress and signed into law by him, "the President has amended two Acts of Congress. . . . There is no provision in the Constitution that authorizes the President to enact, to amend, or to repeal statutes."

What did the president gain when Congress gave him the line-item veto, and what did he lose when the Court took it away? Not much, despite the advantage on particular items. If the line-item veto had survived, Congress would have taken countermeasures to even the playing field. It might have written legislation so as to exempt certain provisions from the president's new veto power, or it might have taken some of his legislative priorities hostage, withholding action on them until he consented not to cancel certain provisions.

Some argue that the president lost a great deal because he cannot veto omnibus measures that contain much of the session's legislative output and many of its budget decisions. But this view does not take account of the political bargaining through which omnibus bills are assembled. These bills materialize during the final stages of the annual budget process, and Congress passes them after extensive negotiations with the president. There is much give and take at this stage, and the president gains quite a lot by wrapping separate bills into an omnibus measure. If he does not, the president has the option of vetoing the measure when there is little in it for him; he generally refrains from exercising the veto just because the measure contains some provisions he dislikes.

CONCLUSION

For every president, budgeting balances what he wants and what he can get. The published words and numbers attest to what the president says he wants but are silent about what he will do in pursuit of his objectives and what he will settle for. How much of the budget is presidential ambition and how much is political

---

BOX 5-5
The Line-Item Veto

The following procedures were established by the Line Item Veto Act (P.L. 104-130), enacted into law in 1996 and invalidated by the Supreme Court in 1998.

1. Congress passes an appropriations bill, a bill providing new direct spending, or a bill containing a "limited tax benefit" and sends the legislation to the president.
2. The president signs the measure in the same manner as he signs other bills passed by Congress. At this point, the measure is enacted into law. Steps 3 through 6 do not apply if a bill becomes law without the president's signature or by congressional override of his veto.
3. Within 5 days after signing the measure, the president notifies Congress that he has canceled certain spending items or limited tax benefits. The president may not cancel legislative language in an appropriations bill.
4. Within 30 days, Congress may pass legislation disapproving the president's cancellation. If it fails to do so, the canceled provision ceases to have legal force or effect. Disapproval legislation would be considered under expedited procedures.
5. The president may veto the disapproval bill in the same manner as he may veto any other bill passed by Congress.
6. Congress may override the president's veto by a two-thirds vote of the House and Senate, in the same manner as it may override any presidential veto.

Source: Line Item Veto Act, P.L. 104-130 (April 9, 1996), 110 Stat. 1200-1212.

---

bluster can be known only after Congress has completed its work and agencies are implementing the approved spending plans.

A review of the budgetary record of the four most recent presidents shows that each approached the annual round of revenue and spending decisions in a distinctive way. Ronald Reagan formulated budgets that he knew would come out of Congress much changed from what went in. He requested a lot more for defense so that he could get more, even though Congress trimmed the increase. He demanded many of the same domestic cuts, year after year, so that the growth of many programs was slowed or halted, even though Congress restored all or most of the money. He railed against deficit spending, but presided over gargantuan deficits that led to the Gramm-Rudman-Hollings laws enacted during his second term.

George H. W. Bush took a less ideological but more rigid posture than Reagan. Locking himself into a "read my lips, no new taxes" pledge, Bush started his presidency opposed to modest tax increases—only to be compelled by soaring deficits and the GRH targets to sign a very large tax increase. Although he also proposed domestic spending cuts, Bush distanced himself from the budget. In contrast to all post–World War II presidents, who introduced their budgets with a message outlining their policies and objectives, Bush merely sent a brief, perfunctory letter of transmittal. The real budget messages published during this period were those of Richard Darman, his budget director, who often seemed to have his own agenda.

Budgetary battles with Congress were a recurring theme of the Clinton presidency. The first battles were with fellow Democrats who were uneasy about some of the tax increases he proposed in 1993; the later ones were with congressional Republicans who opposed his spending priorities and wanted tax cuts. Each of Clinton's battles ended in negotiation, and in each the president attained much of what he wanted. He won enactment of the deficit reduction package in 1993; blocked Republican efforts to slash taxes and certain domestic programs in 1995 and 1996; negotiated a deal with Republicans in 1997 that cut taxes, added some spending, and claimed to produce a balanced budget; and once again blocked Republican tax cuts and achieved some spending gains in his final years in office. In each of his confrontations with Republicans, Clinton scored a political victory, pinning a fiscal irresponsibility label on Republicans for shutting down the government, wanting to trim Medicare, and refusing to go along with increases for education and some of his other priorities. Even when he got much less than he initially asked for, Clinton had no difficulty exulting in his political success.

Balancing the conflicts and tensions of budgeting seemed to come easily to Clinton, though he sometimes discomfited supporters and left others bewildered as to what he really stood for. To Clinton, balancing was not merely compromising on differences or taking a centrist position. It meant embracing seemingly clashing views by promoting government expansion while downsizing government and co-opting conservative positions while advancing liberal ones. It meant taking strong steps to curtail the deficit while proposing program initiatives, and pruning government operations while extracting more tax dollars to pay for government. Budgeting by Clinton often defied conventional classifications and accommodated the constraints and opportunities of the moment. There was a streak of opportunism in Clinton's stewardship of the federal budget, but it was an opportunism that brought triumphs when the odds were stacked against him. As president, he sought new syntheses that appealed to the political middle, which wanted smaller government and more from government. Whether this was the real Clinton or the political one makes little difference; either way, it was a formula that repeatedly bested congressional Republicans.

George W. Bush also has had to balance disparate budget objectives, but he has done so in ways that distinguish him from both his immediate predecessors. In contrast to his father, Bush has not wavered in his determination to reduce the tax burden; in contrast to Clinton, he generally has eschewed open conflict with Congress in spending policies. Taxing less and spending more have left the government with large, persistent deficits that are likely to grow even bigger in the decade after he leaves office. Yet Bush has not been able to ignore budget trends, and midway through his second term, he took a harder line on spending, especially for social programs.

Bush has been consistent on taxes, advocating cuts early in his presidency, when the government was flush with surpluses, and late in his term, when deficits were entrenched. Because of congressional budget rules and divisions among Republican members (especially in the Senate), Bush has had to settle for smaller cuts than he preferred and for sunset provisions that will terminate cuts if they are not removed. But reducing tax rates has been one of his signature accomplishments, and he is not likely to reverse course during his last years as president. Some see Bush's unqualified endorsement of tax cuts as an effort to avoid the political pitfalls that beset his father, while others view it as a "starve the beast" tactic to trim government by denying it revenues.

In fact, however, there has been little starving of government on Bush's watch. During his first year, Bush was forced by the 9/11 terrorist attacks to spend more on defense and homeland security. But within months of the attacks, he also signed a farm bill and a supplemental appropriations act that had been fattened by Congress and added billions to education spending. During his first five years in office, Bush signed every spending bill passed by Congress, even when the amounts greatly exceeded his budget requests. He also promoted additional spending and muscled a costly expansion of Medicare through Congress. Bush took a tougher line on spending increases late in his presidency, but only after the divisions in his own party and unfavorable public opinion ratings threatened to weaken his political influence.

Judging from his budget record, Bush has been a populist president, giving Americans the lower taxes and bigger programs they want. Arguably, this stance has been designed to bolster Republican efforts to become entrenched as the majority party, but the legacy of oversized deficits has undermined this strategy.

6

The Congressional Budget Process

Shortly after the president submits his budget, Congress begins work on a budget resolution that expresses its own policies and priorities. This resolution sets forth budget totals for each of the next 10 (or fewer) years and allocates spending among 20 functional categories. The resolution may also contain reconciliation instructions to change existing revenue or direct spending laws, as well as other provisions relating to the budget. In developing its budget resolution, Congress often deviates from the president's recommendations, but when the Budget Enforcement Act (BEA) was effective, it had to adhere to discretionary spending limits and pay-as-you-go (PAYGO) requirements. With the expiration of the BEA limits, the budget resolution has become the means of setting annual limits on the total that may be appropriated.

Because it is in the form of a concurrent resolution, a budget resolution is not a law. Although both the House and Senate pass it, the resolution is not presented to the president for his signature or veto; hence it does not have statutory effect. In addition to adopting the budget resolution, Congress provides legal authority for the federal government to raise and spend money through revenue laws, appropriation acts, and other spending legislation. The purpose of the budget resolution is to establish the fiscal framework within which Congress takes these statutory actions. If everything goes according to plan, Congress's actions and the amounts actually raised and spent would conform to the levels specified in the resolution. Sometimes budget outcomes are on target or come close; other times there are significant variances. Even though Congress has enforcement tools, such as points of order, section 302 allocations to House and Senate committees, and scorekeeping reports (described later in this chapter), it sometimes enacts policies that differ from the resolution. Moreover, actual revenues and spending often diverge from the amounts set out in the resolution because of factors outside Congress's effective control (for example, the performance of the economy).

In 1998, for the first time since Congress established its own budget process a quarter of a century earlier, it failed to adopt the annual resolution. It also failed to approve a budget resolution in 2002, 2004, and 2006. But these failures did not stop other legislative actions related to the budget. Congress appropriated funds to federal programs and agencies, and it produced a slew of authorization bills. But it did not consider reconciliation legislation, nor did it devise a comprehensive budget policy. Except for the fact that Congress produced truly mammoth omnibus appropriation acts, 1998, 2002, 2004, and 2006 were routine budget years. No significant changes were made in the tax code, entitlement programs, or federal budget rules. The lack of a budget resolution was hardly noticed.

In some years, however, congressional budgeting has big ambitions and large conflicts. These are the years when the budget resolution and the reconciliation bill dominate the legislative agenda and drive Congress to enact substantial changes in revenue or spending policy. In discussing the congressional budget process, therefore, it is necessary to distinguish between status quo and change-oriented years. In the former, the resolution hardly makes a difference; in the latter, it makes all the difference.

WHY CONGRESS HAS A BUDGET RESOLUTION

Why does Congress go through the motions of adopting a budget resolution when it still must pass separate bills that enable the government to tax and spend? In fact, Congress operated for almost two centuries—from its first session in 1789 until 1975—without a budget resolution. During that period, it made numerous financial decisions each year and acted on revenue and spending bills one at a time. But Congress did not vote on the total budget; the totals were simply the sum of its many legislative actions.

To understand why Congress established its own budget process, one must consider three questions. How did Congress manage to operate without a budget resolution in the past? Why did Congress reverse course in 1974 and create a legislative budget process? What purpose is served by having a budget resolution that lacks legal status?

Congress and budgeting do not easily fit together. Congress is inherently a decentralized institution that must, because of the geographical basis on which members are elected, give many committees and their members a voice in budget decisions. Fragmentation is not a legislative disorder, although it sometimes produces messy procedures and unpredictable outcomes. Rather, it is inherent in an institution in which senators come from each of the 50 states and representatives from 435 different places in America. The political job of Congress is to give voice, representation, and access to the diversity of interests in American life. In the budgetary arena, Congress upholds this institutional imperative by widely distributing influence. Most members have some budgetary power by serving on one or more of the committees responsible for revenues, authorizations, or appropriations.

Congress's practice of taking up the many budget-related measures one at a time reinforces its decentralization. But consider the alternative—an arrangement that would give a single set of House and Senate committees control of all budget legislation. Given the size and importance of the budget, these committees would be able to leverage their power to control virtually all significant legislation. Members of these committees would influence substantive legislation, even when it was not in their committee's jurisdiction and only weakly germane to the budget. Most other members would be without a significant role or influence. Such a concentration of congressional power would not be sustainable. Eventually the rank-and-file majority excluded from budgetary power would wrest control away from the few who had it.

Budgetary fragmentation worked reasonably well in the past when Congress followed the president's lead on budget matters and jurisdiction over federal spending was concentrated in the appropriations committees. Although Congress acted on the budget in piecemeal fashion, the president's recommendations guided its actions. Every step of the way, especially in making appropriations and writing tax legislation, Congress used the president's budget as the starting point and typically made many small, incremental changes. The thousands of separate congressional decisions added up to totals that did not veer very far from the president's budget. In effect, the president served as the coordinator of congressional budget action, making it possible for a fragmented Congress to produce seemingly coordinated budget outcomes.

However, for reasons discussed in the previous chapter, the president's legislative influence sagged in the late 1960s and early 1970s. Watergate and Vietnam took a toll, as did conflict between the White House and Capitol Hill over tax increases, deficit spending, and the impoundment of appropriated funds. Impoundment was the final straw; it spurred enactment of the Congressional Budget Act (CBA) in 1974, which conceived of the budget resolution as an opportunity for Congress to stake out an independent position on the budget. For this reason, the budget resolution was to be exclusively a legislative decision. The president would not be involved, and Congress would not be beholden to his economic forecasts or policy preferences in drawing up the resolution. It would rely instead on the new Congressional Budget Office (CBO) for information and analysis.

Relations with the president were not Congress's only concern in establishing its own budget process. During the decade before CBA, congressional control of spending became increasingly difficult. The appropriations committees, which once had jurisdiction over virtually all federal spending, were unable to block the rising tide of entitlements and other backdoor methods that shifted jurisdiction to authorizing committees. As entitlements gained budgetary prominence, it became evident that Congress could not control total federal spending through annual appropriation decisions. It needed a broader process that encompassed all expenditures—one that linked revenue and spending. The budget resolution was to be that coordinating device. It covers all federal spending, regardless of committee jurisdiction, and requires Congress to make explicit decisions on total revenue and spending, budget priorities, and the surplus or deficit.

But in devising a comprehensive budget process, Congress had to ensure that legislative power remained dispersed. CBA balanced budgetary integration and legislative fragmentation by layering the budget resolution on top of existing authorizations, appropriations, and revenue processes. The coexistence of an integrated budget process and decentralized revenue and spending processes has greatly complicated congressional budgeting. All revenue and spending set in the budget resolution is also in the jurisdiction of other congressional committees. The resolution is advisory; the work of other committees is legislative. The resolution deals with aggregates and a small number of major spending categories; other committees get into the details and make specific program decisions. Implementing the "big picture" of the resolution depends on the actions of authorizing, appropriations, and revenue committees. As a fiscal framework, the resolution is highly important when it controls what others do and is unimportant, even irrelevant, when it does not. In some years, the resolution has a lead role in framing the legislative agenda and in determining how much is raised and spent. In other years, it merely ratifies the status quo.

In the more than 30 years that Congress has been producing budget resolutions, the process has rarely been the same two years in a row. Not only has the timing of Congress's actions differed, so too have the content and length of these measures; they have become political variables that expand and contract to suit the current Democratic or Republican agenda. The Democrats' fiscal year 1995 resolution covered 5 years and sought few changes in budget policy. With Republicans winning control of Congress for the first time in 40 years, the fiscal 1996 resolution demanded more than $1 trillion in revenue and spending changes. A 7-year time frame was selected because the resolution targeted fiscal year 2002 as the first year in which the budget would be balanced. The fiscal year 1997 reso-

lution covered 6 years and curtailed the budgeted savings; the fiscal year 1998 resolution reverted to a 5-year horizon with modest policy objectives. The fiscal year 2000 resolution was stretched to 10 years because the Republican majority wanted to show deep tax cuts. Because tax cuts are scored against the baseline, the longer the period covered by the resolution, the bigger the reported size of the cuts. For the fiscal year 2001 resolution, Republicans cut the duration covered by the resolution in half, from 10 to 5 years, because they wanted to show smaller tax cuts (so as to demonstrate that the cuts would not touch the Social Security surplus). Like just about everything else in budgeting, each year is a different story because of changes in budget and political conditions and in relationships of party leaders, other committees, and the budget committees.

The history of the budget process tells us that Congress cannot abide major changes in policy each year—trying to do so would provoke partisan conflict, congest the legislative calendar, and strain relations between the budget committees and other congressional committees. But it is also the case that Congress cannot accept standpat budget policies year after year. Election results, pressure from the White House, emerging spending demands, and concern about the deficit have impelled Congress to use the budget resolution as a platform for redirecting government policies. "Big bang" years in congressional budgeting have tended to be followed by relatively quiet years. Congress enacted major budget changes in 1990, had status quo budget resolutions in 1991 and 1992, launched another round of policy changes the following year, sought few changes in 1994, tried to enact truly significant budget legislation in 1995 (but stirred up so much conflict that some federal departments were shut down for lack of funds), and settled for more modest legislation the next several years. During George W. Bush's first term, the budget resolution was deployed to drive significant tax cuts through Congress. When there were no tax cuts on the agenda, Congress did not bother to complete work on the budget resolution.

The extent to which the budget resolution seeks change can be measured by the scope of its reconciliation instructions. A resolution that does not contain reconciliation merely accommodates the status quo; one that has such instructions seeks to change existing law. The broader the scope of reconciliation—the more committees subjected to it and the more dollars involved—the greater the importance of the resolution in setting Congress's agenda and revising budget policy.

Paradoxically, the budget resolution was intended to manifest congressional independence, but in some reconciliation years, it has been an instrument of presidential power. In 1981 Ronald Reagan seized control of the congressional budget process to win far-reaching changes in revenue and spending laws. Bill Clinton did much the same in 1993, as did George W. Bush in 2001. These presidential triumphs, serving very different political objectives, have been among the most salient accomplishments of congressional budgeting. In practice, the resolution reflects the interdependence of the two branches. Congress can pass any resolution it wants, but to enact its proposals, Congress must win the president's acquiescence. The wider the disagreement between the two branches, the more they have to reach out to one another to bridge their differences. When they fail to do so, not only is the congressional budget process at risk, but the continuing operation of government is also in jeopardy.

In both status quo and policy initiative years, Congress uses the budget resolution as the basis for allocating budget authority and outlays among House and Senate committees. This section 302 process (described later in the chapter) sets the budgetary boundaries within which congressional committees operate. Ideally, for the resolution to serve this purpose, it should be adopted in a timely manner—before committees begin work on appropriations and other budget-related matters. Although the official timetable of the congressional budget process calls for adoption of the budget resolution by April 15, table 6-1 shows that this deadline is often missed by a few weeks, sometimes it is missed by months, and sometimes it is not adopted. In some years, Congress adopted the resolution after the fiscal year had started and some appropriation bills already had been enacted. Delay in the resolution is a barometer of budgetary conflict. In some years, disagreement has been so deep and pervasive that it has been hard to assemble a majority in support of the resolution. However, before 1998 the House and Senate almost always managed to eke out a majority. Box 6-1 discusses the breakdown in the process in 1998 and suggests that the resolution was as much a victim of indifference as of conflict. With the federal budget balanced for the first time in a generation, and with House and Senate budget committee leaders divided on the appropriate strategy for dealing with the new situation, Congress opted for inaction. In 2002, 2004, and 2006, however, it was the deficit that blocked final agreement, as the House and Senate disagreed on steps to deal with the problem.

STRUCTURE AND CONTENT OF THE BUDGET RESOLUTION

A budget resolution may have four types of provisions: budget aggregates and functional allocations, as required by the CBA; optional

TABLE 6-1
Adoption Dates for the Budget Resolution, Fiscal Years 1976–2008[a]

Fiscal year	Date of adoption	Days after deadline
1976	May 14	1
1977	May 13	0
1978	May 17	2
1979	May 17	2
1980	May 24	9
1981	June 12	28
1982	May 21	6
1983	June 23	39
1984	June 23	39
1985	October 1	139
1986	August 1	78
1987	June 27	73
1988	June 24	70
1989	June 6	52
1990	May 18	33
1991	October 9	176
1992	May 22	37
1993	May 21	36
1994	April 1	0
1995	May 12	27
1996	June 29	75
1997	June 13	59
1998	June 5	51
1999	not adopted	. . .
2000	April 15	0
2001	April 13	0
2002	May 10	25
2003	not adopted	. . .
2004	April 11	0
2005	not adopted	. . .
2006	April 28	13
2007	not adopted	. . .
2008	May 17	32

Source: Congressional Research Service, *Congressional Budget Resolutions: Selected Statistics and Information Guide,* CRS Report RL30297, table 2, p. 14, and figure 1, p. 15.

a. The dates pertain to the first budget resolution for fiscal years 1976 through 1982, and to the annual resolution for subsequent years. Before fiscal 1987 Congress was supposed to adopt the resolution by May 15; since then the scheduled adoption date has been April 15.

reconciliation instructions, inserted at the budget committees' discretion; changes in House or Senate rules governing action on the budget; and "sense of the Congress" statements and other nonbinding provisions, included in most resolutions, which give members an opportunity to go on record concerning federal budget issues.

Budget Aggregates

CBA requires four main aggregates (exhibits 6-1 and 6-2):

—total revenue and the amount by which the total should be changed;

—total new budget authority and outlays;

—the deficit or surplus; and

—the public debt.

These totals do not include the receipts and outlays of the Social Security trust funds that are, by law, off-budget. As a result, when the unified federal budget ran a surplus in the late 1990s, the budget resolution continued to show a deficit. The Senate, but not the House, separately sets forth Social Security revenues and outlays in the resolution (see exhibit 6-3). From time to time, Congress has altered the treatment of Social Security in the budget, and it is likely to do so again.

CBA requires members of Congress to vote on, and thereby take responsibility for, budget totals. If there were no resolution, the totals would simply be the arithmetic sum of past decisions, new legislation, current appropriations, and the impact of economic conditions on revenues and expenditures. Voting on total outlays and the deficit has been onerous for many members, who are in the position of endorsing budget outcomes they do not favor. The public debt limit also has been a hard vote. The limit is largely symbolic, for it does not effectively control the amount the government borrows or owes. Nevertheless, because

▼

BOX 6-1
The Budget Resolution That Wasn't: Republicans Fighting Republicans

Both the House and the Senate passed budget resolutions for fiscal 1999, but the two chambers could not agree on a final version. This was the first time since the congressional budget process began that Congress failed to complete its budget work. It should not have turned out this way, for Republicans controlled both the House and Senate. Furthermore, just a year earlier they had negotiated a deal with the president that cut taxes, increased some spending, and promised a balanced budget in fiscal 2002. In 1998, however, a strong economy and bull stock market produced a revenue surge that helped liquidate the budget deficit. But politicians demonstrated that they can quarrel just as much over how to spend a surplus as they can on how to get rid of a deficit, and Republicans showed that they could fight each other with as much zeal as when they battle Democrats.

Even before Congress started work on the budget resolution, Bill Clinton made two astute moves that put congressional Republicans on the defensive and split their ranks. The first, in the 1998 State of the Union Address, was a four-word demand—"save Social Security first"—that put Republicans on notice that the president would oppose using the looming surplus for tax cuts. Clinton did not offer any concrete proposals for strengthening Social Security, but his démarche had the effect of portraying tax cuts as undermining the viability of the Social Security system. His second ploy, in his fiscal 1999 budget, was to use $65 billion in tobacco money (that would come either from a tax on cigarettes or from tobacco litigation) to offset additional spending that he proposed on education and other social programs. The fact that the offset breached budget rules (separating discretionary expenditures from direct spending and revenues) did not hinder Clinton, for he was able to depict the issue as tobacco versus kids.

These two issues—tax cuts and tobacco money—became fault lines in Congress when the House and Senate worked on the budget resolution. Senate Budget Committee Chair Pete Domenici (R-N.Mex.) put together a status quo resolution that contained a token tax cut,

continued

---

the limit on the total debt is set in law, Congress must periodically pass legislation raising the limit. It must do so even when there is a surplus because money borrowed from Social Security and other trust funds is included in the statutory limit on the public debt. To ease the political burden, the House has a special procedure whereby passage of the budget resolution is also deemed to pass the debt limit legislation (in many instances, however, the House uses alternative procedures to pass debt-limit legislation). The Senate does not have a comparable procedure. Hence senators must vote twice: once on the budget resolution and again on raising the statutory debt limit.

Functional Allocations

The budget resolution allocates total new budget authority, outlays, direct loans, and loan guarantees among the 20 budget functions listed in table 6-2. Each function is divided into a number of subfunctions, and each budget account is assigned to a subfunction. The last three digits in an account's identification code represent the subfunction in which it is classified. Although the functions express

▼

BOX 6-1
Continued

rejected Clinton's spending initiatives, and held discretionary spending to approximately the level set in the caps. After some internal battles among Republicans, Domenici got the Senate to pass his resolution unaltered on a mostly party line vote, 57-41, on April 2. He was aided by Senate rules that require a 60-vote approval for the tax cuts that some Republican colleagues wanted.

House Republicans delayed work on the budget resolution, hoping that buoyant revenue estimates would bolster their case for tax cuts. CBO progressively raised the estimated surplus, from $8 billion in March to $63 billion just three months later. House Budget Committee Chair John Kasich (R-Ohio) decided to craft a resolution that would appeal to the conservative wing of the party to enhance his prospects of winning the Republican presidential nomination in 2000. Kasich's proposal had $70 billion in tax cuts, $150 billion in spending reductions, and abolition of one or more cabinet departments. On June 5 his resolution squeaked through the House on a 216-204 vote.

Once the deadline for adopting the resolution passed, the appropriations committees began marking up their spending bills. More important, Congress passed a costly transportation bill that added tens of billions of dollars to federal spending (see box 8-2) and made a mockery of the House Budget Committee's cutback efforts.

In conference, the House and Senate budget resolutions were poles apart. The Senate had tobacco money but no reconciliation instructions; the House had reconciliation but no tobacco money. The Senate did not curb spending or include major tax cuts; the House had both. Kasich wanted an issue more than he wanted a budget resolution; Domenici, one of Congress's leading advocates of biennial budgeting, preferred inaction over a resolution that would reopen budget wounds. De facto, Domenici got a two-year budget when the conference broke up without a resolution. Kasich got an issue, but not what he had hoped for. His proposed spending cuts evaporated and were replaced, as box 5-4 chronicles, by sizable spending increases.

Congress's budget priorities, they do not bind the appropriations committees in recommending funds for federal programs and agencies. As section 302 allocations have become more important as the basis for Congress's internal budget control, the functional allocations have receded in importance.

Functional allocations must add up to the corresponding budget aggregates. This rule of consistency is strictly enforced; it bars members of Congress from proposing increases or decreases in functional amounts without also proposing adjustments in the budget totals. The requirement of arithmetic consistency is fundamental to budgeting, but in politics consistency is not always easy to achieve. Public opinion polls generally show that Americans want bigger programs and a smaller budget. They favor reductions in total federal spending but oppose reductions in particular programs. They prefer larger allocations to the various budget functions but encourage cutbacks in government spending. Arithmetic consistency means that elected politicians may not do what the voters want. Some members of Congress resolve the contradictions in public opinion by voting to raise functional allocations while opposing the

▶ **EXHIBIT 6-1**
Budget Aggregates: Revenue and Budget Authority

The following budgetary levels are appropriate for the fiscal years 2005 through 2010:

(1) FEDERAL REVENUES.—For purposes of the enforcement of this resolution—

(a) The recommended levels of Federal revenues are as follows:

Fiscal year 2005: $1,483,658,000,000.
Fiscal year 2006: $1,589,892,000,000.
Fiscal year 2007: $1,693,246,000,000.
Fiscal year 2008: $1,824,274,000,000.
Fiscal year 2009: $1,928,678,000,000.
Fiscal year 2010: $2,043,916,000,000.

(b) The amounts by which the aggregate levels of Federal revenues should be reduced are as follows:

Fiscal year 2005: $366,000,000.
Fiscal year 2006: $17,758,000,000.
Fiscal year 2007: $26,006,000,000.
Fiscal year 2008: $11,935,000,000.
Fiscal year 2009: $27,553,000,000.
Fiscal year 2010: $22,466,000,000.

(2) NEW BUDGET AUTHORITY.—For purposes of the enforcement of this resolution, the appropriate levels of total new budget authority are as follows:

Fiscal year 2005: $2,078,456,000,000.
Fiscal year 2006: $2,144,384,000,000.
Fiscal year 2007: $2,211,308,000,000.
Fiscal year 2008: $2,324,327,000,000.
Fiscal year 2009: $2,428,613,000,000.
Fiscal year 2010: $2,524,958,000,000.

Source: *Concurrent Resolution on the Budget for Fiscal Year 2006* (conference report to accompany H. Con. Res. 95), H. Rept. 109-62, 109th Cong., 1st sess., April 28, 2005, pp. 2–3. For this and other components of the resolution cited in this chapter, see also www.gpoaccess.gov/serialset/creports/pdf/109-62/109-62_conres_budget_06.html.

(a) The first part of every budget resolution sets forth total revenues, the amounts by which revenues are to be changed, total new budget authority, total outlays, the deficit or surplus, and the public debt. These totals do not include the revenues, new budget authority, or outlays of the off-budget Social Security trust funds. (Revenue and outlay amounts for Social Security are included in another section of the budget resolution for enforcement purposes in the Senate but not the House.)

(b) The budget resolution must cover at least 5 fiscal years—the "budget year" (the upcoming fiscal year) and the four ensuing "outyears"—and may also include revisions for the "current year" (the year then in progress). This resolution was for fiscal year 2006, but it also revised amounts for the then current year, fiscal year 2005. Some recent budget resolutions have covered up to 10 fiscal years. The outyear amounts will be altered by subsequent budget resolutions; nevertheless, these amounts are important because they may influence the impact of current congressional action on future budgets.

(c) Revenue changes may be either increases or decreases, but they pertain only to changes due to new legislation, not those deriving from changes in economic conditions. The resolution displayed here set the stage for congressional action on tax-cut legislation during the 2005 session.

▶ EXHIBIT 6-2
Budget Aggregates: Outlays, Deficit, and Debt Limit

(3) BUDGET OUTLAYS.—For purposes of the enforcement of this resolution, the appropriate levels of total budget outlays are as follows:

Fiscal year 2005: $2,056,006,000,000.
Fiscal year 2006: $2,161,420,000,000.
Fiscal year 2007: $2,215,361,000,000.
Fiscal year 2008: $2,305,908,000,000.
Fiscal year 2009: $2,411,288,000,000.
Fiscal year 2010: $2,514,745,000,000.

(4) DEFICITS (On-BUDGET).—For purposes of the enforcement of this resolution, the amounts of the deficits (on-budget) are as follows:

Fiscal year 2005: $572,348,000,000.
Fiscal year 2006: $571,528,000,000.
Fiscal year 2007: $522,115,000,000.
Fiscal year 2008: $481,634,000,000.
Fiscal year 2009: $482,610,000,000.
Fiscal year 2010: $470,829,000,000.

(5) DEBT SUBJECT TO LIMIT.—Pursuant to section 301(a)(5) of the Congressional Budget Act of 1974, the appropriate levels of the public debt are as follows:

Fiscal year 2005: $7,962,000,000,000.
Fiscal year 2006: $8,645,000,000,000.
Fiscal year 2007: $9,284,000,000,000.
Fiscal year 2008: $9,890,000,000,000.
Fiscal year 2009: $10,500,000,000,000.
Fiscal year 2010: $11,105,000,000,000.

Source: *Concurrent Resolution on the Budget for Fiscal Year 2006* (conference report to accompany H. Con. Res. 95), H. Rept. 109-62, 109th Cong., 1st sess., April 28, 2005, p. 3.

(a) The outlay amounts in the budget resolution are estimates. The actual deficit is determined by congressional revenue and spending decisions and the amounts collected and spent, not by the entries in the budget resolution. The Budget Enforcement Act imposed limits on discretionary outlays, as explained in chapter 4.

(b) These aggregates exclude Social Security (which is displayed in the next exhibit). If Social Security were included, the deficit would be significantly lower for each year listed here. For example, the budgeted deficit for fiscal year 2006 would have been $383 billion instead of the $572 billion amount shown here.

(c) For the outyears covered by the resolution (2007–10), Congress will adopt new budget resolutions, undoubtedly revising the totals. The fiscal year 2010 amounts will be revised at least four times (assuming Congress adopts a budget resolution each year).

(d) Each year's increase in the public debt is greater than that year's deficit because amounts borrowed from Social Security and other trust funds reduce the deficit but add to the public debt. Another part of the budget resolution (not shown here) provides amounts for "debt held by the public," which excludes amounts borrowed from trust funds. Of the $8.6 trillion recommended in this budget resolution for the public debt limit for fiscal year 2006, $5 trillion involves debt held by the public; the remaining $3.6 trillion represents money owed by the federal government to its trust funds.

▶ **EXHIBIT 6-3**
Budget Aggregates: Social Security

(a) SOCIAL SECURITY REVENUES.—For purposes of Senate enforcement under sections 302 and 311 of the Congressional Budget Act of 1974, the amounts of revenues of the Federal Old-Age and Survivors Insurance Trust Fund and the Federal Disability Insurance Trust Fund are as follows:

    Fiscal year 2005: $573,475,000,000.
    Fiscal year 2006: $604,777,000,000.
    Fiscal year 2007: $637,792,000,000.
    Fiscal year 2008: $671,688,000,000.
    Fiscal year 2009: $705,849,000,000.
    Fiscal year 2010: $740,343,000,000.

(b) SOCIAL SECURITY OUTLAYS.—For purposes of Senate enforcement under sections 302 and 311 of the Congressional Budget Act of 1974, the amounts of outlays of the Federal Old-Age and Survivors Insurance Trust Fund and the Federal Disability Insurance Trust Fund are as follows:

    Fiscal year 2005: $398,088,000,000.
    Fiscal year 2006: $415,993,000,000.
    Fiscal year 2007: $429,254,000,000.
    Fiscal year 2008: $443,235,000,000.
    Fiscal year 2009: $460,443,000,000.
    Fiscal year 2010: $479,412,000,000.

Source: *Concurrent Resolution on the Budget for Fiscal Year 2006* (conference report to accompany H. Con. Res. 95), H. Rept. 109-62, 109th Cong., 1st sess., April 28, 2005, pp. 3–4.

(a) Almost all Social Security revenues and outlays are off-budget and are excluded from the budget aggregates (displayed in the previous two exhibits). However, a small portion for administrative expenses, and for transfers from the general fund to the trust funds for taxes paid on Social Security benefits, is included.

(b) This exhibit pertains only to the Senate; there are no parallel provisions in the House. The Senate chose to protect the Social Security balances against erosion through legislative action by enforcing revenue and outlay levels under sections 302 and 311 of the 1974 Congressional Budget Act, which bar certain floor actions that would breach the amounts in the budget resolution. The House achieves the same purpose by means of a provision in law (section 13302 of the Budget Enforcement Act of 1990) establishing a point of order against legislation that would reduce Social Security balances over a 75-year period.

(c) The House and Senate also differ on the treatment of administrative expenses for Social Security. These expenses, which were set in the budget resolution at $4.6 billion in new budget authority for fiscal year 2006, are subject to annual appropriations. For enforcement purposes in the Senate (but not in the House), amounts of new budget authority and outlays for administrative expenses are specified in a separate subsection of the budget resolution (not shown here); amounts are provided for each year covered by the resolution.

(d) The 1974 Congressional Budget Act bars the inclusion of changes in Social Security in reconciliation acts. This prohibition may be waived by a simple majority vote in the House and by a three-fifths vote in the Senate.

TABLE 6-2
Functions in the Budget Resolution[a]

Code	Function
050	National Defense
150	International Affairs
250	General Science, Space, and Technology
270	Energy
300	Natural Resources and Environment
350	Agriculture
370	Commerce and Housing Credit
400	Transportation
450	Community and Regional Development
500	Education, Training, Employment, and Social Services
550	Health
570	Medicare
600	Income Security
650	Social Security[b]
700	Veterans' Benefits and Services
750	Administration of Justice
800	General Government
900	Net Interest
920	Allowances
950	Undistributed Offsetting Receipts

Source: *Concurrent Resolution on the Budget for Fiscal Year 2006* (conference report to accompany H. Con. Res. 95), H. Rept. 109-62, 109th Cong., 1st sess., April 28, 2005, pp. 4-11.

a. Allocations of new budget authority and outlays are made to each function in the budget resolution for each covered year.

b. Only the on-budget portion of Social Security is included in the functional allocations of spending.

budget resolution on the grounds that total spending is too high.

The budget resolution does not allocate funds among specific programs or accounts; doing so would trespass on the jurisdiction of the spending committees. The lack of line-item detail in the budget resolution complicates its passage, for members cannot readily take credit for earmarking funds to particular programs. Congressional rules require members to vote on budget resolutions without getting credit for spending on popular programs and often without knowing how much particular programs will get. Although the resolu-

tion rarely mentions programs, the committee report accompanying it often specifies the program assumptions underlying the functional allocations (exhibit 6-4). In some years, the budget committees' reports have recommended specific amounts for particular programs. But the amounts are not binding, and the appropriations committees may disregard them. However, to the extent that the functional allocations reflect consensus or majority sentiment in Congress, they may influence the appropriations committees' actions. Since appropriators value their independence, it is rare that they implement all the budget resolution's expectations.

BINDING RULES AND NONBINDING SENTIMENTS

Recent budget resolutions have tended to be lengthier than those adopted in the past because they have contained new (usually temporary) rules for congressional action on budget-related matters and nonbinding views on current budget issues. In contrast to the budget aggregates and functional allocations, these provisions typically pertain to only one chamber. The House or Senate may have different rules for dealing with certain budget matters, and they may also express different sentiments on current matters.

The budget resolution is a convenient vehicle for the House and Senate to deal with the budget because it also includes key rules for enforcing budget decisions and allows those rules to be changed each year, as desired. Even when a rule is enacted in law, it functions only as a rule of the House and Senate and can be changed by a budget resolution. Through the budget resolution, the House or Senate can establish new points of order for revenue or spending legislation and can modify existing points of order. Inasmuch as the House and

> **EXHIBIT 6-4**
> **Program Assumptions Underlying the Functional Allocations**

Education, Training, Employment and Social Services: Function 500

Discretionary spending levels for both the budget year and the outyears reflect the President's recommended levels, as re-estimated by CBO, with the following adjustments: the discretionary levels are increased by $1.04 billion in BA in fiscal year 2006 for Department of Education programs. These increases include $0.6 billion above the President's request to maintain funding for Community Development Block Grants at 2005 levels, and an additional $0.4 billion to accommodate a $100 increase in Pell Grants in 2006. Mandatory spending levels reflect the CBO baseline, adjusted to support state-based abstinence grants. The conference agreement also includes a reserve fund to accommodate potential legislation addressing the shortfall in BA in the Pell Grant Program, and procedures modifying the budgetary treatment of Pell Grant funding. . . .

Although the Congress strongly supports the Federal student loan programs, it is increasingly concerned that the subsidy estimates for the Ford Direct Loan Program do not reflect the program's true cost to the Federal Government. For example, the President's 2006 budget reveals that although the program was expected to result in a net savings of $2 billion from its inception through fiscal year 2004, the actual experience is that the program resulted in a net cost to taxpayers of $3 billion over the same period. This represents a $5-billion underestimate of the program's actual cost to taxpayers over roughly 10 years.

Source: *Concurrent Resolution on the Budget for Fiscal Year 2006* (conference report to accompany H. Con. Res. 95), H. Rept. 109-62, 109th Cong., 1st sess., April 28, 2005, pp. 41–42.

(a) This excerpt, pertaining to function 500 (Education, Training, Employment and Social Services), explains some of the assumptions underlying the fiscal year 2006 budget resolution adopted by Congress. The conference report on this budget resolution also discussed assumptions for the other budget functions. With some exceptions, the discussions of assumptions have tended to become more detailed in recent years, and the language increasingly resembles that found in appropriations committee reports.

(b) On occasion, program assumptions appear in the text of the budget resolution; most assumptions, however, are discussed in the accompanying committee reports. Although these assumptions do not bind congressional action on revenue and spending bills, to the extent that they reflect understanding among committees or members, they may influence the amounts appropriated or other legislative decisions. The appropriations committees often do not adhere to the program assumptions; doing so would make them subservient to the budget committees.

(c) The assumptions in this exhibit for discretionary spending are referenced either to the amounts requested by the president in his budget or to the amounts appropriated for the previous year, thus orienting them to the benchmarks used in the appropriations process. Assumptions about mandatory spending are referenced to the CBO baseline, which the budget committees use in formulating the budget resolution.

Senate separately enforce their rules, they do not have to agree on rules changes in the budget resolution.

In fact, the House and Senate have reacted differently to the expiration of BEA rules. The budget resolution for fiscal year 2004 contained discretionary spending caps and PAYGO rules for Senate consideration of revenue and spending legislation; the House did not have comparable provisions. But both chambers adopted new rules in the same resolution restricting the use of advance appropriations (that is, funds that become available in a later fiscal year) and defining emergency spending. Even when both chambers adopt the same rules, as they did with respect to PAYGO in 2007, enforcement may differ. The House, acting through its Rules Committee, can (and often does) waive points of order on budget legislation; the Senate, however, requires a three-fifths vote for setting aside critical budget rules.

Finally, the budget resolution often contains provisions that either express nonbinding sentiments or attempt to influence budget policy. For example, the fiscal year 1998 resolution specified discretionary spending limits for each of the next six years, prescribed how revenue from the sale of government assets should be accounted for in the budget, and established reserve funds to cover possible legislation. The resolution also contained more than two dozen "sense of the Congress" (or of the House or Senate) statements expressing views on budget issues. One of these called for a change in baseline scoring practices, another for legislation authorizing the sale of loan assets held by the federal government, and a third for tax cuts to benefit working families. These types of statements usually serve as substitutes for legislative action; they enable members to go on record for or against certain matters, even when no legislation is forthcoming. Some

statements have appeared in the budget resolution year after year.

THE BUDGET COMMITTEES

The House and Senate budget committees are responsible for developing the budget resolution and shepherding it through their respective chambers. The resolution can originate in either the House or Senate, in contrast with revenue bills, which must originate in the House, and appropriation bills, which until the late 1990s always did. In most years, there is extensive consultation between the two committees before they mark up the resolution.

The budget committees appear to be like other congressional committees, with their own jurisdiction, membership, and staff. But they are different—their jurisdiction is very circumscribed yet also very broad. The budget resolution and reconciliation bills are their only legislative products: the former cannot become a law, and the latter must be assembled without changing the substantive provisions that other committees insert. The budget committees keep busy year-round monitoring budget developments and the work of other committees. Occasionally, they issue reports on topical budget issues, but they do not produce legislation dealing with these issues.

The budget committees are both powerful and weak—powerful because they can initiate sweeping changes in federal tax and spending policy, and weak because they are dependent on other committees to carry these changes through the legislative labyrinth. They are strong when the budget resolution propels changes in policy, weak when the resolution merely accommodates the status quo. When they were established in 1974, there was fear that these committees would become congressional bullies, forcing other committees to produce legislation against their will. More than 30 years later, it should be apparent that these committees are only as strong as the House and Senate allow them to be. As Congress's budget mood changes from year to year, so too does the legislative standing of the budget committees.

Fear that the budget committees would become too powerful was especially pronounced in the House, where liberals were concerned that the fiscal discipline imposed by the new congressional budget process would be used as a club against social programs. To ease these fears, CBA limited service on the House Budget Committee to two consecutive Congresses (this was later increased to three Congresses) and assigned more than half the seats to members of the House Appropriations and Ways and Means Committees and to the majority and minority leadership. These provisions were designed to deter members from using the budget committee as a power base; they could make a splash, but not a career, on the committee. The Senate Budget Committee does not have a comparable limitation, and some of its leaders have used the committee to enhance their legislative careers.

Over the years, the budget committees have evolved into instruments of the House and Senate party leaderships. Rather than operating autonomously (as most committees do), the budget committees shape the resolution to reflect the preferences of the majority party's leaders in Congress. They consult with Democratic or Republican leaders before drafting the resolution and rely on the leadership to win its passage. Several factors account for the strong role of party leaders in determining the resolution's policy orientation.

First, the budget resolution covers a broad swath of legislative issues: it deals with defense, agriculture, transportation, and just about every other area of legislative activity. Congress's budget policies affect most major legis-

lation, and there inevitably are disputes between the budget committees and other committees over the priority and dollars to be accorded to particular areas. Party leaders often iron out differences among the committees and settle disputes over budget aggregates and functional allocations.

Second, the budget resolution is one of the most partisan matters Congress takes up each year. What is at stake is not just the legislative preferences of one or another committee, but the Republican budget or the Democratic budget. When the president is of the other party, as has been the case for more than two-thirds of the years since the congressional budget process was inaugurated, the resolution is seen as Congress's alternative budget policy. Only party leaders can represent the range of views needed to formulate and defend the party's position on the budget.

Finally, because of party line voting and fissures within Democratic and Republican ranks, in many years it has been hard to assemble a majority in favor of the budget resolution. Party leaders make deals and apply pressure to get the resolution through the House and Senate. In lining up the votes, they have gained a strong voice in determining the orientation and content of the budget resolution.

THE CONGRESSIONAL BUDGET OFFICE

The Congressional Budget Office (CBO) was established by the same 1974 law that created the congressional budget process. Both were designed to give Congress the capacity to act independently of the president on revenue and spending matters. Yet despite their common roots and objectives, CBO has flourished while the congressional budget process has languished. Through three decades of economic and political cycles, CBO has secured a niche as an objective, skilled, and relevant producer of budgetary information and policy analysis. Its estimates have become influential, sometimes decisive, elements of policy debate, and the periodic appointment of a new director has become one of the important actions taken by congressional leaders.

The main reason for CBO's rise is the prominence accorded scoring—measuring the budgetary impact of new legislation and other policy changes. As discussed in chapter 4, CBO's score can doom legislation or smooth the way to passage; it can compel committees and members to modify pending legislation, even after political deals have been negotiated; and it can complicate or thwart the president's legislative ambitions.

As scoring has become more salient, in-depth analysis of programs and issues by CBO staff appears to have lost ground. CBO publishes a slew of analytic reports each year, but it has no monopoly in this area, and its findings do not often sway legislative decisions. In policy analysis, CBO is but one of many voices, and it is rarely the main one heard. In scoring, however, CBO's only authoritative rival is OMB, which is usually viewed by the media and policy elites as more partisan and less reliable.

To succeed in the congressional environment, CBO must be both independent of Congress and subservient to it. If it is not subservient, CBO will not be useful to legislators, and they may weaken its capacity to perform; if it is not independent, it will lack the legitimacy and stature that give its pronouncements authority.

Balancing these opposite imperatives has made for a sometimes feisty relationship between Congress and its budget experts, especially every fourth (or eighth) year when a new CBO director is appointed. But the fact that CBO has persisted as an effective institution attests to its agility in upholding its independence while serving Congress. Yet it is not only CBO that must balance these cross-pressures; Congress itself must be of two minds about CBO. The contemporary Congress needs CBO just about as much as CBO needs Congress. Obviously, CBO depends on Congress for resources, authority, and access; it could not function well if resources were inadequate, statutory authority were withdrawn or diluted, or its staff were kept at a distance from legislative action. But it is also the case that Congress needs CBO, not only for the data it produces but also for the respectability and occasionally the political advantage it gives the legislative branch in budgetary conflicts. Congress is generally viewed by the media and other elites as holding the high ground when it disagrees with the president on budgetary matters, largely because of the esteem in which CBO is held and the credibility accorded its estimates.

The 1974 Congressional Budget Act artfully designed CBO to serve multiple legislative demands—but according to priorities that make it more beholden to the budget committees than to any other committees. According to the Budget Act, CBO's "primary duty and function" is to provide the budget committees information on "all matters within their jurisdiction." The act also authorizes CBO to assist other committees, and accords lowest priority to assisting individual members. The act further reinforces CBO's relationship with the budget committees by directing it to produce various reports, including annual baseline projections and a periodic scorekeeping report on the status of the budget and the impact of pending or enacted legislation.

Over the years, modifications in congressional budgeting have boosted CBO's scorekeeping role. These include extension of the resolution's time horizon from 1 year to 10 years, the use of reconciliation, and budget enforcement rules. Although the BEA has expired, it has left a legacy of heightened interest in scoring, especially in the Senate, where a PAYGO rule has been enforced since 1993. (The House adopted a PAYGO rule in 2007, at the beginning of the 110th Congress.) Reconciliation also has elevated the importance of scoring because only legislation within the amounts specified in reconciliation instructions is free from the threat of filibuster in the Senate.

The wide gulf between Democrats and Republicans on major issues has complicated CBO's mission. It was established to function as a nonpartisan body that is indifferent to political considerations. The Budget Act provides that the director and staff are to be appointed "without regard to political affiliation and solely on the basis of their fitness to perform their duties." Maintaining political neutrality can be exceedingly difficult because CBO's projections and analyses often bolster one party's position against the other's. CBO often is in the line of fire, lauded by those who like its findings, decried by those who do not. The extreme partisanship that has beset Congress in recent times has made CBO independence more urgent and more difficult. CBO exists to give neutral advice to politicians who are not neutral on the issues of the day. CBO does not have a single vote in Congress, but its findings may affect how members vote on critical issues. CBO enjoys the influence it has, but it must act as if it were bereft of influence.

CBO's core activities are driven by the budget cycle or the legislative calendar. It produces 10-year projections of budget and economic conditions in January, before the president submits his budget to Congress, and updated estimates around the time Congress returns from its summer recess. Other budget-related work includes an annual analysis of the president's budget, assessment of the long-term budget outlook, and reports to Congress on the current status of the budget.

Scoring is CBO's most important responsibility—and the most controversial. CBO scores had a marked effect on two of the most prominent legislative initiatives considered by Congress since the early 1990s: President Clinton's failed effort to reform the American health care system, and President George W. Bush's successful extension of Medicare coverage to prescription drugs. Early in his presidency, Clinton made universal health insurance a leading priority of his new administration. His fiscal year 1995 budget estimated that health care reform would generate outlay savings in excess of $50 billion over the next six years. CBO Director Robert Reischauer, however, scored the proposal as more than a $70 billion increase in federal spending over the same period. While it would be misleading to conclude that the CBO score doomed the plan, projections showing that the budget, which then had a sizeable deficit, would be adversely affected made the president's task much more difficult.

In 2003 CBO again played a key role in determining the fate of pending legislation. After years of failed attempts, Congress passed a bill adding prescription drug coverage to Medicare (P.L. 108-173). For 2007 most participants pay the first $265 in annual drug costs, Medicare pays 75 percent of costs between $265 and $2,400, individuals are then responsible for all expenses between $2,400 and $5,451, and finally Medicare pays all but nominal costs above $5,451. This unusual configuration has been labeled a "donut" because of the hole in the middle ($2,400–$5,451). The size of the hole (which changes each year) was dictated by a budget constraint that limited projected additional spending to $395 billion over the first 10 years. As CBO scored the bill and the numerous changes made in the course of its consideration, the size of the hole was expanded or reduced to keep within the $395 billion limit.

CBO scores legislation when it is pending in Congress or has just been enacted. All scores are based on assumptions about future conditions, including the behavior of those affected by the policy changes. Inasmuch as the score has a 10-year horizon, it is prone to significant error. But CBO does not rescore previously enacted legislation to correct for differences between projected and actual results. The only score that matters is the one produced at the time legislation is considered or enacted. Because subsequent developments do not affect the score, CBO always is right, even when its numbers prove to be wrong.

One of the most difficult tasks in scoring is to estimate the extent to which changes in policy will change Americans' behavior. For example, in scoring the Medicare legislation, CBO had to estimate the additional volume of drugs that eligible persons would purchase if all or part of the cost were shifted to the federal government. In measuring the revenue effects of tax legislation, CBO has to estimate the extent to which investors would cash in capital gains if tax rates were lowered. Until recently, CBO resisted demands (mostly from congressional Republicans) that it adopt dynamic scoring methods. The term "dynamic scoring" is fuzzy, but it usually refers to changes in macroeconomic conditions that may ensue from policy changes. For example, some critics of CBO have argued that it should factor increases in GDP, profits, and individual incomes that would result from reducing the tax burden on business, investors, and workers. CBO (and others) were concerned that this version of dynamic scoring would enable legislators to claim that just about every tax cut would produce additional revenue.

In 2003 CBO Director Douglas Holtz-Eakin evaluated dynamic scoring by constructing baselines that used different macroeconomic assumptions and showing the scores that derived from each of them. CBO projected that future deficits would be similar regardless of the assumptions used. While its estimates did not end the debate on dynamic scoring, CBO once again demonstrated its capacity to serve Congress while maintaining its independence.

FORMULATING THE BUDGET RESOLUTION

The budget committees cannot mark up the budget resolution in a normal legislative manner. Although the resolution is a brief document, it touches the interests of virtually all House and Senate committees. The resolution is the budget committees' business, but it also happens to be the business of the revenue, appropriations, and most authorizing committees. It is not enough that the budget committees comprehend the budget and its policy implications; they must also know what is important to other committees. They hold hearings and rely on CBO data and reports, as well as on "views and estimates" reports submitted by other committees. But their most important sources of information come from informal, behind-the-scenes discussions with party leaders, committee chairs, and rank-and-file members. These discussions deal with big issues (such as changes in tax levels and legislative initiatives), but they also fill in some of the program detail that is of interest to members of Congress but missing from the resolution.

CBO's baseline provides a useful starting point for preparing the resolution. It enables the budget committees to focus on policy changes rather than on the myriad line items that constitute the budget. The committees also rely on CBO's annual *Budget and Economic Outlook* that projects the budget on the basis of economic assumptions over the next 10 years.

By mid-March each year, committees submit their views and estimates on budgetary matters in their jurisdiction to the budget committees. An excerpt from one such report appears in exhibit 6-5. These documents are supposed to alert the budget committees to the plans and preferences of other committees; over the years they have become less revealing and less useful. Although a few committees treat this report as an opportunity to lay out their legislative agenda or to comment on the president's budget, many have come to regard it as one of the things they have to do to get through the annual budget cycle. Because the views and estimates are prepared early in the session, most committees avoid locking themselves into specific budgetary or legislative positions. Instead, they practice defensive budgeting—seeking to derail presidential recommendations they oppose while keeping congressional options open for opportunities that may materialize later in the session. Most committees prefer informal channels of communications to advise the budget committees of their preferences and to obtain assurance that their interests are protected in the resolution.

Budget committee chairs use the period between the hearings and the markup to develop the majority party's position on budget issues and to consult with others on their preferences. The chairs usually convene their committees to mark up the resolution after reaching an understanding in the majority party. In 1998, however, House Budget Chair John Kasich (R-Ohio) drafted a resolution calling for a new round of spending cuts without first obtaining consensus in Republican ranks. The ensuing friction and disarray delayed adoption of the resolution and contributed to Congress's failure to complete its budget work. In the House, the budget committee's preresolution consultations have always been partisan. In the Senate, during the early years of the process, the chair reached out to the minority party in an effort to broaden support for the resolution. Since the early 1990s, however, partisanship has driven a wedge between Democrats and Republicans on the Senate Budget Committee.

The markup is organized around the "chairman's mark," a document that proposes the aggregates, functional allocations, and other provisions to be included in the resolution. If agreement among majority party members has been secured in advance and everything goes according to script, the committee will ratify the chair's proposal with almost all Democrats voting on one side and almost all Republicans on the other. The committee may alter the chair's mark, but doing so can be difficult because the markup is usually conducted under "budget neutral" rules, which require proposed spending increases to be offset by proposed cuts or by increased totals.

Although the resolution does not itself mention programs, much of the discussion at markup concerns particular programs. In committee, members often try to obtain assurance that the amount allocated for a particular function can accommodate the programs in which they are interested. These discussions create a legislative history that might make a difference later in the year when appropriations are decided.

FLOOR ACTION

House and Senate rules and practices guide debate on the budget resolution. In the House, the Rules Committee usually devises a "special rule" (in the form of a simple House resolution), which, once approved, sets the terms

> **EXHIBIT 6-5**
> **Views and Estimates Report**

Key provisions of the Farm Security and Rural Investment Act of 2002 (2002 Farm Bill) will expire on September 30, 2007. The farm bill establishes the basis for economic support to agriculture, promotes the efforts of producers to conserve natural resources, and provides for the nutritional needs of the nation's poorest. The primary focus of our Committee will be to seek timely enactment of a 2007 Farm Bill. Your Committee's work on the Concurrent Resolution on the Budget for FY 2008 is crucial to our efforts and we appreciate your consideration of our views. . . .

When the 2002 bill was written, the baseline for agricultural safety net programs and their expected cost was 140 billion dollars over ten years. Under the most recent CBO baseline (which assumes continuation of current programs), the comparable amount for the coming ten years is 80 billion dollars. The baseline has increased for some Farm Bill programs—particularly food stamps, which account for 67 percent of our budget—that need to be maintained, not cut to fund other programs. The bottom line is that additional resources are needed to produce a policy that facilitates a strong farm sector and helps our nation move toward energy independence in a fiscally responsible way.

Source: House Agriculture Committee, "Budget Views and Estimates Letter," from Chair Collin C. Peterson and Ranking Minority Member Bob Goodlatte to the chair of the House Budget Committee, Representative John Spratt, March 1, 2007; available on the House Agriculture Committee website (agriculture.house.gov/inside/pubs/FinalBudgetViewsLetter2008.pdf).

(a) Section 301(c) of the 1974 Congressional Budget Act provides for each House and Senate committee to report to the budget committee of its chamber its views and estimates on budgetary matters within its jurisdiction. These views and estimates are sometimes published by the House or Senate Budget Committee in the report on the resolution or in a committee print. The excerpts shown here are from the House Agriculture Committee's views on the fiscal year 2008 budget.

(b) There is no standard practice concerning the views and estimates reports. For fiscal year 2008, for example, the House Agriculture Committee responded with a letter signed jointly by the chairman and ranking minority member, but the two leaders of the House Energy and Commerce Committee submitted letters separately. While the letters from the two committees were brief (less than four pages), the Democratic response from the Energy and Commerce Committee included a 40-page attachment that reviewed in depth the president's proposals for various programs.

(c) This excerpt, like other views and estimates reports, focuses on major legislation scheduled for reauthorization in the coming session. Such reports also discuss proposals in the president's budget, indicating areas of agreement and disagreement. Few committees comment on all programs in their jurisdiction.

under which the budget resolution is considered. Typically, the rule allows the minority party to offer a substitute resolution and may also permit amendments on particular provisions. The minority never gets its way, for party lines are sharply drawn in the House, where (as table 6-3 shows) Democrats and Republicans have almost always taken the opposite position on passage of the resolution. In most years, the majority party has supplied almost all the votes needed to pass the resolution; it can count on little or no help from the minority. This condition prevailed in the 1970s and 1980s, when the Democrats were the majority in the House, and it has persisted since the mid-1990s, when the Republicans gained majority status. Regardless of which party is the majority, it often encounters deep fissures within its ranks on budget policy. For years the Democrats had difficulty bridging differences between the liberal and conservative wings of the party. More recently, Republicans have had difficulty balancing the preferences of those in its ranks who want to downsize government and those who prefer to maintain existing programs.

The situation was different in the Senate during the early years of the congressional budget process, when bipartisan cooperation facilitated adoption of the resolution (as table 6-4 shows). Partisanship emerged when the Republicans gained control of the Senate in 1981 and has persisted in most years since. In some recent years, every minority party senator has voted against the resolution, requiring the majority party to shop among its own members for the necessary votes. Senate rules limit debate on the resolution to 50 hours, thus precluding filibusters and other dilatory tactics.

In both the House and Senate, amendments must preserve the arithmetic consistency of the resolution. An amendment changing any functional allocation must make reciprocal adjustments in other parts of the resolution. This rule makes it difficult to win adoption of amendments that increase expenditures or cut revenues.

WHY THE RESOLUTION IS RARELY ADOPTED ON SCHEDULE

In the final stages of the budget resolution process, a conference committee resolves differences between the House and Senate versions. As shown by the entries in table 6-1, adoption of the conference report often occurs long after the CBA deadline. The original target date was May 15; in the mid-1980s, Congress moved it one month earlier, but it still has difficulty adopting the budget resolution on schedule.

Deadlines are missed because members often have more reasons to vote against the resolution than for it. It is easier to vote against big deficits than for them, easier to vote for individual spending items than for spending totals, easier not to vote on the public debt limit than to vote for a $8 trillion debt. Deadlines are missed because nothing stops if the budget resolution is behind schedule or even if it is not adopted. Congress still makes appropriations, and federal agencies continue to operate.

Getting the budget resolution adopted is a political ordeal. Republicans have one plan for disposing of the surplus or dealing with the deficit; Democrats have another. The president presents his priorities; Congress has others. Debate on the budget sets one wing of each party against another, the House against the Senate, the parts against the whole, the preference for smaller government against the push for bigger programs, the tax cutters against the deficit cutters. The budget resolution is not a law, but it may spawn more strife

TABLE 6-3
House Votes on Adoption of the Budget Resolution, by Party,
Fiscal Years 1976–2008[a]

Fiscal year	Total		Democrats		Republicans	
	Yes	No	Yes	No	Yes	No
1976	200	196	197	68	3	128
1977	221	155	208	44	13	111
1978	213	179	206	58	7	121
1979	201	197	198	61	3	136
1980	220	184	211	50	9	134
1981	225	193	203	62	22	131
1982	270	154	84	153	186	1
1983	219	206	63	174	156	32
1984	229	196	225	36	4	160
1985	250	168	229	29	21	139
1986	258	170	234	15	24	155
1987	245	179	228	19	17	160
1988	230	192	230	19	0	173
1989	319	102	227	24	92	78
1990	263	157	157	96	106	61
1991[b]	218	208	218	34	0	174
1992	261	163	243	17	18	145
1993[c]	215	201	214	44	0	157
1994	243	183	242	11	0	172
1995	223	175	222	11	0	164
1996	238	193	8	191	230	1
1997	226	195	5	190	221	4
1998	333	99	132	72	201	26
1999	216	204	3	194	213	9
2000	221	208	4	205	217	2
2001	211	207	2	201	208	5
2002	222	205	3	202	218	2
2003	221	209	1	206	219	2
2004	215	202	1	199	214	12
2005	215	212	0	201	215	10
2006	218	214	0	201	218	12
2007	218	210	0	197	218	12
2008	214	209	214	13	0	196

Sources: *Congressional Quarterly Almanac, 1975–2000;* Clerk of the House of Representatives, "Roll Call Votes Only" (clerk.house.gov/art_history/house_history/index.html).

a. Votes are on adoption of the budget resolution in the House, not on the conference report. In years that Congress adopted two resolutions, the vote shown here is on the first resolution. Breakdown by party excludes Independents.

b. A second budget resolution was passed on October 9; the votes shown here are for the first resolution.

c. The House passed two budget resolutions, Plan A and Plan B; the votes shown here are for Plan A.

TABLE 6-4
Senate Votes on Adoption of the Budget Resolution, by Party,
Fiscal Years 1976–2008[a]

Fiscal year	Total		Democrats		Republicans	
	Yes	No	Yes	No	Yes	No
1976	69	22	50	4	19	18
1977	62	22	45	6	17	16
1978	56	31	41	14	15	17
1979	64	27	48	8	16	19
1980	64	20	44	5	20	15
1981	68	28	49	6	19	22
1982	78	20	28	18	50	2
1983	49	43	3	41	46	2
1984	50	49	29	17	21	32
1985	41	34	1	31	40	3
1986[b]	50	49	1	45	48	4
1987	70	25	38	6	32	19
1988	56	42	53	0	3	42
1989	69	26	44	6	25	20
1990	68	31	38	17	30	14
1991	Voice vote					
1992	Voice vote					
1993	54	35	36	15	18	20
1994	54	45	54	2	0	43
1995	57	40	55	0	2	40
1996	57	42	3	42	54	0
1997	53	46	0	46	53	0
1998	78	22	37	8	41	14
1999	57	41	3	41	54	0
2000	55	44	1	44	54	0
2001	51	45	0	43	51	2
2002	63	35	15	35	50	0
2003	Not considered					
2004[c]	56	44	6	42	50	1
2005[c]	51	45	1	43	50	1
2006[c]	51	49	0	44	51	4
2007[c]	51	49	1	43	50	5
2008[c]	52	40	48	0	2	40

Sources: *Congressional Quarterly Almanac, 1975–2006;* Congressional Quarterly Weekly Report, March 20, 2006, p. 790.

a. Votes are on adoption of the budget resolution in the Senate, not on the conference report. In years that Congress adopted two resolutions, the vote shown here is on the first resolution.

b. Vice President George Bush voted "yes" to break the tie.

c. Senator Jeffords (I-Vt.) and Senator Lieberman (I-Conn.) changed party affiliation from Republican to Independent and from Democrat to Independent, respectively. For 2004–08, in the case of Jeffords, and for 2008, in the case of Lieberman, their votes are counted in the totals but not in the party breakdown.

than if it were. It is a symbol of what divides the parties, of what Americans want from and think is wrong with government, and of failures of will and leadership. If it were a law, and federal revenue and spending were dependent on it, the resolution would have to be enacted. Missing statutory deadlines matters in ways that missing symbolic ones does not.

Until 1998 the budget was a conflict that had a resolution. One way or another, Congress managed to produce a budget resolution—in one session, almost half a year after the official deadline. The actual adoption dates suggest a patternless process, budgeting without stable, predictable routines. Some years the resolution made it through only because enough members felt that having a congressional budget was better than not having one. In quite a few years, majority party whips garnered the necessary votes by persuading recalcitrant members "to vote the process, not the numbers"—to keep the process alive by voting for the resolution, even through they did not agree with the policies expressed in it.

Evidently, this appeal no longer suffices, for Congress failed to complete action on a budget resolution in four of the nine years between 1998 and 2006. In these years, a majority just did not care enough to supply the votes needed to pass a resolution. Quite probably, these will not be the last times that Congress fails to complete its budget work. Each failure has its particular causes—a surplus in one year, a deficit in another, fighting among congressional Republicans one year, and between Republicans and Democrats in another. But the failures also have a deeper cause that lies in the transformation of the budget process into a significantly different activity than was envisioned when CBA was enacted a generation ago. At the start of the twenty-first century, the process has a different purpose than it had at the initiation of con-

gressional budgeting. Despite its brief existence, congressional budgeting has gone through four distinct stages, each with its own procedural and political features.

Stage one (1975–80) was characterized by the building of new budget institutions (House and Senate budget committees and CBO) and the adoption of budget resolutions as an expression of congressional independence from the executive branch. Most members saw the budget resolution as an instrument for taking responsibility for the fiscal outcomes and spending policies of the government. But the process was inherently weak because the budget resolution was unable to regulate revenues or spending that ensued from existing law. Legislative committees were able to thwart the budget process by doing nothing.

Stage two (1980–90) remedied this weakness by establishing reconciliation procedures (described below) that enable Congress to compel changes in existing revenue and spending law. The budget process came to be regarded as a key instrument in combating the high deficits that persisted in those years. Congressional independence receded in importance, as the president gained new means to influence legislative action.

Stage three (1990–2001) was dominated by the budget enforcement rules discussed in chapter 4. These rules substituted fixed constraints for congressional discretion. In contrast to the original CBA design, which permitted Congress to adopt any budget policy supported by majorities in the House and Senate, budget enforcement rules restricted revenue and spending decisions. During this period, the budget resolution came to be seen merely as a means of facilitating passage of a reconciliation bill. When there was no reconciliation bill, there was no compelling reason to adopt a budget resolution.

Stage four (2001–06) was characterized by the use of budget resolutions and reconciliation to legislate reductions in taxes. Not only has the resolution been narrowed in purpose, but reconciliation has been narrowed in scope. In years that Congress is not considering tax cuts, it can avoid the difficulties of the budget resolution by not adopting it.

With the election of Democratic majorities in the House and Senate, it is likely that congressional budgeting will enter a new phase in 2007 and beyond.

THE RECONCILIATION PROCESS

Reconciliation is the procedure Congress uses to bring revenue and direct spending under existing laws into conformity with the levels set in the budget resolution. The process has two distinct phases: issuance of reconciliation instructions in the budget resolution and enactment of a reconciliation bill (or bills) changing revenue and spending laws. Two separate procedures are needed because the budget resolution cannot change laws.

Reconciliation is an optional process. Although it has been used frequently since 1980, its scope has varied. As explained earlier, it is used in years in which major changes are made in budget policy and not at all in years when status quo budgets are adopted.

Table 6-5, which lists all the reconciliation bills enacted into law, demonstrates that the process is now somewhat different than it was at the outset. For one thing, reconciliation bills have become less frequent. Nine reconciliation bills were passed by Congress in the 1980s, but only seven in the next decade. None of the bills passed in the 1980s was vetoed by the president; two of the bills passed in the 1990s were vetoed, both by Bill Clinton. So far in the 2000s, five more reconciliation bills have been passed, one of which was

vetoed (by Clinton). The original purpose of reconciliation was to trim the deficit by increasing revenues or reducing outlays; in the late 1990s, and continuing into the new century, the primary focus of reconciliation was to reduce taxes. This shift was propelled by the emergence of surpluses as well as by Republican ascendancy in Washington. Tax cutters looked to reconciliation as their primary legislative vehicle because it cannot be filibustered and can therefore pass the Senate by majority vote. In a closely divided Senate, where the majority party often has been unable to muster 60 votes to break a filibuster, reconciliation has made it possible to get tax legislation through Congress. Conflict over tax policy in reconciliation bills has intensified partisan strife in the Senate and was an important factor in the abrupt firing of the Senate parliamentarian (as discussed later). This extraordinary move indicates how important interpretation of the rules is in complex legislative processes such as reconciliation.

Reconciliation begins with instructions in a budget resolution directing designated committees to report legislation that changes existing law. Exhibit 6-6, taken from the fiscal year 2006 resolution, shows instructions when one or multiple committees are directed to propose changes in existing law. The instructions have three components: they name the committees directed to recommend legislation, they specify the amounts by which existing revenue or direct spending laws are to be changed, and they usually set a deadline by which the committees are to recommend legislation implementing the changes. The Senate and House issue separate instructions to their committees, allowing each chamber to fine-tune the text to its own practices. The instructions usually cover the same fiscal years specified in the budget resolution but do not specify how the changes are to be made or

TABLE 6-5
Reconciliation Acts, 1980–2006

Calendar year	Fiscal years covered	Reconciliation act(s)	Date enacted (or vetoed)
1980	1980–81	Omnibus Reconciliation Act of 1980 (P.L. 96-499)	12-05-80
1981	1981–84	Omnibus Budget Reconciliation Act of 1981 (P.L. 97-35)	08-13-81
1982	1983–85	Tax Equity and Fiscal Responsibility Act of 1982 (P.L. 97-248)	09-03-82
		Omnibus Budget Reconciliation Act of 1982 (P.L. 97-253)	09-08-82
1983	1984–86	Omnibus Budget Reconciliation Act of 1983 (P.L. 98-270)	04-18-84
1985	1986-88	Consolidated Omnibus Budget Reconciliation Act of 1985 (P.L. 99-272)	04-07-86
1986	1987–89	Omnibus Budget Reconciliation Act of 1986 (P.L. 99-509)	10-21-86
1987	1988–90	Omnibus Budget Reconciliation Act of 1987 (P.L. 100-203)	12-22-87
1989	1990–91	Omnibus Budget Reconciliation Act of 1989 (P.L. 101-239)	12-19-89
1990	1991–95	Omnibus Budget Reconciliation Act of 1990 (P.L. 101-508)	11-05-90
1993	1994–98	Omnibus Budget Reconciliation Act of 1993 (P.L. 103-66)	08-10-93
1995	1996–2002	Balanced Budget Act of 1995	12-06-95 (vetoed)
1996	1997–2002	Personal Responsibility and Work Opportunity Reconciliation Act of 1996 (P.L. 104-193)	08-22-96
1997	1998–2002	Balanced Budget Act of 1997 (P.L. 105-33)	08-05-97
		Taxpayer Relief Act of 1997 (P.L. 105-34)	08-05-97
1999	2000–09	Taxpayer Refund and Relief Act of 1999 (H.R. 2488)	09-23-99 (vetoed)
2000	2001–05	Marriage Tax Relief Reconciliation Act of 2000 (H.R. 4810)	08-05-00 (vetoed)
2001	2002–07	Economic Growth and Tax Relief Reconciliation Act of 2001 (P.L. 107-16)	06-07-01
2003	2004–08	Jobs and Growth Tax Relief Reconciliation Act of 2003 (P.L. 108-27)	05-28-03
2005	2006–10	Deficit Reduction Act of 2005 (P.L. 109-171)	02-08-06
		Tax Increase Prevention and Reconciliation Act of 2005 (P.L. 109-222)	05-17-06

what programs are affected—these details are left to the discretion of the committees receiving the instructions.

The number of designated committees indicates the scope of the year's reconciliation process and may also affect the procedures applied to move the bill through Congress. Because of their jurisdiction over taxes and major entitlements, the House Ways and Means and the Senate Finance Committees are always among the designated committees. In a few years (1981 and 1995 are leading examples), just about every committee with direct spending jurisdiction was drawn into the reconciliation process. Reconciliation instructions are not issued to the appropriations committees or to authorizing committees whose jurisdiction is limited to discretionary programs.

▶ EXHIBIT 6-6
Reconciliation Instructions

SEC. 201. RECONCILIATION IN THE HOUSE OF REPRESENTATIVES.
SINGLE COMMITTEE

(b) Submission Providing for Changes in Revenue.—The House Committee on Ways and Means shall report to the House a reconciliation bill not later than September 23, 2005, that consists of changes in laws within its jurisdiction sufficient to reduce revenues by not more than $11,000,000,000 for fiscal year 2006 and by not more than $70,000,000,000 for the period of fiscal years 2006 through 2010.

MULTIPLE COMMITTEES

(a) Submissions to Slow the Growth in Mandatory Spending.—(1) Not later than September 16, 2005, the House committees named in paragraph (2) shall submit their recommendations to the House Committee on the Budget. After receiving those recommendations, the House Committee on the Budget shall report to the House a reconciliation bill carrying out all such recommendations without any substantive revision.

(2) Instructions.—

(A) Committee on agriculture.—The House Committee on Agriculture shall report changes in laws within its jurisdiction sufficient to reduce the level of direct spending for that committee by $173,000,000 in outlays for fiscal year 2006 and $3,000,000,000 in outlays for the period of fiscal years 2006 through 2010.

(B) Committee on education and the workforce.—The House Committee on Education and the Workforce shall report changes in laws within its jurisdiction sufficient to reduce the level of direct spending for that committee by $992,000,000 in outlays for fiscal years 2005 and 2006 and $12,651,000,000 in outlays for the period of fiscal years 2005 through 2010. . . .

Source: *Concurrent Resolution on the Budget for Fiscal Year 2006* (conference report to accompany H. Con. Res. 95), H. Rept. 109-62, 109th Cong., 1st sess., April 28, 2005, pp. 11–14.

(a) Separate instructions, usually with different wording, are issued for House and Senate committees. The wording is altered from time to time in each chamber, and it is not uncommon for the text of reconciliation instructions to differ materially from those issued in previous years.

(b) When instructions are issued to only one House and one Senate committee, those committees report their reconciliation legislation directly to their chambers. When two or more committees are instructed, each committee submits its recommendations to the budget committee in its chamber, which consolidates all recommendations (without any substantive revision) into an omnibus bill.

(c) Both the House and Senate set September 23, 2005, as the deadline for the tax committees to report recommended changes in revenue law. When the instructions provide for two or more reconciliation bills in a chamber, the deadlines may differ for each bill. In this case, the deadline for the spending reconciliation bill was September 16, and the deadline for the debt limit reconciliation bill (not shown here) was September 30.

(d) The amounts in the instructions are computed as changes against the CBO baseline.

Additionally, by law, reconciliation may not be used to legislate changes in Social Security.

The dollar amounts in the resolution are computed with reference to the CBO baseline. The changes specified in the instructions are the amounts by which revenues or spending are to be changed from baseline levels. These computations are based on assumptions about the future levels of revenue and spending under current law and the impact of the changes that would ensue from new legislation. Hence the savings that reconciliation generates are assumed savings; the actual savings often diverge, sometimes significantly.

The instructions do not specify how the dollar changes are to be realized or the programs altered. Mentioning programs in the instructions would violate the legislative division of labor between the budget committees and other congressional committees. This relationship gives the budget committees control of money and authorizing committees control of programs. Reconciliation would break down if the budget committees become so powerful that they could dictate which programs and laws should be altered. Nevertheless, the instructions are based on assumptions concerning the programs reconciliation will affect. Voting on the instructions in the budget resolution is not a pig-in-a-poke exercise in which members of Congress blindly endorse spending changes without awareness of what these changes are likely to be. As noted earlier, program assumptions often are set forth in budget committees' reports on the resolution. Like other assumptions linked to the resolution, those pertaining to reconciliation are typically based on understandings worked out in advance between the budget committees and the committees of jurisdiction.

Even when they are mentioned, the program assumptions are not binding. Each committee has discretion to decide on the legislative changes to be made in complying with the instructions. Committees sometimes fall a bit short of the mark, producing less than 100 percent of the targeted revenue or spending changes, but it is rare that a committee ignores or significantly shortchanges the instructions. The budget committees monitor compliance, but even when they find that a committee has not followed the instructions, they cannot unilaterally change the committee's recommendations.

When more than one committee in the House or Senate is subject to reconciliation, the legislative changes are sent to the budget committee, which consolidates the proposals into an omnibus bill. CBA bars the budget committees from making substantive revisions in the legislation that the committees of jurisdiction send to them. This restriction pertains even when the proposed legislation fails to meet the dollar targets specified in the reconciliation instructions. As a last resort, the budget committee can take the fight to the floor. In the House, it needs a cooperative Rules Committee to enable it to offer an amendment to the legislation.

Consolidating the legislative work of many committees into an omnibus reconciliation bill serves several purposes. First, it simplifies the task of coordinating the various pieces of legislation and monitoring their compliance with the instructions. Rather than congest the legislative calendar with numerous bills, the House and Senate take up all proposed legislation in an omnibus measure. Second, all committees subject to reconciliation are treated alike; no committee has to be concerned that Congress might enact the savings it has proposed but not act on the cutbacks proposed by other committees. Finally, consolidating the legislation in an omnibus bill transforms the vote from cutting particular programs into saving the surplus or reducing the deficit. This is not the case when program elements are voted on separately.

Sometimes, however, Congress deems it advantageous to split reconciliation into two or more bills. It did so in 1982, 1996, and 2005—years of intense conflict between Democrats and Republicans on budget policy. By splitting various components into separate measures, the House and Senate voted on provisions that had broad support, leaving other items to their own fate. In 1995 the Republican-controlled Congress produced an omnibus reconciliation bill that packaged Medicare cutbacks, tax cuts, and many other provisions into a single measure. President Clinton vetoed that bill and accused Republicans of using cuts in Medicare to pay for tax reductions that would benefit upper income earners. To avoid being attacked again, Republicans devised three separate reconciliation bills the following year; Congress passed the one that reformed federal welfare programs but did not act on the other two dealing with Medicare and taxes.

In most years, reconciliation is considered as a package, under rules and procedures that restrict the time available for debate and opportunities to amend the measure. Budget rules require that amendments be revenue-neutral—that they not increase the deficit nor reduce the surplus. To satisfy this restriction, an amendment reducing revenues or increasing spending must contain offsets. The House takes up the reconciliation bill pursuant to a special rule (drafted by the Rules Committee) that specifies which amendments may be considered. Despite the enormous size of some reconciliation bills—the 1995 version covered more than 1,500 pages—the Rules Committee typically permits consideration of fewer than half a dozen amendments. One of these usually is a substitute bill offered by the minority party. In most years, the House passes the reconciliation bill compiled by the budget committee with few or no changes.

The Senate allows only 20 hours of debate on the reconciliation bill, which works out to only 12 minutes per member. In some years, this amounts to less than one minute per page. When the 20 hours are up, the Senate votes on the bill, including pending amendments, without further debate. During this "vote-a-thon," many pending amendments are withdrawn and the bill is approved.

The net effect of the special House and Senate rules is that once the process is initiated by instructions in the resolution, the implementing legislation is passed. Only in 1995, 1999, and 2000—when President Clinton vetoed bills produced by congressional Republicans—did instructions fail to lead to a reconciliation act.

Because there is a strong probability that a reconciliation bill will pass once it is initiated, it is an attractive vehicle for provisions that are unrelated to the budget. In response to this problem, the Senate adopted the "Byrd rule," which restricts the inclusion of extraneous matter in a reconciliation bill. According to this rule, a provision is extraneous if it does not change revenues or outlays, increases outlays or decreases revenues for a committee not in compliance with its reconciliation instructions, is outside the jurisdiction of the committee that inserted the provision, has outlay or revenue provisions that are merely incidental to nonbudgetary items, or would increase future deficits. The Byrd rule may be waived by a three-fifths vote of the Senate. Because of the rule's complexity, its application depends on parliamentary interpretation. The rule has blocked provisions that some may have deemed relevant to deficit reduction while permitting others that have had little impact on the deficit. In 1993 House-passed provisions establishing a procedure for reviewing entitlement expenditures were struck from the bill in the Senate on the grounds that they were not germane to deficit reduction. In 1996, however, the Senate parliamentarian ruled that tax cuts that would have caused the deficit to rise did not violate the Byrd rule. This issue was one of the partisan disputes that led to the dismissal of the parliamentarian (see box 6-2).

Reconciliation procedures are cumbersome because they must balance divergent perspectives and interests. Congress's impulse to legislate drives it to expand programs; its need to curtail the budget drives it to contract them. The budget committees have a fiscal outlook; authorizing committees have a programmatic perspective. The budget committees control the budget resolution, which targets savings. Authorizing committees control the reconciliation bill; they select the programs. Reconciliation would be a lot simpler if the budget committees did the whole job, but such an unbalanced arrangement would not be acceptable to other committees.

Balance comes at some cost. Reconciliation is a leaky process in which not all the savings promised at the start are achieved at the end. Its tight timetable discourages committees from making truly substantive changes in affected programs. Instead, reconciliation puts a premium on short-term financial adjustments that enable Congress to come close to the dollar targets without restructuring the affected programs. Since its inauguration in 1980, reconciliation has claimed more than $2 trillion in deficit reduction, almost $1 trillion (over 10 years) in 1990 and 1993 alone. Yet few programs have been terminated or significantly altered through this process. Over the years, Medicare has been the most "reconciled" federal program, yet not a single major benefit available in 1980 was unavailable two decades later.

In the past, reconciliation was applied almost exclusively to deficit reduction, but with the advent of a balanced budget in the late 1990s, reconciliation had a new use. Its procedures were applied to cut taxes. During the presidency of George W. Bush, the reconciliation process increased the deficit by cutting the revenues flowing to the federal government.

ENFORCING CONGRESSIONAL BUDGET DECISIONS

Achieving the outcomes set forth in the budget resolution depends on the actions of Congress and the president, the performance of the economy, and the accuracy of the estimates and assumptions on which the resolution is based. Some critical variables lie beyond Congress's direct control. When economic conditions—growth, employment, inflation, and interest rates—vary from the forecast, so too do actual federal revenues and spending. Budget results also veer off mark when program assumptions, such as the number of participants in entitlement programs, are faulty.

The budget resolution is enforced by Congress when it considers new revenue or spending legislation. However, Congress is not required to act when actual budget outcomes diverge from the amounts set in the resolution because of unanticipated changes in economic conditions, or inaccurate estimates of future revenues or spending under existing law. Variances between budgeted and actual outcomes since 1980 are shown in table 6-6. In roughly three-fifths of the years covered in this table, the actual deficit was higher, or the surplus was lower, than the amount budgeted by Congress. The variances are not random and appear to be influenced by changes in economic performance and in total revenue. In each of the dozen years between 1980 and 1992, the actual deficit exceeded the level

---

▼

BOX 6-2
Senate Parliamentarian a Casualty of Reconciliation Wars

In 2001 the fate of the trillion dollar tax cut (over 10 years) sought by President George W. Bush rested largely on the rulings of an unelected official, Senate Parliamentarian Robert Dove. Partisan conflict between Democrats and Republicans over proposed tax cuts was cloaked in a dispute over reconciliation procedures, impelling Dove to issue rulings that influenced budget outcomes and cost him his job. Although the parliamentarian is a nonpartisan position, Dove was not protected against the strong political forces that dominate contemporary budgeting.

Early in his presidency, George W. Bush made sweeping changes in tax policy his number one legislative priority. Congressional Republicans decided that the path to enactment would be eased by folding tax cuts into one or more reconciliation bills because such measures cannot be filibustered in the Senate. At the time, the Senate was divided equally, with 50 Democrats and 50 Republicans. Without reconciliation, the tax cuts would have almost certainly been doomed in the Senate. In opting for this procedure, House Republicans decided to move forward with multiple reconciliation bills, each containing a portion of the proposed tax cuts. Republicans favored multiple bills because, they hoped, this tactic would attract support for popular tax cuts (such as a reduction in the marriage tax penalty) and would lead to deeper overall cuts than might be obtained in a single reconciliation bill. However, congressional Democrats challenged this approach, arguing that the Congressional Budget Act (CBA) allows only one reconciliation bill a year and that this procedure should be reserved for legislation that reduces the deficit.

In ruling on these disputes, Dove was guided by the provisions of the CBA and Senate precedents. While his rulings could be appealed, the expectation was that they would be decisive. Key senators from both parties lobbied Dove, offering their interpretations of what the CBA says and means. During floor debate on the fiscal year 2002 budget resolution (which contained the instructions that would trigger the reconciliation process), Senate Budget Committee Chair Pete Domenici (R-N.Mex.) argued that there is no language in the CBA that expressly bars use of reconciliation to reduce taxes. "We decide, we vote. And if we have the votes, we use reconciliation because this law permits it," Domenici argued. Kent Conrad (D-N.Dak.), ranking minority member of the Senate Budget Committee, vigorously disputed this claim.

continued

---

specified in the budget resolution; in each year between 1993 and 2000, the deficit was lower or the surplus was higher than the budgeted amount. One plausible explanation of this pattern is that Congress (and CBO) tends to be unduly optimistic when the budget is mired in deficit, and they therefore underestimate the shortfall. However, they err on the side of caution when fiscal conditions are improving.

Throughout the period covered in table 6-6, unbudgeted policy changes added to the deficit or trimmed the surplus, but their budgetary impact was smaller than the changes deriving from economic conditions or estimation errors. Policy changes averaged $21 billion a year and accounted for one-third of the variance between budgets and outcomes. It should be noted, however, that in almost all the years, policy changes increased spending or

▼

BOX 6-2
Continued

"It would be a perversion of the reconciliation process to use it for spending or for tax cuts. That is not deficit reduction. . . . That is for what reconciliation ought to be reserved. Everything else ought to be under the regular order of the Senate, permitting Senators the right to extended debate, permitting Senators to amend, because that is the Constitutional role for this body."

Juggling the two parliamentary issues, Dove displeased both Republicans and Democrats, the former by ruling that the reconciliation process protects only one bill against filibuster, and the latter by permitting tax cuts in reconciliation bills. The first ruling compelled Republicans to abandon their multiple bill strategy, leading them to accept smaller tax cuts than they wanted. Dove did not formally rule on the use of reconciliation for tax cuts because the Democrats refrained from raising a point of order, fearing that an adverse ruling would establish a precedent for future reconciliation bills.

Although Dove survived these battles, he soon was at the center of another controversy over budget procedures. This time, the issue was a provision added in the conference report on the budget resolution establishing an emergency fund that would allow spending above the discretionary caps. This issue pitted the chair of the Senate Appropriations Committee, Ted Stevens (R-Alaska), who opposed the emergency fund, against Senate Majority Leader Trent Lott (R-La.), who supported it. Dove indicated that the emergency fund language might not be permissible under the Congressional Budget Act and could, therefore, be subject to a point of order. This was the last straw for Lott. He promptly fired Dove, demonstrating that conflict within a party can be as divisive as conflict between Democrats and Republicans.

Out of office, Dove appeared to have the final word on the subject, for Congress settled for one rather than two reconciliation bills and scaled down the tax cuts to fit within the constraints of the budget resolution. Dove's stance will influence future budget battles and reconciliation bills, as future Senate parliamentarians will look back at the actions taken in 2001 to guide their own rulings.

Rules and procedures are critical to everything Congress does, but nowhere more so than on budget matters. Jockeying over the rules usually occurs behind the scenes; reconciliation and the firing of Robert Dove brought it out into the open.

---

reduced revenues. Significantly, policy add-ons were modest during the years that budget enforcement rules were in effect.

Various enforcement mechanisms promote legislative compliance, including revenue floors and spending ceilings, spending allocations to committees (and control of the legislation they produce), cost estimates and scorekeeping reports, and various points of order to block legislation that violates budget rules.

Revenue Floors and Spending Ceilings

During the more than 30 years of congressional budgeting, enforcement rules have been tightened and new points of order added. The original budget resolution process enforced ceilings on total budget authority and outlays and established a floor for total revenue. CBA bars consideration of any measure that breaches the revenue or spending aggregates. This prohibition applies only to the totals;

TABLE 6-6
CBO Computation of Differences between Budgeted and Actual Deficits, by Source, Fiscal Years 1982–2006[a]

Billions of dollars

Fiscal year	Policy changes	Economic conditions	Estimation errors[b]	Total differences
1982	−12	76	9	73
1983	22	59	11	92
1984	15	3	−14	4
1985	23	15	−16	22
1986	16	11	22	49
1987	−15	15	6	6
1988	9	8	29	46
1989	17	−20	20	17
1990	20	49	50	119
1991	−19	32	2	15
1992	12	25	−26	11
1993	12	9	−93	−72
1994	11	−21	−40	−50
1995	2	2	−15	−11
1996	25	−48	−40	−63
1997	−5	−37	−89	−131
1998	7	−71	−96	−160
1999	. . .	. . .	. . .	. . .
2000	61	−79	−77	−95
2001	95	−26	−26	43
2002	56	119	202	376
2003	. . .	. . .	. . .	. . .
2004	44	−27	10	27
2005	. . .	. . .	. . .	. . .
2006	69	−82	−122	−135
Mean	21	1	−13	−8
Absolute average[c]	26	38	46	74

Source: Congressional Budget Office, *The Budget and Economic Outlook: Fiscal Years 2008–2012*, January 2007, table C-3, pp. 130–31.

a. Differences are computed in reference to the deficit or surplus in the first (or only) budget resolution adopted for the fiscal year. Positive differences denote an increase in the deficit (or a decrease in the surplus); negative differences denote a reduction in the deficit (or an increase in the surplus). No budget resolutions were adopted for fiscal years 1999, 2003, and 2005.

b. CBO designates estimation errors as technical factors.

c. The absolute average disregards whether the differences are positive or negative.

there is no restriction on measures that would cause functional allocations to be exceeded.

It did not take long for the shortcomings of this arrangement to become apparent. When only the totals are enforced, legislation can proceed as long as there still is room in the budget, even if the inevitable effect would be to cause violations later in the fiscal year. Once the totals were reached, however, no spending legislation could proceed—not even measures that had been assumed in the budget resolution. Of course, Congress would not allow coveted legislation to be blocked just because total spending would be exceeded. At times, Congress has stopped minor bills, but it has never applied the rule against important bills such as regular or supplemental appropriations.

In budgeting, the totals are not effective enforcement tools. This lesson, which was learned when congressional budgeting was inaugurated in the 1970s, was relearned when the Gramm-Rudman-Hollings Act sought to control the deficit in the 1980s. Totals do not provide a reliable basis for control because there is an inherent tension between them and the various parts of the budget. As has already been mentioned, most Americans want the totals to be smaller and the parts to be larger; they want more programs and less government. Unless the pressure for more programs is contained, it is difficult to constrain the totals (even when Congress passes laws such as Gramm-Rudman-Hollings that purport to limit the deficit). The totals do not hold because program advocates are stronger than the guardians of the budget. It does not take much daring for those who want more money to disable or outmaneuver aggregate controls. They can ignore or waive the rules, play fast and loose with the numbers to make it appear that spending is lower than it actually is, frontload spending cuts and backload the increases, and use other bookkeeping tricks to get what they want while pledging fidelity to budget discipline.

Section 302 Committee and Subcommittee Allocations

Although revenue and spending totals are still controlled, nowadays Congress relies principally on allocations to legislative committees and appropriations subcommittees to enforce its budget decisions. These allocations, required by section 302 of the Congressional Budget Act, recognize that Congress operates through its committee system. To effectively limit spending, it is necessary that each committee be given a budget for the legislation in its jurisdiction. The basic rule is that committees cannot generate more spending than has been allocated to them in the budget.

Section 302 prescribes a two-step procedure. First, the spending totals in each budget resolution are allocated among House and Senate committees; then the appropriations committees subdivide the amounts allocated to them among their subcommittees. This procedure forms a chain of control that links individual appropriations to the budget totals. The amounts allocated to committees cannot exceed the budget authority and outlay aggregates in the budget resolution; the amounts distributed to appropriations subcommittees cannot exceed the amount available to the parent committees; and the budget authority and outlays provided or ensuing from appropriation bills cannot exceed the amount available to the relevant appropriations subcommittee.

The House and Senate budget committees take the first step, a section 302(a) allocation, which is usually incorporated in the statement of managers that accompanies the conference report on the budget resolution. Although budget committees make these allocations, they are based on assumptions and under-standings developed in formulating the resolution. By the time the budget committees mark up the resolution, the other committees have a good idea of the amounts that will be allocated to them. Allocations are made to the appropriations committees and to authorizing committees that have direct spending jurisdiction; section 302 allocations are not made for discretionary authorizations, whose funding is provided in appropriation bills. The new budget authority and outlays allocated to committees may not exceed the corresponding totals in the budget resolution.

The House and Senate budget committees have different allocation practices. The House Budget Committee (as exhibit 6-7 shows) allocates amounts to each committee, distinguishing between the "current level" (spending under existing law) and "discretionary action" (spending that will ensue from new legislation, including annual appropriations). In addition to section 302 allocations for the next fiscal year, the House Budget Committee issues total allocations for the next five years.

The Senate Budget Committee avoids detailed allocations. It does not distinguish between current level and discretionary action. Instead, it gives each committee lump sums for budget authority, outlays, and entitlements funded in annual appropriations (as exhibit 6-8 shows).

After the appropriations committees receive their allocations, they subdivide their amounts among their subcommittees in a section 302(b) report (discussed in chapter 9). When an appropriation is considered in the House or Senate, the budget authority and outlays resulting from the bill are compared to the relevant subcommittee's allocation. A point of order can be raised against a measure that exceeds its section 302(b) allocation. Box 6-3 discusses enforcement during years that Congress fails to complete action on a budget resolution.

▶ **EXHIBIT 6-7**
Section 302 Allocations to House Committees

	2005 total	2005–09	2006 total	2006–10
	(in millions of dollars)			
Armed Services Committee				
Current law				
Budget authority (BA)	85,355	473,465	91,209	494,600
Outlays (OT)	85,245	473,045	91,129	494,215
Energy and Commerce Committee				
Current law				
BA	161,936	1,155,178	207,337	1,293,242
OT	161,946	1,157,483	207,955	1,295,935
Discretionary action				
BA	. . .	1,525	100	2,000
OT	. . .	1,525	100	2,000
Reconciliation				
BA	. . .	. . .	−2	−14,844
OT	. . .	. . .	−2	−14,734
Reauthorizations				
BA	. . .	10,080	. . .	15,120
OT	. . .	5,985	. . .	10,845

Source: *Concurrent Resolution on the Budget for Fiscal Year 2006* (conference report to accompany H. Con. Res. 95), H. Rept. 109-62, 109th Cong., 1st sess., April 28, 2005, p. 86.

(a) The House and Senate Budget Committees make separate allocations to the committees of their respective chambers. The two committees use different formats and terms in making these allocations. As required by section 302(a) of the 1974 Congressional Budget Act, the allocations are included in the joint explanatory statement accompanying the conference report on the budget resolution.

(b) The House Budget Committee classifies allocations into at least three categories: (1) "current law" refers to new budget authority and outlays that derive from existing law; (2) "discretionary action" refers to spending from legislative action expected during the session; and (3) "reauthorizations" refers to the extension of mandatory spending in expiring authorizations. (The term "discretionary" used here has a different meaning in budget enforcement rules. See chapter 4.) When the budget resolution includes reconciliation instructions, there also is an allocation for this purpose under the term "reconciliation." Negative amounts reflect the assumption that the committee will report legislation to reduce spending.

(c) The allocations cover a one-year (fiscal year 2006) and five-year (fiscal years 2006–10) time period consistent with the time frame of the budget resolution text. One- and five-year allocations are also provided for fiscal year 2005 because the budget resolution revised the amounts for that fiscal year. The point of order that enforces the spending allocations is keyed to these time periods.

(d) Allocations to the House legislative committees (two of which are shown here) cover mandatory spending; allocations of discretionary spending made to the appropriations committee are provided in a separate table.

(e) In this case, the allocations to the Armed Services Committee do not assume that the committee will report legislation affecting spending beyond what is covered in the baseline. The allocations to the Energy and Commerce Committee, on the other hand, reflect assumptions that the committee will report legislation, as part of the reconciliation process, that will reduce outlays by $14.7 billion over fiscal years 2006–10 and, as discretionary action, will increase outlays by $2 billion during the same period.

▶ EXHIBIT 6-8
Section 302 Allocations to Senate Committees

(in billions of dollars)	Direct spending jurisdiction		Entitlements funded in annual appropriations act	
Committee	Budget Authority	Outlays	Budget Authority	Outlays
Agriculture, Nutrition, and Forestry	111.747	111.108	341.876	260.136
Armed Services	494.585	494.199	0.200	0.270
Banking, Housing, and Urban Affairs	74.258	9.668	0	−0.028
Commerce, Science, and Transportation	68.875	40.886	5.076	5.054
Energy and Natural Resources	19.461	18.898	0.268	0.277
Environment and Public Works	180.812	0.994	0	0
Finance	5,505.551	5,517.365	2,424.576	2,423.728
Foreign Relations	63.726	60.966	0.794	0.794
Governmental Affairs	402.936	387.261	99.879	99.879
Judiciary	32.071	31.766	2.941	2.979
Health, Education, Labor, and Pensions	68.205	62.245	21.289	20.734
Rules and Administration	0.366	0.323	0.640	0.639
Intelligence	0	0	1.314	1.314
Veterans' Affairs	6.327	6.498	185.814	185.182
Indian Affairs	2.555	2.682	0	0
Small Business	0	0	0	0

Source: *Concurrent Resolution on the Budget for Fiscal Year 2006* (conference report to accompany H. Con. Res. 95), H. Rept. 109-62, 109th Cong., 1st sess., April 28, 2005, p. 89.

(a) The Senate Budget Committee allocates new budget authority, outlays, and entitlement spending to Senate committees for the current fiscal year (if appropriate), the next fiscal year, and the five-year total. Only the five-year total allocation is shown here. Allocating a five-year total instead of separate amounts for each of the five years affords more flexibility to committees in drafting their legislation.

(b) "Direct spending" has a different meaning in this context from the meaning it has in the PAYGO rules. Here it includes all spending in each committee's jurisdiction; in PAYGO, it covers spending by committees other than the appropriations committees.

(c) "Entitlements funded in annual appropriations" includes programs such as Medicaid and food stamps that receive annual appropriations. These programs are included both in the amounts allocated to the appropriations committee as well as in the amounts allocated to relevant authorizing committees.

(d) In the Senate, legislation exceeding either the budget authority or outlay allocation to the committee of jurisdiction may be subject to a point of order that can be waived only by a three-fifths vote of the membership.

▼

BOX 6-3
Budgeting without a Resolution

When Congress fails to adopt a budget resolution, it is bound by the revenue and spending policies specified in the previously adopted resolution, as well as by the committee allocations made pursuant to it. The reason for this is that each resolution sets revenue and spending levels for the next 10 years, not just for the year immediately ahead. These levels remain in effect until they are superseded by a new budget resolution. The old decisions are likely to be quite stringent, for they do not take account of developments that occurred subsequent to adoption of the last budget resolution, such as revised revenue or spending estimates, the enactment of presidential spending initiatives, and new authorizing legislation. Although it may be unable to adopt a budget resolution, Congress is likely to have difficulty with the constraints of the old resolution.

This problem was especially urgent during the 2004 session. The House and Senate passed different budget resolutions; the conference committee then reported a compromise that was approved by the House but not by the Senate. In contrast to the House, which had allocated spending limits to the appropriations committee for only the next year, the Senate had made allocations for each of the next two years. The discretionary spending limit for the second year was $814 billion, about $7 billion below the amount set in the conference report. Without a new resolution, the Senate Appropriations Committee would be restricted to the lower amount allowed by the old resolution.

In recent years, the House and Senate have compensated for the lack of a new budget resolution by adopting a special measure known as a "deeming resolution," which is considered to have the same effect for budget enforcement purposes as a regular resolution. There is no standard format or procedure for deeming resolutions; they can be simple resolutions that have been passed by either the House or the Senate, or provisions inserted into bills that are signed into law. Their common purpose is to establish spending limits for annual appropriations.

In 2004 the deeming resolution approved by the House provided that "for purposes of Title III of the Congressional Budget Act, the conference report shall be considered adopted by the Congress," even though the Senate had not approved the conference report. (Title III is the part of the Budget Act that prescribes enforcement rules.) The Senate inserted a deeming provision in that year's Defense Appropriations Act. This provision set discretionary budget authority at $821 billion, rather than the $814 billion that otherwise would have taken effect.

In some years, the deeming resolution is the best of all solutions, for it enables Congress to set budget amounts without going through all the trouble of reconciling different House and Senate views.

Scoring and Scorekeeping

Enforcing congressional budget rules requires information on the budgetary impact of pending or passed legislation and on the status of the budget. The first type of information is known as scoring, the second as scorekeeping (see chapter 4 for a fuller discussion). Scoring pertains to a particular measure, scorekeeping to the cumulative impact of past and current legislation on the budget. Scoring is done by

CBO, which prepares cost estimates of legislation reported by House and Senate committees (exhibit 6-9). These estimates are especially important in assessing the budgetary impact of open-ended entitlement legislation. Scorekeeping reports are issued on an irregular basis, much less frequently than was the practice in the early years of congressional budgeting. A sample of one such report—the current level report—appears in exhibit 6-10. It compares congressional action affecting the budget with the amounts set forth in the budget resolution.

Scorekeeping is not just an informational exercise; its most important use is in ruling on points of order against pending legislation. Since 1975 Congress has come to rely heavily on procedural and substantive points of order to enforce budgetary rules. The original process was permissive: it operated on the notion that Congress should be allowed to take any budgetary action it wanted, provided that it was informed on the financial implications of its actions. Procedural points of order were devised to ensure that Congress complied with budget rules. For example, it is out of order to consider revenue or spending legislation before adoption of the budget resolution.

As the deficit mounted in the 1980s, Congress prescribed tougher enforcement mechanisms. The use of reconciliation to bring existing revenue and spending laws in line with the resolution was an important step in this direction. Congress also tightened enforcement by enacting discretionary spending caps and PAYGO rules for direct spending and revenues. Through these and other changes, Congress shifted from procedural enforcement to substantive rules—from the notion that it should be free to adopt any budget outcome that a majority prefers to the notion that its budget actions must conform to preset policy guidelines. The procedural requirements have been continued, but the current emphasis is on ensuring that Congress adheres to the budget resolution and section 302 allocations. As part of this shift, budget information is now used to regulate congressional action, not merely to inform Congress on the status of the budget.

Section 302 bars the House and Senate from considering any measure that would cause an appropriations subcommittee's allocation to be exceeded. In the House, points of order can be waived by a special rule that is voted on before consideration of the measure to which it pertains; such rules need only a majority to pass. In the Senate, however, many budgetary points of order can be waived only by a three-fifths vote (60 votes) of the membership (some of these are listed in box 6-4). In light of the party lineup in the Senate, neither Democrats nor Republicans can waive affected budget rules without obtaining some support from the other side.

One reason that the Senate is stricter in enforcing budget rules is that the Senate Budget Committee, with its permanent committee assignments, is stronger than the House Budget Committee (whose members must leave the committee after several terms). The Senate Budget Committee is more likely to fight for institutional power; the House Budget Committee is inclined to accommodate other committees. The various points of order and supermajority rules give the Senate Budget Committee a strong voice in determining whether proposed legislation is admissible under the budget rules. The relatively lax House budget rules, and the ease with which they can be swept aside, reflect the strength of the majority party leaders and the weakness of the House Budget Committee.

The differences between the two chambers on budget matters are also rooted in institutional culture. The rules of the House are designed to facilitate the passage of legislation

▶ **EXHIBIT 6-9**
CBO Cost Estimate

H.R. 720
Water Quality Financing Act of 2007

CBO estimates that implementing this legislation would cost about $9.2 billion over the next five years, assuming the appropriation of the necessary amounts. . . . The Joint Committee on Taxation (JCT) estimates that enacting H.R. 720 would reduce revenues by $50 million over the 2008–2012 period and by $541 million over the next 10 years. CBO estimates that enacting title VI would increase vessel tonnage charges. . . . Those charges would increase offsetting receipts, which are credits against direct spending, by $615 million over the 2008–2017 period.

	Fiscal year (in millions of dollars)					
	1998	1999	2000	2001	2002	2003
Changes in revenues						
Changes to tax-exempt financing						
Estimated revenues	0	*	−1	−4	−13	−31
Changes in direct spending						
Vessel tonnage charges						
Estimated budget authority	0	−40	−41	−41	−67	−68
Estimated outlays	0	−40	−41	−41	−67	−68
Spending subject to appropriation						
Spending under current law						
Budget authority	1,300	0	0	0	0	0
Outlays	1,412	1,211	781	562	430	409
Proposed changes						
Clean water SRF grants						
Authorization Level	0	2,000	3,000	4,000	5,000	0
Estimated outlays	0	100	450	1,250	2,350	3,150
Technical assistance and research grants						
Authorization level	0	75	75	75	75	75
Estimated outlays	0	38	60	71	75	75

*Revenue loss of less than $500,000

Source: Congressional Budget Office, "Cost Estimate, H.R. 720, Water Quality Financing Act of 2007" (as ordered reported by the House Committee on Transportation and Infrastructure on March 1, 2007), March 5, 2007 (www.cbo.gov/ftpdocs/78xx/doc7838/hr720.pdf).

(a) The 1974 Congressional Budget Act requires CBO to prepare five-year cost estimates of all public bills (other than appropriations bills) reported by House or Senate committees. CBO sometimes provides cost estimates on bills before they are reported and on pending amendments, thereby informing Congress of costs before it acts. Cost estimates of reported bills usually are published in the report accompanying each bill. Some cost estimates are provided to members or committees on a private basis.

(b) The cost estimate shown here involves revenues (as estimated by the Joint Committee on Taxation), direct spending (in the form of offsetting receipts), and spending subject to appropriation (which assumes that the authorized amount will be appropriated in full).

(c) Cost estimates are computed in reference to CBO's baseline projections. Thus the estimates shown here are the estimated changes from baseline levels that would result from the policy changes in the legislation.

> ### ▶ EXHIBIT 6-10
> **Scorekeeping Report**
>
> Report to the Speaker from the Committee on the Budget—
> Status of the Fiscal Year 2007 Congressional Budget Adopted in House Concurrent Resolution 376
> Reflecting Action Completed as of January 1, 2007—
>
> | | Fiscal year 2007 | Fiscal years 2007–11 |
> |---|---|---|
> | *Appropriate level* | (On-budget amounts, in millions of dollars) | |
> | Budget authority | 2,283,029 | 1 |
> | Outlays | 2,325,998 | 1 |
> | Revenues | 1,780,666 | 10,039,909 |
> | | | |
> | *Current level* | | |
> | Budget authority | 2,266,002 | 1 |
> | Outlays | 2,273,560 | 1 |
> | Revenues | 1,771,853 | 10,146,069 |
> | | | |
> | *Current level over (+) / under (-) appropriate level* | | |
> | Budget authority | −17,027 | 1 |
> | Outlays | −52,438 | 1 |
> | Revenues | −8,813 | 106,160 |

1. Not applicable because annual appropriations acts for fiscal years 2008 through 2011 will not be considered until future sessions of Congress.

Source: Remarks of Representative John Spratt, *Congressional Record,* January 5, 2007, p. H92.

(a) The 1974 Congressional Budget Act requires the House and Senate Budget Committees to issue scorekeeping reports on the status of the congressional budget. The committees insert these reports, based on CBO data, into the *Congressional Record* from time to time; there is no fixed schedule.

(b) The "appropriate level" is the level set in the most recently adopted budget resolution; the "current level" is the level based on all completed congressional action. The current level includes both new legislation enacted during the session and revenue or spending resulting from existing law.

(c) These reports are used in determining whether a pending measure would violate section 311 of the 1974 Congressional Budget Act by causing total budget authority or outlays to exceed, or total revenues to fall below, the levels set in the budget resolution.

(d) The format of these reports has changed from time to time, and the House and Senate have somewhat different practices. The House report (an excerpt shown here) compares the budgeted and current levels for the current fiscal year (2007) and the five-year total (2007–11). In this report, for fiscal year 2007, revenues were $8.8 billion below the revenue floor, and budget authority and outlays were $17 billion and $52.4 billion below the spending ceiling, respectively. Thus any legislation reducing revenues would violate section 311, but legislation providing spending up to these amounts would not.

(e) No amounts are shown for budget authority or outlays for the five-year period because appropriations for the outyears have not yet been enacted.

▼

BOX 6-4
Prohibitions in Selected Senate Budget Rules Requiring 60 Votes to Waive

- Consideration of an appropriations bill before the appropriations committee has filed a section 302(b) report on its spending suballocations.
- Consideration of a measure providing spending in excess of a committee's section 302(a) spending allocation (or, in the case of the appropriations committee, its section 302(b) spending suballocations).
- Consideration of new spending, revenue, or debt-limit legislation for a fiscal year before adoption of the budget resolution for that year.
- Consideration of spending legislation that would violate the spending ceilings for the budget year, or revenue legislation that would violate the revenue floor for the budget year or the total for the budget year and the ensuing outyears.
- Consideration of an amendment to a reconciliation bill that would increase the deficit.
- Inclusion of extraneous matter in a reconciliation bill (Byrd rule).
- Inclusion of Social Security legislation in a reconciliation bill.
- Consideration of revenue or direct spending legislation that would increase the deficit for the periods covering the current fiscal year and the next 5 years, and the current fiscal year and the next 10 years (PAYGO rule).

Source: Senate Budget Committee, "Points of Order Applicable to All Legislation," June 2005 (www.senate.gov/~budget/republican/analysis/2005/PointsOfOrder.pdf). Some of the points of order requiring 60 votes to waive stem from provisions in the 1974 Congressional Budget Act and others stem from provisions included in annual budget resolutions. The Senate Budget Committee document cited here provides a comprehensive listing. Consideration of a measure providing spending in excess of a committee's section 302(a) spending allocation (or, in the case of the appropriations committee, its section 302(b) spending suballocations).

that the majority party favors and its committees produce; the Senate's rules accommodate more floor amendments and produce less partisan outcomes. When it is unified, the majority party in the House can remove any rule that would act as a barrier to floor action while also thwarting the legislative ambitions of the minority. The House majority often waives budget rules, especially when the violations are procedural. It also waives substantive points of order when the violation is deemed to be minor or technical, or when the leadership is determined to have its way. Because it does not restrict floor amendments and is more vulnerable than the House to proposals that would

breach budget rules, the Senate has to be more circumspect in considering budget legislation. The ease with which members can filibuster or otherwise block action has acculturated the Senate to behave in a less partisan manner. The extreme partisanship of recent times has complicated the Senate's work and made it even more difficult than in the past to complete all required budget actions.

WOULD A PRESIDENTIAL ROLE STRENGTHEN CONGRESSIONAL BUDGETING?

As discussed earlier in this chapter, the budget resolution process established in 1974 was conceived as a way for Congress to stake out its own position on the budget and avoid dependence on the president's recommendations. For this reason, the budget resolution was devised as an internal congressional procedure without any involvement by the president. Over the years, however, both the resolution process and Congress's budget relations with the president have changed. During the 1990s, there were frequent budget summit negotiations between the president and Congress. These typically took place near the end of the session, after Congress unilaterally passed its own budget resolution but before it completed work on appropriations.

The president and Congress are interdependent on budget matters. The president cannot get his budget adopted without legislative action, and Congress cannot get its budget resolution implemented without the president's concurrence. If they have become interdependent, would it make sense for the president and Congress to seek agreement early in the process? Why wait until the last minute when positions have hardened and shutdown is imminent? Why should Congress unilaterally formulate a budget resolution when it cannot unilaterally enact the legislation needed to implement the resolution?

In considering these questions, it is necessary to take account of how switching from a concurrent to a joint resolution (that would require the president's signature to become law) might affect the willingness and capacity of warring politicians to make budgetary peace. Conflict is ubiquitous in budgeting because it is a process in which some pay and others benefit. But precisely because conflict is unavoidable, it is essential that the process be engineered so as to encourage opposing sides to seek accommodation.

One of the virtues of the existing congressional budget process is that it is tailored to each year's circumstances. Congress takes up reconciliation bills in some years but not in others. In some years, it adopts status quo budgets; in others it reaches for major policy changes. In some years, the president and Congress go to the summit on budget disputes; in others they work out disagreements through routine work on legislation and appropriations. The elasticity of the process has enabled the two branches to formally negotiate when the prospect of agreement is favorable and to go their separate ways when the gap between them is so wide that agreement is beyond reach.

It is true that by the end of the process, when the final appropriations bills are negotiated, there has to be some meeting of the minds. But resolving appropriations disputes is usually a more placid matter than resolving budgetary differences. The former typically deal with discrete activities and spending items, the latter with budget totals and program priorities. Appropriations fragment budget conflict into bite-size decisions that can be resolved one at a time; the budget resolution aggregates them into comprehensive statements of national policy. Congress often makes appropriations decisions in a bipartisan manner, though to a lesser extent than in the past; budget resolutions generate partisan wrangling and party-line votes. In view of this voting pattern, giving the president a formal role may make it more difficult for the two sides to bridge their differences. Each would be emboldened to uphold its position by emphasizing the differences between it and the other political branch.

Some have suggested that involving the president in the budget resolution process would spur the two branches to reach agreement early in the session and not wait until the last moment, when federal agencies are about to run out of money. In budgeting, however, real deadlines encourage compromise, but contrived deadlines merely postpone the day of reckoning. Congress and the president know that if they fail to agree on the resolution, they still have until much later in the session to work out their differences. Moreover, even if they do agree on a budget framework in the spring, they may still fight later in the year when appropriations and other implementing measures are considered.

The budget resolution must be a process for all political seasons—when big policy shifts are in the air and when only incremental adjustments are made; when the two branches lock horns on the budget and when they see things the same way. The best way to ensure that the budget resolution works under all conditions is to keep it flexible. Arming the president with a pen might leave him with nothing to sign or veto.

CONCLUSION

During its more than 30-year history, the congressional budget process has been frequently remade—either through formal changes in the rules or informal adaptation. At the outset, there were two budget resolutions a year, at least one too many for those in Congress who did not want to vote repeatedly on the deficit and other difficult matters. By the early 1980s, the second resolution was discarded, and the surviving resolution was transformed from a target into a constraint. In line with this new arrangement, Congress shifted reconciliation from the end of the annual budget cycle to the beginning. It stretched the period covered by the resolution from 1 year to 3, then to 5, and finally to 10. It tinkered with the legislative calendar by accelerating action on the budget resolution and permitting House consideration of appropriations bills after May 15, even without adoption of the resolution.

The budget resolution has played many roles. In some years, it has rubber-stamped previous decisions; in others it has taken the lead in recasting budget policy. Often the resolution has accommodated the demands of revenue and spending committees; sometimes it has challenged them. Once the budget committees largely controlled the resolution; now these committees have nominal jurisdiction, with much budget policy being dictated by party leaders or developed in negotiations with the president. Over the years, the president has moved from being an outsider to being a vital participant in changing congressional budget policy. He does not have a formal veto power over the resolution, but he can block implementing legislation.

The variability of the budget resolution manifests weakness and instability in the process. Even after 30-plus years, the resolution has not earned a secure niche in Congress. Each year it is only as important as Congress wants it to be, only as relevant as the budget committees are. The resolution is a strange breed, more than a symbolic statement but less than a law. Nothing stops if Congress fails to adopt it, and nothing has to be changed if the numbers prove faulty or if they are overtaken by economic circumstance. The budget resolution cannot be ignored, but neither is it always followed.

In this makeshift environment, the congressional budget process has attracted contradictory reform proposals. Some would weaken or do away with the budget resolution; others would strengthen it. Abolishing it, along with the budget committees and the budget rules that have accreted over the years, would return Congress to the pre-1974 situation, in which the totals were added up without anyone having to vote on them. The case for terminating the congressional budget process rests on the argument that it has spawned confusion and conflict, complicated Congress's budget work, and has not effectively controlled federal spending. Some critics have argued that the process has weakened presidential responsibility and has spurred increased spending.

The problem with abolishing the budget process is that doing so would not return Congress to the old status quo. The appropriations committees now control a much smaller share of federal spending, and entitlements consume a much larger share. Without a budget process, there would be no reconciliation mechanism, eliminating the most effective means available to Congress to curb entitlements and impel revenue changes. Perhaps the budget committees, shorn of a role in making legislative policy, could serve as monitors of the fiscal behavior of other congressional committees. Yet it is doubtful they would be effective in an advisory role. Perhaps party leaders could make budgetary policy, for this is a role to which they have gravitated over the years. But they would not likely enforce budgetary discipline with the same determination that the budget committees have.

The congressional budget process is a malleable tool. It served Congress during the decades of high deficits and assisted Congress in balancing the government's books in the late 1990s. If it survives, it will be because the process enables Congress to set the policies and priorities it wants, not because it prevents a legislative majority from working its will.

7

Revenue Legislation

Almost all of the revenues collected each year derive from permanent law, not from current legislative decisions. Congress has the option of doing nothing and allowing existing law to continue or of revising the tax code to change either the volume of revenues or the incidence of taxation. In some years, the president's budget and Congress's budget resolution do not propose significant changes in tax policy; these documents merely estimate the receipts that will be generated from existing tax laws. In other years, one or both branches seek to change the amount collected or the distribution of the tax burden, and revenue policy is among the most controversial features of the budget.

Two variables are important in defining the process and politics of revenue legislation. One is whether the aim is to raise or lower tax rates; the other is whether the president or Congress initiates proposed changes. When deficit reduction is the priority, as it was from 1982 through 1993, legislation to increase revenues is usually a prominent part of the reconciliation package. When the budget moved to a surplus in the late 1990s, controversy flared over whether to lower the tax burden, and reconciliation was deployed to expedite the enactment of tax cuts. Even when tax issues are on the back burner, Congress considers some revenue measures, tinkering with relatively minor tax provisions or extending some expiring provisions.

Congress usually takes up major tax legislation pursuant to the president's recommendations to change specific revenue provisions. However, Congress typically deviates from his proposals. Occasionally, Congress acts on its own initiative. This occurred in 1982 (the second year of the Reagan presidency), when Senate Republicans were alarmed by the growing budget deficit and pushed through tax increases to reverse some of the revenue losses enacted the previous year. Congressional initiatives were aborted in 1995 and 1999, when Republican leaders sought to cut taxes in the face of strong opposition from President Clinton, who vetoed the legislation sent to him. The most common pattern, however, is for Congress to act only after the president has proposed major changes in revenue legislation. For example, in 1993 Clinton prodded Congress to enact tax increases as part of a deficit reduction package. Once Congress becomes involved, it usually exercises considerable independence, altering the volume or composition of taxes to suit its preferences. Even when it meets the president's revenue target, Congress does so in its own manner.

Two intrinsic features of tax policy propel congressional independence: tax policy directly affects most Americans, and it is controversial. Revenue legislation is intensively lobbied and closely monitored by interest groups, which actively use political access to influence the outcome. Members of the tax-writing committees (the House Ways and Means and the Senate Finance Committees) often receive more campaign money from political action committees than do the members of any other congressional committees. With the money comes pressure to benefit certain taxpayers by changing the tax code.

During the high-deficit era, Congress frequently boosted federal revenues. When the president took the initiative by proposing the increases, he gave Congress political cover to raise taxes. But the growing budget surpluses of the late 1990s emboldened congressional leaders to take the initiative in seeking tax cuts. Both types of action—tax increases and cuts—spark conflict between the president and Congress, between the major political parties, and sometimes between the House and Senate as well. Getting tax legislation through Congress can be a difficult chore but one that has been accomplished frequently during the past two decades (table 7-1). Often the task has been eased by treating revenue legislation as an opportunity to benefit particular interests or taxpayers. Just about every tax bill that makes it through Congress contains tax breaks, even measures whose ostensible purpose is to increase federal revenue. With increases and decreases combined in the same measure, producing tax legislation is almost always a redistributive activity in which some gain and others lose. The winners and losers are selected through complex legislative procedures and political maneuvers that often produce gargantuan bills, which revise hundreds of sections of the tax code and make it more complex.

More than two centuries ago, Americans revolted against taxation without representation; nowadays many do not even like taxation with representation. Yet the federal government has an enormous need for revenues to finance the many programs that Americans want. As difficult as the task is, Congress and the president have devised a tax system that raises more than $2.5 trillion a year. More than two centuries ago, tax disputes were settled in battle; today's disputes are settled through political action and legislative procedures.

REVENUE LEGISLATION IN CONGRESS

The Constitution grants Congress the power to levy taxes but says little about how to exercise

TABLE 7-1
Major Tax Legislation, 1980–2006

Billions of dollars

Year	Legislation	Estimated revenue impact[a]
1980	*Omnibus Budget Reconciliation Act* First use of the reconciliation process	+4 (1 year)
1981	*Economic Recovery Tax Act* Enacted six months after Ronald Reagan became president; indexed major features of the individual income tax	−749 (1 year)
1982	*Tax Equity and Fiscal Responsibility Act* Initiated by the Senate; repealed some of the tax breaks enacted the previous year	+98 (3 years)
1983	*Social Security Amendments* Increased revenue for Social Security system, which was on the brink of insolvency	+165 (7 years)
1984	*Deficit Reduction Act* Revenue gains and spending cuts were packaged together in a reconciliation bill	+51 (4 years)
1986	*Tax Reform Act* Designed to be revenue-neutral; lowered rate on highest individual income tax bracket from 50 to 28 percent; revenue loss offset by eliminating many tax expenditures	+11 (1 year)
1987	*Budget Reconciliation Act* Canceled Gramm-Rudman-Hollings sequestration of $23 billion	+23 (2 years)
1989	*Omnibus Budget Reconciliation Act* Included approximately $10 billion in spending cuts	+6 (1 year)
1990	*Omnibus Budget Reconciliation Act* Contained the Budget Enforcement Act, which introduced new controls on revenue and spending legislation	+137 (5 years)
1993	*Omnibus Budget Reconciliation Act* Raised highest individual tax rate to 39.6 percent	+240 (5 years)
1997	*Taxpayer Relief Act* Part of the balanced budget agreement between the president and Congress; expanded several major tax expenditures; estimated revenue loss much higher after first five years	−95 (5 years)
2001	*Economic Growth and Tax Relief Reconciliation Act of 2001* Reduced income tax rates and added significant tax breaks shortly after George W. Bush became president	−1,349 (11 years)
2003	*Jobs and Growth Tax Relief Reconciliation Act of 2003* Accelerated reductions in tax rates enacted two years earlier and reduced capital gains and dividend rates	−350 (11 years)
2005–06	*Tax Increase Prevention and Revenue Reconciliation Act of 2005* Extended reduced rates for capital gains and dividends and expanded business expensing provision for two years; final action carried over into 2006	−69 (5 years)

Sources: *Congressional Quarterly Almanac, 1980–97;* Joint Committee on Taxation: (1) *Estimated Budget Effects of the Conference Agreement for H.R. 1836,* JCX-51-01, May 26, 2001; (2) *Estimated Budget Effects of the Conference Agreement for H.R. 2, The "Jobs and Growth Tax Relief Reconciliation Act of 2003,"* JCX-55-03, May 22, 2003; and (3) *Estimated Revenue Effects of the Conference Agreement for the "Tax Increase Prevention and Reconciliation Act of 2005,"* JCX-18-06, May 9, 2006, available at the committee's website (www.house.gov/jct/).

a. Revenue impact estimated at time of enactment; actual revenue impact usually diverges from these estimates. The number of years in parentheses is the number of years covered by the estimate.

TABLE 7-2
House Ways and Means Committee: Pre-Reform and Post-Reform

Pre-reform (before 1975)	Post-reform (since 1975)
Democratic members of Ways and Means appointed Democratic members of other committees.	Committee appointments are made by Democratic Steering and Policy Committee; Ways and Means no longer has a role.
Ways and Means had complete jurisdiction over Medicare and Medicaid.	Medicare Part B is shared with Energy and Commerce Committee, which also has complete jurisdiction over Medicaid.
No subcommittees. All legislation was developed and marked up by the full committee, which thereby kept controversial matters off the congressional agenda.	Ways and Means is required to have at least six subcommittees, though major tax legislation is still considered by the full committee.
The committee was small, with only 25 members. It was dominated by a coalition of Republicans and conservative Southern Democrats.	Committee was enlarged to 37 members, and the ratio of Democrats to Republicans was increased from 15-10 to 25-12. In the 110th Congress, the ratio is 24 Democrats to 17 Republicans.
Almost all markups were closed. Staff was small and controlled by the chair.	Most markups are held in open session (though premarkup in party caucuses is closed). Staff was increased but is still mostly controlled by the chair.
Most bills reported by the committee were considered in the House under a closed rule that barred floor amendment.	Most bills are considered under a limited rule that permits designated floor amendments.

this power. One of its few requirements is that revenue legislation must originate in the House. This sequence—first the House, then the Senate—has given rise to differences in the way the two chambers handle revenue measures. However, the congressional budget process and pay-as-you-go (PAYGO) rules have narrowed the differences, and the House and Senate now often behave similarly.

In the House

Almost all tax measures begin their legislative journey in the House Ways and Means Committee—a panel whose vast jurisdiction covers Social Security, trade legislation, unemployment benefits, and some health programs. Reforms that swept through the House in the

1970s greatly affected this committee; it is much less independent and powerful than it was before the reforms. Some of the changes are listed in table 7-2, which compares the pre-reform and post-reform Ways and Means Committee.

The full committee generally develops major revenue legislation; subcommittees may handle minor matters. At one time, the Ways and Means Committee shielded itself from lobbyists by marking up legislation behind closed doors. House rules now require it (and other committees) to conduct business in the open unless it expressly votes to meet in executive session. Openness has exposed Ways and Means to more intense political pressure, but the chair often brokers deals in private and then convenes the committee to approve the bargains that have already been struck. Ways and Means once thrived on bipartisan cooperation; Democrats and Republicans worked together to produce legislation that commanded overwhelming support on the floor. But bipartisanship was attacked by reformers who saw it as the means by which a conservative coalition of Republicans and Southern Democrats controlled tax legislation and blocked consideration of measures that liberal Democrats favored. The reformers broke the conservative hold on the committee by enlarging Ways and Means and changing the ratio of Democrats to Republicans. Since the 1970s, the committee has been polarized (as has been the House as a whole), and voting often splits along party lines.

Heightened partisanship has been accompanied by an increase in the frequency and size of tax legislation. It has been common for issues decided one year to be reconsidered one or two years later, and for Congress to change hundreds of sections of the tax code in a single bill. Partisanship has also reduced the committee's insularity and independence, making it more susceptible to outside influence. Ways and Means does not have a completely free hand in initiating and drafting tax legislation: it must be mindful of party leaders' preferences, the revenue levels set in the budget resolution, and the reconciliation instructions. Much of what the committee produces by way of revenue legislation is at the behest of other congressional actors, in particular the Speaker of the House and the House Budget Committee. Ways and Means still enjoys great latitude in the details of legislation, but external pressures often drive overall policy. In response to these pressures, the majority party members on Ways and Means usually caucus in advance of formal committee meetings to hammer out legislation that comports with their party's position.

After Ways and Means reports a bill, it seeks a rule (in the form of a House resolution) that prescribes the terms and conditions under which the measure is considered on the floor. The Rules Committee, which the Speaker controls, has three basic options. One is to write a closed rule, which bars floor amendments and forces members to approve or reject the entire measure. Another option is to draft an open rule, which permits members to offer any amendment. The third is to compose a limited rule, which permits consideration of designated amendments. Ways and Means used closed rules routinely from the 1950s until the early 1970s, during the 18-year reign of Chair Wilbur Mills (D-Ark.). This procedure gave Ways and Means enormous leverage, and it almost always got the House to pass the legislation that it reported. Nowadays the House often changes some parts of reported measures and rarely permits closed rules on tax legislation.

But open rules on revenue bills are unworkable. Operating under open rules, the House can disregard the compromises crafted in committee and rewrite legislation from scratch. This makes for wonderful political theater but not for sound legislation. Open rules encourage members, for whom the next election is always less than two years away, to turn a measure raising revenue into one that cuts taxes. Instead, most tax legislation is considered under a limited rule, which enables the majority party to decide which amendments the House may consider. Typically, the majority crafts the limited rule to permit amendments that improve the bill's chance of passing; it blocks amendments that might split or embarrass their party. The House must approve the rule drafted for a bill before it takes up the measure. Those opposing the legislation try to defeat the rule. If they succeed, the bill will not be considered unless a new rule has been drafted and approved. After the rule is approved, the House acts on the bill and any permitted amendments. Once the rule passes, it is almost always the case that the bill also passes.

In the Senate

Senate work on revenue measures begins in the Finance Committee, whose legislative jurisdiction is even broader than that of its House counterpart. Although the Senate is supposed to wait until the House has completed action, it sometimes gets around this requirement by stripping a minor House-passed bill (such as a measure renewing an expiring tariff) of all text except the enacting clause and then substituting its own revenue provisions. Box 7-1 describes one of the most prominent Senate initiatives: a 1982 tax increase that the president did not propose and that was not included in any House-passed legislation. Although this procedure did not adhere to the spirit of the constitutionally prescribed sequence, it did follow the strict letter of the requirement. Federal courts have consistently refused to pass judgment on the legality of congressional procedures; hence tax legislation initiated by the Senate is valid law.

In most cases, the Senate takes up tax measures only after the House has acted. For decades this sequence differentiated the Senate's behavior from that of the House. Considering the bill first, the House was constrained by strict rules that limited members' ability to vote for tax cuts or to give breaks to favored interests. Tax legislation that passed the House was adorned with few amendments and had almost no extraneous provisions. The Senate outcome was altogether different. In both the Finance Committee and on the floor, senators added numerous amendments that awarded tax breaks and other benefits. At times, hun-dreds of amendments were added—a process that came to be known as "Christmas treeing" the bill. It was not uncommon for the Senate to turn a House bill that raised revenue into one that reduced revenue.

These amendments gave the Senate considerable advantage vis-à-vis the House in the ensuing conference convened to resolve differences in the two bills. It is widely understood on Capitol Hill that tax bills, more than other types of legislation, are rewritten in conference. Much of what the House or Senate passes may be cast aside by the conferees, who sometimes insert provisions that were not in either chamber's revenue measure. When the conference drafts the final bill, Senate conferees use many of their added provisions as bargaining chips to extract concessions from the House. Because of this, the conference report often hews more closely to the Senate's position.

PAYGO RULES

As detailed in the next section, the PAYGO rules prescribed by the Budget Enforcement Act of 1990 changed the Senate's incentive to add provisions to revenue bills, as well as other aspects of tax legislation. The basic rule (which is more fully discussed in chapter 4) was that congressional action on revenue and direct spending legislation should not add to the budget deficit nor diminish the surplus. Legislation reducing federal revenues had to be offset by an increase in revenues or a decrease in direct spending. If Congress failed to fully offset the net revenue loss, funds were to be sequestered from certain direct spending programs. The House and Senate also have internal PAYGO rules.

In enforcing the statutory PAYGO rule, congressional scorers distinguished between baseline revenues deriving from existing laws and changes in revenues resulting from new

▼

BOX 7-1
Senate Initiative on Revenue Legislation: The 1982 Tax Increase

Barely one year after he signed a massive tax cut into law, President Ronald Reagan signed the Tax Equity and Fiscal Responsibility Act (TEFRA), which increased federal revenue by an estimated $98 billion over three years. TEFRA was an extraordinary policy reversal that bypassed normal legislative procedures and was enacted without any House consideration of the measure before the conference report. TEFRA was cobbled together in the Senate, taken to conference, and passed with little House influence on its final provisions.

The Congress that enacted TEFRA was

1981
August 13
Reagan signs tax cuts into law ($749 billion over five years).

1982
July 23
Senate passes, 50-47, tax increase bill.

August 19
Conference report passes House, 226-207, and Senate, 52-47.

September 3
Reagan signs TEFRA into law.

split along party lines. The Democrats had a majority in the House, and the Republicans had the Senate and the White House. In 1981 this political lineup spawned a bidding war between House Democrats and the president as to who could produce the bigger tax cuts. When the bidding ended, Reagan was the winner, but his triumph soon presented the president with a political quandary: how to deal with an escalating budget deficit that was far higher than he had estimated earlier in the year. Reagan's solution, presented in a September 24, 1981, television address was to propose that $22 billion be raised by eliminating "abuses and obsolete incentives in the tax code."

Inasmuch as this proposal came late in the legislative session, Congress did not act on it. Reagan renewed his call for revenue enhancements early in the next session, but House Ways and Means Committee Chair Dan Rostenkowski (D-Ill.) refused to act. He feared that House Democrats would be blamed for increasing taxes, and he did not want another bidding war with the White House.

That would have been the end of the matter were it not for the determination of Senate Finance

continued

legislation. Congress was not required to offset a drop in revenues resulting from changing economic conditions, nor could it use an increase in revenues resulting from improved economic circumstances to offset legislated revenue losses. However, Congress was required to offset projected decreases resulting from new legislation.

The North American Free Trade Agreement (NAFTA), which Congress approved in 1993, illustrates how PAYGO worked. At the time it was considered, NAFTA was estimated to reduce tariffs and increase direct spending by $2.7 billion over its first five years. Some NAFTA proponents argued that it would actually increase tax collections by stimulating trade

▼

BOX 7-1
Continued

Committee Chair Robert Dole (R-Kans.) to do something about the deficit. Dole negotiated the deals and compromises between committee Republicans and the White House that enabled him to draft a bill that would pass on a straight party-line vote.

But how could the bill be reported? The House had not acted, and the Constitution requires it to initiate revenue legislation. Dole's solution was to attach his committee's tax increases to a minor revenue bill that the House had passed late in the previous session. The enlarged bill passed the Senate without any Democratic support.

Action then shifted to the House, which could have been expected to produce its own bill so as to position itself for the ensuing conference with the Senate. But Ways and Means Committee Democrats, still fearful that they would be tarred as tax increasers, opted to go straight to conference. The conferees then hammered out a final bill based almost entirely on the Senate-passed version.

By this time, there were deep fissures in the Republican ranks—especially in the House—where the midterm elections were only a few months away. With the Republicans split, the bill needed substantial Democratic support in the House to be enacted. House Democrats could no longer remain on the sidelines, but they would not supply the needed votes until they got three political protections. First, the House took up the conference report under a closed rule that precluded separate votes on controversial provisions. Second, Reagan promised to give Democrats who supported the bill letters thanking them for their votes. And finally, each party produced a majority of its House members in support of the conference report.

As a revenue raiser, the 1982 measure had relatively little impact on the deficit, which soon passed the $200 billion mark. But it had a lingering impact on subsequent legislation and on political fortunes. The bill set a precedent for political sleight of hand that remained through the 1980s; revenue enhancements were not to be treated as tax increases. TEFRA earned Senator Dole the label "tax collector for the welfare state," a stigma he could not shake off among some Republican voters when he ran for president 14 years later, in 1996. As for Ronald Reagan, he signed the 1982 tax increase without comment and went on to sign more than half a dozen additional increases before leaving office. Yet he is remembered as the tax-cutting president.

and increased economic activity, but assumptions about the overall macroeconomic impact were not included in the official estimates. Hence they had no bearing on Congress's need to find $2.7 billion in offsets. Although PAYGO did not require that the NAFTA legislation itself offset the $2.7 billion—the offsets could have been included in other revenue or direct spending bills passed by Congress—it would not have been possible to muster majority support unless the measure contained the offsets. The administration first proposed to generate additional revenue by doubling customs fees and adjusting other charges. However, House Republicans, whose votes were needed to pass NAFTA, labeled the proposal a tax increase and threatened to vote against it. The administration then negotiated a compromise in which most of the additional revenue came from bookkeeping changes in several taxes, with only a small increase in customs fees.

When Congress acts on a measure, it lacks certain knowledge of the legislation's future budgetary impact. Knowledgeable people, using slightly different assumptions, can come up with widely divergent estimates. The 1990 Budget Enforcement Act decreed that Office of Management and Budget (OMB) estimates were determinative in scoring legislation for statutory PAYGO purposes. For purposes of enforcing budget resolution policies, however, Congress relies on Congressional Budget Office (CBO) estimates, which use data prepared by the Joint Committee on Taxation, when it is considering revenue legislation—even when they diverge significantly from OMB's figures.

OMB and CBO often differ because they use different assumptions about the future behavior of taxpayers in response to changes in tax rules. Scoring is often routine, with little dispute about the assumptions used and the estimates deriving from them. Sometimes, however, conflict between the president and Congress or between Democrats and Republicans complicates the scoring of tax policy. When this occurs, scoring becomes a weapon one side or the other uses to promote or impede legislation. During the George H. W. Bush administration, for example, the president argued that reducing capital gains tax rates would increase federal revenue by spurring owners to sell long-held assets. Using different assumptions, however, CBO advised Congress that a lower tax rate would reduce federal revenue over a five-year period. At one level, this was a technical argument, where experts who had information on the past actions of taxpayers disagreed on how their behavior might change in response to future

rate changes. At another level, it was a political dispute between protagonists who differed over tax policy; each side used the assumptions that supported its position. Because Congress relied on CBO, its projection that lower rates would lose revenue doomed the legislation. But this was not the end of the matter; the dispute flared in every subsequent session until Congress reduced capital gains rates.

IMPACT OF PAYGO ON CONGRESSIONAL BEHAVIOR

During the years it was in effect, the statutory PAYGO rule influenced both the actions of Congress and the revenue legislation it produced. Some of the effects were procedural; many were substantive.

PAYGO diminished the Senate's advantage in going second on tax legislation. It became less practicable for the Senate to "Christmas tree" tax bills by inserting revenue-losing provisions as bargaining chips for the conference. Every step of the way, senators had to be mindful of whether a proposal would cause a drop in revenue. All revenue losses had to be offset, even if the revenue loss was incidental to the bill's main objectives. In 1998, for example, the Senate Finance Committee reported a bill that restricted certain practices that the Internal Revenue Service used to enforce tax laws. Although the legislation did not aim to change federal revenues, it was scored as causing a $6 billion loss over five years. Before reporting the bill, the Finance Committee had to devise offsets that satisfied PAYGO but were not perceived as tax increases. Approximately half of the offset came from changing the timing of when businesses could claim deductions for the payment of certain compensation to employees.

PAYGO forced both the House and the Senate to play the offsets game—that is, to include revenue-raising provisions whose sole purpose is to make room for tax cuts. Gaming the process occurs because neither chamber or party relishes the task of voting for tax increases. Accordingly, each seeks revenue enhancements while avoiding the blame for raising taxes. In this game, timing is important. When the revenue change takes effect and when it expires strongly influence the score accorded legislation. Another tactic is to exploit the fact that scoring covers a finite period—typically 5 or 10 years. What happened earlier or is projected to happen after this period has no bearing on the score.

One popular timing ploy is to extend an expiring tax. For example, the federal tax on airline tickets expired in 1996, was renewed for a brief period that year, and then renewed again (in a somewhat different form) the following year. In contrast to a permanent tax, which is scored as a revenue increase only once, a temporary tax is scored whenever it is renewed. The reverse of this game is to structure tax cuts so that they are effective for only a portion of the scored period, thereby reducing the amount that has to be offset.

Congress has become adept at turning long-term revenue losers into short-term (5- to 10-year) revenue gainers. The trick is to structure the tax law so that more money flows into the Treasury during the first part of the scored period and the majority of revenue loss occurs during the last part or later. A good example of this device was the 1996 legislation that contained a variety of breaks for small businesses, which were estimated to cause a $10 billion loss over 5 years and $20 billion loss over 10 years. A portion of the required offsets was obtained by temporarily suspending a 15 percent surcharge on certain distributions from pension funds. This tax cut was scored as a revenue producer because it gave taxpayers an incentive to withdraw money from their pension funds. In so doing, they would not pay the 15 percent surcharge, but they still would be subject to ordinary income taxes, which would result in a revenue increase during the scored period. Although there would be revenue loss after this period, it did not affect the score. Congress used a similar tactic in 1998 legislation that reformed the internal revenue system and in a 2005 measure that extended access to Roth IRAs to upper-income taxpayers.

In 1993 the Senate adopted an internal PAYGO rule that required that any revenue or direct spending measure be deficit neutral. Under the rule, any measure providing tax cuts or direct spending increases had to include offsets to them. Over the years, the Senate modified the rule significantly, first to allow tax cuts (or direct spending increases) that did not exceed the on-budget surplus, and later, to exempt any tax cut or direct spending increase assumed in the budget resolution. In 2007 the House adopted an internal PAYGO rule requiring direct spending and revenue legislation to be deficit neutral over 6-year and 11-year time periods (including the current year), without providing for any exemptions; the Senate revised its PAYGO rule in a similar manner.

TAX EXPENDITURES

The old practice of "Christmas treeing" revenue bills and the new practice of structuring revenue legislation to get a favorable score indicate that Congress does not simply view such legislation as a means of generating revenue: it also is an opportunity to give benefits to certain firms or households through adjustments in the tax code. These benefits appear in the budget as tax expenditures, a term defined in law as revenue losses resulting from deductions, exemptions, credits, and other exceptions to the normal tax structure. Tax expenditures are breaks and loopholes that reduce both the tax liabilities of certain taxpayers and the revenue collected by government.

Tax expenditures are means by which the federal government pursues certain public objectives. They may be regarded, as the term denotes, as alternatives to direct spending and other policy instruments. A preferential rate on capital gains aims to stimulate investment, deducting mortgage interest payments from taxable income promotes home ownership, credits for child care expenses enable parents to work outside the home. The government can also promote these objectives through grants (which are budgeted as expenditures) rather than through tax breaks. It can provide cash subsidies to homebuyers (or owners), to families whose parent or parents work outside the home, or to firms that invest in physical or human capital. The budget facilitates comparison of direct and tax expenditures by classifying both into functional categories, but there is relatively little explicit trading off between the two types of expenditures.

The budget publishes two different measures of tax expenditures—a broad measure based on taxation of all income, and a "reference" measure based on the existing tax structure. The two differ in the treatment of certain types of income. For example, the broad measure includes transfer payments from government to households; the reference measure excludes this income.

The budget lists more than 150 tax expenditures; each of the 50 largest had estimated annual revenue losses in excess of $1 billion in fiscal 2007. Table 7-3 lists some of the largest tax expenditures and compares their estimated revenue losses at five-year intervals. Most of the major tax expenditures have been in effect since the early years of the federal income tax, but some—such as the earned income credit, individual retirement accounts, and the child credit—were enacted in the 1970s or later.

Despite the availability of budgetary information on tax expenditures, Congress does not have a formal mechanism for substituting between them and direct expenditures. The two types of spending are likely to be in the jurisdiction of different committees and are usually considered in different types of legislation.

Tax expenditures are a form of entitlement. Like the entitlements that appear in the direct spending part of the budget, they generally are governed by permanent legislation, are not normally reviewed by Congress each year, are not controlled by the appropriations process, and grow in response to exogenous factors without any congressional action. The estimated revenue loss from exclusion of employer contributions for medical insurance and care rose automatically from an estimated $67 billion in 1996 to $126 billion 10 years later. During the same period, the loss from mortgage interest on owner-occupied homes grew from $54 billion to $76 billion (see table 7-3). As a form of entitlements, tax expenditures can be altered by Congress through reconciliation legislation or ordinary revenue measures. But if Congress does nothing, the volume of tax expenditures, like the cost of other entitlements, depends on requirements already mandated in law.

Although they are defined in law and are reported in the president's budget, tax expenditures are highly controversial. Conservatives don't like the concept because, they argue, it implies that all income belongs to the government except for the portion it permits taxpayers to retain. Liberals don't like them because the value of tax expenditures is much greater for upper-income earners than for low-income people. For example, a $1,000 deduction for home mortgage interest is worth $350 for someone in the 35 percent tax bracket, but only $150 for someone taxed at the 15 percent rate. Because tax expenditures are a function of tax liabilities, their value rises when tax rates are increased. This produces the anomalous circumstance that taxpayers are paying higher

TABLE 7-3
Major Tax Expenditures: Estimated Revenue Losses, Fiscal Years 1996, 2001, and 2006

Billions of dollars

Tax expenditure	Revenue forgone		
	1996	2001	2006
Exclusion of employer pension plan contributions and earnings	59	92	48
Employer contributions for medical insurance and medical care	67	81	126
Mortgage interest on owner-occupied homes	54	61	76
Deduction of certain state and local taxes	29	42	35
Preferential capital gains tax rate	6	42	28
Rebasing of capital gains at death	30	28	29
Charitable contributions	24	27	40
Interest on public purpose bonds	13	23	27
State and local property taxes	16	23	15
Child credit[a]	. . .	20	33
Capital gains exclusion on home sales	18	19	36
Social Security benefits for retired workers	17	19	20
Interest on life insurance savings	11	16	24
Individual retirement account contributions and earnings	6	16	7

Sources: *Budget of the United States Government, Analytical Perspectives, Fiscal Year 1996*, table 5-6, p. 64; *Analytical Perspectives, Fiscal Year 2001*, table 5-3, p. 117; *Analytical Perspectives, Fiscal Year 2006*, table 19-3, p. 324.

a. The child credit was enacted in 1997.

taxes at the same time they are given greater tax breaks.

With liberals and conservatives disenchanted with tax expenditures, the concept survives because it is a useful measure of the revenue forgone because of provisions in the tax code. This information is useful for policymakers when they rewrite the tax laws. It enables them to assess the difference between nominal and effective tax rates, that is, the difference between the tax rates published in official documents and the actual percentage of income paid in taxes. It also enables them to examine the interaction between tax breaks and tax rates.

RATES VERSUS BREAKS:
THE 1980S VERSUS THE 1990S

Virtually every deficit reduction package enacted in the 1980s and 1990s curtailed some tax expenditures (the major exception was 1981). In these bills, the critical trade-off was between tax breaks and tax rates: the more breaks in the tax code, the higher the rates have to be to meet revenue targets. During the first decade of the new century, however, Congress and the president reduced tax rates and increased tax breaks, thereby contributing to revenue losses that boosted the budget deficit.

The rates-versus-breaks contest played out very differently in the 1990s than in the previous decade. The 1980s began with more than a dozen individual tax brackets, the highest of which was 70 percent on certain types of income. In 1981, President Ronald Reagan's first year in office, Congress enacted a 25 percent cut (over three years) in income taxes, indexed the tax brackets (they have been adjusted each year since 1985 for changes in consumer prices), reduced the top rate on "unearned" income (investment income such as dividends) from 70 percent to 50 percent, and introduced or expanded tax breaks. The breaks included accelerated depreciation of assets, a tax credit for research and development expenses, an increase in the maximum contribution to individual retirement accounts, a reduction in estate taxes, exclusion of some interest income, and an increase in the child care tax credit. The 1981 Economic Recovery Tax Act decreased revenue by both lowering rates and increasing breaks. At the time it was enacted, the law was estimated to reduce federal revenues by $749 billion over the next five years. Although some of these breaks were eliminated the next year, that law reduced fiscal 1990 revenue by an estimated $323 billion.

This was the high-water mark for tax breaks in the 1980s. During the remainder of the decade, Congress passed and Republican presidents signed almost a dozen tax increases, which chipped away at the breaks while steeply reducing tax rates. The first step in this direction was a 1982 law that increased federal revenue by an estimated $98 billion over three years (see box 7-1). The law curtailed various corporate tax preferences, such as provisions that let firms sell unused tax breaks. It also mandated that a portion of interest and dividend income be withheld. Congress also trimmed tax breaks through reconciliation legislation enacted in 1984, 1986, 1987, and 1989. But the biggest shift from breaks to lower rates was made by the Tax Reform Act of 1986—a measure whose main purpose was to simplify the tax code, not to change the amount of federal revenue. Congress decided that this legislation should be revenue-neutral, which compelled it to trade off rates and breaks. The only way it could lower the former was to eliminate some of the latter. The 1986 tax reform collapsed the 14 individual tax brackets into two and lowered the top rate from 50 percent to 28 percent. It also reduced

effective tax rates by increasing the personal exemption as well as the standard deduction for taxpayers who do not itemize deductions. These rate reductions were paid for by eliminating the deduction for state and local sales taxes, raising the capital gains tax rate, phasing out the deduction for consumer interest payments, taxing unemployment benefits, and making numerous other adjustments in tax expenditures.

The rates-versus-breaks trade-off was very different during the 1990s. The highest individual income tax rate was raised from 28 percent to 39.6 percent, and corporate income tax rates (which were reduced in 1986) were also raised. Congress passed rate increases in 1990 when Republican George Bush was in the White House and again in 1993 when Democrat Bill Clinton was president. These laws made many relatively minor adjustments in tax expenditures, but the 1997 balanced budget agreement (discussed in chapter 2) added a handful of major breaks: a new individual retirement account (Roth IRA) allowing tax-free distribution of pension funds, education tax credits and education savings accounts, a new tax credit for children, deductibility of student loan interest payments, lower capital gains rates, increases in estate tax exemptions, full deductibility (phased in over a number of years) of health insurance premiums paid by self-employed taxpayers, and many other revenue-losing provisions. The estimated revenue losses were $95 billion during the first 5 years, $275 billion over 10 years, and vastly higher amounts beyond that period.

Why the reversal in the rates-versus-breaks trade-off? The answer comes in at least three parts and is indicative of how the political climate and budget behavior changed from one era to the next: changes in public perception of tax breaks, a difference in the importance of the deficit on the political agenda, and the introduction of PAYGO budget rules.

First, there was a shift in public sentiment on taxes. In the 1980s, supply-side arguments that high marginal tax rates lowered saving, investment, and output carried the day. Even liberal Democrats joined the bandwagon for lower tax rates, though some were motivated more by their dislike of tax breaks than by their acceptance of the new economic doctrine. In the 1990s, by contrast, the supply-side position lost favor, and there was growing concern that high-income earners had not paid their fair share. The widening income gap—low-income households losing ground and high earners reaping the dividends of an expanding economy—contributed to this shift in political sentiment. In fact, virtually all the rate increases enacted during this decade were imposed on upper-income taxpayers, who bore a rising share of the income tax burden.

Second, there was a more sustained effort to curtail the deficit during the 1990s than in the previous decade. In the 1980s, the White House was occupied by presidents who were less concerned about reducing the deficit than about reducing the tax burden. Although Reagan did sign many tax increases into law, most were small, and the additional revenue was obtained by closing loopholes, not by across-the-board tax increases. Reagan's only big tax increase was the 1982 legislation, which he was persuaded to accept on the expectation that each dollar of increased revenue would be matched by three dollars of spending cuts. When the expected spending cuts did not materialize (because majority support was lacking in Congress for such deep cutbacks), Reagan felt cheated and resolved not to sign any other tax increases. He grudgingly relented from time to time, only agreeing to as little new revenue as he could get away with.

Presidential behavior was different in the decade after Reagan left office. George H. W. Bush promised "no new taxes," but his own aides maneuvered him into accepting a large tax increase when it became apparent that the Gramm-Rudman-Hollings deficit targets would be breached. If this were to occur, the required sequestration would have had dire consequences for many federal programs, including defense. Furthermore, Congress would not agree to a new budget deal unless it included hefty tax increases. As noted in chapter 5, Bush generally distanced himself from budgetary matters, which gave his aides broad scope to negotiate a package that contradicted his oft-stated "no new taxes" position and thereby damaged his political career. Clinton's tax increase was enacted on his initiative, and he had to fight a reluctant Congress to get it. Bush's increase took effect during a recession, Clinton's at the start of an economic boom. Bush left office long before the deficit had receded; Clinton continued in office as the deficit vanished.

Finally, PAYGO narrowed the options open to Congress in dealing with revenues. The requirement that revenue losses be offset biased congressional action against broad rate cuts and in favor of targeted tax breaks. In contrast to rate cuts, which lose substantial revenue because they benefit most taxpayers, the losses from breaks can be limited by targeting particular taxpayers or by structuring them in ways that defer the revenue loss beyond the scored period. This is exactly what Congress did in 1997 when it enacted costly tax breaks within the PAYGO budget constraint.

CUTTING RATES AND ADDING BREAKS: TAX POLICY IN THE NEW MILLENNIUM

The rates-versus-breaks trade-off ended with the inauguration of George W. Bush in 2001. Making tax cuts the centerpiece of his domestic agenda, the president successfully pushed Congress to pass legislation that lowered income tax rates and significantly increased certain tax expenditures. In fact, the House and Senate passed tax cuts in every year from 2001 to 2006, though the 2005 cuts were not enacted into law because the two chambers were unable to reconcile their different versions. Using its standard 10-year horizon, CBO has estimated that the enacted tax cuts trimmed more than $2 trillion from federal revenues. Because some of the biggest cuts had sunset provisions, the full 10-year revenue loss would be significantly higher if they were made permanent. Clearly, Bush's tax agenda differed from the one that prevailed during both the 1980s and 1990s. In contrast to Reagan, Bush has not retreated from his tax-cutting preferences; in contrast to his father and Clinton, he cut tax burdens rather than raised them.

Bush's first tax cut, enacted shortly after he entered office in 2001, pared an estimated $1.35 trillion from federal revenue over 10 years. It reduced the lowest tax bracket to 10 percent and the highest to 35, doubled the child tax credit to $1,000, phased out the estate tax, increased the amounts that could be sheltered in retirement funds, and provided relief for married taxpayers. However, to keep the total revenue loss within the bounds set by that year's budget resolution (and to comply with Senate rules), the law provided for all of its tax cuts to expire at the end of 2010 (see box 7-2). Congress passed a small tax cut targeted at businesses in 2002 and a larger one in 2003 that included reduction in taxes on dividends and capital gains. It also produced relatively small tax reductions in 2004 and 2006.

The sharp change in sentiment during the new millennium was due to several changed circumstances. Foremost was the arrival of budget surpluses and the election of George W. Bush. The former spurred the new president and members of Congress to trim federal revenue; the latter put into power a person who doggedly promoted tax cuts even when the surplus vanished. The surplus disabled PAYGO, which was still on the books but no longer deterred Congress from boosting spending or reducing revenues. Arguably, tax cuts would have been significantly smaller, and Congress would have been compelled to choose between rates and breaks, if PAYGO were still effective. By the time the surplus vanished, PAYGO was a dead letter. Bush did propose reenactment of PAYGO, but he favored a version that covered only spending increases, not revenue losses.

Even when federal defense and homeland security spending rose in the aftermath of the 9/11 terrorist attacks, George W. Bush continued his drive to cut taxes. Unlike his father, who approved tax increases, Bush was determined to stay the course, despite deterioration in the government's financial condition. Bush may have been motivated by a "starve the beast" tactic, that the only way to curtail federal spending is to take away some of the tax revenue available to it.

In 2000, the year before Bush became president, federal revenues totaled 20.9 percent of GDP, a level that matched the peak achieved in 1944, when the United States was mobilized to wage a world war. This elevated level of revenue emboldened the president and Congress to cut taxes, but the impulse to cut taxes continued when revenues plunged to 16.3 percent of GDP (in 2004), as many Republican leaders embraced the view that lower tax burdens would spur economic growth. Tax cuts were the main cause of the steep drop in revenue, but economic weakness also played a role. In a $12 trillion economy, each one percentage point decline translated into a $120 billion revenue loss. All told, federal revenues were about $500 billion less in

2004 than they would have been if the government had retained the same share of revenue it had four years earlier.

Bush's main objective has been to reduce tax rates, for he believes that high rates discourage savings, investment, enterprise, and other actions that expand the economy. But he signed legislation that also augmented tax breaks for families and businesses. This "rates and breaks" outcome was due in part to the behavior of Congress, which tends to be responsive to particular constituencies, and in part to the fact that rate cuts would provide little benefit to persons in low tax brackets. Tax breaks targeted at lower-income filers enable them to benefit from the reductions. In other words, lower marginal tax rates largely benefited one segment of taxpayers, while new or expanded breaks largely benefited another segment. It was this political imperative that produced the massive tax cuts of the new millennium.

DYNAMIC REVENUE SCORING

In 2006 President Bush asked Congress for funds to establish a dynamic analysis unit in the Treasury Department to estimate the impact on the economy of changes in tax laws. Although the proposal deals with the technical issues in economic analysis, it has stirred considerable controversy, for it has the potential to alter the way Congress handles tax legislation. Using dynamic analysis, tax reductions that are conventionally estimated to lower future federal revenues might be projected to raise them instead. Conversely, legislation raising tax rates might be scored as reducing federal revenue. Inasmuch as the fate of legislation often is influenced by the score it receives, converting to dynamic scoring methods would likely affect the tax policies enacted by Congress.

As discussed in chapter 4, all revenue measures reported by committee or passed by the House and Senate are scored by CBO on the basis of estimates supplied by the Joint Committee on Taxation. The score determines whether the legislation is consistent with the adopted budget resolution and congressional rules, both of which generally limit the total revenue loss that Congress can pass. To the extent, therefore, that dynamic analysis lowers the estimated revenue loss, it enables Congress to pass steeper reductions in tax rates.

In conventional (or static) scoring, CBO takes account of probable behavioral changes that would ensue from modifications to the tax code. For example, when Congress lowered the capital gains tax rate, CBO estimated the additional revenue that would accrue because taxpayers had incentives to sell appreciated assets. Although these microeconomic responses are incorporated into the score, possible changes in total economic activity are not reflected in the score. Dynamic scoring would assess pending or enacted legislation to estimate its impact on the overall economy. If it is assumed that national output will rise because of new incentives for businesses to invest and employees to work, dynamic scoring would show that lowering tax rates boosts revenue.

This is what makes dynamic scoring so controversial, for it would embolden Congress to reduce tax rates even when the budget is mired in deficit. In 2003 the House adopted a rule requiring a "macroeconomic impact analysis" for revenue measures reported by the Ways and Means Committee. The rule does not specify the type of macroeconomic analysis, thereby permitting the use of alternative models of how the economy and tax policies interact. Applying different models to the tax cuts reported by the Ways and Means Committee in 2003, the Joint Committee on Taxation estimated that the revenue feedback resulting from increased economic activity would range from 6 to 28 percent over the next 5 years, and

▼

BOX 7-2
Sunsetting Tax Legislation: Political Reality and Budget Tricks

Most of the tax cuts enacted during George W. Bush's presidency have sunset provisions. They will automatically expire at the end of 2010 (in some cases, earlier) if they are not extended by Congress. If Congress does nothing, individual income tax rates will revert to the levels in effect before Bush took office. The estate tax will disappear in 2010 but will reappear at rates as high as 55 percent the next year, and the special 15 percent rate on dividend income and capital gains will lapse.

Tax cuts have been the signature domestic policy initiative of Bush and congressional Republicans. Why would they make these legislative accomplishments temporary rather than permanent? The answer has to do with budget rules that limit the total revenue loss that may be enacted. Sunsets are means of cutting taxes while staying within the letter of budget rules. Because these rules are effective only in the Senate, sunsets have been a means of resolving conflicts between it and the House over tax legislation. They enable Congress to cram more tax cuts into law than would be feasible if the revenue loss were permanent.

The most important impediment to permanent tax cuts is the Byrd rule, which pertains only to reconciliation bills. One provision of this complex rule bars the Senate from considering tax legislation that is projected to lose revenue beyond the period covered by the congressional budget resolution (which typically ranges from 5 to 10 fiscal years). This restriction may be waived by a 60-vote majority, but at the time the 2001 tax cuts were considered, the Senate was split 50-50 between Democrats and Republicans, putting the 60 votes beyond reach. The simplest way for the Senate to keep within the Byrd rule was to sunset all the tax cuts at the end of 10 years (the budget window used in the budget resolution that year). Actually, the Senate had another option—to place the tax cuts in an ordinary bill rather than a reconciliation bill; but doing so would have exposed the legislation to a filibuster. Reconciliation avoided a filibuster but limited the tax cuts that could be enacted.

The House does not have a comparable restriction, nor does it require 60 votes to waive budget rules. Operating through the Rules Committee, which often devises special rules to waive points of order against pending bills, the House can set aside budget restrictions by majority vote. It turns out, however, that because the Senate is handcuffed by its own rules, it is in a stronger bargaining position when it goes to conference with the House. In tax legislation, as in

continued

from 3 to 23 percent over a 10-year budget horizon. This additional revenue would offset all or a portion of the revenue loss.

If reductions in tax rates have beneficial effects on the economy, why are these not included in scoring revenue legislation? Part of the answer is that dynamic scoring is dependent on assumptions and subjective judgments about the economic response to tax policy changes. Slight shifts in assumptions can lead to enormous swings in the estimates. Another part of the answer is that dynamic scoring would spur Congress to reduce tax rates and make it more difficult to boost taxes

▼

BOX 7-2
Continued

other matters, the Senate can insist on its position, arguing that it cannot yield because the Byrd rule bars it from approving positions favored by the House.

This occurred in 2003 when Congress once again trimmed federal taxes. The House and Senate were unable to agree on the amount of revenue loss prescribed in the budget resolution, so each chamber devised its own reconciliation instructions, with the House providing for $550 billion in cuts and the Senate providing for $350 billion. Each chamber then produced a reconciliation bill geared to the revenue loss targeted in the budget resolution. In conference, the Senate insisted that it could not consider revenue losses in excess of $350 billion and the House was compelled to retreat. This time, sunsets were used to enact more tax cuts than would have been possible if they had been made permanent. Some provisions were set to expire in only a few years, thereby holding down the estimated revenue loss.

Do sunsets produce larger or smaller tax cuts? The answer depends on whether the temporary provisions are extended before they expire. If they are continued, then sunsets have the effect of understating the full revenue loss; if they are not, then the long-term revenue loss will be lower. When the 2001 and 2003 tax bills were enacted, it was widely expected that in due course they would be made permanent. But as of this writing (in 2007), this has not happened yet. The cost of making lower tax rates and other revenue-losing provisions permanent is one barrier; opposition by Democrats and fissures in Republican ranks are another. CBO has estimated that the federal government would lose an additional $1.5 trillion in revenue during fiscal years 2007–16 if the 2001 and 2003 tax cuts were extended, and another $350 billion if other expiring provisions were extended. These additional revenue losses would occur at just about the time that baby boomers were entering the retirement stream and claiming the pension and health care benefits promised to them. Predicting future tax legislation is difficult, but it is highly unlikely that all the sunsetted provisions will be extended.

Those who oppose making the tax cuts permanent have one big advantage: if Congress does nothing, the sunsets expire and the pre-2001 (or 2003) provisions are restored. In the end, the sunsets may turn out to be real sunsets and not merely legislative tricks to evade budget controls. The architects of the Bush tax cuts may have misplayed their hand and may end up with less than if they had trimmed their ambitions at the outset and eschewed all sunsets.

when the government is in need of additional revenue. Perhaps the most important factor is that the fight over dynamic scoring reflects deep divisions between Democrats and Republicans over tax policy. As long as the two parties hold fundamentally different views on taxes, dynamic scoring will be more a battle cry than a means of estimating the revenue impact of legislation.

TRENDS IN FEDERAL REVENUE

Annual revenues reached $100 billion in 1963; less than 30 years later (in 1990), they exceeded $1 trillion. Exactly a decade later (in 2000), they passed the $2 trillion mark. CBO has projected that total revenues will double to $4 trillion by 2016. These revenue increases have been driven principally by inflation and economic growth—not by tax legislation. Federal revenues are elastic; they grow automatically as the economy expands and as personal and corporate incomes rise.

Despite their rise, until recently, federal revenues moved within a narrow band as a proportion of the gross domestic product (GDP). In 1960 they totaled 17.8 percent of GDP, and in 1996, 18.9 percent. During this period there was much less variability in revenues than in outlays. The gap between the highest and lowest ratios of revenue to GDP was 2.7 percentage points; the spread on the expenditure side was more than twice as wide, at 6.3 percentage points. However, revenues varied significantly as a share of GDP during the past decade, peaking at 20.9 percent in 2000 and declining to 16.3 percent in 2004. During these four years, the gap was almost double what it was during the previous 25 years. Both past stability and recent instability are rooted in tax policy.

Revenue stability was due to legislative action, not to happenstance. If Congress had not acted, revenues would have been propelled upward by inflation, which boosts nominal incomes, and by economic expansion, which raises real incomes. Before income tax brackets were indexed to inflation (automatically adjusted for changes in consumer prices), Congress periodically responded to rising revenue trends by lowering tax rates or increasing breaks. Thus when budget receipts soared from 17.2 percent of GDP in 1976 to 19.6 percent in 1981, Congress cut tax rates and indexed individual income tax brackets to the rate of inflation. Revenues then receded to 17.5 percent of GDP in 1986, only slightly higher than they had been a decade earlier.

Indexation narrowed Congress's legislative options. Before indexation, when Congress compensated for rising tax yields, it typically redistributed the tax burden, giving more reductions to some taxpayers than to others. This arrangement enabled both branches to take credit for reducing taxes, even though some taxpayers may not have been fully compensated for inflation. But inasmuch as the legislative response lagged inflation, there usually was a period during which tax burdens were above the trend line.

Indexation (which took effect in 1985) enables the president and Congress to avoid the blame for inflation-induced tax increases. The adjustment is swift and automatic, but it is not complete because not all relevant features of the tax system have been indexed. Indexation also means that politicians no longer have the expedient option of reducing nominal tax rates to compensate for inflation. Instead, their role has been to raise taxes in order to curtail the budget deficit or to lower taxes when surpluses appear or to stimulate the economy. In fact, since enactment of indexation, Congress has passed more than a dozen revenue-changing measures. The targeted tax cuts enacted in 1997 significantly reduced the taxes paid by certain earners, but the overall impact on federal revenues was much more modest (at least during the first five years) than its proponents and opponents claimed. According to official estimates, the 1997 legislation was projected to reduce total federal revenues by only about 1 percent during its first five years. Unlike previous tax cuts, which reduced revenue as a percentage of GDP, the revenue-to-GDP ratio continued to rise after the 1997 legislation.

Arguably, indexation reoriented revenue legislation from stabilizing and redistributing tax burdens to producing more revenue. Partly because of indexation, bureaucrats cut taxes and politicians raised them during the 1990s. This role reversal generated revenues in excess of the levels realized in the past and set the stage for George W. Bush's campaign to cut federal taxes. It also caused extraordinary instability in revenue policy, as the government lurched from Clinton's strong opposition to big tax cuts to Bush's embrace of a strategy that cut revenues as a share of GDP below the 1950–2000 trendline.

The contrast between Clinton and Bush indicates that the two parties differ on tax policy. They clash on how to dispose of surpluses in the few years they occur, and more frequently on how to reduce deficits. Near the end of his presidency, Clinton thwarted Republican demands to cut taxes by insisting that "saving" Social Security should have first claim on the surplus. When he inherited the Oval Office, however, Bush pushed large tax cuts through Congress, even when the surplus vanished.

In tax policy, elections matter. Clinton was able to boost taxes in 1993 because he had a Democratic majority in both houses of Congress; Bush succeeded in cutting taxes in 2001 because he had (before the defection of Senator Jeffords) Republican majorities in both chambers. If the past is a guide to the future, the 2008 election will set the course for tax legislation, especially if one party controls both the White House and Congress. Yet, regardless of the 2008 election results, pressure to generate additional revenue will influence tax policy. Congress and the president may also be impelled to rewrite tax laws to deal with problems created by the Alternative Minimum Tax (AMT), which is discussed later in this chapter.

Changes in the political lineup and in the condition of the budget spawn instability in tax policy. Tax rates and breaks do not remain the same for an extended period. Every rise in tax rates intensifies pressure to lower them, just as every reduction gives rise to pressure to raise them. The only constants in tax policy are that the government requires vast amounts to finance its programs and that proposals to change revenue laws usually rank high on the legislative agenda.

SOURCES OF FEDERAL REVENUE

Over the years, there have been both stability and change in the composition of federal revenues. Individual income taxes have been the largest revenue source for an extended period, accounting for almost 47 percent of total receipts since 1960 (table 7-4). But the portion of revenues derived from corporate income taxes is only about half of what it was after World War II (although it has edged up a bit since the early 1990s). The share from social insurance taxes (for Social Security and Medicare) has more than doubled, while excise taxes have dropped to about 4 percent of total revenues.

One cause of the decline in corporate taxes is reduction in the marginal tax rates on business profits; another has been relatively low profits. Corporate profits amounted to 10 percent of GDP in 1960; in 1990 they were 7 percent. Greater reliance on debt financing, generous tax breaks, and more aggressive tax avoidance practices may have also contributed to the decline in corporate tax revenues. Whatever the reasons, corporations paid more than 40 percent of their profits as taxes in 1960 but less than 25 percent in 2004.

The increase in social insurance taxes has been accompanied by higher spending on Social Security and Medicare. Note, however, that the rise in the share of revenue coming from these taxes has been negligible since 1990. This reversal of the long-term trend may appear surprising, as an aging population will

TABLE 7-4
Federal Revenues, by Source, as Share of Total Receipts and GDP, by Decade, 1960–2000, and 2005

Revenue source	1960	1970	1980	1990	2000	2005
Percentage of total receipts						
Individual income taxes	44.0	46.9	47.2	45.2	49.6	43.0
Corporate income taxes	23.2	17.0	12.5	9.1	10.2	12.9
Social insurance taxes	15.9	23.0	30.5	36.8	32.2	36.9
Excise taxes	12.6	8.1	4.7	3.4	3.4	3.4
All other receipts	4.2	4.9	5.1	5.4	4.5	3.8
Percentage of GDP						
Individual income taxes	7.8	8.9	9.0	8.1	10.3	7.6
Corporate income taxes	4.1	3.2	2.4	1.6	2.1	2.3
Social insurance taxes	2.8	4.4	5.8	6.6	6.7	6.5
Excise taxes	2.3	1.6	0.9	0.6	0.7	0.6
All other receipts	0.8	0.9	1.0	1.0	0.9	0.7
Total receipts	17.8	19.0	19.0	18.0	20.9	17.6

Source: *Budget of the United States Government, Historical Tables, Fiscal Year 2008,* table 2.2, pp. 31–32, and table 2.3, pp. 33–34.

require more government spending on pensions and health care. While it is true that the amount collected from social insurance has continued to rise, the Social Security and Medicare trust funds will nonetheless face serious financial imbalances once the baby boom generation retires. Why has the government not boosted social insurance taxes to shore up the financial condition of these funds?

A powerful clue comes from the data presented in table 7-5, which are drawn from CBO calculations. The table shows that in 1995, 38 percent of all taxpayers paid more Social Security taxes than income taxes. With the employer's share of social insurance taxes added in, the percentage almost doubles to 73 percent. The relative burden of social insurance taxes is highest for the lowest-income taxpayers. Payroll taxes exceeded income taxes for 99 percent of those earning less than $10,000 and for 92 percent of individuals and families in the lowest income quintile.

Not surprisingly, taxpayer resistance to higher social insurance taxes has increased as these taxes have taken a bigger bite out of paychecks. From 1950 until 1990, Congress frequently raised the social insurance tax rate, boosting it from 1.5 percent each for employees and employers at the start of this period to 7.65 percent each at the end. All told, there were 19 tax rate increases during this 40-year stretch, on average one every other year (table 7-6). Since 1990 the tax rate has not been changed, though the maximum earnings on which the tax is imposed climbed from $51,300 to $90,000 in 2005. Raising the maximum taxable wage base does not require new congressional action and affects only those workers whose earnings exceed the previous base. Since most employees earn less than the maximum taxable earnings, the increase does not affect them.

Resistance to raising the social insurance tax rate may compel politicians to rely on other

TABLE 7-5
Percentage of Taxpayers Whose Payroll Taxes Exceeded Their Income Taxes, by Cash Income and Income Quintiles, 1995

Percent

	Employee share	Employee and employer share
Cash income (dollars)		
0 to 10,000	99	99
10,000 to 20,000	69	91
20,000 to 30,000	46	81
30,000 to 40,000	34	78
40,000 to 50,000	25	74
50,000 to 75,000	14	71
75,000 to 100,000	6	52
100,000 to 200,000	3	20
200,000 or more	3	4
All incomes	38	73
Quintile		
Lowest	92	97
Second	48	82
Middle	31	77
Fourth	16	72
Highest	5	37
All quintiles	38	73

Source: Congressional Budget Office, "Estimates of Federal Tax Liabilities for Individuals and Families, by Income Category and Family Type," memorandum, May 1998, tables 8 and 13.

TABLE 7-6
Social Insurance Tax Rate and Maximum Taxable Earnings, Employed and Self-Employed People, 1937–2005[a]

Year	Employee tax rate[b] (percent)	Self-employed tax rate (percent)	Maximum taxable earnings[c] (dollars)
1937–49	1.0	. . .	3,000
1950	1.5	. . .	3,000
1951	1.5	2.25	3,600
1954	2.0	3.0	3,600
1957	2.25	3.375	4,200
1960	3.0	4.5	4,800
1962	3.125	4.7	4,800
1963	3.625	5.4	4,800
1966	4.2	6.15	6,600
1967	4.4	6.4	6,600
1969	4.8	6.9	7,800
1971	5.2	7.5	7,800
1973	5.85	8.0	10,800
1978	6.05	8.1	17,700
1979	6.13	8.1	22,900
1981	6.65	9.3	29,700
1982	6.7	9.35	32,400
1984	7.0	14.0	37,800
1985	7.05	14.1	39,600
1986	7.15	14.3	42,000
1988	7.51	15.02	45,000
1990	7.65	15.3	51,300
2005	7.65	15.3	90,000

Source: Social Security Administration, *Social Security Bulletin: Annual Statistical Supplement: 2005,* table 2.A3, p. 99.
a. This table only includes the years in which the rates were changed (except for 2005).
b. The same percentage is paid by the employer.
c. From 1966, when Medicare was first implemented, until 1990, taxable earnings for the hospital insurance contribution were the same as the earnings base for Social Security. During 1991–93, maximum taxable earnings were higher for the hospital insurance contribution than for Social Security. Since 1994 the hospital insurance tax has been levied on all earnings, while Social Security has been capped at the amounts shown in this column.

measures to sustain the Social Security and Medicare trust funds. If this resistance persists, social insurance taxes will account for a declining share of future federal revenues, in contrast to the period before the 1990s, when these taxes provided a rising share.

Social insurance taxes are earmarked to particular uses; they do not finance the general expenses of government. However, the government borrows the balances in the Social Security trust funds (and in other trust funds), paying prevailing interest rates and using the money to finance other expenditures. Earmarking decreases the portion of revenues that

is available for the general purposes of government. These federal funds include a small amount of earmarked revenue, which is deposited into special funds. Federal fund revenues dropped steeply from almost 15 percent

TABLE 7-7
Federal Funds Receipts by Decade, 1960–2000, and 2006

Measure	1960	1970	1980	1990	2000	2006
Federal funds receipts as percent of						
GDP	14.6	14.1	12.9	11.1	13.7	11.6
total receipts	81.8	74.2	67.8	61.6	65.5	64.4
federal funds outlays	101.1	91.6	80.9	65.1	100.1	73.9
Net interest as percent of federal funds receipts[a]	8.6[b]	10.0	15.0	29.0	16.8	14.9
Gross interest on the public debt as percent of						
federal fund receipts	11.4[b]	13.5	21.3	41.6	27.3	26.7

Source: *Budget of the United States Government, Historical Tables, Fiscal Year 2008,* table 1.2, pp. 23–24, table 1.4, pp. 27–28, and table 3.2, pp. 53–70.

  a. Net interest is gross interest paid by the government minus the interest earned by trust funds and other federal entities.

  b. Data for 1962.

of GDP in 1960 to only 11 percent in 1990 (table 7-7). The tax increases of the 1990s boosted this percentage to 14 percent in 2000, but subsequent tax cuts lowered it to less than 12 percent in 2006. At the start of the new century, federal funds accounted for only 66 percent of total receipts, compared with 82 percent four decades earlier. Federal fund receipts financed all general outlays in 1960, but in 2006 they covered less than three-quarters of federal fund expenditures, with the remainder financed by borrowing. During the same period, net interest payments soared from less than 9 percent of general receipts to 15 percent. This share was even greater when computed in terms of gross interest, almost all of which is paid by the general fund.

When the deficit peaked at about $400 billion in 2004, general expenditures exceeded $1.7 trillion dollars a year, but general revenues were $600 billion less. This shortfall was greater than the consolidated budget deficit because a portion of the deficit was offset by trust fund surpluses that were almost $200 billion. In fact, if general revenue had been the same share of GDP in 2004 as it was 40 years earlier—before Medicaid, food stamps, Head Start, and other multibillion dollar programs financed by general funds were established—

the federal budget would have been balanced.

The sharply different financial condition of the general fund compared with trust funds has its roots in the American dislike of being taxed to pay for government. Historically, taxes have been somewhat more acceptable when the proceeds are earmarked for specific purposes such as highways, Social Security, or Medicare. Although opposition to general taxes certainly is not new—throughout most of U.S. history, major increases in these taxes occurred only in wartime—the deterioration in the general fund during the 1970s and 1980s suggests that enacting tax increases to pay for the expenses of government became more difficult during these decades. Factors that may have contributed to the erosion of general taxation include decreased confidence in government, protracted conflict between the president and Congress over tax policy, increased attentiveness of interest groups to revenue legislation, and indexation of individual income taxes.

Viewed in historical context, the 1990 and 1993 income tax increases were an anomaly. In neither case was the United States at war, nor was there a significant upswing in public approval of government performance. Despite this, Congress and the president boosted general revenues because of growing alarm over the size of the deficit. In both years, tax increases were not formulated in free-standing legislation but as part of a deficit-reducing reconciliation package negotiated by the president and congressional leaders. Moreover, most of the additional revenue came from high-income taxpayers. The vast majority of taxpayers were not affected by increases in marginal tax rates, the removal of the cap on the Medicare tax base, and the phase-out of certain exemptions and deductions. In fact, by the end of the 1990s, millions of low- and moderate-income households had lower effective income tax rates than they had at the start of the decade. By concentrating the tax increases on a sliver of taxpayers, Congress and the president defused political opposition.

The 1990 and 1993 measures improved the condition of the general fund, which received most of the new revenue. In a temporary reversal of budget trends, general revenues grew more rapidly during the 1990s than general outlays. These revenues were approximately $500 billion higher at the end of the decade than they had been at the start, but general outlays rose by less than $300 billion. Just as deterioration in general fund revenues led to the high-deficit era, the recovery in these revenues made it possible to incur budget surpluses. But tax cuts for the new century once again weakened the general fund, which reverted to trend and declined as a share of total revenue. With general fund receipts falling far short of general outlays, big deficits returned.

WHO PAYS FEDERAL TAXES?

In considering revenue legislation, Congress is not only concerned with the amount of money the government collects but also with the distribution of the tax burden among seg-

ments of the population. Calculating the incidence of federal taxes is a complex and controversial task—it entails assumptions about how taxes paid by others (such as the employers' share of social insurance taxes and corporate income taxes) affect particular income earners, such as workers and shareholders. It stirs disputes about the definition of income and requires that the impact of the many preferences and special provisions in the tax code be measured.

The nominal income tax rate American taxpayers use in preparing their returns is not an accurate measure of actual tax burdens. These rates do not indicate how preferences and breaks reduce taxable income or the taxes actually paid. The two principal measures used in calculating actual tax burdens are taxes as a percentage of adjusted gross income and the effective tax rate. The former covers only income that is subject to taxation; the latter is a broader measure that covers all cash income but excludes noncash income such as in-kind benefits from government and health care premiums paid by employers. The effective tax rate is calculated by dividing total cash income into the amount of taxes paid. For example, a person making $100,000 a year who pays $10,000 in federal income taxes has an effective tax rate of 10 percent. The effective tax rate is negative when taxpayers receive refunds from the government in excess of the taxes they paid.

Table 7-8 shows that the individual income tax is highly progressive. At all income levels, those who earn more pay a higher percentage of their income in taxes than those who earn less. Moreover, the income tax became more progressive during the 1990s and continued to be so after the large Bush tax cuts in 2001 and 2003. In the lowest income level, taxpayers had a 0 percent share of individual income tax liability in 1980 but a –3 percent share in

TABLE 7-8
Shares of Income and Tax Liability, and Effective Tax Rates by Income Quintiles, 1980, 1990, 2000, and 2004[a]

Percent

Income group	Share of pretax income (in 2004 dollars)				Share of individual income tax liabilities				Share of social insurance taxes			
	1980	1990	2000	2004	1980	1990	2000	2004	1980	1990	2000	2004
Lowest quintile	3	3	3	3	0	0	−2	−3	4	4	4	4
Second quintile	7	7	7	7	4	3	1	−1	12	11	10	10
Middle quintile	11	11	11	12	11	9	6	5	20	18	16	16
Fourth quintile	21	20	20	20	20	18	14	14	27	27	26	25
Highest quintile	57	61	61	60	65	70	81	85	37	41	43	44
Top 10 percent	39	42	45	42	48	54	68	71	19	22	26	26
Top 5 percent	25	29	33	30	35	42	56	58	9	12	15	15
Top 1 percent	10	14	20	15	17	24	37	37	1	2	4	4

Source: Congressional Budget Office, *Historical Effective Federal Tax Rates: 1979 to 2004*, December 2006, tables 1A and 1B in accompanying supplemental spreadsheet file.

a. The table is based on a comprehensive measure of income that includes all cash income, both taxable and tax-exempt, as well as imputed income from taxes paid by businesses and in-kind income from governmental and nongovernmental sources such as Medicare, Medicaid, and employer-paid health insurance premiums. Sum of quintiles may be slightly less or more than 100 percent due to rounding errors.

2004. At the other end of the income spectrum, the top 5 percent of income earners had a 35 percent share of individual income tax liability in 1980 and 58 percent share in 2004.

The steep progressivity of the income tax has had a great deal to do with the revenue surge experienced by the government during the 1990s. As noted earlier in this chapter, the highest marginal tax rate was increased during this decade from 28 percent to 39.6 percent. During this period, upper-income earners gained ground, earning a higher share of national income, while low-income earners lost ground. In effect, the government muddled through to a policy in which the winners were more heavily taxed on their gains while the losers were taxed less. Arguably, this was a fortuitous combination of good economic and social policy, for it allowed markets to function efficiently and allowed for some redistribution of income. It also suggests, however, that the boom in federal revenues

depends upon sustained financial gains by upper-income taxpayers.

The income data on which table 7-8 is based is a comprehensive measure of relative tax burdens because it includes, as the note to the table indicates, types of income that are not subject to taxation. Table 7-9, which shows effective tax rates, also is based on a comprehensive measure of income. Social insurance taxes are inherently nonprogressive because they are levied at a flat rate and the Social Security portion is imposed only up to the maximum earnings listed in table 7-6. Middle-income taxpayers have a higher effective social insurance tax rate than do individuals and families in the highest income quintile. But in considering the overall progressivity of the Social Security system, it is appropriate to take into account the benefits government pays out. Social Security replaces a higher percentage of the lifetime earnings of low-income workers. The more one makes, the lower the

TABLE 7-9
Effective Tax Rates by Income Quintiles, 1980, 1990, 2000, and 2004[a]

Percent

Income group	Effective individual income tax rates				Effective social insurance tax rates				Total effective federal tax rates			
	1980	1990	2000	2004	1980	1990	2000	2004	1980	1990	2000	2004
Lowest quintile	0	−2	−8	−10	7	9	11	10	9	9	5	2
Second quintile	5	4	1	−2	9	11	11	11	16	17	14	10
Middle quintile	9	7	5	3	10	12	12	11	20	20	18	15
Fourth quintile	11	9	8	5	9	12	12	11	22	22	21	18
Highest quintile	17	15	19	15	6	7	7	7	26	25	29	26
Top 10 percent	18	17	22	18	4	6	5	5	28	26	31	28
Top 5 percent	20	18	24	20	3	4	4	4	29	26	32	29
Top 1 percent	21	21	26	21	1	2	2	2	32	28	34	32

Source: Congressional Budget Office, *Historical Effective Federal Tax Rates: 1979 to 2004,* December 2006, table 2A in accompanying supplemental spreadsheet file.

a. The table is based on a comprehensive measure of income that includes all cash income, both taxable and tax-exempt, as well as imputed income from taxes paid by businesses and in-kind income from governmental and nongovernmental sources such as Medicare, Medicaid, and employer-paid health insurance premiums. The total effective tax rate includes the imputed share of corporate income and excise taxes, as well as the employers' share of social insurance taxes.

percentage one gets back from Social Security. Moreover, the earned income tax credit, which was significantly expanded during the 1990s, compensates low-income earners for all or a portion of their social insurance taxes.

Even with social insurance and other taxes factored in, the total effective tax rate (which includes the impact of excise and corporate income taxes on each cohort of taxpayers) is higher for each income class than for the next lower class. Low-income earners bear a heavier burden in excise taxes but a much lower one in individual income taxes. The total effective tax rate on individuals and families with cash income in the highest income quintile is almost double the rate on those in the middle income quintile.

The progressivity of the tax system pertains to vertical equity—the taxes paid by people who differ in the amounts they earn. Economists are also concerned with horizontal equity—the taxes people earning the same

amount pay. The myriad preferences and breaks in the tax code impair horizontal equity, as they are not evenly distributed among taxpayers or among those with similar incomes. Consider two families, each earning $100,000 a year: one owns a home, the other rents; one has capital gains, the other does not; one has a pension fund, the other does not. In these and numerous other ways, the two taxpayers are differentiated in the income taxes they pay. One family might have a $15,000 tax bill; the other might pay only $5,000. Tax expenditures are the great unequalizer of the federal tax system, for they are not evenly distributed across or within income ranks. To ameliorate some of the inequity, Congress established an Alternative Minimum Tax (AMT) that requires taxpayers who benefit from certain preferences to pay more taxes than would be required by the regular tax system. However, the AMT has become a huge headache for politicians and taxpayers and is likely to be revised significantly while this book is still in print.

The AMT was enacted in 1969 to deter wealthy persons from sheltering their income from taxes. It requires certain taxpayers (typically those who itemize deductions) to calculate their tax liability twice, first through the regular income tax schedules filed by millions of Americans each year, then through an alternative schedule that adds back various exclusions and deductions. The amount owed in taxes is the higher of the two amounts. The AMT has only two tax brackets, 26 and 28 percent, but these often leave many taxpayers with higher liabilities than they owe under the regular system. The reason for this is that the amounts deducted due to certain popular tax breaks, such as deductions for dependents and state and local taxes, are added back in when calculating the AMT.

For decades the AMT occasioned little notice. Few Americans were subjected to it, and most did not even bother to calculate their AMT liability. In recent years, however, the AMT has affected a rapidly rising number of taxpayers. According to some estimates, more than 20 million households will be subject to the AMT by 2010. The main reason for this projected rise is that the AMT is not indexed for inflation. To make matters worse, most of those newly affected by the AMT are middle-income earners. Very affluent Americans generally are not affected because they already pay taxes above the amounts that the AMT would require.

Why doesn't Congress simply repeal the AMT? The straightforward answer is that as more Americans are covered by it, the AMT generates much more tax revenue for the government. By some calculations, if current laws remain in place, it will not be long before the AMT will produce more revenue than the regular income tax. Instead of repealing the AMT, Congress has annually adjusted some of its features to reduce the number of taxpayers affected by it. A longer-term solution would require simplification of the tax code by eliminating many of the breaks that are now excluded from the regular tax schedules but included in the AMT.

USER CHARGES

The federal government collects more than $240 billion a year in user charges. These charges differ from taxes in that they are levied on recipients of particular benefits or services, or on activities that the government regulates. The government, in the exercise of its sovereign powers, collects taxes; it collects user fees in carrying out business-type activities. In contrast to taxes, which are accounted for as budget receipts, most user fees are budgeted as offsetting collections.

CBO has identified four types of user charges. The largest category consists of fees individuals or businesses pay for goods and services the government provides. These typically resemble business transactions in that the payer voluntarily obtains the good and services. These fees include the premiums paid for participating in the Medicare part B program, purchases of postal services, and charges for using federal parks.

The second category consists of charges paid for activities the government regulates. These transactions are partly voluntary because they can be avoided by not engaging in the regulated activities. They include copyright and patent fees, and licenses required as a condition for engaging in certain activities.

Third, certain taxes are levied on beneficiaries of federally provided goods and services. But unlike most user fees, they generally are budgeted as tax receipts, not as offsetting collections. Benefit charges include taxes on airline tickets and on gasoline.

Finally, liability-based charges are imposed on various activities to compensate for damage to the environment or injury to those affected by the activities. These charges usually are earmarked to trust funds set up to remedy the harm or compensate those injured by it. Taxes on coal mining compensate miners afflicted with black lung disease (or their survivors); taxes on vaccines compensate those injured by measles shots or other prescribed vaccinations; and taxes on crude oil finance the cleanup of oil spills and provide compensation for damages resulting from them.

Since the mid-1980s, Congress and the president have viewed user charges as a means of generating additional revenue. Before then, the prevailing policy was to charge beneficiaries the cost of providing goods or services. A 1952 statute expressed the sense of Congress that benefits and services provided by federal agencies "shall be self-sustaining to the full extent possible." But the law also provided that fees should be fair and equitable and should take into account the public interest. The implementing guidelines issued by OMB provided for user charges to be imposed only for special benefits available to identifiable recipients.

The Consolidated Omnibus Budget Reconciliation Act of 1985 expanded user fees to cover not only the cost of providing services but also some or all of the federal agency's operating expenses. For example, the law directed the Nuclear Regulatory Commission to recover one-third of its annual operating expenses; the 1990 reconciliation legislation raised the target to 100 percent. Other agencies that have been directed to recover all or a portion of operating costs include the Customs Service, the Patent and Trademark Office, and the Food and Drug Administration.

Efforts to curtail the budget deficit through budget enforcement rules have stimulated increases in user charges. The rules distinguish between discretionary and mandatory user fees. The former are authorized and made available in appropriations acts and are scored as offsetting collections. They enable Congress to make an equivalent amount of additional appropriations. Mandatory fees authorized in substantive legislation, however, do not affect the amount that may be appropriated. This distinction gives the president and Congress a strong incentive to structure user fees so that they are classified as discretionary. Some groups complain that various user fees have been set above the amounts required to recover costs and that the excess revenue has been spent on other federal programs.

OFFSETTING COLLECTIONS

Offsetting collections reduce budget authority or outlays by an equivalent amount. For example, $50 million of offsetting collections credited to an account reduce budget outlays in that account by $50 million. Most user charges are scored as offsetting collections, as are income from the sale of assets, interest earned by federal entities, and certain flows of money between federal accounts or funds.

When is a receipt budgeted as revenue and when is it accounted for as an offsetting collection? The basic rule, laid down by the President's Commission on Budget Concepts in 1967, is that activities "essentially governmental in character, involving regulation or compulsion, should be reported as receipts," but that business or market-oriented activities should be offset against expenditures. This is not a clear-cut distinction, as evidenced by the manner in which Medicare premiums are budgeted. Until 1983 these premiums were recorded as receipts; since then they have been budgeted as offsetting collections. However, these premiums, which amount to more than

$55 billion a year, are still recorded as receipts in the national income and product accounts.

Classifying revenue as an offsetting collection rather than as a receipt does not affect the size of the deficit or surplus because it reduces total revenue and spending by equal amounts. But it can affect the consideration of legislation under the budget enforcement rules.

CONCLUSION

Congress processes revenue legislation in much the same manner as it did 200 years ago. These measures still originate in the House, and the House Ways and Means and Senate Finance Committees still have virtually exclusive jurisdiction. But there have been important changes—some impelled by the proliferation of budget rules, some by the growth of earmarked and trust fund revenues. Revenue legislation is now formulated in the context of a budget resolution and often is enacted in a reconciliation bill. Tax measures may abide by budget rules that limit the amount of revenue loss enacted. Behavioral differences between the House and Senate have been narrowed; nowadays, the Senate is usually the more constrained chamber in considering tax legislation.

Additional changes in the revenue process are likely in the years ahead, especially as Congress confronts the budgetary impact of an aging population. Despite the urgings of economists and others who argue that stable, predictable tax policy contributes to national efficiency, revenue legislation will continue to be active on the congressional agenda. Future legislation will change the amounts the government collects and redistribute the tax burden. Whether the budget is in surplus or deficit, Congress will take up proposals to cut or raise taxes. And whether Democrats or Republicans control the House and Senate, Congress will produce legislation cutting taxes for some groups. Tax rates versus tax breaks will continue to be a point of contention, and the more Congress legislates on this subject, the more complex the tax code will become. Additional procedural changes, such as a restoration of the statutory PAYGO rule or the use of dynamic revenue scoring, may be considered.

If the past is any guide, tax legislation will be cyclical: rates will be raised, then reduced, and then raised again. There is no such thing as equilibrium in taxes; there is only the legislative impulse to tinker with the tax code.

8

Authorizing Legislation

Congress has two distinct processes for establishing and funding federal programs and agencies. One leads to the enactment of *authorizing legislation,* which establishes the legal basis for the operation of federal agencies and programs. The other culminates in the *appropriation of money,* which enables agencies to incur obligations and expenditures. These steps are usually taken in separate measures, but sometimes they are combined in direct spending legislation. The distinct actions are prescribed by House and Senate rules, which bar unauthorized appropriations and the insertion of legislation into appropriation bills. Although the rules are sometimes waived or disregarded and allow for certain exceptions, they define the boundaries of authorizing legislation and appropriation measures.

The distinction between the two types of measures was incorporated into House rules in the 1830s and into Senate rules two decades later; it is now codified as House Rule XXI and Senate Rule XVI. However, the practice predates the establishment of Congress and was probably adapted from the British Parliament. The First Congress, which convened in 1789, took it for granted that substantive legislation should not be combined with appropriations. It thus passed one law establishing the War Department and another law appropriating funds to this department and other newly established agencies. The separation of authorizations and appropriations was placed in the rules decades later, in response

▼

BOX 8-1
Democrats versus Republicans: Fighting over Legislation in Appropriations Bills

The prohibition against legislation in appropriations is not strictly enforced by Congress, which often inserts relatively minor legislation in appropriations bills. During the 1990s, however, the volume and significance of such legislation increased to the point where entire laws were sometimes enacted in appropriations acts.

Senate Republicans removed restrictions to legislation in appropriations bills in 1995 by overturning a parliamentary ruling on Rule XVI. Four years later, the roles were reversed, and Republicans voted to restore the bar against legislation in appropriations bills, while Democrats voted to permit legislation. Both times the parties were motivated by short-term considerations, but their actions had long-term consequences for Congress.

Round One: Republicans Disable Rule XVI
During Senate consideration of a supplemental appropriations bill on March 16, 1995, Senator Kay Bailey Hutchison (R-Texas) offered an amendment to nullify certain court orders concerning the Endangered Species Act and to prohibit the Fish and Wildlife Service from using appropriated funds to determine that particular species were endangered. Senator Harry Reid (D-Nev.) raised a point of order that the amendment was legislation in an appropriations act, and the chair sustained the point of order. Senator Hutchison appealed this ruling, and the ruling was rejected 42-57. Following this vote, the Senate parliamentarian let it be known that he would no longer advise the Senate to enforce Rule XVI.

Round Two: Democrats Use Appropriations Bills to Force Action on Legislation
With Rule XVI disabled, there was no impediment in the Senate to inserting legislation in appropriations bills. Senate Democrats, led by Minority Leader Tom Daschle (D-S.Dak.), realized that they now had a clear path to wrest control of the legislative calendar from Republicans. By long-standing tradition, the majority leader decides which bills the Senate should consider. This role enables the majority party to block legislation the minority wants. Senator Trent Lott (R-Miss.) actively deployed this power when he became majority leader in 1996. In response, his Democratic counterpart, Senator Daschle, boldly attached controversial legislation favored by his party but opposed by Republicans to pending appropriations bills. In one case, he added minimum wage legislation; in another, a bill regulating health care organizations. Rather than

continued

to the frequent insertion of riders and other legislative provisions in appropriation bills.

House Rule XXI provides that "an appropriation may not be reported in a general appropriation bill . . . for an expenditure not previously authorized by law." It also provides that "a provision changing existing law may not be reported in a general appropriation bill. . . ."

Note that these restrictions apply only to general appropriations bills. Through House precedents, a continuing resolution (providing stopgap funding for agencies that have not yet received regular appropriations) is not a general appropriation bill. Hence it may contain both unauthorized appropriations and substantive legislation.

BOX 8-1
Continued

take up these and other measures on Democratic terms, Senator Lott pulled various appropriations bills from the Senate floor, delaying their passage and risking a government shutdown. The impasse ended, not surprisingly, with Republicans agreeing to take up Democrat-supported measures and Democrats withdrawing the legislation they had attached to appropriations bills.

Round Three: Republicans Restore Rule XVI
With the Democrats gaining the upper hand despite their minority status, Senator Lott reversed course in July 1999, offering a motion to restore Rule XVI. During the debate, he vented his frustration on how action on appropriations had been stymied:

> "Every Senator dumps his out basket on the floor of the Senate with every amendment he or she has ever dreamed of . . . [and] whole bills or major amendments are offered on the floor of the Senate to appropriations bills . . . where the committees have not been allowed to act, where the committee chairman has not had any input. It is time to bring this process under control."

Senator Daniel Moynihan (D-N.Y.), nearing the end of an illustrious 24-year career in the Senate, bemoaned that when Rule XVI was vitiated "a century or more of fixed senatorial practice crashed and burned and has been burning all around us ever since. Our government became incomprehensible. . . . The authorizing committees are gradually being marginalized and have no role." When debate ended, the Senate by a 53-45 party-line vote restored Rule XVI. However, too much had changed since 1995 for the Senate to fully restore the old practice.

Rule XVI only bars legislation in the form of Senate amendments to appropriations bills. From the time this rule was devised more than a century ago until the late 1990s, these "amendments" included both changes made by the Senate Appropriations Committee to House-passed spending bills and floor amendments. The reason, explained in the next chapter, is that the House traditionally acts on appropriations bills first, and the Senate does not produce its own bill but merely amends the House-passed version. If the Senate Appropriations Committee reports a bill before the House has completed action, as has sometimes been the case since the late 1990s, it does so in the form of an original bill, not an amendment. The net effect is that the Rule XVI prohibition does not apply to legislation added by the Senate Appropriations Committee to any spending bill initiated by the committee. The rule continues to apply, however, to floor amendments.

Senate Rule XVI provides that the "Committee on Appropriations shall not report an appropriation bill . . . proposing new or general legislation." It also bars appropriations that are not "made to carry out the provisions of some existing law. . . ." But the Senate rule is not as strictly enforced as the House one. The Senate allows more exceptions and has procedures that enable it to insert legislation in appropriation bills. Box 8-1 highlights some Senate disputes on legislating in appropriations bills during the 1990s.

Nineteenth-century debates in the House and Senate indicate two reasons for separating authorizations and appropriations. One was a concern that conflict over legislation would impede the flow of funds to federal agencies. The other was that the urgency of funding ongoing agencies would impel Congress to enact ill-considered legislation in appropriations bills. Both concerns have contemporary relevance for Congress. Conflict over legislation, not disputes over the amount that should be made available, is the primary cause of protracted delay in enacting appropriations. Moreover, many legislative provisions that probably would not be enacted on their own are enacted in appropriations bills.

TYPES OF AUTHORIZING LEGISLATION

Authorizations represent the exercise of the legislative power accorded to Congress by the Constitution. (At one time, what is now referred to as authorizing legislation was referred to simply as legislation.) In legislating, Congress can place just about any kind of provision in an authorization. It can prescribe what an agency must or may not do in carrying out assigned responsibilities. It can spell out the agency's organizational structure and its operating procedures. It can grant an agency broad authority or restrict its operating freedom by legislating in great detail. Authorizing measures do not have a uniform structure—some are only one or two pages long, a few run to hundreds of pages. Some are divided into titles, others into chapters; most are subdivided into sections. Some enable agencies to obligate money; most do not.

The broad scope and variety of authorizing measures spawn confusion about them. The term authorization is part of the problem, for it has several meanings in federal budgeting. An authorization law looks in two directions: inward to Congress, where it serves as a license for the House and Senate to consider appropriations, and outward to federal agencies, where it licenses them to operate. To sort out

the different types of measures and their functions, it is necessary to distinguish between discretionary authorizations and direct spending, as well as between substantive legislation and the authorization of appropriations. The distinctions affect both the legal status of authorizing legislation and the manner in which Congress handles it.

Discretionary Authorizations and Direct Spending Legislation

Budget rules distinguish between discretionary authorizations, which do not provide budget resources, and direct spending legislation, which provides budgetary resources or enables the affected agency to obligate funds. Figure 8-1 diagrams the contents of both types of legislation, which contain substantive provisions specifying such matters as the organization and duties of the agency. However, they differ in their relationship to appropriations. Discretionary authorizations provide authority to appropriate; direct spending provides authority to obligate. Discretionary authorizations may be spent only to the extent provided in appropriations acts; direct spending may be spent as provided in authorizing legislation.

This difference can be further clarified by referring to table 8-1, which shows the sequence of four key steps in federal budgeting: authorizations, appropriations, obligations, and outlays. The second and third steps are reversed in the two types of measures: in discretionary spending, appropriations precede obligations; in direct spending, authorizations precede obligations. The action that immediately precedes obligations defines the type of measure. Although this distinction might appear to be merely a technical matter, it has important political and legislative consequences. Enabling federal agencies to incur obligations in advance of appropriations shifts

FIGURE 8-1
Authorizing Legislation

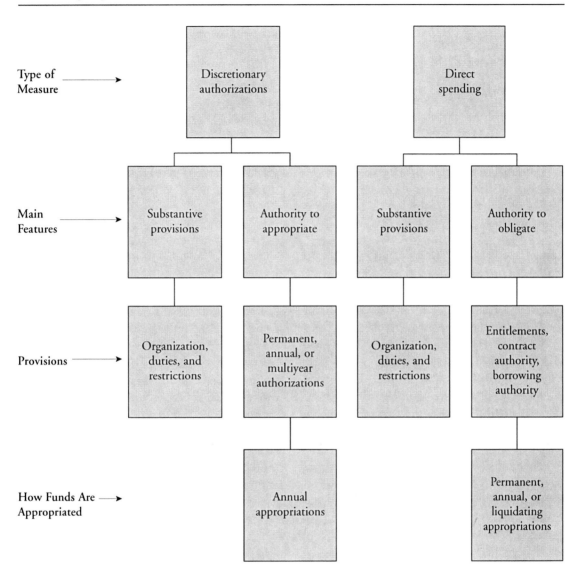

Type of Measure →

Main Features →

Provisions →

How Funds Are → Appropriated

Discretionary authorizations

Direct spending

Substantive provisions

Authority to appropriate

Substantive provisions

Authority to obligate

Organization, duties, and restrictions

Permanent, annual, or multiyear authorizations

Organization, duties, and restrictions

Entitlements, contract authority, borrowing authority

Annual appropriations

Permanent, annual, or liquidating appropriations

legislative power from the appropriations committees to authorizing committees. The appropriations committees have the upper hand in controlling discretionary spending; authorizing committees have the lead role in determining the amount of direct spending.

Throughout this book, the term *authorizing legislation* generally refers to discretionary programs. Although direct spending is also provided in authorizing legislation, the differences in budget rules and legislative procedures dictate that it be labeled differently.

TABLE 8-1
Comparison of Sequence for Discretionary and Direct Spending

Discretionary	Direct
1. Authorization	1. Authorization
2. Appropriation	2. Obligation
3. Obligation	3. Appropriation
4. Outlay	4. Outlay

Substantive Legislation and Authorization of Appropriations

Authorizing legislation typically has two main components, corresponding to the characteristics mentioned earlier. Looking outward to federal agencies, it contains substantive provisions that prescribe the terms and conditions under which they operate. Looking inward to Congress, it authorizes the making of appropriations. The two components are usually combined in the same measure, as in the legislation shown in exhibit 8-1, which established the National Integrated Drought Information System and authorized appropriations for that program. The "authorized to be appropriated" language is the formula used to indicate that the rule requiring authorization before appropriation has been satisfied. For reasons explained below, while Congress sometimes appropriates funds to agencies whose "authorized to be appropriated" language has expired, it does not appropriate funds for programs lacking substantive provisions.

Temporary and Permanent Authorizations

Authorizing legislation—both the substantive provisions and "authorized to be appropriated" language—is permanent unless the law expressly limits its duration. The permanent provisions continue in effect until they are repealed or amended by new authorizing legislation. (However, an appropriations act and

any substantive legislation in it are effective for only a single fiscal year unless the act expressly provides a longer period of effectiveness.) In many areas of federal activity, the permanence of authorizing law eliminates the need for new legislation. Of course, even when authorizations are permanent, Congress has the option of writing new law on the subject.

Although the substantive provisions are almost always permanent, the "authorized to be appropriated" language often pertains to a specific period. These authorizations of appropriations may be permanent, annual, or multiyear (examples of these three types of authorizations are shown in exhibit 8-2). *Permanent authorizations* do not mention specific years and continue in effect until Congress changes them. These authorizations typically are for "such sums as may be necessary"; they do not mention amounts of money. An agency having a permanent authorization only needs to obtain annual appropriations to continue in operation. *Annual authorizations* are for a single fiscal year and usually for a fixed amount of money. Under House and Senate rules, these authorizations have to be renewed every year in order for appropriations to be made. All Congress is required to do is extend the "authorized to be appropriated" provision for another fiscal year. In practice, however, Congress often uses the reauthorization to legislate changes in substantive law. *Multiyear authorizations* are typically in effect for two to five years and have to be renewed when they expire. These provisions often authorize escalating amounts for each fiscal year.

Until the 1960s, virtually all authorizations of appropriations were permanent. But most programs established over the past four decades have had annual or multiyear authorizations, and many older programs have been converted from permanent to temporary status. It is important to keep in mind that even

▶ **EXHIBIT 8-1**
Basic Features of Authorization Acts

ESTABLISHMENT OF AGENCY OR PROGRAM

SEC. 3. NIDIS PROGRAM
(a) IN GENERAL.—The Under Secretary, through the National Weather Service and other appropriate weather and climate programs in the National Oceanic and Atmospheric Administration, shall establish a National Integrated Drought Information System.

DUTIES AND FUNCTIONS

(b) SYSTEM FUNCTIONS.—The National Integrated Drought Information System shall
   (1) provide an effective drought early warning system . . . ,
   (2) coordinate, and integrate as practicable, Federal research in support of a drought early warning system; and
   (3) build upon existing forecasting and assessment programs and partnerships.

AUTHORIZATION OF APPROPRIATIONS

SEC. 4. AUTHORIZATION OF APPROPRIATIONS.—
There are authorized to be appropriated to carry out this Act—
   (1) $11,000,000 for fiscal year 2007;
   (2) $12,000,000 for fiscal year 2008;
   (3) $13,000,000 for fiscal year 2009;
   (4) $14,000,000 for fiscal year 2010;
   (5) $15,000,000 for fiscal year 2011; and
   (6) $16,000,000 for fiscal year 2012.

Source: *National Integrated Drought Information System Act of 2006*, P.L. 109-430, December 20, 2006.

(a) These excerpts illustrate the basic elements of authorizations: establishment of federal agencies or programs, specification of the agency's duties and functions (including any restrictions), and authorization of appropriations. The first two of these are referred to in the text as substantive legislation.

(b) Authorizing legislation does not always prescribe how an agency should be organized, but the trend has been to specify major organizational units in law.

(c) There has also been a trend to spell out the agency's functions in detail. In this example, the specification of "system functions" is relatively brief compared to many other authorizations.

(d) The office was given temporary (six-year) authorizations of fixed amounts. Authorizations typically are made for multiyear periods with fixed amounts, which often increase over the period of authorization. In some instances, authorizations are for "such sums as may be necessary."

▶ **EXHIBIT 8-2**
Examples of Duration of Authorization to Appropriate

PERMANENT

SEC. 4. AUTHORIZATIONS OF APPROPRIATIONS.—There are authorized to be appropriated such sums as may be necessary to carry out this Act.

ANNUAL

SEC. 101. ARMY.—Funds are hereby authorized to be appropriated for fiscal year 2007 for procurement for the Army as follows:

(1) For aircraft, $3,451,429,000.
(2) For missiles, $1,328,859,000.
(3) For weapons and tracked combat vehicles, $2,278,604,000.
(4) For ammunition, $1,984,325,000.
(5) For other procurement, $7,687,502,000.
(6) For National Guard Equipment, $318,000,000.

MULTIYEAR

(d) Authorization of Appropriations.—Section 379B of the Public Health Service Act (42 U.S.C. 274m) is amended to read as follows:
"SEC. 379B. AUTHORIZATION OF APPROPRIATIONS.
For the purpose of carrying out this part, there are authorized to be appropriated $34,000,000 for fiscal year 2006 and $38,000,000 for each of fiscal years 2007 through 2010."

Sources: *Buffalo Soldiers Commemoration Act of 2005*, P.L. 109-152, December 30, 2005 (permanent authorization); *John Warner National Defense Authorization Act for Fiscal Year 2007*, P.L. 109-364, October 17, 2006 (annual authorization); and *Stem Cell Therapeutic and Research Act of 2005*, P.L. 109-129, December 20, 2005 (multiyear authorization).

(a) The three examples shown here differ in the period covered by the authorization of appropriations. The first example is of a permanent authorization. It has no time limit, and under the rules, Congress can make annual appropriations without any new authorizing legislation. Permanent authorizations usually are indefinite (no dollar limit) and authorize "such sums as may be necessary."

(b) Annual authorizations must be renewed each year, unless Congress terminates the program or makes unauthorized appropriations. Annual authorizations usually authorize definite amounts for the fiscal year. A single amount may be authorized, or, as shown here, the authorizations may be broken down by program components. In annually reauthorized programs, there is usually little difference between the authorized and appropriated amounts.

(c) Multiyear authorizations, for two or more years, often specify escalating amounts with higher amounts authorized for the next year than for the prior year. In these cases, the subsequent appropriation is often much lower than the authorization. Oftentimes, authorizations of appropriations take the form of an amendment to an underlying law, as shown here.

when a program or agency is put on temporary authorization, substantive law governing its operations continues to be permanent.

There are two main reasons for the trend toward temporary authorization, which correspond to the two functions of authorizing legislation. First, a temporary authorization gives Congress and its authorizing committees frequent opportunities to review agency activities and to make changes as they deem appropriate. Congress strengthens its capacity to oversee and control when it lacks confidence in federal agencies, as happened after the Watergate scandal, when Congress shifted the Justice Department and intelligence agencies to temporary authorization. Second, congressional committees seek temporary authorizations to increase their legislative influence, especially with respect to the amounts appropriated to federal agencies. Some temporary authorizations itemize the amounts for particular projects and activities. Notice, for example, the breakdown of authorizations for Cooperative Threat Reduction programs of the Defense Department in exhibit 8-4. Although the amount authorized does not determine the amount appropriated—under the rules, the appropriation can be equal to or less than the authorization—there is often a close correspondence between the two. This is particularly so in annually authorized programs, where the appropriation typically exceeds 90 percent of the authorized level. Inasmuch as both the annual authorization and the annual appropriation are enacted in the same session and under the same political and budgetary conditions, the authorization strongly influences the subsequent appropriation. The annual defense authorization and appropriation acts exemplify this pattern.

The link tends to be considerably weaker in multiyear authorizations because these typically specify escalating amounts for each fiscal year. Since appropriations are made one year at a time, there is often a widening gap between the authorized and appropriated resources. Moreover, committees that specialize in multiyear authorizations, such as the House Committee on Transportation and Infrastructure, tend to be strong advocates for their programs, leading them to give more weight to program needs than to budget conditions. The gap between authorized and appropriated levels spurs interest groups to demand full funding for their programs, by which they mean that Congress should appropriate the amounts promised in authorizations.

Congress often sets aside (or ignores) its rules and makes unauthorized appropriations for programs whose "authorized to be appropriated" language has expired. As mentioned earlier, an appropriation in excess of the authorized amount is also deemed to be unauthorized. In fact, unauthorized appropriations have become commonplace. More than 160 programs whose authorization had expired, some more than a decade earlier, received appropriations for fiscal year 2005 (the largest such programs are listed in table 8-2). Congress made $170 billion in unauthorized appropriations for that year for nondefense discretionary programs; this amounted to almost 40 percent of all nondefense discretionary spending. Since the early 1990s, national defense has been the only major area whose expiring authorizations have consistently been renewed year after year. In many other areas, Congress has skipped the authorization process and continued federal programs by providing them with annual funding. As the list in table 8-2 shows, some prominent programs have been continued despite their lack of a current authorization—including veterans' medical care, NASA space activities, the Department of Justice, and the Customs Service.

TABLE 8-2
Major Federal Programs with Expired Authorization of Appropriations, Fiscal Year 2005[a]

Billions of dollars

Program	Fiscal 2005 appropriation
Veterans' medical care	27.9
NASA	16.2
Housing assistance (Section 8)	14.9
Head Start	6.9
Diplomatic and consular services	5.9
Federal Bureau of Investigation	5.2
Immigration and Naturalization Service	5.1
Community Development Block Grants	4.7
Customs Service	4.7
Federal Prison System	4.6
Centers for Disease Control	4.5
Substance Abuse and Mental Health Administration	3.3
Indian Health Services	3.0
Low-Income Home Energy Assistance	2.2
International organizations	1.7
Superfund	1.3

Source: Congressional Budget Office, *Unauthorized Appropriations and Expiring Authorizations*, January 14, 2005.

a. This annual report, required by law, lists all programs that received appropriations for the current fiscal year, even though their authorizations had expired.

In most cases, unauthorized appropriations are fully available for obligation and expenditure. The main exception is when there is a statutory bar against the obligation or use of unauthorized funds, as exemplified by the middle entry in exhibit 8-3. When Congress appropriates money for programs whose "authorized to be appropriated" provision has expired, the funds are spent according to the permanent substantive laws in effect. Congress, however, rarely makes appropriations for programs that lack substantive legislation. Doing so would infringe on the authorization process and would leave the affected agency without statutory guidance on how the funds are to be spent.

AUTHORIZING LEGISLATION IN CONGRESS

There is no prescribed legislative path for authorizations. Some originate in the House, others in the Senate. Many are considered by only one committee in each chamber; some are jointly or sequentially referred to two or more committees.

Authorizing legislation defines the jurisdiction of most House and Senate committees. Most of the work of congressional committees involves their authorizing responsibilities; for most members of Congress, legislative influence derives from their service on these committees. Table 8-3 shows the authorizing committee jurisdiction of selected programs, and it indicates that the House and Senate do not have parallel authorizing committee structures. Moreover, authorizing committees differ greatly in legislative activity and output. Some have robust agendas and produce significant legislation each session; others are inactive and go through long spells without much legislative activity. The active committees tend to have jurisdiction over programs with temporary authorization or matters of current interest. The strength of committee leadership also makes a difference, as does the extent to which changes in budget policy that arise through the reconciliation process affect the matters in a committee's jurisdiction.

Three other factors affect authorizing activity in Congress. One is the extent to which the White House takes the lead in promoting new legislation; another is the extent to which funds are available to pay for new or expanded programs; and the third is the capacity of the House or Senate to pass legislation its committees produce. Authorizing activity has been relatively low since the 1980s, when President Reagan sought to curtail many domestic programs and chronic deficits ruled out major legislative initiatives. Nevertheless, some committees continue to generate streams of legislation.

▶ **EXHIBIT 8-3**
Examples of Reauthorization Requirements in Law

RESTRICTION ON APPROPRIATION

(b) No funds may be appropriated after December 31, 1960, to or for the use of any armed force of the United States for the procurement of aircraft, missiles, or naval vessels unless the appropriation of such funds has been authorized by legislation enacted after such date.

RESTRICTION ON OBLIGATION

(a)(1) Notwithstanding any provision of law enacted before the date of enactment of the State Department/USIA Authorization Act, Fiscal Year 1975, no money appropriated to the Department of State under any law shall be available for obligation or expenditure with respect to any fiscal year commencing on or after July 1, 1972—
(A) unless the appropriation thereof has been authorized by law enacted on or after February 7, 1972; or
(B) in excess of an amount prescribed by law enacted on or after such date.

RESTRICTION ON APPROPRIATION FOR UNAUTHORIZED PROJECT

Notwithstanding any other provisions of this Act—
(1) no amount appropriated pursuant to this Act may be used for any program deleted by Congress from requests as originally made to either the Committee on Commerce, Science, and Transportation of the Senate or the Committee on Science, Space, and Technology of the House of Representatives;
(2) no amount appropriated pursuant to this Act may be used for any program in excess of the amount actually authorized for that particular program by section 4 (a), (b), and (d). . . .

Sources: *Military Construction Authorization Act of 1959*, P.L. 86-149; *Department of State/USIA Authorization Act, Fiscal Year 1975*, P.L. 93-475; and *NASA Authorization Act, Fiscal Year 1992*, P.L. 102-195.

(a) The first of the three excerpts shown here was the genesis of annual authorization for the Defense Department. When the department was established, it had a permanent authorization. Annual authorization was initially applied to certain procurement expenditures; since then it has been extended to the entire department. Inasmuch as the bar is only against appropriations, the funds would be available for expenditure if appropriations were made for unauthorized programs.

(b) The second example is the provision of law that converted the State Department from permanent to temporary authorization. In this case, unauthorized appropriations may not be used because the bar is against obligation, unless the appropriation act expressly waives the prohibition.

(c) The final example is from an annual authorization act for the National Aeronautics and Space Administration. Once again, there is a bar against using unauthorized appropriations, but in this instance (unlike the previous example) it pertains only to that year's appropriations.

TABLE 8-3
House and Senate Authorizing Committee Jurisdictions for Selected Programs[a]

Program	House committee	Senate committee
Civil service	Oversight and Government Reform	Homeland Security and Governmental Affairs
Coast Guard	Transportation and Infrastructure	Commerce, Science, and Transportation
Highways	Transportation and Infrastructure	Commerce, Science, and Transportation
Medicaid	Energy and Commerce	Finance
Medicare–Part A	Ways and Means	Finance
Medicare–Part B	Energy and Commerce	Finance
NASA	Science and Technology	Commerce, Science, and Transportation
National Institutes of Health	Energy and Commerce	Health, Education, Labor, and Pensions
National parks	Natural Resources	Energy and Natural Resources
Private pensions	Education and Labor	Health, Education, Labor, and Pensions
Rural development	Agriculture	Agriculture, Nutrition, and Forestry
School lunch	Education and Labor	Agriculture, Nutrition, and Forestry
Social Security	Ways and Means	Finance
Veterans' pensions	Veterans' Affairs	Veterans' Affairs

Sources: House Rule X and Senate Rule XXV.

a. The authorizing jurisdictions of House and Senate committees are not parallel. Thus a House committee may be paired with a Senate committee on some matters but not on others. On major legislation, two or more House or Senate committees may claim jurisdiction. Since the House has more committees than the Senate, it has more overlapping jurisdictions. When two or more committees have jurisdiction over portions of the same bill, the measure may be assigned to them concurrently (multiple referral) or sequentially. In the case of sequential referral, after the first committee has completed its work, the remaining committees are usually given a deadline by which to report the bill.

The House and Senate Armed Services Committees produce annual authorizing legislation covering the Defense Department; the House Ways and Means Committee and the Senate Finance Committee (which have broad authorizing jurisdiction in addition to their responsibilities in tax policy) formulate important legislation concerning Medicare, other health programs, and trade.

Overall, however, there has been a steep decline in the volume of laws (most of which are authorizations) enacted by Congress. When Dwight Eisenhower was president in the 1950s, each two-year Congress produced as many as 1,000 public laws. Since the 1990s, Congress has averaged fewer than half as many. The factors accounting for this trend include conflict within Congress, differences between Capitol Hill and the White House, closer monitoring of congressional action by interest groups (which guard against legislation adverse to their interests), the tendency to consider legislation in terms of its budgetary impact, and the proclivity of Congress to package legislation into broad, program-oriented bills.

The trend has affected the way most authorizing committees work. In some sessions, much of the year's legislation is folded into an omnibus reconciliation or appropriations bill. The process feeds on itself—the more difficult it is to pass ordinary legislation, the more committee chairs and others in Congress seek a legislative vehicle, such as an omnibus bill, on which their stalled measure can ride to enactment. The upshot is a stunted authorizations process in which some bills make it through on their own, some are enacted as parts of other measures, and some do not get enacted.

THE RELATIONSHIP OF AUTHORIZATIONS AND APPROPRIATIONS

It is a basic rule of federal law that appropriated funds are to be spent according to the terms set in authorizing law. Appropriations determine the amounts available for expenditure; authorization acts determine how the money is spent. In practice, however, the relationship is not always clear-cut, and there may be considerable friction between the two types of congressional action. Some authorizations provide budget authority; most appropriations acts contain substantive law. Differences in the reports filed by the relevant authorizing and appropriations committees sometimes further complicate the relationship.

There has been intermittent conflict between the two sets of committees since the appropriations committees were established during the Civil War era. At times appropriators have been dominant, using their control of the purse to influence the course of legislation. At other times, authorizers have had the upper hand, using their much larger numbers to outvote the appropriations committees when their jurisdictions and interests clash. One of the purposes of the House and Senate rules is to diminish conflict by walling off the appropriations and authorizations processes from one another. Despite the rules, however, the committees often get in each other's way—the appropriations committees by inserting legislative provisions in spending bills, the authorizing committees by providing budget resources in legislation. Other factors have also altered the division of legislative work: extensive earmarking of funds, an increase in direct spending, and the insertion of appropriation-forcing language in authorizing legislation. Legislation in appropriations bills is discussed in the next chapter; other practices generating conflict between authorizations and appropri-

ations are considered in the remainder of this chapter.

Earmarks in Legislation and Reports

Authorizing legislation is as general or as detailed as Congress makes it. When it is general, as was once the usual practice, agencies have considerable discretion in spending appropriated funds. When authorizing legislation details exactly how agencies operate and funds are spent, however, the possibility of conflict with the preferences of the appropriations committees escalates. Since the 1970s, there has been a pronounced trend toward greater specificity in authorizing legislation, indicating specific amounts for particular projects or activities, as displayed in exhibit 8-4. Authorizing committees are not the only ones to earmark funds; the appropriations committees also specify how funds are to be spent. As chapter 9 shows, the appropriations committees extensively earmark funds and dictate other conditions in the reports that accompany bills.

Quite often, the details in authorizing legislation differ from those set forth in appropriations bills or reports. One frequent source of friction between the two sets of committees is the appropriation of funds for unauthorized projects or activities. In 1993, for example, fighting broke out into the open when the House Transportation Appropriations Subcommittee earmarked more than $300 million to 58 highway projects that had not been included in authorizing legislation passed by Congress two years earlier. This precipitated a bitter clash between the appropriations subcommittee and the Public Works and Transportation Committee and delayed enactment of the transportation appropriations bill for many months. This battle between authorizers

▶ EXHIBIT 8-4
Authorizations by Program

(a) Funding for Specific Purposes.—Of the $372,128,000 authorized to be appropriated to the Department of Defense for fiscal year 2007 in section 301(19) for Cooperative Threat Reduction programs, the following amounts may be obligated for the purposes specified:

(1) For strategic offensive arms elimination in Russia, $76,985,000.

(2) For nuclear weapons storage security in Russia, $87,100,000.

(3) For nuclear weapons transportation security in Russia, $33,000,000.

(4) For weapons of mass destruction proliferation prevention in the states of the former Soviet Union, $37,486,000.

(5) For biological weapons proliferation prevention in the former Soviet Union, $68,357,000.

(6) For chemical weapons destruction in Russia, $42,700,000.

(7) For defense and military contacts, $8,000,000.

(8) For activities designated as Other Assessments/Administrative Support, $18,500,000.

(b) Report on Obligation or Expenditure of Funds for Other Purposes.—No fiscal year 2007 Cooperative Threat Reduction funds may be obligated or expended for a purpose other than a purpose listed in paragraphs (1) through (8) of subsection (a) until 30 days after the date that the Secretary of Defense submits to Congress a report on the purpose for which the funds will be obligated or expended and the amount of funds to be obligated or expended. . . .

(c) Limited Authority to Vary Individual Amounts.—

(1) In general.—Subject to paragraphs (2) and (3), in any case in which the Secretary of Defense determines that it is necessary to do so in the national interest, the Secretary may obligate amounts appropriated for fiscal year 2007 for a purpose listed in any of the paragraphs in subsection (a) in excess of the specific amount authorized for that purpose. . . .

Source: *John Warner National Defense Authorization Act for Fiscal Year 2007*, P.L. 109-364, October 17, 2006, section 1302 ("Funding Allocations"), 120 Stat. 2431.

(a) Some authorizing measures, such as the one excerpted here, specify amounts for particular programs and activities. Specification by program or activity increases the likelihood of conflict between the authorizing and appropriations committees.

(b) Agencies often determine that it is necessary to shift funds from one program to another within an account; this action is known as a reprogramming. The appropriations committees routinely include restrictions on reprogramming in appropriations acts, but authorizing committees sometimes restrict the reprogramming of authorized amounts as well. Reprogramming is more fully discussed in chapter 10.

(c) In this example, the authorizing committee has sought to control agency actions by restricting the obligation and expenditure of appropriated funds above the specified authorization levels unless prior notification procedures are followed.

and appropriators is chronicled in box 8-2. It turned out to be only one round in an ongoing turf battle in Congress over who should control billions of dollars of transportation money. The next round was played out in 1997 and 1998, when Congress reauthorized highway programs, and is discussed in box 8-3. The conflict in the transportation area continued with the enactment of another major highway bill in 2005, the Safe, Accountable, Flexible, Efficient Transportation Equity Act.

Appropriation-Forcing Language

Discretionary authorizations do not enable agencies to incur obligations or spend money: the authorized funds are available only to the extent provided in appropriations acts. But authorizing committees sometimes expand their budgetary influence by inserting appropriation-forcing language in legislation. In some instances, the authorizing legislation stipulates that not less than a certain amount of appropriated funds shall be made available for a particular purpose. In others, it bars spending appropriated funds for activities that the appropriations committees favor unless a threshold amount is also appropriated for activities that the authorizing committees favor. The appropriations committees are not legally required to provide the threshold amount, but if they do not, funds appropriated for their preferred activities might become unavailable.

Dealing with Conflicts

Several principles guide the resolution of conflicts between authorizations and appropriations, but application of the principles hinges on the precise wording of the statutes in question. One principle is that legislation in an appropriations act is valid law, even when it is enacted in disregard of House or Senate rules. Substantive provisions in appropriations acts generally have the same legal status as provisions enacted in authorizing legislation. One major difference, however, is that in contrast to authorizing law, which is permanent unless the law expressly limits its period of effectiveness, appropriations are effective for only one fiscal year unless the text of the law gives it a longer duration. In practice, much legislation in appropriations bills is effective for a single fiscal year but is reenacted annually.

The second principle is that appropriations can repeal or amend authorizing law but only if this action is done expressly or in a manner that manifests Congress's intent to revise or terminate the earlier law. Whenever possible, laws that seem to conflict are to be interpreted in ways that reconcile their intent or effect. Suppose, for example, that Congress passes legislation that bars an agency from obligating unauthorized funds but then makes an unauthorized appropriation to the agency. On the surface, this may appear to be a collision between two laws—one providing money, the other barring its use. But an alternative explanation may resolve the conflict: in making the appropriation, Congress conditions its availability on enactment of authorizing legislation. Because repeal of a statute must be explicit or manifest, it has become common to insert "notwithstanding any other provision of law" into legislation. This language is designed to ensure that the new law prevails, regardless of any previous enactment to the contrary.

Even without this language, when two laws conflict, the more recent statute governs. Inasmuch as the normal sequence is for appropriations to follow authorizations, direct conflict between the two usually results in the application of appropriations law. Complications may arise if one of the laws passes Congress first but is signed by the president after

▼

BOX 8-2
Authorizations versus Appropriations: Who Controls Transportation Money?

In 1991 Congress earmarked $6.2 billion in contract authority (over six years) to more than 600 highway and mass transit projects. Two years later, the House Transportation Appropriations Subcommittee tried to redirect $300 million of this money to 58 different projects—many of which happened to have been in the home state of the subcommittee's new chair, Representative Bob Carr (D-Mich.). He argued that the reallocations were based on economic and environmental criteria, but it turned out that more than half of the earmarked money would have gone to states that had members on his subcommittee.

On June 24, 1993, Carr's subcommittee requested that the Rules Committee grant a blanket waiver of House Rule XXI, which prohibits unauthorized appropriations. This request was opposed by Representative Norman Mineta (D-Calif.), the new chair of the Public Works and Transportation Committee, who complained that the appropriation infringed on his committee's jurisdiction. Four days later, the Rules Committee sided with Mineta, making it likely that the disputed projects would be struck from the bill by a point of order.

On June 29, Speaker Tom Foley (D-Wash.) tried to broker a deal in which the Public Works Committee would report a new bill authorizing the disputed projects, after which the House would take up the appropriations bill. But Mineta refused to go along, arguing, "I'm not a rubber stamp; the Public Works Committee is not a rubber stamp." The next effort at compromise came in July, when the leadership proposed a new procedure for handling disputes between the two committees. However, Mineta insisted that his committee must have the final say on disputed projects. Carr refused to concede veto power to Public Works, insisting that "any policy that impacts on money is of interest to us and is within our jurisdiction."

To break the impasse, which blocked House passage of the transportation appropriations bill for months, Carr's subcommittee drafted a new bill, which reclassified the disputed projects. On September 23, when the House was finally set to vote on the bill, nearly all of the disputed projects had been removed. The bill passed by a vote of 312-89, giving Mineta a clear victory and stymieing the appropriators' raid on authorization jurisdiction.

Why did the battle take place, and why did the Public Works Committee win? The protagonists were new to their posts, they were not familiar with the informal means of working out accommodations, and each wanted to prove his mettle. Moreover, the projects added by the appropriations subcommittee were to be funded by taking money from previously authorized projects, not by providing more for transportation. This set up a zero-sum conflict between the two committees.

The authorizers won for two main reasons. First, with 63 members, Public Works was the largest committee in the House. Moreover, the authorizers drew support from members of other House committees who felt that Appropriations had overstepped its jurisdiction and had become too powerful. But this was not the last round in the battle, for as exhibit 8-3 shows, the appropriations committees have other powers in their legislative arsenal. The next round occurred four years after the Carr-Mineta confrontation, when the multiyear transportation program came up for reauthorization. The stakes were much higher this time and many of the combatants were different, but once again the battle lines were drawn in the House between the authorization and appropriations committees.

BOX 8-3
The 1998 Washington TEA Party: Revenge of the Transportation Committee

Weighing in at 500 statute pages, the Transportation Equity Act for the 21st Century (TEA-21) is no ordinary law. It was the product of prolonged budgetary strife between the House Transportation Committee and the Appropriations Committee. One facet of this conflict (recounted in box 8-2) revolved around highway projects; an even bigger battle pertained to control of the Highway Trust Fund—the more than $20 billion collected each year from taxes on gasoline and other products. Each side had its power base—the Transportation Committee had its own trust fund, and the Appropriations Committee had its annual spending bills. Each had allies—Transportation could count on support from many in Congress who had highway or mass transit money earmarked to their states or districts; Appropriations made common cause with the budget committees and the White House, both of which wanted to constrain this area of spending.

1997
May 21
Shuster's amendment to the fiscal 1998 budget resolution fails, 214-216.

September 30
ISTEA, set to expire, is extended for six months.

1998
March 27
Shuster's new bill is reported in the House.

April 1
TEA-21 passes the House, 337-80.

April 2
TEA-21 passes the Senate amended, by unanimous consent.

May 22
TEA-21 conference report passes the Senate, 88-5, and the House, 297-86.

June 9
Clinton signs TEA-21 into law.

Periodically, the Transportation Committee produced a law, such as the Intermodal Surface Transportation Efficiency Act of 1991 (ISTEA), in which the trust fund money was allocated according to its preference. The Appropriations Committee would then limit the amount that could be obligated each year. Representative Bud Shuster (R-Pa.), the tough chair of the Transportation Committee, vowed that this time would be different. He would get revenge by passing a bill that granted his committee full control of the trust fund and eliminated the appropriators' role in transportation funding.

His chance came when ISTEA's six-year authorization was scheduled to expire. Without a new authorization, the flow of highway money from Washington to the states would stop. Just about everyone in Congress took it for granted that there would be a new transportation bill in 1997. What they did not know was whether the appropriators or authorizers would dictate its terms. When Clinton signed TEA-21 in 1998, there was no doubt who had won; the law was an unqualified victory for the Transportation Committee, which got more money and more control through Shuster's shrewd legislative maneuvers.

Shuster's first move was to enlarge his committee to 73 members—making it the largest in Congress. Members were eager to volunteer for seats on the committee, confident that their loyalty would be amply rewarded with money for their districts. His second ploy was to demand

continued

▼

BOX 8-3
Continued

---

that the fiscal 1998 budget resolution be amended to add $12 billion for transportation. This demand put House Republican leaders in a quandary, since they had just signed a deal with the president that was thought to have settled budget issues for the next several years. Despite this, Shuster pressed forward with his amendment, but an all-out effort by the leadership produced just enough votes to narrowly defeat it. However, the Transportation Committee would not be subdued by a single vote. "We'll be back," Shuster warned.

This close call convinced party leaders that Shuster's demands would have to be accommodated. They negotiated a brief extension of ISTEA, promising Shuster that he would get favorable treatment the following year. This delay played into Shuster's hand, for 1998 was an election year, and members could be counted on to vote for local projects. Moreover, by 1998 the previous year's balanced budget deal was no longer news, and the surging surplus made it feasible to spend money without appearing to bust the budget. With adoption of the fiscal 1999 budget resolution delayed (discussed in box 6-1), transportation advocates had a clear field to demand more money without being constrained by budget decisions.

Shuster exploited these advantages to produce his dream bill, which proposed $217 billion over six years for highway and mass transit programs (including $9 billion on 1,467 specified projects). Rather than resorting to the usual stealth methods for funding members' projects, Shuster explicitly listed all of them in the text of the bill—a display of the heady combination of money and power. This was ten times the number of projects in a highway bill Reagan vetoed in 1987 and nearly three times more than the Democratic Congress distributed in the 1991 ISTEA. The bill moved the highway trust fund off-budget and beyond the reach of the Appropriations Committee's control. To gain legislative backing, the bill included such provisions as a subsidy for ethanol producers, which drew support from corn producing states.

When the House took up his bill, Shuster set forth his budget philosophy in plain terms: "Spend the revenue coming in [the Highway Trust Fund]. This is honesty in budgeting. If we are not going to spend the revenue coming in, then we should reduce [highway] taxes." The bill sailed through the House unaltered.

But Shuster still had three hurdles: the Senate, the president, and the need to offset the additional spending. The Senate version had less spending, had fewer earmarks, and did not disturb existing budget rules and relationships. But the House-Senate conference reached enough compromises to enable the bill to pass both chambers. One compromise kept the Highway Trust Fund on-budget but built a "firewall" around the fund that ensured reductions in highway or mass transit spending would not be used for increased spending in other programs. Clinton criticized the bill but stopped short of explicitly threatening a veto. In due course, the price for support from the White House became known—a stricter drunken driver standard. Clinton accepted this concession because his bargaining power was limited and he knew that Congress would not sustain a veto. The offsets required by budget rules were a bit complicated; an estimated $18 billion was needed. Most of this was realized by curtailing disability payments to veterans for smoking-related ailments.

Its victory thus achieved, TEA-21 brought several years of budgetary peace in the transportation arena. But congressional action on another massive highway bill in 2005 showed that this kind of conflict does not have a final chapter.

the other. This situation occurred in 1992, when Congress inserted different provisions in the defense authorization and appropriations acts. Although the authorization act passed Congress first, it was signed into law after the appropriations act. Legal counsel representing Congress argued that the "last law prevails" rule is determined by the sequence of legislative action. The White House took the position, however, that this rule should be applied on the basis of the sequence in which the bills become law.

Conflict between authorizations and appropriations also arises from differences in the reports that accompany these bills. As is discussed in the next chapter, the appropriations committees usually express legislative intent in their reports, not in the text of their bills. By contrast, authorizing committees express much of their legislative intent in the bills themselves. When an authorization law and an appropriations report collide, legal rules may clash with political expedience. On strictly legal grounds, the authorization should take precedence, but the affected agency may nevertheless feel compelled to abide by the dictates of the appropriations report. If it does not, it risks being penalized in the next round of appropriation decisions.

DIRECT SPENDING LEGISLATION

Authorization law provides or effectively controls more than half the budget resources federal agencies spend. This type of authorization is termed "spending authority" by the Congressional Budget Act and "direct spending" by the Budget Enforcement Act (BEA). The terms are not precisely synonymous, but they are sufficiently similar to be used interchangeably, except when the specific provisions of law pertaining to them are being discussed. *Direct spending* is the term preferred here because it distinguishes this type of measure from *discretionary authorizations.*

The classification of an expenditure as direct or discretionary depends on which committee controls it. Appropriations committees control discretionary spending; all other spending is classified as direct because it is directly controlled by authorizing committees. This "fingerprints" rule ignores the type of spending and considers only committee jurisdiction. Direct spending includes entitlements funded in annual appropriations acts because eligibility criteria and payment schedules set in authorizing law determine the amounts spent. For example, although annual appropriations finance Medicaid, these expenditures are classified as direct spending because authorizing law determines the amount to be spent.

Entitlements are the most prominent form of direct spending. Direct spending takes several other forms, including *borrowing authority* (provisions authorizing agencies to spend borrowed funds), *contract authority* (provisions authorizing agencies to incur obligations in advance of appropriations), and *authority to forgo the collection of user fees* or certain other charges. The Congressional Budget Act bars Congress from considering new contract or borrowing authority legislation unless this authority is made effective only to the extent provided in appropriations acts. However, trust funds, such as the Highway Trust Fund, are exempted from this restriction. Exhibits 8-5 and 8-6 provide examples of entitlement and contract authority.

Entitlements are a form of direct spending that gives eligible recipients a legal right to payments from the government. The government is obligated to make such payments even if the budget and appropriation acts do not provide sufficient funds. Most entitlement laws are open-ended—they do not specify or limit the amount to be spent. Instead, they

▶ **EXHIBIT 8-5**
Entitlement Programs

ENTITLEMENT LEGISLATION

ENTITLEMENT TO HOSPITAL INSURANCE BENEFITS

Sec. 266. (a) Every individual who—

(1) has attained the age of 65, and

(2) is entitled to monthly insurance benefits under section 202 or is a qualified railroad retirement beneficiary, shall be entitled to hospital insurance benefits under part A of title XVIII for each month for which he meets the condition specified in paragraph (2), beginning with the first month after June 1966 for which he meets the conditions specified in paragraphs (1) and (2).

PERMANENT APPROPRIATION

Sec. 1817. (a) There is hereby created on the books of the Treasury of the United States a trust fund to be known as the "Federal Hospital Insurance Trust Fund" (hereinafter in this section referred to as the "Trust Fund"). The Trust Fund shall consist of such amounts as may be deposited in, or appropriated to, such fund as provided in this part. There are hereby appropriated to the Trust Fund for the fiscal year ending June 30, 1966, and for each fiscal year thereafter, out of any moneys in the Treasury not otherwise appropriated. . . .

ANNUAL APPROPRIATION

For payment to the Federal Hospital Insurance and the Federal Supplementary Medical Insurance Trust Funds, as provided under section 1844, 1860D-16, and 1860D-31 of the Social Security Act, sections 103(c) and 111(d) of the Social Security Amendments of 1965, section 278(d) of Public Law 97-248, and for administrative expenses incurred pursuant to section 201(g) of the Social Security Act, $177,742,200,000.

Sources: *Social Security Amendments of 1965*, P.L. 89-97; and *Labor, Health and Human Services, Education Appropriations Act for Fiscal Year 2006*, P.L. 109-149, December 30, 2005 (119 Stat. 2851).

(a) These entries pertain to Medicare: the first provision established entitlement to Medicare, the second made a permanent appropriation to the Medicare Health Insurance Trust Fund, and the third made an annual appropriation to the Medicare Supplementary Medical Insurance Trust Fund.

(b) The Congressional Budget Act defines entitlements as authority "to make payments (including loans and grants), the budget authority for which is not provided for in advance by appropriations acts, to any person or government if, under the provisions of law containing such authority, the United States is obligated to make such payments to persons or governments who meet the requirements established by such law."

(c) When an entitlement has a permanent appropriation and is financed through a trust fund, as in the case of the Health Insurance Trust Fund, all receipts of the trust fund become available for obligation without further action by Congress. Hence the receipts of these trust funds are scored as budget authority.

▶ **EXHIBIT 8-6**
Contract Authority

AUTHORIZING LEGISLATION

(1) OUT OF HIGHWAY TRUST FUND—There shall be available from the Highway Trust Fund (other than the Mass Transit Account) the following sums:

(A) NATIONAL MAGNETIC LEVITATION PROTOTYPE DEVELOPMENT PROGRAM—For the national magnetic levitation prototype development program under this section $5,000,000 for fiscal year 1992, $45,000,000 for fiscal year 1993, $100,000,000 for fiscal year 1994, $100,000,000 for fiscal year 1995, $125,000,000 for fiscal year 1996, and $125,000,000 for fiscal year 1997.

LIMITING APPROPRIATION

None of the funds in this Act shall be available for the planning or execution of the National Magnetic Levitation Prototype Development program as defined in subsections 1036(b) and 1036 (d)(1)(A) of the Intermodal Surface Transportation Efficiency Act of 1991.

LIQUIDATING APPROPRIATION

For grants and payment of obligations incurred in carrying out the provisions of the High Speed Ground Transportation program as defined in subsections 1036(c) and 1036(d)(1)(B) of the Intermodal Surface Transportation Efficiency Act of 1991, including planning and environmental analyses, $7,118,000, to be derived from the Highway Trust Fund and to remain available until expended: *Provided,* That none of the funds in this Act shall be available for the implementation or execution of programs the obligations for which are in excess of $5,000,000.

Sources: *Intermodal Surface Transportation Efficiency Act of 1991*, P.L. 102-240; and *Department of Transportation and Related Agencies Appropriations Act for Fiscal Year 1996*, P.L. 104-50.

(a) This exhibit shows the often-fractious relationship between authorizations and appropriations. The first entry, from the 1991 transportation authorization act, provided contract authority to the national magnetic levitation prototype development program for each of the subsequent six years. The phrase "there shall be available" enables an agency to incur obligations in advance of appropriations. The amounts made available by this act were to rise from $5 million in 1992 to $125 million in 1996 and 1997.

(b) The middle entry, drawn from the fiscal 1996 transportation appropriations act, imposed a limitation on obligating funds for the magnetic levitation program. In fact, it barred the use of any funds for this program. Without the limitation on obligations, $125 million would have been available from the authorization; the limitation in the appropriation act reduced this to zero.

(c) The final entry is of a liquidating appropriation, which is made to pay off obligations incurred pursuant to contract authority provided in authorizing legislation. A liquidating appropriation does not provide additional resources nor does it change the amount that may be obligated.

(d) No liquidating appropriation was needed for the magnetic levitation program because the limitation in the middle entry barred any obligations for this purpose.

spell out eligibility criteria and establish formulas for payments. The total paid depends on the number of those eligible and the amount each person is entitled to receive.

Some entitlements (such as Social Security) have permanent appropriations—the mandated payments are made without annual congressional action. Most entitlement programs, however, go through the annual appropriations process, although Congress does not really control them at this stage. If the amount appropriated is not sufficient, Congress has to provide supplemental funds. A few entitlements are formally contingent on appropriations, but the control is not effective. At one time, the law authorizing the food stamps program specified that the amount spent shall be limited by annual appropriations. But food stamp spending has never been constrained by appropriations decisions, and Congress classifies this program as direct spending.

The Growth of Direct Spending

Chapter 2 discussed the transformation of the federal budget from a means of financing government agencies and programs into a means of assisting American families and households. Whatever the reasons for this transformation, it has resulted in a steady expansion of the share of the budget defined as direct spending.

Although the growth in direct spending has been remarkable, most of these increases have been in three areas: Social Security, Medicare, and Medicaid. Almost all the growth in these expenditures has resulted from pre-1980s legislation, not from new congressional action. In fact, Congress has taken repeated, though usually relatively modest, steps since 1980 to cut these expenditures. Most cuts have been achieved through reconciliation bills, not through the PAYGO process. When it was in effect, the statutory PAYGO rule stemmed

spending increases due to new legislation; it was not effective in dealing with increases generated by existing law.

The rise in direct spending has had an enormous impact on federal outlays and congressional operations. It has made the control of federal spending more difficult than was the case when discretionary authorizations and annual appropriations governed most of the budget. It has put Congress in the politically uncomfortable position of having to vote for spending cuts rather than increases. Furthermore, it has made the budget more sensitive to changes in economic conditions.

The surge in direct spending has, by definition, shifted budgetary power in Congress from the appropriations committees to certain authorizing committees. Although the appropriators still have vast budgetary power—the nearly $1 trillion in annual spending that they control is a lot of money by anyone's count—they review a shrinking percentage of total expenditures. The growth in direct spending has been partly propelled by efforts of various authorizing committees to augment their power by freeing programs in their jurisdiction from the control of appropriators. This is not to say, however, that direct spending programs are exempt from recurring congressional scrutiny. Some are, while others are not—Social Security is rarely subject to new legislation while Medicare is adjusted frequently by Congress.

CONCLUSION

Conflict between authorizers and appropriators is inherent in an institution that looks at the same issues through both program and financial perspectives, and in which the two sets of committees have different members. Sometimes conflict breaks out in the open, as occurred in both 1993 and 1997–98 on transportation programs. Most often, however, it is waged behind the scenes and fought over relatively small amounts of money—earmarks, unauthorized projects, and the like. From time to time, reformers have proposed to simplify congressional procedures by merging the authorization and appropriation functions in a single set of committees. Although Congress has shown little interest in restructuring its committee system along these lines, it has merged the authorization and appropriation processes for direct spending. For all practical purposes, the authorizing committees control direct spending. As this part of the budget has expanded, the relative jurisdiction of the appropriations committees has shrunk in relative size. The appropriations committees accepted spending caps in the 1990s as part of a quid pro quo that protected their jurisdiction against new raids by authorizing committees. Despite some continuing skirmishes, the bargain was maintained for a decade, enabling appropriations committees to hold on to control of one-third of federal spending.

The Budget Enforcement Act of 1990 walled off the discretionary portions of the budget from direct spending programs and slowed the raid on the appropriations committees' control. The current rules and practices of the congressional budget process, including internal PAYGO rules and other procedures, also sharpen the distinction between discretionary spending and direct spending and constrain efforts to convert discretionary programs into entitlements. Although PAYGO rules have made it more difficult to legislate new or expanded entitlements, it is highly unlikely that direct spending will shrink as a share of the federal budget

in the years ahead. Even if new direct spending programs are not added, the aging of the U.S. population will impel future increases in spending on pensions and health care—the two biggest direct spending programs.

BEA had a mixed impact on the authorizations process. It did not directly influence discretionary authorizations, which Congress can enact for any amount. Nevertheless, because the caps constrained discretionary spending, Congress was less inclined than it once was to authorize programs at amounts well in excess of appropriated levels. BEA placed formidable legislative obstacles in the way of new entitlements, but it did not control spending resulting from existing law. New direct spending legislation had to run the gauntlet of PAYGO rules, but increases caused by past legislation were not limited, even when they exceeded budgeted levels.

BEA moderated budgetary conflict between the appropriations and authorizing committees. Each operated according to its own rules and in its own orbit. If direct spending exceeded budgeted levels, Congress still could appropriate as much as was allowed by the discretionary caps. Moreover, the rules made it difficult to convert discretionary spending into direct spending or to take money from one category and spend it on another. But the rules were not airtight and not self-enforcing—they did not put an end to conflict between authorizers and appropriators. On a number of occasions, Congress raided PAYGO accounts to spend more on discretionary programs than the caps allowed. On other occasions, it simply manipulated the rules to obtain more spending than would otherwise be permitted.

9

The Appropriations Process

An appropriations act is a law passed by Congress that enables agencies to incur obligations and the Treasury to make payments for designated purposes. Congress's power to appropriate derives from the Constitution, which provides that "no money shall be drawn from the Treasury but in consequence of appropriations made by law." An agency may not spend more than the amount appropriated to it, and it must use available funds only for the purposes, and according to the terms, that Congress sets. Over time, appropriations have also come to be regarded as mandates requiring that agencies carry out prescribed activities by spending all of the funds appropriated to them. Impoundment rules (discussed in the next chapter) that restrict the president's power to delay or withhold the expenditure of funds reflect this newer concept of appropriations. Executive discretion is now limited by appropriations in two ways: by imposing a ceiling on the maximum and a floor on the minimum that may be spent.

Although appropriations provide legal authority for outlays, with few exceptions the amounts set forth in appropriations acts pertain to budget authority. Appropriations make money available for obligation; they do not specify the amounts to be disbursed during the fiscal year. In contrast to most states and local legislatures, which appropriate to cover cash payments, Congress does not normally require that appropriations be spent in the fiscal year for which they are made. In many cases, outlays occur years after the appropriation was enacted. This practice provides agencies with funding for activities (such as procurement and construction) that span a number of years, but it weakens the ability of Congress to control annual outlays.

The Constitution does not require annual appropriations, but since the First Congress in 1789, the practice has been to appropriate each year. From time to time, Congress has been urged to adopt a biennial budget (and make appropriations every other year) as many state legislatures do. But the appropriations committees have resisted such proposals, preferring the short-term control that comes from annual action to the longer-term perspective that might be gained from biennial decisions. Change does not come easily to the appropriations committees; appropriators hold on to traditions even when external conditions change. Although strong pressure has built up in recent years to shift from an annual to a biennial appropriations cycle, at this writing Congress appears unlikely to adopt this change.

Appropriations must be obligated during the fiscal year for which they are provided, unless (as often happens) Congress expressly makes the money available for a longer period. In contrast to authorizing legislation, which is presumed to be permanent, an appropriations act and any substantive provisions in it expire at the end of the fiscal year—unless the text makes them permanent or effective beyond the fiscal year. The annual nature of appropriations explains why Congress often reenacts the same or similar provisions (such as restrictions on using federal money to pay for abortions) year after year.

TYPES OF APPROPRIATIONS ACTS

The Constitution does not prescribe the type of measure in which appropriations are made.

Appropriations can be inserted in any law, but practice that predates the Constitution is to appropriate in acts that are distinct from other types of legislation. This distinction is codified in House and Senate rules, which distinguish between legislation and appropriations.

Congress produces four types of appropriations. *Regular appropriations* provide budget authority for the upcoming fiscal year, or if it has already started, for the year in progress. *Supplemental appropriations* provide additional budget resources when the regular appropriation is deemed insufficient or for activities the regular appropriation did not fund. *Continuing appropriations* (usually referred to as continuing resolutions because they are enacted as joint resolutions rather than as bills) fund agencies that have not received regular appropriations by the start of the fiscal year. *Permanent appropriations* (usually enacted in substantive legislation) become available without current action by Congress. Because interest charges, Social Security, and other expenditures are financed by permanent appropriations, less than half of federal spending requires new annual appropriations.

The number of supplementals and continuing resolutions (CRs) varies from year to year. For fiscal year 2002, for example, there were two supplementals and eight continuing resolutions, while for fiscal year 2005, there were five supplementals and three continuing resolutions. Jurisdiction over these measures is vested in the House and Senate appropriations committees, each of which is divided into subcommittees that do almost all of the work that goes into producing the various spending bills. Each House and Senate subcommittee handles one regular appropriations bill, as well as the portions of supplementals and continuing resolutions pertaining to matters in its jurisdiction.

In some years, several or all of the regular appropriations bills have been folded into an omnibus measure, often together with large amounts of legislation. Omnibus bills represent a strong break with the tradition that each appropriations bill be enacted separately. Other important deviations are discussed in the next section.

TRADITION AND CHANGE

In describing the appropriations process, it is necessary to distinguish between the way things have been done over the years and recent changes that have uprooted or challenged long-established practices.

From afar, the appropriations process does not appear to be much different from what it was in the past. The appropriations committees initiate their work in response to the president's budget. Each appropriations bill is in the jurisdiction of a single subcommittee that operates largely independently of other subcommittees and the full committee. Each bill is structured on the basis of accounts, and agency officials appear at subcommittee hearings to justify their budget requests.

But a closer look reveals significant change in the world of appropriations. Once the appropriations committees controlled virtually all federal spending; now they have effective jurisdiction over only one-third. Once they had no rival in Congress for determining how much was spent on the programs in their jurisdictions; now they must reckon with budget resolutions and (in some years) preset spending caps. Once they worked almost entirely behind closed doors; now they mark up almost all bills in the open. Once just about every appropriations bill was enacted by the start of the fiscal year; now many—in some years most—are not. These and other breaks with tradition are spelled out in table 9-1.

For generations, tradition was centered in the House Appropriations Committee. Much

more than its Senate counterpart, the committee was bound by norms and practices that insulated it from pressures within Congress and from changes in the role and scope of government. The House Appropriations Committee was the custodian of the spending process: it initiated all spending bills, its members spent long days reviewing spending plans, it operated in a bipartisan manner, and it took pride in guarding the Treasury against federal agencies' demands for more money. Members on the House Appropriations Committee rarely served on any other committee; appropriations was their sole committee assignment. They did not legislate, advocate, or evaluate programs, nor did they prepare budgets; they only appropriated money.

For decades, tradition was a buffer against change. Over time, however, it weakened the appropriations committees by rendering them less malleable and less responsive to congressional spending demands. To understand how traditional practices once sheltered the appropriations process and now undermine its effectiveness, the evolution of appropriations in Congress must be reviewed.

Congress had an appropriations process for three-quarters of a century before it had appropriations committees. But even before Congress had separate appropriations committees, the notion was branded into the political mind-set of the appropriators that their job was to restrain the spending ambitions of executive agencies, not to legislate. Appropriators were to decide how much the agencies, established through previous congressional decisions, should spend.

Early in the history of the appropriations process, it became apparent that spending pressures do not only emanate from the executive branch; they also come from members of Congress who favor particular expenditures. The appropriators were also pressured to add

TABLE 9-1
Tradition and Change in the Appropriations Process

Traditional practice	Current practice
Committee	
Had jurisdiction over virtually all federal spending	Has jurisdiction over only one-third of spending
Experienced members from relatively safe districts appointed to the committee[a]	Many junior members, often from swing districts, selected[a]
Exclusive committee; members had no other major committee assignment[a]	Many appropriations members serve on other House committees[a]
High bipartisan cooperation; many bills passed with overwhelming majorities	Partisan conflict; many bills passed on party-line votes[a]
Party leaders had no role in committee decisions	Party leaders often have lead role in making appropriations decisions
Parallel House and Senate subcommittees	
Procedures	
Each regular appropriations bill was enacted separately	Regular appropriations often enacted in omnibus appropriations
House originated all appropriations bills	In some years, a few bills originate in Senate
Small amount of legislation inserted in appropriations bills	Appropriations often contain vast amounts of legislation
Decisions made in executive session	Bills marked up in open session
All (or almost all) appropriations enacted by the start of the fiscal year	Many (in some year most) appropriations bills enacted after the fiscal year has started
Spending and control	
Authorizing legislation rarely specified amounts authorized to be appropriated	Authorizing legislation often specifies amounts authorized to be appropriated
Appropriations committees were not constrained in the total appropriated	Total constrained by section 302(a) allocations and (in some years) discretionary spending caps
Subcommittees decided spending amounts independently of one another	Subcommittee decisions coordinated by section 302(b) allocations
OMB gave little formal attention to appropriations process	OMB monitors appropriations bills and prepares statements of administration policy on each bill
No procedure for assessing whether appropriations bills were within budget	OMB and CBO score each appropriations bill enacted into law
Appropriations only limited expenditure, they did not mandate that funds be spent	Impoundment rules limit discretion of the president to withhold appropriated funds

a. Applies only or predominately to the House Appropriations Committee.

legislative provisions to their bills. To ward off these internal pressures, the House (in the 1830s) and the Senate (in the 1850s) adopted rules against unauthorized appropriations and legislation in appropriations bills. Though they have been modified over the years, these rules still define the basic relationship between appropriations and other congressional activ-ity. More important, they set appropriations apart from just about everything else Congress does. Despite these rules, Congress makes of the appropriations process what it wants, and it often redefines the relationship between appropriations and other legislative business.

Before the 1860s, jurisdiction over both revenue and spending bills was entrusted to the House Ways and Means and Senate Finance Committees, but the demands of the Civil War and the expansion of government impelled the House to establish a separate appropriations committee in 1865; the Senate followed suit three years later. The new committees' perceived duty was to control federal spending by resisting the entreaties of those inside and outside Congress who wanted to spend more. There then ensued a 50-year war between the appropriations and legislative committees. The former won the first round when the House adopted the Holman Rule, authorizing the appropriations committee to insert legislation retrenching expenditures in its bills. The latter retaliated by seizing jurisdiction over various spending bills, beginning with the pork-laden rivers and harbors bill and ending with control of half of the appropriations bills. Thus, at the start of the twentieth century, spenders had the upper hand in Congress.

The contest between spenders and guardians is never-ending; economic conditions and the mood of the country as much as the internal rules of Congress determine the balance of power between the two. By the end of World War I, sentiment had shifted in favor of the appropriators. Federal spending ballooned more than 25-fold during the war years; big deficits emerged, making Congress receptive to demands for fiscal discipline. It passed the Budget and Accounting Act of 1921, which enlisted presidential power on behalf of spending control. The president was made an ally of the appropriations committees; together they would constrain the spending demands of federal agencies and congressional committees. To strengthen the new presidential budget process, Congress returned jurisdiction of all spending bills to the appropriations committees.

This was the environment in which tradition hardened in the House Appropriations Committee. The world of appropriations was cloistered and patterned. The committee did not consider any spending demands until the president submitted his budget. Then subcommittees held hearings but invited only agency officials to testify. Agencies prepared justification books that focused on the extent to which the amount requested differed from the previous year's appropriation, and the committee issued reports that focused on the extent to which the amount it recommended differed from the previous appropriation and the president's request. The committee did not compare the appropriation to the amount authorized. In many cases, it did not even know how much had been authorized.

As guardian of the Treasury, the House Appropriations Committee sheltered itself from the spending pressures that buffeted Congress. It recruited members from safe districts, put them through a long apprenticeship, had them work long hours poring over agency requests and reviewing spending details with agency witnesses, and taught them how to give agencies what they needed while cutting their requests. The long hours and closed process molded members into a cohesive, nonpartisan group that rarely aired differences to outsiders. Appropriations staff were part of this small community. They typically were recruited from federal agencies, not from other congressional committees or from the ranks of political campaigners or law school graduates. Appropriations staff paid attention to what agencies did and maintained close relations with agency budget staff. Periodically, House Appropriations and agency staff went on retreat to guzzle beer, play cards, and trade war stories.

Appropriations bills were structured distinctively, by accounts rather than sections, and most of the committee's intent was expressed in report language, not in the bill.

Senate amendments were worded and numbered in a way that often made it difficult for outsiders to follow the action. When conferees met to resolve House-Senate differences, they convened in a small room that was barely big enough to seat all of them plus the one or two staff members who kept the tally sheets. This was a world in which government talked to itself—everybody else was an outsider.

This closed world could not survive the enlargement of government ushered in by the New Deal and World War II, and was further expanded by Great Society legislation in the 1960s. Authorizing legislation took on a new look; it was broader, more programmatic, and often sought to influence the amount appropriated or to bypass the appropriations process. As they held on to tradition, the appropriations committees became increasingly dysfunctional. The account structure was poorly aligned with federal programs and activities. It had an annual perspective, but Congress was determined to establish long-term commitments through income support programs, such as Social Security and Medicare. Appropriators protested the raid on their jurisdiction, but they were too weak to resist the expansion of entitlements. They railed against "backdoor spending," a term invented by appropriators to convey the notion that spending through authorizing legislation is illicit. They continued to hold onto tradition, even though it left them with a shrinking jurisdiction.

In the post–Vietnam/Watergate era, reformers seeking a more open, responsive institution attacked congressional tradition. Rule changes forced all committees to open their doors. In the House, the ratio of Democrats (who were the majority party) to Republicans on Appropriations was increased, giving the committee a more partisan orientation. The Democratic Caucus was given a voice in selecting House Appropriations subcommittee chairs. Furthermore, voting procedures in the House were changed to permit recorded votes in the Committee of the Whole, where appropriations bills and much other legislation are considered.

The insulation of the appropriations process was further undermined by the Congressional Budget Act of 1974, which established House and Senate budget committees to police congressional action on revenue and spending legislation. The clear message was that the appropriations committees cannot effectively control federal spending because much spending is outside their jurisdiction, and appropriations bills are not adequately related to one another, or to total spending, revenues, and the deficit.

The appropriations committees now have to operate within budget constraints set by others. Over time these constraints have been codified in budget rules and procedures (discussed later in this chapter) that divide discretionary funds among the appropriations subcommittees. Impoundment procedures, also enacted in 1974, were another blow to tradition, for they gave statutory recognition to the reality that as much as Congress limits what agencies spend, it wants them to spend what it appropriates.

The weakening of tradition has made the appropriations process somewhat more similar to other congressional activities and much less insulated from the political tides affecting Congress. The appropriations process is more permeable than it once was, although it still stands apart from other legislative activities. The loss of tradition is reflected in a number of conditions, such as partisan strife, tardy enactment of appropriations bills, recourse to omnibus bills, Senate initiative on appropriations bills, the weakening of subcommittee independence, increased legislation in spending bills, and the enlarged role of party leaders.

Congress is conflicted by the need to make appropriations and the difficulty of doing so. The need to complete action pushes the appropriations process to the center, but the political polarization of Congress pushes it to the extremes. The problem is more pronounced in the House, where partisanship is more strident and the majority party can ignore the interests of the minority.

In the traditional relationship between the two chambers, the House Appropriations Committee starts the process. If partisan strife blocks the House from completing its work on time, the Senate cannot complete its work in a timely manner either. The House Appropriations Committee used to be a unifying institution in Congress; now it often is a polarizing force. It is the forum to which many partisan legislative disputes are brought when there are no other avenues for resolution. Rather than being walled off against conflict, the appropriations process has become a conduit for amplifying and spreading friction and for forcing action on other issues, sometimes at the expense of stalemating appropriations bills.

This tendency began during the long spell of Democratic control, but it picked up momentum with the Republican takeover of the House in 1995. Even before he was sworn in as Speaker, Newt Gingrich (R-Ga.) demanded that each appropriations subcommittee chair pledge fealty to the Republican legislative agenda. Republican Party leaders preempted many decisions that the appropriations committees traditionally had made, such as the insertion of controversial riders and the timing of various actions, which further ensnared appropriations in partisan strife. In most years, key appropriation decisions have been made in summit negotiations between party leaders and the president or his aides. Sometimes appropriations committee leaders have been consulted; often they have not.

The pent-up anger of the House Appropriations Committee, provoked by its loss of independence, burst into the open in an extraordinary letter sent by Chair Robert Livingston (R-La.) to Speaker Gingrich on November 6, 1998—three days after that year's midterm elections and one day before Gingrich announced his resignation from Congress (exhibit 9-1). Livingston demanded that he be empowered to run the Appropriations Committee "without being subject to the dictates of any other Member of Congress" and that he "be the final authority to determine the content of legislation within the Appropriations Committee, and the schedule under which legislation is produced, without interference." Livingston's plea was a throwback to a past legislative era in which the appropriations committees operated according to their own rhythm, largely indifferent to the tides of change in Congress and the nation. That world can be rebuilt only by distancing the work of appropriations from the political context in which budgets are made.

Recent developments indicate, however, that the appropriations process has become even more enmeshed in party politics. Six years after Livingston argued for independence, House Republicans met to select a new Appropriations Committee chair. The vacancy occurred because the incumbent was limited by House Republican party rules to three terms (six years) as chair. The rule, which applies to all House committees as well as to appropriations subcommittees, is intended to undermine the seniority rule, which enables long-serving members to hold on to their chairmanships even when their views are out of step with party doctrine.

In the 2004 contest for the new House Appropriations Committee chair, Representative Harold Rogers, one of the three candidates, boasted of his prowess in raising campaign

▶ **EXHIBIT 9-1**
Appropriations versus Party Leadership

The following excerpts are from a letter sent by House Appropriations Committee Chair Robert Livingston (R-La.) to Speaker Newt Gingrich (R-Ga.) on November 6, 1998:

In consideration of the deep respect and friendship that I hold for you, I have set forth herewith a list of requirements that I believe are critical and vital to the success of the 106th Congress. In order for the majority to complete its work and demonstrate that we can properly govern, I believe it imperative that you acknowledge and agree to these suggested changes in House procedure, without exception:

1. I, as Chairman of the Appropriations Committee, shall run the Committee as I see fit and in the best interest of the Republican majority, with full consultation with the Leadership, but without being subject to the dictates of any other Member of Congress.
2. That I be the final authority to determine content of legislation within the Appropriations Committee, and the schedule under which legislation is produced, without interference.
3. That all future budget resolutions be completed for House approval between April 15 and April 30, and that thereafter all appropriations bills are free to proceed with or without a Budget Resolution, for completion in the House of Representative by the end of June of every calendar year. The Senate will be urged to do likewise so that all conferences can be completed before the August break of each calendar year.
4. I, as Appropriations Chairman, shall be present in all Leadership discussions of the budget affecting Appropriations matters. No decisions on Appropriations issues will be made within the context of budget negotiations without consultation (not necessarily approval) with me.
5. There will be no amendment in Rules or Law affecting Appropriations jurisdiction without my approval.
6. No Member or Subcommittee Chairman will be removed from my committee or from their post on my committee without my approval. . . .
9. Members should not be assigned to Committees 'because of their districts.' Fragile Members are afraid to cast tough votes, and that inhibits the passage of credible legislation.
10. No Republican will be assigned to the Appropriations Committee without my approval.
11. No Member should hold more than 5 subcommittees without waivers, and waiver should never be issued except under the strictest of conditions or dire emergency or importance. No Member of the Appropriations Committee shall serve on any Committee or Subcommittee other than that of the Budget Committee. . . .
13. I, as Chairman of the Appropriations Committee, during last minute negotiations with Democrats or with representatives of the White House on all appropriations bills, will make all final decisions, but with full consultation with the leadership.
14. There should be weekly meetings with Democrats to last no more than one hour, and I as Chairman of the Appropriations Committee should be included. . . .
16. The Speaker shall insist that the Senate concur and conform to our expedited schedule on Appropriations and budget, with the understanding that should either house fail to pass an appropriations bill by July 30, that the respective bill which has been passed by the remaining House of Congress will become the actionable vehicle for conference.

funds for Republican candidates (see exhibit 9-2). In soliciting the support of Speaker Dennis Hastert, Rogers argued that he would help Republicans retain their majority in the House. In contrast to Livingston, who wanted to preserve the special status and prerogatives of the Appropriations Committee, Rogers and the other candidates pledged to work with party leadership.

Appropriations is not the only committee that has been affected by partisanship, but the impact has been greater there than on others because of its bipartisan traditions. In the past, the timely enactment of appropriations was facilitated by cooperation between Democrats and Republicans. In the present period, the majority party has the task of shepherding spending bills through the House, but it sometimes does so without reaching out for support of the minority. Yet the fact that Republicans and Democrats alike earmark funds for their districts and projects shows that the two parties do cooperate in promoting the electoral interests of incumbents.

THE APPROPRIATIONS COMMITTEES AND THEIR SUBCOMMITTEES

Despite attrition in jurisdiction and independence, the appropriations committees are among the most coveted assignments in Congress. In both the House and Senate, members actively campaign for these posts by calling on party leaders, getting senior members to intervene on their behalf, and pointing to the political or geographical strengths they would bring to the committee.

These committees are powerful because they control the portion of federal spending that is subject to annual congressional action. The more than $900 billion in discretionary money they control is, by a wide margin, the largest pool of dollars over which Congress has

recurring influence. This is the part of the budget on which money is spent because of current rather than past decisions. Almost all the rest is governed by statutory rules that continue in effect unless Congress changes them. Appropriating $900 billion of discretionary money requires legislative action; spending $2 trillion of mandatory money does not. The appropriations committees' legislative prominence derives not only from the huge pot of money they control but also from the small amounts they dole out to thousands of projects.

In many regards, the appropriations committees resemble other congressional committees. Subcommittees conduct hearings, and staff draft bills and reports. The full committee takes up each bill after the relevant subcommittee has completed its work. Bills go from the committee to the floor, and disagreements between the House and Senate versions are worked out in conference. But the differences are more illuminating.

The three critical distinguishing characteristics are the bounded jurisdiction of the appropriations committees, the near certainty of congressional action, and the prominence of their subcommittees. On almost every House and Senate committee, the most important decisions each year revolve around setting a legislative agenda and deciding which issues and bills are to be taken up. In the case of appropriations, these decisions are predetermined by jurisdiction. These committees must act on the regular appropriations bills and continuing resolutions made necessary by failure to complete the regular bills on time. The committees have some discretion in deciding whether to report supplemental spending bills, but almost all of their agenda is set for them in advance. Just about every other congressional committee must be concerned with whether the House and Senate will take up the measures it reports

▶ **EXHIBIT 9-2**
Appropriations Have Become Subservient to Party Leaders

The following excerpts are from a letter sent by Representative Harold Rogers (R-Ky.) to Speaker Dennis Hastert on December 10, 2004, shortly before House Republicans selected the new chair of the Appropriations Committee. Rogers was one of three candidates vying for support from Republican colleagues. He did not receive the Speaker's support and did not win. Representative Jerry Lewis (R-Calif.) was selected.

I am writing to ask for your support of my candidacy to serve as the next Chairman of the House Appropriations Committee.

Our Republican majority is on the line in the 2006 elections, and who you select to lead the Appropriations Committee will be crucial in neutralizing our biggest vulnerability—the soaring, historically-high deficit. . . .

What I'm proposing is a sweeping attitudinal change of the entire Committee. . . . We need someone who can work with the Budget Committee, Leadership, and out Members—not against them. . . . As this year's Omnibus clearly illustrated, the Appropriations process is broken and in dire need of repair. . . .

Finally, I believe Appropriators must help maintain our Republican Majority through aggressive fundraising. On my watch, Members of the Committee will raise, at a minimum, $15 million dollars per cycle towards that goal. As I've proven—raising and giving over $5 million to our candidates—I am ready to lead by example.

Source: Harold Rogers, "Dear Colleague Letter," December 20, 2004.

TABLE 9-2
House Votes on Passage of Appropriations Acts, Three-Year Intervals, Fiscal Years 1996–2005[a]

	1996			1999		
Bill	Total	Democrats	Republicans	Total	Democrats	Republicans
Agriculture	313-78	120-63	193-14	373-48	173-25	199-23
Commerce-Justice-State	272-151	66-129	206-21	225-203	28-175	197-27
Defense	294-125	85-105	209-19	358-61	149-47	209-13
District of Columbia	224-191	31-155	193-35	214-206	3-194	211-11
Energy and Water	400-27	175-23	225-3	405-4	187-0	217-4
Foreign Operations	333-89	133-57	200-31	255-161	69-126	186-34
Homeland Security[b]	. . .	. . .	. . .	. . .	. . .	. . .
Interior	244-181	31-166	213-14	245-181	38-162	207-18
Labor-HHS-Education	219-208	6-189	213-18	c	c	c
Legislative Branch	337-87	110-85	227-1	235-179	36-158	199-20
Military Construction	319-105	125-74	194-30	396-10	179-7	216-3
Transportation[d]	361-61	144-50	217-10	391-25	193-2	197-23
Treasury-Postal Service[d]	216-211	15-181	200-30	218-203	26-169	192-33
VA-HUD	228-193	27-165	201-27	259-164	54-145	205-18

Source: *Congressional Quarterly Almanac,* 1995, 1998, 2001, and 2004.

a. The votes listed here are on passage of the bill in the House, not on adoption of the conference report. The votes of Representative Bernard Sanders (I-Vt.) are included in the totals but not in the breakdowns by party.

b. The Homeland Security Appropriations Act was first enacted for fiscal year 2004.

and whether disagreements between the two chambers will be worked out in conference. The appropriations committees do not have any such doubts; they have absolute certainty that their spending bills will be enacted. They may not know when each bill will be considered or whether all the regular appropriations will be enacted by the start of the fiscal year. They also may not know whether all the bills will be enacted in normal fashion (one at a time) or will be combined in an omnibus bill. But they do know that theirs is "must-pass" legislation—one way or another, all the work will be completed.

The special status of the annual spending bills shapes the behavior and operations of the appropriations committees. As noted previously, these traditionally were among the least partisan committees in Congress, markedly less divided along party lines than the budget committees. Over the years, even when Democrats

and Republicans have disagreed on budget policy and spending priorities, they often joined ranks in passing appropriations bills. The money these committees distribute mutes their partisanship—Democrats and Republicans each get funds for their projects and constituencies, giving members from each party strong incentive to vote for appropriations.

Fiscal years 1996 and 1999 were years of elevated partisan strife. For fiscal years 2002 and 2005, however, tables 9-2 and 9-3 show that all appropriations bills passed the House with lopsided majorities or by voice vote, in sharp contrast to the votes on the budget resolutions. The overwhelming votes of approval on appropriations bills have occurred during periods of inflamed partisanship in Congress. In recent times, party-line voting (in which a majority of Republicans are on one side and a majority of Democrats on the other) has been near a record high. Nevertheless, Republicans

2002			2005		
Total	Democrats	Republicans	Total	Democrats	Republicans
414-16	207-2	205-14	389-31	184-15	204-16
408-19	203-3	203-16	397-18	192-2	204-16
406-20	187-19	217-1	403-17	181-16	221-1
327-88	188-11	138-76	371-54	188-14	182-40
405-15	204-2	199-13	370-16	180-3	189-13
381-46	199-10	181-35	365-41	187-7	177-34
. . .	. . .	. . .	400-5	186-3	213-2
376-32	198-1	177-30	334-86	129-69	205-16
373-43	201-2	170-41	388-13	192-0	195-13
380-38	184-16	195-21	327-43	154-16	173-27
401-0	192-0	207-0	420-1	198-1	221-0
426-1	209-0	215-1	397-12	197-2	199-10
334-94	161-46	172-47	. . .	. . .	. . .
336-89	132-73	203-15	not considered	. . .	. . .

c. This bill was not voted on separately, but was included in an omnibus appropriations act.

d. The Treasury–Postal Service Appropriations Act was incorporated into the new Transportation-Treasury Appropriations Act beginning with fiscal year 2004; see "Transportation" for fiscal year 2005.

and Democrats often have joined ranks to produce spending bills that win broad support in both chambers.

Bipartisanship is rooted in the culture of the appropriations process and is reinforced by the fact that these bills distribute federal money to states and districts. During George W. Bush's first term, bipartisanship was strengthened by the president's willingness to accept large spending increases. Democrats voted for spending bills because they had more money; Republicans voted for the bills because they had more money for their priorities and were backing their president. But there is another side to bipartisanship: with both parties joining in to spend more, it is difficult to use the appropriations process to cut federal spending. The appropriators have a self-image that they are guardians of the Treasury; it is closer to the truth to label them as guardians of their spending interests.

When one party tries to use the process to trim appropriations, Democrats and Republicans go their separate ways. This happened in 1995 when partisan strife was so intense and widespread that for fiscal year 1996, none of the regular appropriations bills were enacted on time. Moreover, Congress and the president fought over the terms of continuing resolutions, as evident in his veto of the second CR and the shutdown of major federal agencies for several weeks. The conflict over fiscal year 1996 appropriations is one of the truly extraordinary political stories of our time; its causes and implications are discussed in box 9-1. The unthinkable happened: Congress failed to complete action on must-pass appropriations, and many government operations were suspended. The protracted impasse and forced closing of federal agencies are additional indications that the old order on appropriations has broken down.

TABLE 9-3
Senate Votes on Passage of Appropriations Acts, Three-Year Intervals, Fiscal Years 1996–2005[a]

Bill	1996			1999		
	Total	Democrats	Republicans	Total	Democrats	Republicans
Agriculture	95-3	45-0	50-3	97-2	44-0	53-2
Commerce-Justice-State	voice vote	. . .	. . .	99-0	45-0	54-0
Defense	voice vote	. . .	. . .	97-2	43-2	54-0
District of Columbia	voice vote	. . .	. . .	not considered	c	c
Energy and Water	voice vote	. . .	. . .	98-1	44-1	54-0
Foreign Operations	91-9	42-4	49-5	90-3	41-1	49-2
Homeland Security[b]	. . .	. . .	. . .	. . .	. . .	. . .
Interior	92-6	41-4	51-2	not considered	. . .	. . .
Labor-HHS-Education	c	c	c	not considered	. . .	. . .
Legislative Branch	voice vote	. . .	. . .	90-9	43-2	47-7
Military Construction	84-10	35-8	49-2	voice vote	. . .	. . .
Transportation[d]	98-1	44-1	54-0	90-1	43-0	47-1
Treasury-Postal Service[d]	voice vote	. . .	. . .	91-5	42-1	49-4
VA-HUD	55-45	1-45	54-0	voice vote	. . .	. . .

Source: *Congressional Quarterly Almanac*, 1995, 1998, 2001, and 2004.
    a. The votes listed here are on passage of the bill in the Senate, not on adoption of the conference report.
    b. The Homeland Security Appropriations Act was first enacted for fiscal year 2004.

In normal times, the appropriations committees excel at turning big policy disputes into routine matters of a little more or a little less money. Historically, appropriating has meant making decisions at the margins for programs and agencies already in operation, not questioning whether the programs and agencies should continue or whether the government should make fundamental changes in policy. If members of Congress want to review the role of government in alleviating malnutrition around the world, the appropriate forum might be the agriculture or foreign relations committees. These committees have little must-pass legislation; they usually have as much time as they want to probe an issue, even if it means that action will be delayed to next year or later. But the appropriations committees must act. Over the years, they have done so by narrowing controversial issues to marginal spending questions: how much

higher or lower should appropriations be to combat hunger? Should the amount be more or less than the president requested? Which countries should get more and which less?

TRADITION AND CHANGE ON APPROPRIATIONS SUBCOMMITTEES

Work and power in the appropriations process are concentrated in the subcommittees. Except for a brief overview session (which is skipped in some years), the subcommittees conduct all appropriations hearings. Each has its own staff, produces its own bill, maintains year-round relations with agencies in its jurisdiction, and operates independently of the other subcommittees. The chairs of the subcommittees are commonly referred to as cardinals, in recognition of the authority each exercises in his or her domain. Their power comes from tradition, control of the purse strings, their

	2002			2005		
Total	Democrats	Republicans	Total	Democrats	Republicans	
91-5	49-0	41-5	not considered	. . .	. . .	
97-0	47-0	49-0	not considered	. . .	. . .	
voice vote	. . .	. . .	98-0	47-0	50-0	
75-24	49-0	25-24	unanimous consent	. . .	. . .	
97-2	50-0	46-2	not considered	. . .	. . .	
96-2	47-2	48-0	voice vote	. . .	. . .	
. . .	. . .	. . .	93-0	45-0	47-0	
voice vote	. . .	. . .	not considered	. . .	. . .	
89-10	48-1	40-9	not considered	. . .	. . .	
88-9	47-2	40-7	94-2	44-1	49-1	
97-0	47-0	49-0	91-0	43-0	47-0	
voice vote	. . .	. . .	not considered	. . .	. . .	
voice vote	. . .	. . .	. . .	. . .	. . .	
94-5	49-1	44-4	not considered	. . .	. . .	

c. This bill was not voted on separately, but was included in an omnibus appropriations act.

d. The Treasury–Postal Service Appropriations Act was incorporated into the new Transportation-Treasury Appropriations Act beginning with fiscal year 2004; see "Transportation" for fiscal year 2005.

capacity to channel funds to favored activities and areas, and the deference accorded them by executive officials and members of Congress. Traditionally, each cardinal has had considerable autonomy in running the subcommittee, free from interference by the full committee chair or party leaders.

One of the distinctive features of the traditional appropriations process was the perfect jurisdictional alignment of the House and Senate subcommittees. Every federal agency was assigned to parallel House and Senate subcommittees; each paired set of subcommittees had the same jurisdiction. In fact, all the activity of each set of House and Senate subcommittees revolved around a single appropriations bill and the supplemental appropriations and continuing resolutions related to their bill. The subcommittees did not produce any other legislation, nor did they wage jurisdictional wars of the sort that frequently beset other congressional committees. Their patterned jurisdiction eased the task of House and Senate conferees when they met to resolve differences on appropriations bills.

The boundaries of the appropriations subcommittees rarely were changed, except to accommodate new programs or agencies. From 1971 to 2005, the House and Senate had 13 sets of parallel appropriations subcommittees. The most significant adjustment during this period occurred in 2003 when the House created a Homeland Security subcommittee to handle the budget of the newly created Department of Homeland Security. To maintain 13 subcommittees, the Transportation and Treasury subcommittees were merged. Some Senators were miffed that the House acted without consulting them, but after a short delay, the Senate adopted the same changes.

This long-standing parallelism was ended temporarily in 2005, during the 109th

BOX 9-1
From Revolution to Shutdown: The 1995–96 Battle of the Budget

When Republicans gained control of Congress in the 1994 midterm elections, they took it for granted that they were elected to change the way things were done in Washington and that President Clinton would be unable to impede their revolution. Favoring big rather than incremental changes, Republican leaders sought to use appropriations bills as a vehicle for enacting their agenda by inserting significant changes in substantive law. However, they underestimated Clinton's willingness to use his veto power. The result was a massive breakdown of the appropriations process; many spending bills were delayed for more than half a year, and portions of the government were shut down twice. In an attempt to keep the government operating, a record 14 continuing resolutions were enacted, a record at that time.

The fight started over efforts to reduce spending levels; it ended without much spending being changed. The early rounds were over congressional efforts to rescind previous appropriations; the final rounds were over congressional efforts to enact new appropriations. While this was the first budget clash between Clinton and congressional Republicans, it was not the last one in which Clinton emerged victorious.

Republicans passed a budget resolution in June 1995 that proposed to sharply reduce the size of the federal government. In addition to deep cuts in discretionary programs, their plan made room for hundreds of billions of dollars in tax cuts (over seven years) by curtailing Medicare, Medicaid, and other social programs. Because the president has no formal role in the budget resolution, Clinton could not impede adoption of the Republican version. However, almost half a year later in December 1995, Clinton derailed Congress's budget revolution by vetoing the reconciliation bill that would have enacted many of the proposed tax and entitlement changes.

1995
June 29
House, 239-194, and Senate, 54-46, pass conference report on budget resolution.

October 1
Fiscal 1996 begins; first continuing resolution enacted the previous day.

November 14
First partial government shutdown follows veto of second CR.

November 17
House, 237-189, and Senate, 52-47, pass conference report on reconciliation bill.

November 20
Government reopens.

December 6
Clinton vetoes reconciliation bill; only seven appropriations bills enacted thus far.

December 16
Second partial government shutdown ensues.

December 18
Two appropriations bills vetoed; another is vetoed the next day.

1996
January 6
Government reopens.

April 25
House, 399-25, and Senate, 88-11, pass conference report on the omnibus appropriations bill for fiscal year 1996; Clinton signs the bill April 26.

continued

▼

BOX 9-1
Continued

After passing the budget resolution, Republicans moved ahead on the fiscal 1996 appropriations, producing spending bills with even deeper cuts than those originally assumed by the budget resolution. Both long-held Democratic priorities and Clinton's pet initiatives were targeted. But the appropriations process was delayed by these efforts to shrink the government, and by the time the new fiscal year started, only two of the regular spending bills had been sent to the president. Congressional Republicans were forced to break their "no continuing resolutions" pledge and pass one to prevent a government shutdown.

At this point, Republicans believed they held the advantage and that Clinton would capitulate to their demands. They did not expect him to risk shutting down the government by vetoing a continuing resolution. House Appropriations Chair Robert Livingston (R-La.) confidently asserted that the

Continuing Resolutions, 1995–96

	President		
Number	Signed	Vetoed	Expiration
First	9/30/95		11/13/95
Second		11/14/95	(12/1/95)
Third	11/19/95		11/20/95
Fourth	11/20/95		12/15/95
Fifth	12/22/95		1/3/96
Sixth	1/4/96		1/25/96
Seventh	1/6/96		9/30/96[a]
Eighth	1/6/96		1/26/96[a]
Ninth	1/6/96		1/26/96
Tenth	1/26/96		3/15/96
Eleventh	3/15/96		3/22/96[a]
Twelfth	3/22/96		4/3/96
Thirteenth	3/29/96		4/24/96
Fourteenth	4/24/96		4/25/96

a. These expiration dates applied to the majority of the programs; additional continuing resolutions were necessary for the other programs.

president has "to accept actions that must be taken to accomplish the desires expressed by the American people last November." Certain they would win, Republicans presented Clinton with a rider-laden continuing resolution. The president vetoed the measure, forcing federal agencies that lacked appropriations to close their doors. Although the federal government had been closed nine times previously, none of the shutdowns had lasted for more than three days. While it was Clinton's veto that forced the shutdown, he was not blamed for the impasse; Republicans were. Both sides finally negotiated a new temporary continuing resolution that reopened the government and gave each side some of its most salient demands. Clinton agreed to a tax cut and the goal of a balanced budget in seven years. In exchange, Republicans agreed to protect important Democratic priorities.

But this respite in the budget war did not bring lasting peace. House Republican leaders linked action on appropriations to tax and spending cuts they sought in the vetoed reconciliation bill. Clinton stood his ground, declaring, "I won't yield to these threats. . . . I won't be forced into signing a budget that violates our values." Clinton brokered a deal with Speaker Newt Gingrich (R-Ga.) and Senate Majority Leader Robert Dole (R-Kans.) on a new continuing resolution that would avert another shutdown. However, Republican freshmen in the House refused to accept the deal, and parts of the government closed for three weeks. Dole

continued

▼

BOX 9-1
Continued

claimed that "Clinton's fingerprints" were "all over the shutdown," but the public again blamed the Republicans.

As weeks of budgetary impasse stretched into months, both sides hardened their positions. House Budget Committee Chair John Kasich (R-Ohio) stated the Republican case for staying the course: "If you don't worry about getting beaten up, you can do great things." But when Congress reconvened in 1996, Republicans acknowledged that their confrontational strategy had failed; it was time to reopen the government and keep it open by passing the remaining appropriations bills. After further delay and several more continuing resolutions, the five remaining appropriations were folded into an omnibus measure that finally cleared Congress in April and was quickly signed into law.

House Republicans had misinterpreted the 1994 election and the attitudes of most Americans. They also underestimated Clinton's steely use of the veto power and determination to get his way. Senate Republican leaders were reluctantly drawn into the fight and sensed that budgetary brinksmanship would lead their party into a quagmire. On the other side, Clinton and congressional Democrats never wavered in protecting their priorities; they rescued programs slated for elimination and forced Republicans to drop most of the controversial riders. Throughout, Clinton managed to sidestep blame, portraying himself as committed to a balanced budget and to keeping the government open. The 1996 election results cemented Clinton's victory—he defeated Dole in the presidential race, and Republicans lost seats in the House.

Congress, when House leaders unilaterally eliminated three subcommittees and realigned the jurisdictions of several others (see table 9-4). The official justification was that the need to consider 13 separate bills each year congests the legislative calendar and impedes timely enactment of the spending bills. The biggest casualty was the Veterans' Affairs–Housing and Urban Development subcommittee, whose jurisdiction included environmental and science programs, space exploration, housing, community development, and veterans' programs. Politics undoubtedly came into play as the restructuring enabled House Republican leaders to tighten their grip on the appropriations process by reshuffling both subcommittee jurisdictions and chairman-

ships. As in the past, each subcommittee had jurisdiction over a single bill, but in a break with tradition, the full House Appropriations Committee retained jurisdiction over the Legislative Branch appropriations bill.

This time, however, the Senate did not follow suit. It reorganized into 12 subcommittees, retaining the Legislative Branch and District of Columbia subcommittees, which had been eliminated in the House. The new lineup left the House and Senate with different subcommittee structures for the first time in decades. In 2007, at the beginning of the 110th Congress, the new Democratic majority realigned the appropriations subcommittees once again, establishing 12 parallel House and Senate appropriations subcommittees.

TABLE 9-4
House and Senate Appropriations Subcommittees, 2005–06 (109th Congress)

House	Senate
Agriculture–Rural Development	Agriculture–Rural Development
Science-State-Justice-Commerce[a]	Commerce-Justice-Science[a]
Defense[a]	Defense[a]
. . .	District of Columbia[a]
Energy and Water	Energy and Water
Foreign Operations[a]	State–Foreign Operations[a]
Homeland Security	Homeland Security
Interior and Environment	Interior
Labor-HHS-Education	Labor-HHS-Education
. . .	Legislative Branch
Military Quality of Life and Veterans Affairs[a]	Military Construction and Veterans Affairs[a]
Transportation-Treasury-HUD-Judiciary-District of Columbia[a]	Transportation-Treasury-Judiciary-HUD[a]

a. Indicates significant jurisdictional differences between House and Senate subcommittees. Relatively minor differences existed among some other subcommittees.

Despite their parallel subcommittee structure, the House and Senate appropriations committees are different institutions. The House Appropriations Committee has twice as many members as its Senate counterpart, many of whom do not serve on any other major committee. Representatives on the appropriations committee are expected to concentrate on committee work, to master the details of programs and spending in their subcommittee's jurisdiction, and to view legislative issues from the appropriations perspective. However, every member of the Senate Appropriations Committee concurrently serves on one or more major authorizing committees. Their other obligations limit the amount of time senators devote to appropriations work. More important, many senators fill two conflicting roles—they are both program advocates and spending controllers. Sometimes the conflicts are in the same program area, when senators serve on both an authorizing committee and the appropriations subcommittee that deals with the same subject. Senator Richard Russell (D-Ga.) chaired the Armed Services Committee at the same time that he chaired the Defense Appropriations Subcommittee; Senator John Stennis (D-Miss.) also held both these posts at the same time. More recently, Senator J. Bennett Johnston (D-La.) concurrently chaired the Energy and Natural Resources Committee and the Energy and Water Appropriations Subcommittee.

Multiple committee assignments divide the loyalties of those serving on Senate Appropriations and diminish the time they devote to the committee's work. Senators who serve on several committees inevitably bring their authorizing interests and perspectives to the appropriations process. Some dominate an issue in the Senate (and occasionally throughout Congress) by virtue of their commanding position on both the authorizing committee and the appropriations committee. This dominance has been lessened by Senate rules that bar members from chairing or serving as ranking minority member of both an authorizing committee and appropriations subcommittee.

Until the mid-1990s, the sequence of congressional action also differentiated the House and Senate appropriations committees. Although the Constitution is silent on the matter, by precedent going back to the First Congress, appropriations bills always originated in the House. When its action follows the House's, the Senate does not produce its own bill, but instead it amends the House-passed appropriations by inserting the Senate's changes. Then the conference committee resolves the differences in the measures passed by the two chambers. This sequence, and the time demands of multiple committee assignments, spurred the Senate to concentrate on matters still in dispute after the House had completed its work. Agencies would "reclama"—that is, appeal to Senate Appropriations to give them more money than was voted by the House or make other changes in the House-passed bill. Its role as a court of appeals typically resulted in the Senate appropriating more than the House provided.

The discretionary spending caps that were in effect during the 1990s narrowed the behavioral differences between the House and Senate committees. The caps limited the additional funds the Senate could provide after the House had completed its work. The House usually appropriated up to the allowable limit, putting the Senate in the politically awkward position of having to cut some programs in order to provide more money for others. The Senate Appropriations Committee adapted to the new situation by reporting some of its bills before the House had acted. When this occurs, Congress preserves the notion that the House acts first by inserting the Senate version into the bill subsequently passed by the House. Table 9-5, which lists the sequence of House and Senate appropriations actions in selected years, reveals that the House has reasserted its prerogative to initiate spending bills. In one important regard, however, the old order has not been restored. For generations, the House Appropriations Committee styled itself as the guardian of the Treasury, boasting of the amounts it had cut from the president's budget and resisting some Senate demands to spend more. The spending spree that began in the late 1990s called this self-image into question. Both in the number of earmarks (discussed later in this chapter) and total appropriations, the House Appropriations Committee has cast its lot with those who want to spend more. This behavioral shift has multiple sources: the enlarged role of party leaders who see short-term advantage in accommodating spending demands; the proliferation and activism of interest groups (including state and local governments) that lobby for additional funds; the soaring cost of election campaigns (in which locally targeted appropriations can facilitate raising campaign funds); and the opening up of the appropriations process to outside pressures. President George W. Bush's unwillingness to use the veto power during the first years of his presidency and the use of baselines to score congressional budget actions also have diminished the zeal to cut federal spending.

One final consideration may outweigh all the other factors. Few members of Congress seek posts on appropriations committees because they want to trim federal spending; rather, most gravitate in that direction because they want to do good things for their district or for the programs they favor. Even if they are not big spenders when they enter Congress, they tend to join the spending parade when they become members of an appropriations committee. Most of what they hear from constituents, program advocates, lobbyists, and local officials strengthens the case to spend more. Nothing less than a shift in the mood of the country can countervail against the relentless momentum to boost appropriations.

TABLE 9-5
Which Chamber Acted First on Appropriations Bills, Selected Fiscal Years

Bill	1994 Reported	1994 Passed[a]	1998 Reported	1998 Passed	2005 Reported	2005 Passed
Agriculture	House	House	House	same day	House	House
Commerce-Justice-State	House	House	Senate	Senate	House	House
Defense	House	House	Senate	Senate	House	House
District of Columbia	House	House	Senate	House	House	House
Energy and Water	House	House	Senate	Senate	House	House
Foreign Operations	House	House	Senate	Senate	House	House
Homeland Security[b]	. . .	. . .	. . .	. . .	House	House
Interior	House	House	House	House	House	House
Labor-HHS-Education	House	House	House	Senate	House	House
Legislative Branch	House	House	Senate	Senate	House	House
Military Construction	House	House	House	House	House	House
Transportation[c]	House	House	House	House	House	House
Treasury–Postal Service[c]	House	House	Senate	Senate	[c]	[c]
VA-HUD-Independent Agencies	House	House	House	House	House	[d]

Source: *Congressional Quarterly Almanac,* 1993, 1997, and 2004

a. Refers to chamber that first passed each bill, not that which first adopted the conference report.

b. The Homeland Security Appropriations Act was first enacted for fiscal year 2004.

c. The Treasury–Postal Service Appropriations Act was incorporated into the new Transportation-Treasury Appropriations Act beginning with fiscal year 2004; see "Transportation" for fiscal year 2005.

d. The fiscal year 2005 VA-HUD Appropriations Act was reported by the House and Senate appropriations committees but was not considered separately by either chamber; it was folded into an omnibus appropriations act.

PROCEDURES AND POLITICS OF COMMITTEE ACTION

The appropriations committees have a structured sequence of tasks they perform each year. While the timing may vary from the schedule set forth in table 9-6, the steps are likely to be completed in the sequence displayed in the table.

The annual appropriations process begins with submission of the president's budget to Congress. In contrast to authorizing committees, which typically take up legislation in response to the introduction of a bill, the appropriations committees initiate their work in response to a request by the president for money. These committees rarely act on their own initiative or pursuant to legislative proposals by members of Congress. In fact, a bill does not even exist during the early stages of the appropriations process; usually an appropriations bill is introduced when the committee is about to report the measure. Often the bill is introduced, referred to committee, and reported on the same day. Despite the absence of a bill, there is considerable activity concentrated around hearings, the allocation of discretionary budget resources among the subcommittees, markup, and drafting of the report that accompanies the bill.

Hearings

In some years, soon after the president sends his budget to Congress, each appropriations committee conducts overview hearings at which the director of the Office of Management and Budget (OMB) and others testify concerning overall budget policies and priorities. These are the only sessions in which OMB is formally

TABLE 9-6
Timetable of Appropriation Actions[a]

February	**President submits his budget to Congress** This initiates the appropriations process; appropriations committees rarely act without a presidential request
February	**Full appropriations committees sometimes conduct brief overview hearings** These are the only full committee hearings. In some recent years, the committees have forgone these hearings
February/March	**Each agency submits justification material** These documents are printed in the agency hearings, and they offer a detailed explanation of the agency's budget request
February/April	**Subcommittee hearings held** House appropriations subcommittee hearings usually are held first, followed shortly thereafter by Senate subcommittee hearings
May/July	**Section 302(b) allocations made by the appropriations committees** These allocations to the subcommittees must precede floor consideration of appropriations bills
May/July	**The chair's mark (optional)** Each subcommittee chair issues a "mark" recommending amounts for the accounts in the subcommittee's jurisdiction
May/July	**Subcommittee markup** Each subcommittee marks up its bill and drafts a report explaining its decisions and providing guidance to affected agencies
May/July	**Full committee reports the bill** Full committee normally makes only minor changes (if any) in the bill prepared by the subcommittee
May/July	**House floor action** Each bill is considered individually
July/August	**Senate floor action** The Senate usually acts after the House and takes up the House-passed bill; if it acts first on its own bill, it incorporates the amended Senate-numbered bill into the House bill for final passage
September/October	**Conferences and final passage** Congress passes one or more continuing resolutions if any of the regular appropriations bills have not been enacted into law by October 1

a. While the steps in this schedule occur every year, the timing of actions may vary from the timetable shown here.

involved (other than in hearings on its own appropriation) and the only hearings the full committees hold. In some years, the appropriations committees skip the overview hearings altogether.

Each agency justifies its budget before its appropriations subcommittee. Before the hearings, agencies prepare justification material that compares the president's budget request with the previous appropriation and explains variances between the two. Each sub-

committee dictates the format and content of the justification material; some structure the justifications according to objectives defined in the strategic plans required by the Government Performance and Results Act of 1993 (GPRA). It is common for the spending agencies to break down their budgets into discrete line items and activities and to justify changes from the previous budget. Exhibit 9-3 shows the type of information included in many agency justification books.

▶ **EXHIBIT 9-3**
Agency Justification of Appropriations Request

Smithsonian Institution
Salaries and Expenses
Summary of FY 2008 Change

	FTEs[a]	Amount
FY 2007 Request	4,251	$537,394,000
FY 2008 Changes		
Mandatory Increases		
Legislated Pay Raises and Workers' Compensation		11,406,000
Utilities, Communications, and Rent		10,373,000
Total Mandatory Increases		21,779,000
Program Increases		
Facilities Operations, Security, and Support Security Check and Badging System Improvements	2	1,381,000
National Museum of African American History and Culture	28	9,893,000
National Zoo—Animal Welfare	3	600,000
Inspector General Auditor	1	100,000
Human Resource Workforce Restructuring		200,000
Total Program Increases		12,174,000
FY 2008 Request	4,285	$571,347,000

a. Full-time equivalents.

Source: Smithsonian Institution, "Summary of FY 2008 Change," February 2007, available at www.si.edu/about/budget/2008/04%20-%20Summary%20of%20Change_R.pdf.

(a) Each agency requesting appropriations submits detailed justifications to the appropriations subcommittees with jurisdiction over its budget. The justifications are published as part of the subcommittee's hearings.

(b) Each subcommittee prescribes the form of the material submitted to it; this exhibit displays the traditional format, which concentrates on proposed increases or decreases from the current year's appropri-

ation. As is the case here, the request (for fiscal year 2008) usually is higher than the current appropriation (for fiscal year 2007). The justifications highlight increases or decreases because these increments are what the appropriations committees traditionally have focused on in reviewing spending requests.

(c) Since the mid-1990s, some subcommittees have reformatted the budget justifications to focus on total spending rather than incremental changes, and on outputs and objectives rather than inputs and items of expenditure.

During the hearings and subsequent negotiations, OMB requires agency officials to uphold the president's budget, even when it differs from their own preferences. It is rare for officials to openly stray from the president's budget. When they do, their career may come to an early end. This happened in 2002 when Mike Parker, director of the Army Corps of Engineers, testified that President Bush's budget would have a "negative impact" on the Corps. Immediately afterwards, Parker was given 30 minutes by the White House to resign or be fired. Of course, there are politically acceptable ways of prying information from agencies regarding what they really want. Although they are not permitted to volunteer such information, agencies may do so in response to questions—some of which may be prearranged—from subcommittee members. Behind the scenes, OMB enforces fidelity to the president's budget by reviewing agency testimony (which is submitted to it in advance) and monitoring the hearings and other action on the appropriations bills. OMB also intervenes at various stages to notify the appropriations committees of any objections the president may have to pending measures.

Most (and in some cases, all) of the testimony is by agency officials, many of whom carefully prepare for the hearings by reviewing detailed briefing books, the previous year's appropriation, and reports. A few agency heads stage mock hearings, at which they are questioned by staff on matters that the subcommittee may raise. In large agencies, the top official is accompanied at the hearings by an entourage of aides who are prepared to provide on-the-spot information in response to questions from members. At most hearings, the testifying agency is given interrogatories—questions for the record—to which it must respond within a few days. The responses to these questions are carefully reviewed by senior officials to ensure that they do not damage the agency's budget request.

Do the hearings make a difference in appropriations outcomes? Probably some, but not all that much. Informal contacts with appropriations committee members and staff are more important in shaping congressional decisions than the formal hearings are. Why then do agencies invest so much care and effort in the hearings? One reason is that a poor appearance can damage an agency's case. Agency witnesses are schooled in proper behavior at the hearings. They must be deferential to members of Congress and not challenge them, even when they feel mistreated. They must be responsive to all questions, and they must supply such additional information as is requested. But it is not only the agency's budget that is on trial at the hearings; its officials are also under examination. How they come through the ordeal has a bearing on the extent to which appropriators have confidence in their performance and trust their numbers. Hearings matter because they are rituals that test the agency's mettle. They also matter because they transmit to agencies the concerns and interests of members. Moreover, they put agencies on notice that even though they may get just about all that was requested, Congress controls the purse.

Section 302(b) Allocations

Although the hearings process is decentralized, with each subcommittee arranging its own schedule and examining the witnesses who appear before it, a subcommittee cannot formally mark up its bill until it has received a section 302(b) allocation from the full committee. This allocation limits the total budget authority and outlays available to each subcommittee for all accounts in its jurisdiction. When Congress adopts the annual budget resolution, the budget committees (pursuant to section 302(a) of the Budget Act) allocate budget resources to each House and Senate committee with jurisdiction over discretionary or direct spending. All discretionary spending is allocated to the appropriations committees, which also receive allocations for entitlements funded in the appropriations bills. Each appropriations committee then issues a section 302(b) report subdividing its budget resources among the subcommittees. The sum allocated to all subcommittees may not exceed the amount available to the full committee. House and Senate rules bar floor consideration of spending measures before the appropriations committees have filed the required section 302(b) report. Excerpts from one such report appear in exhibit 9-4.

This report is not simply a formality. Preparing it involves decisions on the relative priority of federal programs, as represented by subcommittee jurisdictions. The process triggers two rounds of zero-sum competition—first among subcommittees and then among the accounts in each subcommittee's jurisdiction. More for one subcommittee means less for another; more for one account means others will get less. The 302(b) allocations have impelled the appropriations subcommittees to coordinate their spending plans. The subcommittees can no longer act wholly independently of one another—they cannot be indifferent to total spending or to the amounts available to other subcommittees. Before each subcommittee marks up its bill, all subcommittees are informed through the 302(b) procedure of how much they have to spend.

Dividing the discretionary spending pie among competing subcommittees combines political judgment and interpersonal negotiation. The chair of the appropriations committee leads the process in each chamber. The chair usually consults with the subcommittee chairs, probing the amounts they want or might settle for, proposing allocations to the subcommittees and gauging reactions, and calling the committee together to approve the section 302(b) report only when informal agreements have been reached. Appropriations staff play an important behind-the-scenes role in developing a database for the allocations and in negotiating understandings that are taken to committee members for their approval.

The House Appropriations Committee usually issues its 302(b) report in May, and the Senate committee does so in June, but the subcommittees cannot wait this long to start preparing their spending bills. Although they might not have exact figures, the subcommittees have ballpark numbers long before the formal allocations are issued. The effect of the section 302(b) process is to move up key appropriations decisions to an earlier stage; the budget fate of many programs is sealed months before formal appropriation decisions are announced.

There are, however, two ways by which programs may obtain more money later in the process. One is through revision in the section 302(b) report; the other is through budgetary negotiations between the president and Congress. The appropriations committees may revise the 302(b) report at any time during the year, provided that the total allocated to all subcommittees remains within budget limits. Typically, the reports are updated periodically to take into account conference committee decisions and other developments affecting spending levels. The section 302(b) reports also are revised to reflect budgetary agreements between the White House and Capitol Hill that generate more appropriations than were contemplated under the original section 302(b) allocations. In some cases, these agreements make room for additional spending by

▶ EXHIBIT 9-4
Section 302(b) Suballocations to Appropriations Subcommittees

REVISED SUBALLOCATIONS TO SUBCOMMITTEES
FISCAL YEAR 2007 BUDGET AUTHORITY AND OUTLAYS

(in millions of dollars)

Subcommittee	Discretionary	Mandatory	Total
Agriculture, Rural Development, Food and Drug Administration			
Budget authority	17,812	70,945	88,757
Outlays	19,497	52,946	72,443
Defense			
Budget authority	377,357	251	377,608
Outlays	393,165	251	393,416
Energy and Water Development			
Budget authority	30,017	...	30,017
Outlays	31,411	5	31,416
Foreign Operations			
Budget authority	21,300	39	21,339
Outlays	23,441	39	23,480
Homeland Security			
Budget authority	32,080	1,017	33,097
Outlays	38,711	1,014	39,725

Source: House Appropriations Committee, "FY2007 Subcommittee Allocations—302(b)s," available on the House Appropriations Committee website (appropriations.house.gov/pdf/FY07 302b.pdf).

(a) It is not in order to consider any appropriations bill until the House or Senate appropriations committee has filed a section 302(b) report allocating the amounts available to it among its subcommittees. (Section 302(b) is the provision in the 1974 Congressional Budget Act that requires these reports.) Each appropriations committee may revise these allocations by filing a new report.

(b) The total amount allocated to the subcommittees may not exceed the amount allocated to the appropriations committee in the joint explanatory statement accompanying the budget resolution.

(c) Separate allocations are made for budget authority and outlays, as well as for discretionary and mandatory spending. Almost all of the mandatory amounts shown here are for entitlements funded in annual appropriations acts. These appropriated entitlements are controlled by various authorizing committees.

designating some items as emergency; in other cases, various resources are used to offset the additional spending, or spending is deferred to the next fiscal year. A fair appraisal of the section 302(b) allocations is that while they are not airtight, they have had a constraining effect on total discretionary spending.

Subcommittee Markup

Markups are sessions at which subcommittees (or committees) review and report legislation. In the appropriations process, the subcommittee markup is particularly important because the full committee rarely makes major revisions in the bill referred to it. (Technically, only committees report legislation; subcommittees refer legislation to the full committee.) Moreover, the subcommittee drafts the report that accompanies the appropriation bill. It, too, is reported by the full committee, usually with little or no change.

Because of the section 302(b) allocations, almost all appropriations decisions have been made by the time the subcommittee markup begins. These decisions usually are distilled in the "chairman's mark," a document distributed by the chair at, or shortly before, the markup that recommends amounts for each account in the bill. The chair's mark recommends spending for just about all the funds available under section 302(b), leaving rank-and-file members little opportunity to add funds for favored programs. Members have an incentive to notify the chair of their preferences in advance, since the markup is usually too late to influence subcommittee decisions.

Most subcommittee markups are conducted under rules requiring budget neutrality—an amendment increasing one account must also propose offsetting cuts in other accounts. This rule heightens explicit competition among programs for scarce appropria-

tions, and trade-offs are sometimes made during markup. This is most likely to occur in subcommittees that have sprawling jurisdiction over programs whose only affinity is that they are funded in the same appropriations bill. Competition for money was especially intense in the recently dismantled Veterans' Affairs (VA)–Housing and Urban Development (HUD) subcommittee, where space programs were pitted against veterans; such competition was one of the factors in the elimination of this subcommittee.

In addition to setting appropriations levels, the markup approves provisions in the appropriations bill and the text of the accompanying report. As will be discussed later in the chapter, these provisions are often among the most controversial features of appropriations bills. Some provisions earmark funds to particular purposes, others limit the use of appropriated funds, and still others contain legislation changing existing law. The limitations and legislative provisions tend to sharpen partisan conflict on subcommittees. In the late 1990s, Republican efforts to limit enforcement of various environmental laws split the House VA-HUD Appropriations Subcommittee. Although these provisions did not survive the legislative gauntlet, they damaged subcommittee cohesion and delayed enactment of appropriations.

Subcommittees do not closely review report language during markup, but they may take up controversial matters brought to their attention. Sometimes controversy is resolved by moving disputed provisions from the appropriations bill to the committee report or by inserting report language that offers guidance on provisions in the bill.

Full Committee Markup

The appropriations committees may revise the bills and reports the subcommittees prepare, but they rarely make major changes. Their markup usually occurs only a few days before the House or Senate takes up the spending bill—often the committee completes work on more than one bill in a single meeting. Normally, the appropriations committees review each bill to ascertain whether it is within the section 302(b) allocation and to make a few adjustments in amounts and report language to reflect their preferences. Overall, however, an informal rule of reciprocity pervades full appropriations committee markups. Members defer to the judgment of the subcommittee of jurisdiction in the expectation that when their subcommittee's bill is taken up, others will defer to it.

Incrementalism

Although they often miss deadlines, the appropriations committees regard the timely completion of their work as a measure of effectiveness. To achieve this goal, they traditionally limit the conflict inherent in the allocation of money among competing claims. In most appropriations cycles, the main behavioral rule is that appropriations should vary only incrementally from the previous year's level. Ongoing programs should be continued, cuts in existing programs should be avoided or minimized, and increases should be modest and broadly distributed among an array of programs.

Making incremental decisions requires that the appropriations committees review each request with reference to the amount provided for the previous year. These committees are the only major congressional budget makers who do not explicitly use baselines to measure the financial impact of their actions. Baselines are grounded on assumptions about future conditions; the appropriators rely instead on actual amounts: the current year's appropriation and

the president's request for the next year. By eschewing baseline projections, the committees strengthen their control of incremental resources. Suppose, for example, that inflation for the next year is estimated at 3 percent, but the appropriations committees recommend nominal increases of 2 percent for particular programs or accounts. If baselines were used, this decision would be scored as a cutback; in appropriations it is counted as an increase, even though it does not fully compensate for expected inflation.

Since the appropriations committees behave incrementally, they focus on nominal year-to-year spending changes at all stages of the process—from the preparation of justification material, through hearings, to markup and committee reports. For most subcommittees, the agencies' justification material highlights the arithmetic difference between the previous appropriation and the budget request. Only rarely do agencies justify their entire request. In normal times, when the president asks for more than was appropriated for the current year, his request and the previous appropriation form the boundaries within which most appropriations decisions fall. That is, most appropriations are higher than the previous year's level and below the president's budget.

Incremental outcomes are not happenstance. Every step of the way, account by account, the appropriations committees calculate how much the amounts they are recommending are more or less than the previous appropriation and the president's request. In fact, as exhibit 9-5 shows, they often publish the arithmetic difference between their actions and these two reference points in the committee reports. They use these calculations to do their own work.

From the vantage point of the appropriations committees, incremental decisions have several compelling advantages. They reduce

▶ **EXHIBIT 9-5**
Incrementalism in the Appropriations Process

HOUSE REPORT

UNITED STATES COAST GUARD
OPERATING EXPENSES

Appropriation, fiscal year 2006	$5,293,771,000
Budget estimate, fiscal year 2007	5,518,843,000
Recommended in the bill	5,481,643,000
Bill compared with:	
Appropriation, fiscal year 2006	+187,872,000
Budget estimate, fiscal year 2007	−37,200,000

SENATE REPORT

OPERATING EXPENSES

Appropriations, 2006	$5,161,771,000
Budget estimate, 2007	5,518,843,000
House allowance	5,481,643,000
Committee recommendation	5,534,349,000

HOUSE COMPARATIVE STATEMENT

Account	FY 2006 enacted	FY 2007 request	Bill	Bill vs. enacted	Bill vs. request
Military pay and allowances	2,974,770	2,788,276	2,788,276	-186,494	. . .
Civilian pay and benefits	526,182	569,434	569,434	+43,252	. . .
Training and recruiting	175,359	180,876	180,876	+5,517	. . .
Operating funds and unit level maintenance	947,400	1,061,574	1,009,374	+61,974	-52,200
Centrally managed accounts	183,150	207,954	207,954	+24,804	. . .
Port security	. . .	. . .	15,000	+15,000	+15,000

Sources: *Department of Homeland Security Appropriations Bill, 2007,* H. Rept. 109-476, pp. 58, 156, and 157, and S. Rept. 109-273, p. 50, 109th Cong., 2d sess., 2006.

(a) In their reports, the appropriations committees often compare the amounts recommended in the bill with both the current year's appropriation and the president's budget request, specifying the amounts they recommend as higher, lower, or the same as each of these benchmarks. They make this comparison for each account in the bill, as well as for the totals in the bill.

(b) Each appropriations committee report has a comparative table listing each account in the bill. The House reports (such as the one exhibited here) have five columns; the Senate statement typically has seven columns: the five contained in the House report and two additional columns showing the House recommendations and the differences between the House and Senate.

(c) The appropriations committees do not use baseline projections to calculate the budgetary impact of their actions. They eschew baselines, which depend on assumptions about future conditions, and rely instead on the amounts actually appropriated for the previous year and requested for the next year.

TABLE 9-7
Accounts for Which the House Appropriations Committee Recommended Increases or Decreases, Fiscal Years 1996 and 1997[a]

Percent

| Bill | Fiscal year 1996 recommendations | | | | | |
| | Compared with FY1995 appropriation | | | Compared with president's request | | |
	Increase	Decrease	No change	Increase	Decrease	No change
Agriculture	33	38	29	11	66	23
Commerce	36	47	17	6	83	11
Energy and Water	25	73	2	12	69	19
Foreign Operations	25	59	16	8	77	14
Interior	16	71	12	4	80	16
Labor-HHS	24	73	3	6	74	20
Transportation	25	57	18	7	57	36
Treasury	19	66	15	7	68	25
VA-HUD	15	56	29	8	64	28
Average percentage	24	60	16	8	71	21

Sources: House Appropriations Committee, *Comparative Statement of New Budget (Obligational) Authority for 1995 and Budget Estimates and Amounts Recommended in the Bill for 1996,* 104th Cong., 1st sess., selected reports, and House Appropriations Committee, *Comparative Statement of New Budget (Obligational) Authority for 1996 and Budget Estimates and Amounts Recommended in the Bill for 1997,* 104th Cong., 2d sess., selected reports.

conflict over spending and facilitate the timely enactment of appropriations. They reduce the legislative workload by enabling the committees to concentrate on changes at the margins rather than on the total request. They often enable the committees to take credit both for cutting the budget (below the president's request) and increasing expenditures (above the previous level). In view of the preference of Americans for smaller government and bigger programs, the capacity of the appropriators to satisfy both sentiments is no small political feat.

Incrementalism is the unseen hand that coordinates the decentralized appropriations process. When most appropriations fall between current spending and the president's budget, the appropriations committees can be confident that the total of all their decisions

will also be between these reference points. Over the years, incrementalism has enabled the appropriations committees to produce seemingly coordinated outcomes without trespassing on the autonomy of the subcommittees.

Incrementalism depends on a cooperative president, who by asking for more enables the appropriations committees to give more while taking credit for cutting back. This condition did not prevail during the 1980s, when Ronald Reagan demanded deep cuts in many established programs. Although he got his way at first, the appropriations committees quickly regrouped and managed to spend more on domestic programs while staying within the president's budget by trimming some of the additional resources he sought for defense. Reagan's unwillingness to play by incremental rules generated intense conflict and delayed

| Fiscal year 1997 recommendations | | | | | |
| Compared with FY1996 appropriation | | | Compared with president's request | | |
Increase	Decrease	No change	Increase	Decrease	No change
33	37	30	2	58	40
47	42	11	5	80	15
32	58	10	16	62	22
17	49	34	10	51	39
36	36	28	11	53	36
53	44	3	7	75	18
34	35	31	10	52	38
47	30	23	18	39	43
45	26	29	14	53	33
38	40	22	10	58	32

a. Table does not include Defense, District of Columbia, Legislative Branch, or Military Construction appropriations bills. The figures include various special types of accounts such as working capital funds, trust funds, estimated loan levels, liquidation and rescission of contract authorizations, and limitations on direct loans, obligations, borrowing authority, and administrative expenses.

the enactment of appropriations bills. George H. W. Bush also confronted Congress on the budget by proposing domestic cutbacks, but he did not have Reagan's early success. During his term, Bush took a more accommodating stance on budgetary increments, accepting spending increases while attacking Congress for excessive spending.

During the Clinton presidency, efforts by congressional Republicans to cut federal spending and the discretionary caps undermined incrementalism. Table 9-7 compares the appropriations reported by the House Appropriations Committee in 1995—the year in which Republicans took control of Congress—with the amounts appropriated the previous year. Hundreds of programs and accounts were slashed below previous levels, leading to an impasse that was broken only

after a partial shutdown of government and restoration of many of the cuts. The table also shows that in the following year, House Republicans adopted a more incremental approach. During the remaining years of Clinton's term, they made feeble efforts to cut some domestic programs, but after working out differences with the Senate and the White House, the appropriations usually were at or above the previous year's level.

The discretionary spending caps had an uneven impact on incremental behavior. Each time the new caps were enacted (in 1990, 1993, and 1997), they made room for additional spending in the years immediately ahead but tightened spending totals in the last years to which the limits applied. If these caps were strictly applied, there would have been robust increments in some years and cutbacks in others. But Congress, with cooperation or pressure from the president, managed to escape the harsh austerity implied by the caps. In some years, it reset the caps to allow additional spending; in others it used bookkeeping tricks and the emergency escape route to appropriate more than the caps specified.

Congress and the president reverted to incremental appropriations during the four years of budget surpluses (fiscal years 1998–2001). These were the final years of the Clinton presidency and the first year of George W. Bush's term. Moreover, incrementalism persisted even when deficits broke through the $400 billion mark, as President Bush requested higher appropriations for defense and homeland security and Congress responded by voting additional spending for domestic programs as well. Conflict over appropriations diminished significantly as both branches got more for favored programs. During his second term, however, George W. Bush reversed course and demanded that Congress hold the line on nondefense appropriations and provide many federal agencies less money (in real terms) than they had the previous year. Despite his tougher stance, real discretionary spending is almost certain to show a greater increase during his eight years in office than during Clinton's presidency.

Projects and Pork

In making appropriations, subcommittee members do more than look at past budgets, the president's numbers, and agency justifications. They also listen to other members of Congress (especially colleagues on the appropriations committees) who want money earmarked to projects in their districts or states. Subcommittees typically receive more of these requests than they can accommodate, but they satisfy enough of them to give the appropria-

tions bill a solid base of support in the full committee and on the floor.

The normal practice is to earmark funds in committee reports rather than in the appropriations bill; exhibit 9-6 shows earmarks in one such report. The subcommittee chair, consulting with the ranking minority member, usually has the final say over the projects, but widely shared distributive norms guide the process. First, subcommittee members get the biggest prizes, with full committee members next in line. Second, the process is usually bipartisan; both Republicans and Democrats bring home some benefits. Third, members who request and receive earmarked funds are expected to vote for the appropriations bill. The operative norm is "do not ask for money if you do not support the bill."

Each subcommittee has its own notions about how much earmarking is appropriate. For years, the two largest appropriations bills moved in opposite directions on this issue. The Labor, Health and Human Services, and Education bill was relatively pork-free; the Defense bill was crammed with earmarks. Representative Bill Natcher (D-Ky.), the longtime chair of the Labor-HHS subcommittee until his death in 1994, did not like earmarks and allowed few in his bill. Defense, however, has been a pork barrel for generations because it funds thousands of military installations and projects. If pork is, as some pundits have quipped, spending with a zip code attached, there are far more zip codes in defense appropriations than in any other bill.

There are cycles in Congress's appetite for pork. When Republicans took control of Congress in 1995, many vowed that they would purge appropriations bills of earmarks, which they believed build congressional coalitions in favor of higher appropriations. Conservatives produced studies showing that the longer a member serves in Congress, the more inclined

▶ **EXHIBIT 9-6**
Earmarks in Appropriations Committee Reports

The conference agreement includes $310,000,000 for the Economic Development Initiative with specific requirements on how these funds can be used. The conference agreement directs HUD to implement the Economic Development Initiatives program as follows:

1. $100,000 to the City of Anchorage, Alaska for facilities construction associated with the SAFE Center at Chester Creek;
2. $400,000 for Bean's Café in Anchorage, Alaska for the expansion of its kitchen;
3. $150,000 for the Alaska Botanical Garden in Anchorage, Alaska for expansion and renovation of its infrastructure;
4. $750,000 for the Bering Straits Native Corporation in Nome, Alaska for Cape Nome Quarry upgrades;
5. $950,000 for the Western Alaska Council, Boy Scouts of America in Anchorage, Alaska for construction of the Boy Scouts High Adventure Base Camp near Talkeetna, Alaska;
6. $750,000 for the construction of the Tongass Coast Aquarium;
7. $750,000 for Alaska Pacific University for the construction of a building;
8. $250,000 for the construction of the Alyeska Roundhouse in Girdwood, Alaska;
9. $500,000 for the People's Regional Learning Center in Bethel, Alaska to construct a vocational school and dormitories;
10. $500,000 for the Dillingham City School District in Dillingham, Alaska to repair the gymnasium in the Dillingham middle/high school;
11. $250,000 National Children's Advocacy Center in Huntsville, Alabama for facilities planning and improvements to the advocacy center;
12. $200,000 to Chambers County, Alabama for the development of the Chambers County industrial park; . . .

Source: *Departments of Transportation, Treasury, and Housing and Urban Development, the Judiciary, District of Columbia, and Independent Agencies Appropriations Act for Fiscal Year 2006* (conference report to accompany H.R. 3058), H. Rept. 109-307, 109th Cong., 1st sess., November 18, 2005, pp. 218–19.

(a) The appropriations committees often earmark funds to designated projects or activities. While some earmarks usually are included in the text of the legislation, most are included in the accompanying committee reports. Agencies are expected to comply with the earmarks, as well as with other guidance issued by the appropriations committees.

(b) The earmarks displayed here were among many hundreds included in the Transportation-Treasury Appropriations Act for Fiscal Year 2006. In this case, the earmarks are presented alphabetically by state, with the first 10 pertaining to Alaska. The 1,125 earmarks listed in this provision covered 49 pages in the conference report.

(c) Earmarks can be for relatively small amounts, such as the $150,000 in the third earmark shown here for the Alaska Botanical Garden, or for much larger amounts in the tens or hundreds of millions.

TABLE 9-8
Earmarks in Appropriations Acts: Even-Numbered Years, Fiscal Years 1994–2004[a]

Act	1994	1996	1998	2000	2002	2004
Agriculture	313	211	284	359	629	660
Commerce-Justice-State	253	171	275	361	1,111	1,454
Defense	587	270	644	997	1,409	2,208
District of Columbia	0	0	3	16	41	78
Energy and Water	1,574	1,421	1,877	1,707	1,437	2,222
Foreign Operations	38	53	81	69	119	245
Interior	314	137	320	479	636	648
Labor-HHS-Education	5	7	25	491	1,606	2,036
Legislative Branch	1	0	1	0	4	3
Military Construction	895	556	461	518	634	580
Transportation	140	167	147	641	1,473	2,282
Treasury	53	33	11	19	73	61
VA-HUD	30	48	140	469	1,500	1,776
Total	4,202	3,084	4,269	6,126	10,692	14,253

Source: Congressional Research Service, "Earmarks in Appropriations Acts," memorandum, March 17, 2004.

a. The Congressional Research Service has cautioned that because of different definitions, the data are not consistent across all appropriations acts and for all fiscal years. It also has cautioned against adding up the amounts for each subcommittee to produce a total for the fiscal year.

she or he is to vote for appropriations bills. They reasoned that many members who enter Congress determined to cut federal spending are co-opted over time to support higher spending by the pork that their seniority earns. But after a few years of boasting that their spending bills had fewer earmarks, congressional Republicans succumbed to the temptation of using their legislative power for political advantage. When it comes to doing good for one's state or district, differences between Democrats and Republicans vanish.

Table 9-8 confirms this view of legislative politics. Drawing on data compiled by the Congressional Research Service, it shows an extraordinary rise in the number of appropriations earmarks during the decade from 1994 to 2004. The only exception to the uptrend during this period occurred in 1996, when congressional Republicans acted on their campaign commitment to curtail earmarks. But this commitment wilted in the *realpolitik* of Capitol Hill, and once they were comfortable with the exercise of power, Republicans outdid Democrats in their zeal to siphon off federal dollars for their states or districts.

The trend in earmarking is truly extraordinary and tells us a lot about contemporary American politics. The over 14,000 earmarks prescribed in 2004 were more than three times the number a decade earlier. In fact, the surge in earmarks has impelled some appropriations subcommittees to formalize the process by which members of Congress request assistance. Exhibit 9-7 is an excerpt from the instructions issued by the House Labor-HHS-Education Appropriations Subcommittee for fiscal year 2006. The information required is similar to that found in grant applications. The main difference is that only members of Congress are eligible to apply for earmarks. There is a political twist to the earmarking process. Republicans send their requests to the chair of the subcommittee; Democrats address their requests to the ranking minority member. But it is noteworthy

▶ **EXHIBIT 9-7**
Formal Procedures for Requesting Earmarks

Letter from House Labor-HHS-Education Subcommittee

As the Chairman and Ranking Member of the Labor, HHS, and Education and Related Agencies Subcommittee of the Committee on Appropriations, we are pleased to provide information regarding . . . procedures for Member appropriation requests for fiscal year 2006 appropriations. . . .

We look forward to reviewing programmatic funding recommendations and project requests from Members of Congress. Members are asked to provide one letter outlining their fiscal year 2006 *program* requests and separate letter requesting funds for individual projects. However, both program recommendations and project request letters should be submitted to the Subcommittee no later than 5:00 p.m. on Friday, April 8, 2005.

Instructions for Information in Requests
Due to the large number of requests received by the Subcommittee, please assemble your request letter as follows . . .
1. Name of Member of Congress
2. Congressional staff contact, phone number and email address
3. Priority ranking: Due to funding constraints, please assign a priority number to each project for which you are requesting funding.
4. Name and address of the grant recipient, and name and telephone number (and email address, if available) of a contact person at the recipient organization . . .
5. Provide a brief description of the *activity* or project for which funding is requested. . . .
6. Funding details: (a) Total project cost (i.e., including all funding sources and all years); (b) Amount you are requesting for this project in fiscal year 2006. . . . (d) What other funding sources are contributing to this project? What amount does each funding source contribute? (e) Has the potential recipient received funding for this project from any federal agency currently or in the past five years?

Source: House Appropriations Subcommittee on Labor, Health and Human Services, and Education, March 2005.

(a) Each subcommittee has its own procedures for processing members' requests. Some are less formal than those used by the subcommittee exhibited here.

(b) The early deadline (April 8) indicates that many, probably most, funding decisions are made early in the annual cycle, months before the appropriations bills are considered by the House and Senate.

(c) The Labor, Health and Human Services, and Education Subcommittee has a history of bipartisan cooperation. The letter exhibited here was signed by both the chair and the ranking member. But it instructed Republicans to submit their views to the chair and Democrats to submit theirs to the ranking member. However, it concluded, "Of course, all are welcome to send letters to both of us."

(d) The instructions pertain to requests from members of Congress. There are no formal procedures for requests from citizens or organizations. It almost always is more effective for lobbyists to work through members than to submit requests directly.

that the instructions were issued jointly by both the Republican chair and the Democratic ranking member. The two parties fight over social programs; they unite on pork by dividing the spoils.

Because there is no standard definition of earmarks, the data presented in table 9-8 have to be interpreted with caution. Some observers label any project mentioned in an appropriations bill or committee report as an earmark; others restrict the term to items designated for a specific state or locality. But despite disagreements over the term, there is no doubt that the practice has escalated in recent times. Why are there so many more earmarks now than 5 or 10 years ago? Why do the appropriations committees earmark an average of 25 items for each member of Congress?

The large number of earmarks indicates that the cost of inducing members of Congress to vote for appropriations bills (and other legislation) has increased. Members are much more individualistic than they were in the past. Furthermore, earmarks benefiting home districts may help them raise the vast sums required to mount reelection campaigns. But this is not the whole explanation. The volume of earmarks has soared because lobbyists and other claimants are much better organized than in the past to demand favors from Congress. Some of the most successful lobbying firms specialize in representing clients who want projects inserted in spending bills or reports. Mayors and governors are less inhibited about asking for benefits than they were in the past; in fact, it is expected that they will come to Washington with annual shopping lists. And members of Congress are less inhibited than they once were in dispensing favors to constituents and others. Many members of Congress define their roles more in terms of representing their state or district than in legislation for the country.

Earmarks also are a barometer of legislative-executive relations. They manifest Congress's willingness to flex its muscle and to dictate in detail how federal agencies should operate and how they should spend appropriated funds. The growth in earmarking has been accompanied by a sharp increase in the amount of detailed guidance contained in appropriations committee reports. This trend, which is examined later in the chapter, suggests that the president and agencies have lost political bargaining power vis-à-vis Congress. With few exceptions, they have been unable to block Congress from telling them what to do or not to do.

Hardly anyone has a nice thing to say about earmarked appropriations. The president and executive agencies do not like congressional earmarks because they narrow agency discretion in using funds. Authorizing committees profess not to like the practice because they would rather have the earmarks in their own bills. Members of Congress who do not get what they regard as a fair share of the money complain that the practice is wasteful and corrupt. Many who come away winners claim to abhor the volume of pork distributed through the appropriations bills but justify their actions by saying that everybody else is earmarking funds, and they have to look after the interests of their states and districts. The news media and critics of Congress see corruption and vote buying behind earmarked projects.

Several instances of corruption that came to a head in the latter part of the 109th Congress were linked in part to some cases of earmarking. This led Congress to reexamine its rules in this area. In 2007, at the beginning of the 110th Congress, the House adopted a rule requiring the identification of earmarks and their sponsors, and the distribution of this information, before legislation containing the earmarks could be considered; it also adopted another rule barring members from requesting or promoting earmarks in which they (or their families) would have a financial interest. The House rules apply not only to earmarks in appropriations acts but also to earmarks in direct spending measures and limited tax or tariff provisions in revenue measures. The Senate, in early 2007, included similar earmarking rules in comprehensive ethics legislation that it passed and sent to the House, but action on the measure was not completed as of this writing. However, the chair of the Senate Appropriations Committee, Senator Robert C. Byrd (D-W.Va.), implemented a policy of complying with the earmark rules proposed in the pending legislation. The House also adopted later in 2007 a rule aimed at preventing earmarks that had not first been considered by either the House or Senate from being added (or "air-dropped") at the conference stage.

Earmarks flourish because members of Congress would rather decide where appropriations are to be spent than let executive officials make the decisions. They survive periodic reform campaigns because the chief political value of serving on appropriations committees lies in bringing home the bacon, not guarding the Treasury. The appropriations committees earmark because a spending bill with projects spread across the country is easier to pass than one without them. Earmarks flourish in good times when incremental resources are plentiful and, it seems, even more in hard times when the budget is tight.

Though the amounts may appear to be very large to ordinary citizens, in budgetary terms, earmarks are relatively inexpensive—many dozens can be crammed into a tight appropriations bill. Eight thousand projects averaging $1 million each would total less than 1 percent of discretionary spending and less than one-third of a percent of all federal spending.

When funds are scarce, pork is prized because it may be the only benefit that members can bring home. Programs, by contrast, are expensive because they typically provide nationwide (rather than local) benefits. Consider, for example, a proposal to improve public education by subsidizing school linkups to the Internet. Even if such a program were started modestly, with only $100 allotted per student, the total cost would exceed $5 billion. Suppose, however, that instead of a national program, a member earmarks $1 million to a school in her district for an Internet demonstration project. In the political arithmetic of budgeting, $100 per student may be too expensive while $1 million for one school is affordable.

To argue that earmarking is relatively inexpensive is not to justify the practice or to claim that the money is well spent. But neither should one conclude that the enormous size of the federal budget is due to pork; it is due to the expensive program commitments undertaken by the government.

If history is a guide, the current cycle of legislative ascendancy will run its course, and a more balanced relationship will be restored between the two branches. It may take a public outcry or a national crisis to turn the tide, for Congress is not likely to restrain earmarks unless it is pressured to do so.

PROCEDURES AND POLITICS OF HOUSE AND SENATE ACTION

The House normally takes up each appropriations bill within a few days after it has been reported. Box 9-2 lists the main steps in House action on appropriations. This sequence is followed for all the regular appropriations bills but differs in some features from that used for some other types of legislation.

Because appropriations bills are privileged for floor consideration, the House can consider

▼

BOX 9-2
Sequence of House Actions on Appropriations Measures

Special Rule
Although appropriations bills are privileged and the House can consider them at any time, the House normally considers them under special rules (in the form of a simple House resolution) waiving certain points of order, such as those arising out of the rule barring unauthorized appropriations.

Committee of the Whole
After the House adopts the rule, it takes up the appropriations bill in the Committee of the Whole rather than in the House itself. The Committee of the Whole has a much smaller quorum requirement than that of the House.

General Debate
The floor managers—the chair and ranking minority member of the relevant appropriations subcommittee—open debate on the bill. Opening statements may also be made by the chair of the Appropriations Committee, who may advise the House on the overall status of appropriations bills, and by the chair of the Budget Committee, who may comment on whether the bill conforms to the subcommittee's section 302(b) allocation.

Amendments
Regular appropriations bills are usually considered under an open rule that does not preclude consideration of any floor amendments. An amendment must be offered in a timely manner, when the portion of the bill to which it pertains is being considered. (An exception to this requirement is made for amendments pertaining to two or more parts of the appropriations bill, whose amounts are completely offsetting.)

Points of Order
Points of order (which also must be timely) may be raised either against the bill reported by the Appropriations Committee or a floor amendment. In the House, it is rare for the ruling of the chair on a point of order to be challenged.

Limitations
Floor amendments inserting certain limitations into an appropriations bill may be offered only after consideration of funding levels has been completed. At this point, it is in order to move that the Committee of the Whole "rise and report." If the motion is adopted, there may be no opportunity to offer limitation amendments.

Final Passage
After the Committee of the Whole reports, final consideration is before the House. Under certain circumstances, the House may reconsider amendments adopted in the Committee of the Whole, but it usually concurs with the previous vote.

them without first obtaining a special rule through the Rules Committee. Nevertheless, most appropriations come to the floor under a special rule waiving one or more of the standing rules, such as the rule against unauthorized appropriations. The House first adopts the special rule (exhibit 9-8), then takes up the appropriations bill.

Special rules on appropriations bills are usually open; they do not restrict floor amendments. During some years in the 1990s, however, the Legislative Branch Appropriations bill was sometimes considered under a closed rule that precluded amendments. The majority party resorted to this tactic to block the minority from offering amendments that might embarrass it.

During House consideration, the subcommittee chair (who manages the bill on the floor) or the budget committee may advise the chamber whether the budget authority and outlays deriving from the bill are within the section 302(b) allocation to the subcommittee; exhibit 9-9 shows one such statement. Appropriations bills rarely exceed the section 302(b) allocation—doing so would indicate that the Appropriations Committee has violated Congress's budget policy. Occasionally, the bill exceeds the allocation for technical rather than substantive reasons. When this occurs, the House usually waives the point of order.

Section 302 rules inhibit the adoption of floor amendments that would change the amounts recommended by the House Appropriations Committee. As reported by committee, spending bills are usually at or slightly below the levels allowed by section 302(b). Amendments boosting appropriations above the 302(b) allocation may be blocked by points of order; those reducing budget authority or outlays may be challenged on the grounds that the reported levels are within the section 302(b) allocations. The only other option is to shift funds from one account to another within the section 302(b) limits. Such amendments rarely win because those whose programs would lose resources strongly oppose them.

Despite these impediments, amendments cutting appropriations below the level that section 302 allows may prevail when an economizing mood takes hold on Capitol Hill. However, because of an anomaly in budget rules, amendments that purport to cut appropriations may not actually accomplish what they set out to do. The reason is that the section 302 process has two linked, but separate, limitations: one on total discretionary spending, the other on spending deriving from each subcommittee's appropriations. A successful floor amendment that cuts an appropriations bill below the subcommittee limit does not itself change the limit on total discretionary spending. Consequently, the resources saved by the floor amendment can be recycled through the section 302 process to other appropriations. When Republicans took control of the House in 1995, they tried to deal with this situation by devising a "lockbox" rule that would lower the discretionary caps by an amount equal to the savings. For example, an amendment cutting $100 million from an appropriations bill would automatically reduce that year's caps by $100 million. The Senate did not adopt such a rule, and lockbox arrangements have rarely been applied.

Before voting on an appropriations measure, the House may be advised of concerns raised by the White House or OMB. This advice takes the form of a Statement of Administration Policy (SAP) (exhibit 9-10). Each statement specifies the administration's concerns as the appropriations bill moves through the House and Senate. SAPs are issued at as many as seven stages of congressional action: House Appropriations subcommittee

▶ EXHIBIT 9-8
Special House Rule on Appropriations Bills

H. RES. 865
In the House of Representatives, U.S.,
June 13, 2006

Resolved, That at any time after the adoption of this resolution the Speaker may, pursuant to clause 2(b) of rule XVIII, declare the House resolved into the Committee of the Whole House on the state of the Union for consideration of the bill (H.R. 5576) making appropriations for the Departments of Transportation, Treasury, and Housing and Urban Development, the Judiciary, District of Columbia, and independent agencies for the fiscal year ending September 30, 2007, and for other purposes. The first reading of the bill shall be dispensed with. All points of order against consideration of the bill are waived. General debate shall be confined to the bill and shall not exceed one hour equally divided and controlled by the chairman and ranking minority member of the Committee on Appropriations. After general debate the bill shall be considered for amendment under the five-minute rule. Points of order against provisions in the bill for failure to comply with clause 2 of rule XXI are waived except as follows: beginning with "to" on page 5, line 23 through the comma on line 24; beginning with the colon on page 6, line 22 through "year" on line 26; beginning with "for" on page 13, line 1 through "Code" on line 6; beginning with the colon on page 13, line 17 through "expended" on line 25; and sections 120, 127, 129, 206, 530, 707, and 931. Where points of order are waived against part of a paragraph, points of order against language in another part of such paragraph may be made only against such other part and not against the entire paragraph. During consideration of the bill for amendment, the Chairman of the Committee of the Whole may accord priority in recognition on the basis of whether the Member offering an amendment has caused it to be printed in the portion of the Congressional Record designated for that purpose in clause 8 of rule XVIII. Amendments so printed shall be considered as read. When the committee rises and reports the bill back to the House with a recommendation that the bill do pass, the previous question shall be considered as ordered on the bill and amendments thereto to final passage without intervening motion except one motion to recommit with or without instructions.

Source: H. Res. 865 (providing for consideration of the bill H.R. 5576—*Departments of Transportation, Treasury, and Housing and Urban Development, the Judiciary, District of Columbia, and Independent Agencies Appropriations Act for Fiscal Year 2007*), 109th Cong., 2d sess., June 13, 2006.

(a) Although appropriations bills are privileged and may be taken up at any time by the House, the practice is to consider each bill pursuant to a special rule (in the form of a simple House resolution) waiving certain points of order that otherwise would apply. The House votes first on the rule; if it is adopted, the House then considers the appropriations bill.

(b) The rule exhibited here waives points of order against under clause 2 of Rule XXI, which bars unauthorized appropriations and legislation in an appropriations bill. Note that the rule waives all points of order against consideration of the bill; further, it waives all points of order against provisions in the bill, with certain exceptions designated by line and page numbers or section number. Moreover, it does not waive points of order against amendments to the bill.

(c) This is an open rule: it does not restrict floor amendments, but it permits the chair to give priority to members whose amendments have been printed in advance in the *Congressional Record.*

▶ **EXHIBIT 9-9**
Section 302(b) Scoring Statement

The appropriations measure before us today provides funding for Transportation, Treasury, and Housing, as well as the Federal Judiciary and the District of Columbia. Under the reorganized subcommittee structure, this bill represents the first time Housing is matched with Transportation and Treasury in the same appropriations bill. I am pleased to report the bill is consistent with the levels established in H. Con. Res. 95, the House Concurrent Resolution on the budget for fiscal year 2006, which Congress adopted as its fiscal blueprint on April 28th.

THE BUDGET RESOLUTION
H.R. 3058 provides $115.2 billion in discretionary budgetary resources. This is a 7 percent increase over fiscal year 2005. Even so, the bill is consistent with the allocation to the subcommittee, and therefore complies with section 302(f) of the Budget Act, which prohibits consideration of bills in excess of an Appropriations subcommittee's 302(b) allocation of budget authority and outlays. The bill does not contain any emergency spending.

To meet the 302(b) limit, the bill rescinds $549 [million] in mandatory contract authority previously provided to the FAA. The bill also rescinds $2.497 billion of previously enacted discretionary budget authority; all but $4 million of the discretionary rescissions come from the Public and Indian Housing certificate fund.

The bill also complies with the provisions in the budget resolution concerning advance appropriations. The bill includes $4.273 billion in such appropriations, all of them in accounts the budget resolution lists as eligible for advances. The House should be aware, however, these provisions—along with the $18.885 billion in advances already passed in the Labor/HHS/Education appropriations bill—reach the ceiling of $23.158 billion in total advance appropriations provided for in the budget resolution. Any further increase in advance appropriations would breach this limit and subject such legislation to a point of order.

Source: Remarks of Representative Jim Nussle (House Budget Committee chair), *Congressional Record* (daily ed.), June 29, 2005, p. H5384.

(a) During debate on an appropriations bill, the chair of the House or Senate Budget Committee may provide a statement on whether the amounts in the bill are within the relevant subcommittee's section 302(b) suballocation. There is no standard format for these statements.

(b) The budget committees are the official scorers of budget actions for Congress; their analysis is authoritative in ruling on points of order concerning breaches of the section 302(b) limits.

(c) As is the case in this exhibit, the budget committee statement usually reports that the appropriations bill is within the subcommittee's suballocation. Note, however, that the subcommittee rescinded previously appropriated budget authority to meet the limit. Some question whether this tactic adheres to the intent of section 302(b) because the rescinded funds might not have been used at all, while the newly appropriated funds were likely to be used.

(d) In addition to the section 302(b) limit, the budget resolution limited the amount of advance appropriations—funds that become available in a future fiscal year. Chair Nussle reported in his statement that any additional advance appropriations, beyond the amount provided in this bill, would be subject to a point of order.

▶ **EXHIBIT 9-10**
Statement of Administration Policy

Bill Clinton
The Administration appreciates efforts by the Committee to accommodate certain of the President's priorities within the 302(b) allocation. However, the allocation is simply insufficient to make the necessary investments in programs funded by this bill. As a result, critical programs are not funded or are underfunded, in particular, key Presidential priorities such as funding for National Service, Superfund, and climate change. Furthermore, the Administration is very concerned that the Committee has included problematic language regarding the Kyoto Protocol and other issues. Finally, the Administration understands that an amendment may be offered to include unacceptable provisions now contained in H.R. 2, such as income targeting. If the bill were presented to the President without responding to these concerns, the President's senior advisors would recommend that he veto the bill. . . .

George W. Bush
The Administration supports House passage of the FY 2007 Science, State, Justice, Commerce, and Related Agencies Appropriations Bill, as reported by the House Committee and commends the Committee for reporting this bill in a timely manner.

The President's FY 2007 Budget holds total discretionary spending to $872.8 billion and cuts nonsecurity discretionary spending below last year's level. . . . The Administration looks forward to working with Congress to adopt the President's proposals to cut wasteful spending in order to maintain fiscal discipline to protect the American taxpayer and sustain a strong economy.

. . . the Committee bill underfunds the Educational and Cultural Exchange Program and the National Endowment for Democracy (NED), which are important to building and supporting democracies around the world. . . . The Administration looks forward to working with Congress to ensure that these programs receive the requested level of funding.

Provisions of the bill that purport to direct or burden the conduct of foreign relations, and of negotiations with foreign countries or international organizations, as well as condition the President's decisions regarding the use of armed forces, should be amended to make the provisions consistent with the constitutional authority of the President to conduct the Nation's foreign relations and his constitutional authority as Commander in Chief. These provisions include sections 405, 406, 624, 625,626, and 628, and under the heading, "Contributions for International Peacekeeping Activities."

Sources: Office of Management and Budget, *Statement of Administration Policy on H.R. 4194—the Departments of Veterans Affairs and Housing and Urban Development, and Independent Agencies Appropriations Bill for Fiscal Year 1999,* July 15, 1998, p. 1; and *Statement of Administrative Policy on H.R. 5672—the Science, State, Justice, Commerce, and Related Agencies Appropriations Bill, FY 2007,* June 28, 2006.

(a) A statement of administration policy (SAP) is issued for each annual appropriations bill and for some other major legislation. The SAPs go through an internal review, usually led by OMB or White House staff. The final version appears on the OMB website. Sometimes the SAP is placed in the *Congressional Record* and referred to during debate on the measure.

(b) Each president has his own style in dealing with disagreements with Congress. As shown here, Bill Clinton often threatened to veto appropriations bills if objectionable provisions were not removed. George W. Bush, who has been reluctant to exercise his veto power through the first six years of his terms, often pledges to work with Congress to reach agreements. This pledge appears twice in the brief excerpt exhibited here.

(c) Presidents sometimes use SAPs to register their disapproval of provisions that they regard as usurping their constitutional authority. This practice has accelerated significantly under George W. Bush.

(d) Whether it explicitly threatens a veto or not, the SAP sets the groundwork for negotiations between the White House and Congress on matters in disagreement between the two branches.

markup, House Appropriations Committee markup, House consideration, Senate subcommittee action, full committee markup, Senate consideration, and conference committee. The SAP comments on items in the most recent version of the appropriations measure that the administration finds objectionable. It is carefully worded and structured to signal the intensity of the administration's objections and the extent to which the bill may provoke a presidential veto. Before the Clinton presidency, it was rare for the SAP to state outright that the president would veto appropriations bills with objectionable provisions. Instead, it averred that the president's advisers would recommend a veto. By not overtly declaring that the president would veto the bill, the SAP opened the door to negotiation and compromise. Bill Clinton, however, changed the formula when he confronted Republican efforts to trim domestic spending and to attach restrictive riders to appropriations bills. Rather than hinting at a veto, Clinton's SAPs declared his intention to veto appropriations bills if funding was not restored or the riders were not removed. George W. Bush, by contrast, has rarely threatened a veto in his SAPs. His tone has been conciliatory, reaching out to Congress to cooperate on spending bills. One should not be surprised, however, if he takes a harder line during the final years of his presidency, confronting the new Democratic majorities in both the House and Senate.

SAPs were introduced in the 1980s in response to protracted conflict between the president and Congress on budgetary matters. Prodded to pay more attention to what Congress does to the president's budget, OMB introduced SAPs as a means of monitoring congressional action and communicating administration concerns. SAPs do not displace the give and take between presidential aides and legislators, but they indicate a more formal, distant relationship between the president and Congress—one that impels the White House to put its differences down on paper and to threaten vetoes. In fact, SAPs often set the stage for negotiations that lead to resolution of differences and enactment of appropriations. Sometimes, however, the process breaks down, and the vetoes turn from threats into reality.

Senate Action

In discussing Senate work on appropriations, one must distinguish between the traditional sequence in which the House acts first and recent variations in which the Senate sometimes takes the initiative and produces appropriations bills before the House does. In both cases, Senate Appropriations subcommittees conduct hearings, recommend appropriations, draft report language, and prepare the bill for floor consideration. The main difference is that when the Senate goes first, it produces an entirely new bill; when it follows the House, the Senate amends the House-passed bill. In years past, multiple Senate amendments were numbered sequentially and inserted in the bill at the point where the changes were made. In numbering Senate amendments, there was no difference between changes the Senate Appropriations Committee made and those adopted on the floor; both were inserted at the relevant point in the House-passed bill. Immediately following each numbered amendment, the Senate bill lined out language in the House bill that the Senate deleted and italicized language (not in the House bill) that the Senate added. In recent years, however, the practice has been to compile all Senate changes in a single amendment to the House-passed appropriations bill.

When it acts first, the Senate produces its own bill but holds it until the House has completed its version. When the House is done, the entire Senate-passed bill is inserted as a single amendment to the House bill. In this way, the prerogative of the House to initiate appropriations is preserved, even though the Senate acted first. An important procedural advantage accrues to the Senate Appropriations Committee when it acts on a Senate bill: although Senate Rule XVI (discussed in chapter 8) bars committee amendments containing legislative provisions to House-passed bills, the prohibition does not apply when the committee reports its own bill.

Senate hearings on appropriations are not as extensive as those held by the House, but the Senate does not routinely defer to the House's actions. Whether it goes first or second, the Senate's appropriations often differ significantly from the House's in amounts and other provisions. When an appropriations bill goes to conference, there are likely to be more than 100 differences between the two versions. Some differences are bargaining chips, which either chamber uses to strengthen its position in conference; others represent real disagreements.

In acting on appropriations bills, the Senate places few restrictions on members' freedom to offer floor amendments. But it does present tough hurdles to provisions, whether in the reported bill or proposed on the floor, that would violate section 302 limits. The Senate restrictions are more stringent than those applied by the House because they can be waived only by a three-fifths vote, in contrast to the House, which requires only a majority vote. Overall, however, Senate debate on appropriations bills is less structured than in the House; the main steps in the Senate process are listed in box 9-3.

After both the House and Senate pass an appropriations bill, a conference committee is convened to resolve differences between the two versions. The conferees go through each of the accounts to iron out disagreements. Appropriations bills cannot become law until the House and Senate pass them in identical form. But the House and Senate do not have to agree on report language, though it is common for some differences to be resolved in the joint explanatory statement that accompanies the conference report.

As with other legislation, appropriations bills are presented to the president after Congress completes action on them. The president has the option of signing or vetoing the entire measure; he cannot veto portions of appropriations bills (the line-item veto is discussed in chapter 5). Before Congress finalizes an appropriations bill, it usually resolves many of its differences with the president. Consequently, by the time Congress completes work on an appropriations bill, it may have a strong expectation that the president will sign the measure, even if he does not approve of all the items in it. However, some recent presidents have vigorously wielded the veto to block appropriations bills at variance with their priorities. Bill Clinton was especially successful in using the veto to strengthen his bargaining power vis-à-vis Congress. George W. Bush has taken the opposite position; in his first five years in office, he did not veto a single appropriations bill. Not surprisingly, annual appropriations rose much more steeply during this period than during Clinton's presidency.

SUPPLEMENTAL APPROPRIATIONS

Supplemental appropriations and continuing resolutions take a route similar to that of regular appropriations bills. There is no fixed number of these measures, but some are passed in every session of Congress.

Supplementals are prepared by the subcommittees with jurisdiction over the programs to be funded, but not on their initiative alone and usually with more coordination than befits regular appropriations. As previously

BOX 9-3
Sequence of Senate Actions on Appropriations Measures

Waiver Motion (Optional)
The Congressional Budget Act bars consideration of revenue or spending measures that would violate certain substantive or procedural budget rules—for example, the rule against considering these measures until the budget resolution has been adopted. The Senate may set aside these rules by unanimous consent or by adopting a waiver motion.

Time Limitation Agreement
Appropriations bills and other major legislation are often considered in the Senate under a time limitation agreement (also referred to as a unanimous consent agreement), which specifies the time set aside for debate, amendments to be considered, and sometimes when voting will take place on final passage. The majority leader usually proposes the time limitation agreement after consultation with the minority leader and other interested senators. In some cases, when a time limitation agreement cannot be reached, the leadership may move to invoke cloture on a bill or amendment.

Managers' Statements
The chair and ranking minority member of the relevant appropriations subcommittee provide an overview of the bill, including comparison with the previous appropriation and with the president's request.

Committee Amendments
Changes recommended by the Senate Appropriations Committee to the House-passed bill are usually voted on en bloc (all together) and approved by voice vote. This procedure pertains only when the Senate takes up an appropriations bill the House already passed.

Floor Amendments
The entire appropriations bill is open to floor amendment at any time. However, the time limitation agreement often specifies the amount of time allotted to debate on each amendment.

Points of Order
Points of order may be raised at any time during consideration of the bill. When a point of order is raised that an item is legislation in an appropriations bill, another member may raise the defense of germaneness. If the Senate decides that the item is germane, the original point of order fails. Some points of order for violating provisions of the 1974 Congressional Budget Act can be waived only by a three-fifths vote.

Final Passage
After all amendments are disposed of (or when the time arrives for voting on final passage, stipulated in the time limitation agreement), the Senate votes on the bill. Some appropriations bills are agreed on by voice—rather than recorded—vote.

noted, section 302 allocations preclude the sub-committees from acting on their own, without regard for whether the additional funding can be accommodated within budget limits. Compiling a supplemental entails decisions on the scope of the bill, the amount of additional resources that should be provided, whether some or all of the supplemental funding should be designated as emergency, and whether emergency spending should be offset by cutbacks in other areas. Resolving these questions may entail negotiations within Congress and with the White House that range across the jurisdictions of the subcommittees whose programs are targeted for supplemental appropriations.

Although they are a recurring feature of the appropriations process, supplementals are no longer as routine and predictable as they once were, and they differ in scope and purpose from those enacted in earlier periods. Recourse to supplementals depends on the budgetary mood of Congress, as well as on external events such as natural disasters and U.S. military operations. A brief survey of supplemental appropriations over the past three decades highlights the changing use of these measures.

Congress averaged more than six supplemental spending bills a year during the 1970s. In most of those years, supplementals accounted for between 4 and 7 percent of annual appropriations, but in a few years, they totaled more than 10 percent. Supplemental spending was highest in the years immediately after passage of the 1974 Congressional Budget Act. Evidently the new budget process did not effectively curtail Congress's proclivity to supplement the resources provided in the regular appropriations. One reason why Congress did not behave differently is that supplementals were used to finance annual pay increases for federal employees. Another was that supplementals were used to stimulate the economy, and a third was their use to finance pro-

grams that lacked reauthorization when regular appropriations were considered.

All three of these uses have faded away. The practice of financing pay increases for federal employees in supplementals was discontinued during the 1990s in response to the Budget Enforcement Act limit on total discretionary spending. Nowadays, federal agencies must absorb the cost of pay increases through savings in ongoing operations. Furthermore, whether recessions now tend to be briefer and shallower than they once were, or because of a loss of confidence in the efficacy of stimulus spending, Congress rarely makes these types of special appropriations as an economic stimulus. In fact, Bill Clinton's first major legislative defeat occurred shortly after he took office when Congress refused to approve $16 billion in supplemental funds he had requested to stimulate the economy. In the case of delayed authorizations, Congress generally appropriates funds by waiving or ignoring the rules.

Because of these adjustments, supplemental spending receded during the 1980s to only about 1 percent of total budget authority. Half of the supplemental resources were for mandatory programs over which the appropriations committees had little or no control. This decline was spurred by concern over the large budget deficits that emerged during the decade. Congress made two policy changes affecting supplementals. One was to use these measures to rescind previously enacted appropriations, thereby offsetting a portion of the additional spending. Although some members have urged that all supplemental spending be offset, Congress has rarely done so, especially when the additional funds have been allocated for disaster relief and national defense. The other change was a declaration first issued in 1987 by Democratic and Republican leaders that henceforth supplemental appropriations would only be considered for "dire emergencies." This pro-

TABLE 9-9
Supplemental Appropriations, Fiscal Years 2000–06

Billions of dollars

	2000	2001	2002	2003	2004	2005	2006
Defense	8.8	19.6	17.1	62.8	92.0	79.2	68.2
Nondefense	8.1	7.9	28.2	18.3	25.7	81.2	26.2
Total	16.9	27.5	45.3	81.1	117.7	160.4	94.4

Source: Congressional Budget Office, *Supplemental Appropriations from 2000 to 2006,* August 2006, unnumbered table, "CBO Data on Supplemental Budget Authority for the 2000's." Available on the CBO website at www.cbo.gov/ftpdocs/66xx/doc6630/3-16-SuppApprop.pdf.

nouncement, made during the height of the Gramm-Rudman-Hollings campaign to liquidate the deficit, had a short-term impact. But inasmuch as the "dire emergency" standard lacks objective criteria or enforcement mechanisms, it did not impede Congress from voting additional spending when it wanted to do so.

During the 1990s, supplemental appropriations were constrained by the Budget Enforcement Act, which limited discretionary spending. However, emergency spending was excluded from the caps, and Congress used this exemption to appropriate supplemental resources for the Gulf War, other military activities, and disaster relief. In its hands, the emergency exemption was quite elastic, for Congress applied it to routine spending. For example, it designated some of the funds appropriated for the 2000 census as emergency, thereby freeing up an equivalent amount of money within the discretionary caps for other purposes. But despite these occasional evasions, the volume of supplementals was relatively modest during the decade. The story has been quite different since the terrorist attacks in September 2001. Table 9-9 shows that (net of rescissions) each year's supplemental appropriations during the 2000–05 period were higher than the previous year's. The main reason for this trend has been President Bush's decision to exclude the costs of military operations in Iraq and Afghanistan

from his budget. This tactic enables him to show a lower deficit in the budget, but it induces Congress to finance these costs in supplementals rather than regular appropriations bills. Supplemental spending for fiscal year 2005 was boosted by Hurricane Katrina, which devastated New Orleans and adjacent areas. As happened in the aftermath of previous disasters, Congress used the supplemental to provide additional funds for purposes that were unrelated to Katrina. When the books were closed on fiscal year 2005, supplementals accounted for more than 15 percent of discretionary budget authority, far above the level of any year covered by this survey.

Like regular appropriations bills, supplementals also carry earmarked funds. The use of earmarks in supplementals may be especially contentious if the bill is widely viewed as a measure that should be reserved for emergency funding needs. Early in 2007, the House and Senate passed a supplemental appropriations act providing about $100 billion in funds requested by the president for the wars in Iraq and Afghanistan, veterans' programs, and other emergency needs. While significant controversy surrounded the bill over the inclusion of a timetable for the withdrawal of troops from Iraq, and President George W. Bush issued a veto threat on this issue, additional controversy arose because about $20 billion in unrequested funds were included in the

House and Senate versions. According to some observers, much of the additional spending involved unjustified earmarks included merely to attract political support for passage of this highly controversial measure (see box 9-4).

CONTINUING RESOLUTIONS AND OMNIBUS APPROPRIATIONS

The period beginning in the late 1970s and continuing to the present has been a time of significant innovation in the use of appropriations measures, including the transformation of the continuing resolution and the development of the omnibus appropriations act. Congress experimented in 1950 with an omnibus appropriations act to fund all of the regular appropriations bills but abandoned the practice the following year and did not return to it for decades.

The traditional CR, which has been enacted routinely for many decades, is a brief, temporary measure that lists the programs or agencies that have not yet received their regular appropriations, provides a continuing rate of funding (usually the lower of the previous year's appropriation or the president's budget request), is scheduled to expire within days or weeks, and has a few technical provisions made necessary by its temporary status (exhibit 9-11). In contrast, some contemporary continuing resolutions have been omnibus measures that fund all or many of the regular appropriations bills, sometimes are in effect through the remainder of the fiscal year, specify amounts for each account in the same manner as regular appropriations acts, may include significant amounts of substantive legislation, and contain other provisions normally found in regular appropriations. The traditional CR is a few pages long; the omnibus version may run for hundreds of pages. In some years, Congress enacts a series

of brief, traditional CRs, each one only providing stopgap funding, and a final omnibus CR covering the remainder of the fiscal year. This omnibus measure is, in effect, a vehicle for enacting the regular appropriations.

Several characteristics of CRs make them ripe for conversion into omnibus measures. First, under House precedents, they are deemed not to be general appropriations bills. Hence the rules against unauthorized appropriations and legislation in appropriations bills do not apply. Just about anything can be placed in a continuing resolution without drawing a point of order. Second, the manner in which these measures are considered—under imminent threat of government shutdown—makes them ideal vehicles for enacting legislation that would not become law under other circumstances. Third, omnibus continuing resolutions are usually hammered out in summit negotiations between the White House and congressional leaders. There is a lot of confusion and give and take, with each side accepting provisions the other wants on condition that some of its preferences are included. The upshot is a bloated CR that few in Congress profess to like but few vote against.

In the late 1990s and into the early 2000s, Congress deepened its reliance on omnibus appropriations acts but did not always cast them in the form of a CR. These measures acquired the label of "consolidated" appropriations acts. Continuing resolutions still were used often, but generally not as the vehicle for wrapping up congressional action for the session. During the decade covering fiscal years 1998 through 2007, Congress enacted more than 70 CRs—on average, providing stopgap funding for nearly the first four months of the fiscal year.

Many observers consider very large, sometimes massive, appropriations bills as evidence of the breakdown of the regular appropriations

▼

BOX 9-4
Earmarks in Supplemental Appropriations Acts

A supplemental appropriations act passed by the House and Senate early in 2007, which provided about $100 billion in funding for the wars in Iraq and Afghanistan, veterans' programs, and other emergency funding needs, also included about $20 billion in additional spending. Some observers criticized both versions of the act for including what they regarded as excessive earmarks. This example shows some of the earmarks in the House and Senate bills (final legislative action still was pending at this point) from one organization's perspective; in some instances, it may be argued whether an item is properly characterized as an earmark.

Millions of dollars

Proposed earmarks	Amount
Senate	
Land acquisition	1.98
Uganda peace process	2
Repairing ditch irrigation systems	2
Sugar cane cooperative (Hawaii)	3
Vietnam, for environmental remediation of dioxin storage sites	3.2
Guided tours of the Capitol	3.5
Flooded crop and grazing land	6
Nepal, for election aid, reintegration of former combatants, and other assistance to the peace process	6
Philippines, for typhoon relief	6
Ewe lamb replacement and retention	13
Save America's Treasures	13
Mormon cricket eradication (Nevada)	20
Sugar beet production (Minnesota)	24
Asbestos abatement at the Capitol power plant	25
House	
Office of Women's Health at Food and Drug Administration	4
Breeding, rearing, and transporting of live fish	5
Detection of avian influenza in wild birds	5.27
Security upgrades to House office buildings	16
Education and cultural exchange programs	20
Emergency conservation program for farmland damaged by freezing temperatures	20
Spinach growers (California)	25
Hurricane Livestock Indemnity Program	25
NASA, for risk-mitigation projects on the Gulf Coast	35
Farm Services Agency, for salaries and expenses	48
Asbestos abatement at the Capitol power plant	50
Disaster assistance for salmon fishing	60.4
Peanut storage (Georgia)	74
Citrus assistance (California)	100

Source: Thomas Schatz, "Pork Goes to War," *New York Times,* March 30, 2007.

▶ **EXHIBIT 9-11**
Continuing Resolution

Joint Resolution
Making continuing appropriations for the fiscal year 2006, and for other purposes.

Sec. 101. (a) Such amounts as may be necessary under the authority and conditions provided in the applicable appropriations Act for the fiscal year 2006 for continuing projects or activities (including the costs of direct loans and loan guarantees) that are not otherwise specifically provided for in this joint resolution that were conducted in fiscal year 2005, and for which appropriations, funds, or other authority would be available in the following appropriation Acts:

1) the Agriculture, Rural Development, Food and Drug Administration, and Related Agencies Appropriations Act, 2006;

2) the Department of Defense Appropriations Act, 2006; . . .

Sec. 103. Appropriations made by section 101 shall be available to the extent and in the manner that would be provided by the pertinent appropriations Act.

Sec. 104. No appropriation or funds made available or authority granted pursuant to section 101 shall be used to initiate or resume any project or activity for which appropriations, funds, or other authority were not available during fiscal year 2005. . . .

Sec. 106. Unless otherwise provided for in this joint resolution or in the applicable appropriations Act, appropriations and funds made available and authority granted pursuant to this joint resolution shall be available until whichever of the following first occurs: (a) the enactment into law of an appropriation for any project or activity provided for in this joint resolution; or (b) the enactment into law of the applicable appropriations Act by both Houses without any provision for such project or activity; or (c) November 18, 2005.

Source: *Continuing Appropriations Act for Fiscal Year 2006*, P.L. 109-77, September 30, 2005.

(a) A continuing appropriations act is enacted in the form of a joint resolution for agencies that have not received a regular appropriation for the fiscal year. Although it is often referred to as a continuing resolution (CR), it has the same legal status as a bill. It may be in effect for only part of the fiscal year or for the remainder of the year.

(b) The continuing resolution lists the regular appropriations covered by it. This continuing resolution, for fiscal 2006, covered 9 of the then 11 regular appropriations acts.

(c) Most continuing resolutions are temporary measures that expire on the date specified in the CR, or are superseded by enactment of the regular appropriations act. This CR was in effect for 49 days, from the start of the fiscal year through November 18, 2005. When it expired, two more continuing resolutions were enacted, providing funds through December 31.

(d) This measure, as is typical of continuing resolutions, barred the use of funds provided in the continuing resolution to initiate any project or activity that was not funded in the previous fiscal year.

process. The problem, however, lies not in appropriations procedures but in sustained and intense conflict over budget policy. Omnibus or consolidated appropriations bills enable the president and Congress to agree on appropriations through extraordinary procedures when normal means do not suffice. When there is a period of budgetary peace, continuing resolutions and omnibus measures become less common and more modest in size.

STRUCTURE AND CONTENT OF APPROPRIATIONS MEASURES

All regular appropriations acts have three standard features: an enacting clause that designates the fiscal year for which the appropriations are made, account-by-account appropriations, and general provisions (exhibit 9-12).

The basic unit of appropriation is an account. Every unnumbered paragraph in an appropriations act is a single account, and all provisions enacted within the paragraph pertain only to that account unless the text gives them broader scope. The unnumbered accounts are the source of the government-wide accounting system maintained by the Treasury. Laws governing the expenditure of funds (for example, that spending may not exceed appropriations and may be used only for the purposes of the appropriation) pertain to each account. Thus an account limits both the amount and purpose of expenditures.

Over the years, appropriations have been consolidated into a relatively small number of accounts. The budget now contains more than 1,000 accounts, but the 200 largest cover more than 90 percent of all federal expenditures. Many federal agencies have a single "salary and expenses" account for all their operating expenditures; some have additional accounts for special purposes such as procurement or construction. When Congress estab-

lishes a new program, the appropriation for it usually is folded into an existing account. Most appropriations provide a lump sum for all the activities or projects financed by the account, though the appropriations committees sometimes specify in their reports how the money is to be allocated among various projects or activities. Sometimes the appropriations act itself specifies that a portion of the money in the account be used for designated purposes. The appropriation might specify that "not less than" a certain amount should be spent on a particular activity. When this or similar language appears in an appropriations act, the spending agency usually "fences off" the money by treating it as a subaccount.

In addition to provisions attached to particular accounts, each appropriations act has general provisions that apply to all accounts in the act. (An appropriations act that covers two or more departments may be subdivided into titles, each of which has its own general provisions.) The general provisions appear as numbered sections at the end of the title or act (exhibit 9-13). Most general provisions contain either limitations (restrictions on the use of appropriations) or legislation (changes in law); some earmark funds to particular uses. Most are reenacted year after year with little or no change. With some new ones added each year, there has been a steady rise in the number of general provisions; table 9-10 shows this increase at 10-year intervals since fiscal year 1964. Overall, in each such period, there were more general provisions than in the previous period. The fiscal year 2004 appropriations acts had more than seven times the number of general provisions than did the fiscal year 1964 appropriations. This steep increase reflects strained relations between Congress and executive agencies, the growing tendency of the appropriations committees to earmark funds and restrict their use, incremental behavior that

---

▶ **EXHIBIT 9-12**
Structure of a Regular Appropriations Act

ENACTING CLAUSE

Making appropriations for the Department of Interior, Environment, and Related Agencies for the fiscal year ending September 30, 2006, and for other purposes.

Be it enacted by the Senate and House of Representatives of the United States of America in Congress assembled, That the following sums are appropriated, out of any money in the Treasury not otherwise appropriated, for the Department of the Interior, Environment, and Related Agencies for the fiscal year ending September 30, 2006, and for other purposes, namely . . .

APPROPRIATIONS

JOHN F. KENNEDY CENTER FOR THE PERFORMING ARTS
OPERATIONS AND MAINTENANCE

For necessary expenses for the operation, maintenance and security of the John F. Kennedy Center for the Performing Arts; $17,800,000.

GENERAL PROVISIONS

Sec. 414. Other than in emergency situations, none of the funds in this Act may be used to operate telephone answering machines during core business hours unless such answering machines include an option that enables callers to reach promptly an individual on-duty with the agency being contacted.

Source: *Department of Interior, Environment, and Related Agencies Appropriations Act for Fiscal Year 2006,* P.L. 109-54, August 2, 2005.

(a) An appropriations act has three main components: the enacting clause; appropriations to specified accounts; and general provisions.

(b) The enacting clause specifies the fiscal year for which appropriations are made. Unless otherwise stipulated, all funds provided in the act are available for obligation only in that fiscal year. All substantive provisions in an appropriations act expire at the end of the fiscal year unless the text gives them a longer period of availability.

(c) Each unnumbered paragraph constitutes a single appropriations account. Most agencies have a single account providing salaries and expenses; some have additional accounts for procurement or other activities. The statement indicating the purposes of the appropriation often references applicable authorizing laws or provisions in the United States Code.

(d) Provisions in an unnumbered paragraph pertain only to that account unless the text provides otherwise. Funds may be transferred between accounts only by authority provided in law.

(e) The general provisions (which may limit the use of funds or contain new legislation) have numbered sections. These provisions usually apply to all accounts in the act. Appropriations that cover several departments are divided into several separate acts, each with its own general provisions.

▶ **EXHIBIT 9-13**
Types of General Provisions

LIMITATION

Sec. 715. No funds appropriated by this Act shall be available to pay for an abortion, or the administrative expenses in connection with any health plan under the Federal employees health benefits program which provides any benefits or coverage for abortions.

Sec. 716. The provision of section 715 shall not apply where the life of the mother would be endangered if the fetus were carried to term, or the pregnancy is the result of an act of rape or incest.

LEGISLATION

Sec. 828. Notwithstanding any other provision of law, a woman may breastfeed her child at any location in a Federal building or on Federal property, if the woman and her child are otherwise authorized to be present at the location. . . .

Sec. 840. Section 4(b) of the Federal Activities Inventory Reform Act of 1998 (Public Law 105–270) is amended by adding at the end the following new paragraph:

"(5) Executive agencies with fewer than 100 full-time employees as of the first day of the fiscal year. However, such an agency shall be subject to section 2 to the extent it plans to conduct a public-private competition for the performance of an activity that is not inherently governmental."

GOVERNMENTWIDE

Sec. 809. No part of any appropriation for the current fiscal year contained in this or any other Act shall be paid to any person for the filling of any position for which he or she has been nominated after the Senate has voted not to approve the nomination of said person.

Source: *Transportation, Treasury, Housing and Urban Development, the Judiciary, the District of Columbia, and Independent Agencies Appropriations Act for Fiscal Year 2006,* P.L. 109-115, November 30, 2005.

(a) General provisions (usually numbered sections) pertain to all accounts in the appropriations act. Some appropriations acts are divided into titles, which are designated as distinct appropriations acts. In these instances, the general provisions pertain only to the particular title in which they are found.

(b) The number of general provisions has increased greatly over the past 20 years. Most are limitations or legislation; many are reenacted year after year.

(c) Limitations typically begin with language similar to that shown here: "no funds appropriated." Some limitations pertain to broad policy matters, such as the use of appropriated funds to pay for abortions; some pertain to specific matters.

(d) Legislation often begins with the words "notwithstanding any other provision of law." The purpose of this phrase is to expressly override any existing provision of law that is contrary to the new measure. In other instances, legislation directly amends an existing law referenced in the provision.

(e) The annual Treasury Appropriations Act (renamed the Financial Services and General Government Appropriations Act in the 110th Congress) contains governmentwide provisions that pertain to all appropriations and all federal agencies. Note the words "in this or any other Act."

TABLE 9-10
General Provisions in Regular Appropriations Acts, 10-Year Intervals, Fiscal Years 1964–2004ᵃ

Bill	1964	1974	1984	1994	2004
Agriculture	7	8	4	28	89
Commerce-Justice-State	15	19	22	31	72
Defense	41	46	111	175	146
District of Columbia	14	18	31	42	36
Energy and Water	13	7	20	9	101
Foreign Operations	20	17	1	75	101
Homeland Securityᵇ	. . .	. . .	. . .	. . .	21
Interior	5	10	33	25	158
Labor-HHS-Education	10	20	31	24	53
Legislative Branch	3	3	21	29	41
Military Construction	12	10	22	24	28
Transportationᶜ	ᵈ	15	22	41	176
Treasury-Postal Serviceᶜ	0	22	25	92	. . .
VA-HUD	7	6	15	18	84
Total	147	201	371	613	1,106

Source: *United States Statutes at Large,* for years specified in the table.

a. Each numbered section, except for those with a sense of the Congress (or House or Senate) provision, is counted as a general provision; administrative provisions are included in the count. Sections with a capital letter following the designation are counted as a separate section.

b. The Homeland Security Appropriations Act was first established for fiscal year 2004.

c. The Treasury–Postal Service Appropriations Act was incorporated into the new Transportation-Treasury Appropriations Act beginning with fiscal year 2004.

d. There was no separate appropriations bill for Transportation in 1964.

impels these committees to retain old provisions while adding new ones, and the inclusion of more legislation in appropriations acts.

General provisions have become the most prominent and controversial features of some appropriations acts. Provisions have been inserted to restrict the use of federal money to finance abortions, to curb the enforcement of environmental protection laws, to bar certain military operations, and to induce changes in the speed limit on federally aided highways. The 146 general provisions in the fiscal year 2004 Defense Appropriations Act sprawl over more than 40 statute pages; the actual appropriations take fewer pages.

Appropriations Accounts
Each appropriation account specifies the purposes for which the appropriation is made and

the amount appropriated (exhibit 9-14). It may also contain one or more provisions limiting or earmarking funds or changing existing law. In contrast to the general provisions, limitations or legislation embedded in an account pertain only to the money spent out of that account unless the language gives them broader application.

An appropriation that does not specify the period for which the funds are available is a one-year appropriation. The funds may be obligated only during the fiscal year mentioned in the enacting clause; they lapse if not obligated by the end of that fiscal year. Congress sometimes makes multiyear appropriations that extend the period of availability for two or more years. The current practice in defense appropriations, for example, is for research and development funds to be available for two years, procurement funds for

▶ **EXHIBIT 9-14**
Structure of an Appropriations Account

FOOD AND DRUG ADMINISTRATION
Salaries and Expenses

For necessary expenses of the Food and Drug Administration, including hire and purchase of passenger motor vehicles; for payment of space rental and related costs pursuant to Public Law 92–313 for programs and activities of the Food and Drug Administration which are included in this Act; for rental of special purpose space in the District of Columbia or elsewhere; for miscellaneous and emergency expenses of enforcement activities, authorized and approved by the Secretary and to be accounted for solely on the Secretary's certificate, not to exceed $25,000; and notwithstanding section 521 of Public Law 107–188; $1,838,567,000: *Provided,* That of the amount provided under this heading, $305,332,000 shall be derived from prescription drug user fees authorized by 21 U.S.C. 379h, shall be credited to this account and remain available until expended, and shall not include any fees pursuant to 21 U.S.C. 379h(a)(2) and (a)(3) assessed for fiscal year 2007 but collected in fiscal year 2006; . . . *Provided further,* That of the total amount appropriated: (1) $443,153,000 shall be for the Center for Food Safety and Applied Nutrition and related field activities in the Office of Regulatory Affairs; (2) $520,564,000 shall be for the Center for Drug Evaluation and Research and related field activities in the Office of Regulatory Affairs; (3) $178,714,000 shall be for the Center for Biologics Evaluation and Research and for related field activities in the Office of Regulatory Affairs; . . . *Provided further,* That funds may be transferred from one specified activity to another with the prior approval of the Committees on Appropriations of both Houses of Congress. . . .

Source: *Agriculture, Rural Development, Food and Drug Administration, and Related Agencies Appropriations for Fiscal Year 2006,* P.L. 109-97, November 10, 2005.

(a) This unnumbered paragraph constitutes a single appropriations account; all provisions in the paragraph pertain only to this account unless the text indicates otherwise. Appropriation accounts generally are referenced by title—in this case, Food and Drug Administration, Salaries and Expenses.

(b) The Food and Drug Administration received an appropriation of $1.839 billion for all its operating expenses. Notice, however, that a portion of this money is reserved for particular purposes and additional funds may be transferred to this account from other sources.

(c) Although the appropriations language provides little detail on how the funds are to be spent, the appropriations committees' reports and other documents specify many of the particular projects and activities on which the funds are to be spent.

(d) As is common in appropriations acts, much of the appropriations language in the account exhibited here consists of a series of provisions—referred to as "provisos"—that limit or dictate the use of funds. Several of the provisions in this account pertain to user fees, but only one proviso pertaining to user fees (regarding prescription drugs) is shown in this exhibit.

three years, and shipbuilding money for five years. Congress also makes no-year appropriations by specifying that the funds shall remain available until expended. No-year funds may be carried over to future years indefinitely, even if they have not been obligated. Exhibit 9-15 shows examples of appropriations with different periods of availability.

Appropriations acts contain a variety of accounts that serve special purposes. These include appropriations to liquidate contract authority, limit administrative expenses paid out of certain trust funds, transfer funds from one account to another, or finance the subsidy cost of direct or guaranteed loans.

LEGISLATION AND LIMITATIONS IN APPROPRIATIONS ACTS

The inclusion of legislative provisions and limitations in appropriations acts (table 9-11) has been referred to several times in this chapter. Despite the rules barring legislation in appropriations acts, the House and Senate manage to insert legislation when a majority so desires. In some cases, entire laws have been enacted in appropriations measures, but the more common practice is to insert particular provisions. Congress legislates by ignoring or waiving the rules, inserting substantive law in continuing resolutions, and making policy in the guise of limitations. Although the appropriations committees are often characterized as interlopers who disregard jurisdictional boundaries and congressional rules, they frequently are force-fed legislation sought by others. They insert legislation sometimes at the behest of authorizing committee members and at other times because congressional leaders see appropriations bills as their only or best opportunity to move stalled legislation.

Limitations are another matter. These provisions, which typically begin with the phrase,

"none of the funds provided in this Act shall be used for" or similar language, have become the stock in trade of members who want to change policy through the appropriations process. Hundreds of limitations are enacted in appropriations measures each year—some in individual accounts, many in general provisions. Many limitations deal with relatively minor aspects of agency operations, such as the relocation of field offices, but some deal with major or controversial issues, such as the deployment of weapons and funding of abortions. Some are straightforward restrictions on the use of appropriations; others have the barely disguised purpose of altering or blocking the implementation of federal laws.

The thin line between limitations and legislation depends on parliamentary precedents and interpretations. If a provision sets conditions on the use of appropriations or requires a federal agency or official to make a determination or take some action, it is likely to be ruled legislation. If it is negative, unconditional, and entails no action, it is likely to be ruled a limitation. Appropriations committee members (and others) are adept at wording provisions negatively so they are held to be limitations, even when the obvious purpose is to change existing policy.

INTERPRETING APPROPRIATIONS MEASURES

In carrying out their responsibilities, agencies need to know the amounts they have to spend, as well as any conditions Congress imposes on the use of funds. The text of the appropriations act usually provides some guidance, but it rarely is sufficiently detailed to cover all the matters of interest to the appropriations committees. In spending money, agencies go beyond the text of relevant appropriations to also consider other legislation, budget justifications, and the reports on appropriations bills.

▶ EXHIBIT 9-15
Period during Which Funds Are Available

ONE-YEAR

FAMILY HOUSING OPERATION AND MAINTENANCE, ARMY
For expenses of family housing for the Army for operation and maintenance, including debt payment, leasing, minor construction, principal and interest charges, and insurance premiums, as authorized by law, $803,993,000.

MULTIYEAR

MILITARY CONSTRUCTION, ARMY RESERVE
For construction, acquisition, expansion, rehabilitation, and conversion of facilities for the training and administration of the Army Reserve as authorized by chapter 1803 of title 10, United States Code, and Military Construction Authorization Acts, $152,569,000, to remain available until September 30, 2010.

NO-YEAR (INDEFINITE)

GRANTS FOR CONSTRUCTION OF STATE EXTENDED CARE FACILITIES
For grants to assist States to acquire or construct State nursing home and domiciliary facilities and to remodel, modify or alter existing hospital, nursing home and domiciliary facilities in State homes, for furnishing care to veterans as authorized by sections 8131–8137 of title 38, United States Code, $85,000,000, to remain available until expended.

Source: *Military Quality of Life and Veterans Affairs Appropriations Act for Fiscal Year 2006*, P.L. 109-114, November 30, 2005.

(a) Appropriations differ in the period for which the budget authority is available for obligation. The three excerpts displayed here are one-year, multiyear, and no-year appropriations. Other variants are appropriations that become available during only a portion of a fiscal year or that become available in advance of the fiscal year for which they were made.

(b) When an appropriations account does not specify a period of availability (as in the first example here), the funds are available for only the fiscal year specified in the enacting clause of the appropriations act. The one-year availability of appropriations, unless otherwise stated, is provided for in a general provision in another part of the act.

(c) The multiyear funds exhibited here are available for four fiscal years (2007–10) beyond the fiscal year for which the appropriation is made (2006). Although these funds are available for four years, the entire amount is scored as budget authority in the year covered by the appropriations act.

(d) The phrase "to remain available until expended" provides a no-year appropriation that does not have to be obligated in a particular fiscal year. The availability of these funds carries over into subsequent fiscal years, even if they have not been obligated.

TABLE 9-11
Legislation and Limitations in Appropriations Acts

Characteristics	Limitations	Legislation
Purpose	To prevent appropriations from being available for specified activities	To change the application of existing law, to amend existing law, or to establish new law
Common phraseology	"None of the funds in this act may be used for . . ."	"Notwithstanding this or any other Act . . ." or "Notwithstanding any other provision of law . . ."
Typical placement	In account language, or general or administrative provisions	In general or administrative provisions; in omnibus appropriations acts, significant legislation may be included in a separate title
Status generally under House Rule XXI and Senate Rule XVI	Permitted	Prohibited

Substantive Law

The basic principle laid down in the previous chapter—that appropriations must be spent according to the requirements and restrictions set in authorizing legislation—makes it essential for spenders to consult substantive laws. These laws may prescribe certain activities and prohibit others, and they often specify reports spending agencies are to file or establish priorities and funding levels for projects and activities. Authorizing law typically covers many matters not dealt with in appropriations acts: how the agency is to be organized and operate, the duties of its officials, and the manner in which finances are to be managed.

In some instances, however, authorizing law and the annual appropriations act cover the same matters but differ on the procedures or policies to be followed. The authorization may earmark funds to certain projects; the appropriations, to others. One law might require that money be spent on a particular activity; the other might bar use of funds for the very same activity. In sorting out conflicts between these laws, slight differences in wording may spawn big differences in legal interpretation.

Interpreting the appropriation and authorization in ways that enable the agency to satisfy both dictates can deflect collisions between laws. When conflict is unavoidable, the basic rule is that the last enacted law prevails. But agencies understand that conflicts between authorizations and appropriations are not merely matters of statutory construction; they often reflect political conflict between different committees and members. Simply following the letter of the law may not enable the agency to stay in the good graces of both the authorizers and appropriators.

Budget Justifications

Agency budget justifications (see exhibit 9-3) normally break down the amount requested by activities and items of expenditure. The appropriations subcommittees generally expect agencies to adhere to their budget justifications to the extent practicable. Of course, agencies must disregard the justifications when the appropriations committees instruct them to spend the money in a different way. In addition, agencies sometimes deviate from the justifications by going through the reprogramming procedures discussed in the next chapter or by unilaterally making minor adjustments that do not require them to notify Congress.

Appropriations Committee Reports

According to long-standing practice, detailed guidance on how funds are to be spent appears in appropriations committee reports rather than in the body of appropriations acts. This arrangement gives both the appropriations committees and spending agencies somewhat more flexibility than if the details were enacted into law (exhibit 9-16). The reports do not comment on every agency request or item of expenditure. Guidance is most likely when the committee disagrees with the president's request or the distribution of money among activities specified by an agency in its budget justification or when it wants to earmark funds, restrict their use, or dictate agency policies or operations. Since the 1970s, guidance and earmarks have become much more detailed and numerous, leading some to complain that Congress is micromanaging agencies and denying them freedom to operate efficiently. Regardless of whether this charge is warranted, there is ample evidence that a generation of conflict between the legislative and executive branches over budget policies and priorities has abraded the relationship between the appropriations committees and spending agencies.

Agencies are expected to follow the guidance of all reports (House Appropriations, Senate Appropriations, and the joint statement of managers on the conference report), except when they conflict with one another. For example, if the House report earmarks a portion of the funds in an account to project A, the Senate report earmarks to project B, and the conference report to project C, the agency is expected to allocate the specified funds to each of the projects. The same rule applies to other types of guidance in appropriations reports.

In these reports, wording is crucial because it conveys the extent to which the committee allows latitude in carrying out instructions; report language is carefully crafted and sometimes is negotiated with the affected agency. The reports frequently use words such as assumes, notes, requests, expects, directs, and requires. These words are not synonymous—each has its own nuance and intent. However, even the most permissive words offer guidance that agencies do not lightly disregard.

What gives the appropriations reports special force is not their legal status but the fact that the next appropriations cycle is always less than one year away. An agency that willfully violates report language risks retribution the next time it asks for money. It may find this year's report language relocated to the next appropriations act, thereby giving it even less leeway than it had before. Or it may find that the guidance from next year's appropriations committee is even more detailed and onerous or that its appropriation has been cut. The appropriations committees also punish noncompliant agencies by writing tough limitations into the appropriations act, cutting the agency's priority programs, trimming the offending official's staff, issuing more earmarks, or curtailing its operating flexibility. In most cases, the committees do not have to use these weapons because agencies comply with the report language. When they find it difficult to do so, their best course of action may be to explain their predicament to subcommittee staff (or less frequently to members) and seek an accommodation that satisfies the committee's interest while enabling them to run their operations. An agency that maintains ongoing contact with subcommittee members

▶ **EXHIBIT 9-16**
Appropriations Committee Report: Guidance to Agencies

STANDARDS FOR CHECKPOINT TECHNOLOGIES
The conferees recommend TSA work with the National Institute of Standards and Technology to develop standards for checkpoint technologies, as discussed in the Senate report.

REMOTE BAGGAGE SCREENING
The conferees are aware of TSA's participation with airports and airlines in pilots at various airports around the country to evaluate off-site baggage check-in models. The conferees encourage TSA to widely test remote baggage screening, including coupling off-site check in with off-site screening within the airport grounds at secure sort facilities before the baggage is introduced into the terminal and other critical airport infrastructure.

RAIL SECURITY INSPECTORS AND CANINES
The conferees are very disappointed with TSA's reluctance to quickly hire rail inspectors and deploy canine units at transit systems nationwide. Although these activities were funded in fiscal year 2005, TSA does not have a full contingent of rail inspectors on board and only announced the deployment of canine teams on September 27, 2005. This is unacceptable. The conferees direct TSA to report to the Committees on Appropriations no later than February 10, 2006, on the deployment of the 100 rail security inspectors and canine teams funded in fiscal year 2005 and any new inspectors or canine teams planned for fiscal year 2006.

Source: *Department of Homeland Security Appropriations Act for Fiscal Year 2006* (conference report to accompany H.R. 2360), 109th Cong., 1st sess., September 2005, pp. 51–53.

(a) The reports of the House and Senate appropriations committees, which are drafted by their subcommittees, provide detailed guidance to agencies on spending appropriated funds and carrying out activities. Although report language does not have statutory effect, agencies generally heed these directives. The guidance might be positive—specifying how the funds are to be spent—or negative—directing the affected agency not to undertake certain activities or expenditures.

(b) The reports comment on most items in the appropriations bills, but they concentrate on changes from the previous year's level, earmarks, restrictions on the use of funds, and disagreements with the agency or the president's budget. For virtually all appropriations bills, report language has become more detailed and pointed than it was one or two decades earlier.

(c) The language used here to convey the conference committee's views is varied. Phrases such as "the conferees recommend" or "the conferees encourage" (which appear in this exhibit) might soften the guidance. In the case of rail security and canines, however, the committee sends a much stronger message, finding the Transportation Security Administration's actions "unacceptable." In instances like this, the committee may direct the agency to report back on the matter by a fixed date during the fiscal year. Regardless of wording, the appropriations committees expect agencies to follow their guidance.

(d) This exhibit is drawn from the joint explanatory statement of the conference report on a fiscal 2006 appropriations act. Additional guidance appears in the reports of the House and Senate appropriations committees. As a general rule, all guidance should be followed, except when there is a conflict, in which case the conference report is determinative.

and staff and consults with them on problems in implementing report language will obtain more flexibility than one that acts unilaterally.

CONCLUSION

For more than two centuries, making appropriations has been a source of congressional power and a key factor in organizing the legislative calendar. The process has always revolved around the annual review of spending requests and congressional decisions on the amounts to be made available. In making these decisions, the appropriations committees have usually decided on what should be provided for the next year by looking back at what was provided for the current year.

This tradition-bound process has evolved incrementally, with a premium placed on both procedural continuity and program stability. As the political-budgeting world in which they operated was transformed, the appropriations committees held on to tradition—retaining the same subcommittee structure and boundaries despite the vast expansion of government, allowing each subcommittee substantial operating autonomy, and holding on to quaint practices. This unresponsiveness contributed to a shrinkage of their effective jurisdiction with the advance of entitlements and the creation of the congressional budget process. With little choice in the matter, the committees made modest concessions to the growth of government (by consolidating accounts), new congressional budget rules (by fitting their spending decisions into predetermined totals), spending limits (by paying greater attention to outlays), and conflict with the president (by producing omnibus spending measures).

But even when they produce an omnibus measure, the appropriations committees uphold tradition by treating each of the regular appropriations bills enacted in it as if it were separate legislation. The 950-page omnibus appropriations act for fiscal year 1999 contains eight regular appropriations acts, dozens of "emergency supplemental" appropriations, and a substantial amount of unrelated legislation. The content of the omnibus act would be virtually incomprehensible to most Americans; it has no table of contents or other information to indicate when one appropriations act or substantive law ends and another begins. Furthermore, each appropriations act and substantive law has its own numbering arrangement so that the same section number appears numerous times in the omnibus measure. This closed world has been penetrated, however, by outsiders who have an interest in what the appropriations committees are doing. Through the Internet and other modern information technologies, it is possible to quickly locate provisions in an appropriations act or report.

Tradition leaves the appropriations committees in charge, but only over the discretionary accounts. The fact that a shrinking portion of total spending is in their domain is of less consequence to the appropriations committees than that they still effectively control large amounts of money.

Traditions erode when they are at variance with practice. In the case of the appropriations process, the progressive elaboration of budget rules and the escalation of budget conflict have undermined its old ways. The former calls into question the logic of annual appropriations; the latter weakens the special conflict-abating procedures and norms of the appropriations committees. In the 1990s, Congress enacted caps that limited discretionary spending for each of the next five years. Arguably, multiyear caps weaken the case for annual appropriations. Why fight over marginal amounts each year when the boundaries for appropriations have been set in advance? The annuality of appropriations has as much to do with norms and behavior as with legislative calendars and fiscal years. The appropriations committees have been acculturated through two centuries of congressional work to control spending one year at a time. Making annual appropriations is what these committees do—just about the only thing they do. If Congress were to switch to two-year appropriations (which is discussed in chapter 11), the leverage exercised by these committees vis-à-vis spending agencies and other congressional participants would be weakened. It also is highly likely that a two-year cycle would break down, thereby opening the door to much wider use of supplemental appropriations.

Every discretionary program has the potential for duplication of effort in Congress and friction between the two sets of committees. Duplication and conflict tend to be low for programs that have permanent authorizations and high for those that are reauthorized annually. The increase in temporary authorizations has raised the odds that authorizers and appropriators will get in each other's way, even when they go about their own business. Yet there are enormous differences in the relationships between the two types of committees—ranging from defense programs, where the armed services committees and the defense appropriations subcommittees review the same budget submissions and decide many of the same spending issues each year, to various natural resources programs, which have continued for years without significant authorizing legislation.

Because of these differences, merging the authorizations and appropriations processes would have modest impact on some programs and profound impact on others. Some have argued that merging the two sets of committees would weaken congressional spending control while generating more conflict over appropriations. If the appropriations function

were folded into authorizing committees, Congress's responsibility for the federal budget would be even more fragmented than it now is. Others counter that with section 302 allocations in place, effective control can be maintained even when many committees share jurisdiction.

Combining the two processes might make for a more efficient Congress but one less open to divergent perspectives. Congress benefits from authorizing committees that emphasize program needs and objectives, and from appropriating committees that emphasize costs and financial constraints. Both perspectives need to be considered in making public policy; having separate committees gives each a platform for presenting its views. If the two processes were combined, appropriations actions would be hostage to conflict over substantive legislation, and the tendency of Congress to attach unrelated riders to appropriations measures might become more pronounced.

Although change comes slowly to the appropriations processes, it does come. By increments, the process has been made more open and transparent, more partisan and programmatic, and more closely linked to overall budget policies. Innovations discussed in this chapter—the statements of administration policy, section 302(b) allocations, Senate initiative on appropriations bills, omnibus spending measures, the role of party leaders, and summit negotiations between presidential aides and congressional leaders across a range of spending issues—were unknown three decades ago. Even as they uphold tradition, the appropriations committees have been molded and transformed by changes in national politics and congressional institutions. Thirty years hence additional reforms will have been introduced to modernize the appropriations process and adapt it to changing conditions.

Managing Federal
Expenditures

Appropriations are supposed to be made by the time the fiscal year begins. But even when they are delayed, the start of a fiscal year compels agencies to shift to the next stage of budgeting, which involves managing federal expenditures by spending available funds to carry out authorized activities and by accounting for their actions.

The fiscal year starts on October 1, approximately 18 months after most federal agencies begin preparing their budgets and eight months after the president submits his budget to Congress. Key conditions affecting the budget are likely to change during these long intervals. The cost of goods and services may vary from earlier estimates, turnover within agency staff will be higher or lower than expected, and new problems and priorities will come to the fore. In spending appropriated funds, agencies must adhere to congressional intent while adjusting to changing conditions and emergency needs. They must be compliant and flexible—responsive to the will of Congress and responsible for getting the job done.

Implementing the budget is a balancing act that begins before the fiscal year starts and ends after the fiscal year is over. From beginning to end, agencies make thousands of operating decisions that affect spending. Many decisions are routine and conform to original plans, but some agencies adjust spending plans in light of new conditions. Implementing the budget receives much less attention than do presidential and congressional actions, but what an agency does with the money appropriated to it materially affects its performance. Agency budget staffs generally spend more time and effort on this phase of the process than on any other.

Decisions made and problems encountered while executing one year's budget strongly influence future budgets. Agencies often free up resources in their current budget for seed money to initiate activities that may become priorities in the next budget cycle. They may shift staff from old tasks to new ones or redirect operating resources (such as money for contracts or consultants) to new activities. Sometimes they make the adjustments internally, without notifying congressional committees or the Office of Management and Budget (OMB). Sometimes, they formally transfer or reprogram funds and adjust their accounts to reflect the changed allocation.

Managing expenditures is decentralized; within broad rules and guidelines, each spending agency handles its own finances. The federal government is too big and its activities too diverse to centralize financial operations in a single command post. Each agency receiving appropriations or other budget resources from Congress has primary responsibility for assuring the legality, propriety, and efficiency of its expenditures. Agencies usually make their own decisions on these matters, but they sometimes consult the Government Accountability Office (GAO), which serves as the government's principal auditing and evaluation agency, or OMB, which shares responsibility with the Treasury Department for financial management. OMB's role in executing the budget is necessarily selective and limited. On any particular matter, it may intervene to influence the use of federal dollars, but it is much too small to oversee all transactions. Each department has its own budget and accounting staffs; major

subunits are also staffed with budget and finance specialists.

The next section of this chapter traces the normal sequence in which funds are spent as intended by the appropriation, as well as variances from the normal pattern due to reprogramming, impoundment, or other actions. A subsequent section examines financial management practices in federal agencies, including the relationship of budgeting and accounting, internal control, and changes spurred by the Chief Financial Officers Act of 1990, the Government Performance and Results Act of 1993, and OMB's Program Assessment Rating Tool.

SPENDING BUDGET RESOURCES

Appropriated funds are not instantly available to agencies. They become available only upon apportionment by OMB. The Antideficiency Act requires that appropriations be apportioned by periods within the fiscal year (typically by quarters) or among specific projects. The purpose of apportionment is to deter agencies from spending at a rate that would exhaust their budget resources before the end of the fiscal year. Normally, therefore, apportionment spreads available budget resources throughout the year. In some instances, however, such as for national defense and threats to health and safety, funds may be apportioned at a rate that would necessitate supplemental appropriations.

The amount apportioned may not exceed the amount available for obligation. Only unobligated resources are subject to apportionment. OMB reviews the requests agencies submit via the form shown in exhibit 10-1. This form has a complete listing of the types of unobligated budget resources in each fund or account. These resources may derive from current or permanent appropriations, transfers from other accounts, direct spending, unobligated balances carried forward from previous years, income earned from user charges, and other sources. OMB may withhold resources from apportionment but must report any such action to Congress via the impoundment procedures discussed later in this chapter.

Although apportionment is largely a technical procedure, it is the last point at which OMB formally controls agency spending. OMB sometimes uses apportionment to impose conditions on agency spending or to demand changes in agency practices.

Allotment

OMB makes a single apportionment for each appropriation account or fund; it does not formally subdivide the money among programs or organizational units, although it may advise them that particular funds are to be used for specified purposes. However, agencies need to notify program managers of the resources that will be available to them during the year. This information is provided through allotments, which distribute funds among bureaus, divisions, field offices, and other organizational subunits. Allotment procedures vary among agencies—they tend to be formal in large agencies, informal in small ones—and the total allotted may not exceed the OMB apportionment.

The allotment gives each operating unit its budget for the fiscal year. Within its allotment, a unit hires and pays staff, purchases supplies and equipment, and keeps track of its obligations. In most agencies, units do not have to obtain approval from headquarters before taking these actions, although special circumstances may intervene to restrict spending discretion. For example, an agency concerned that available resources will not suffice through the fiscal year might impose a hiring freeze or take back some of the money allotted to subunits at the start of the year. Normally, however, program managers plan activities and expenditures for the full year based on allotted resources.

Allotments, like much of the information agencies produce in the course of implementing their budgets, are not confidential, but neither are they public. Nowadays allotments are usually held in computerized databases and distributed internally as printouts that are updated throughout the year to show the status of obligations and other spending actions. These internal budgets have more program and financial detail than is available in public budget documents. They show the money flows within departments and how funds are parceled among programs and activities, as well as provide insight into how the department is structured and operates.

Obligations

Once funds have been allocated, managers may obligate them. An obligation is an agency's binding commitment to another party concerning goods or services to be provided, amounts to be paid, and other material elements of the transaction. Internal actions, such as setting aside funds for particular purposes, are not bona fide obligations. Each obligation has to be supported by documents—such as purchase orders, signed contracts, letters of credit, or personnel records—attesting to the transaction.

Funds may be obligated only during the period that they are available. Beyond that period, the funds lapse and authority to obligate expires. In addition, exhibit 10-2 shows that the obligation must be for a public purpose, not for a private benefit. Also, the obligation must be related to the purpose for which the appropriation was made. In recent times,

▶ EXHIBIT 10-1
Apportionment of Budgetary Resources

Description	Amount on Latest S.F. 132	Agency request	Action by OMB
BUDGETARY RESOURCES			
1 Unobligated balance:			
1A Brought forward, October 1 (+ or −)			
2 Recoveries of prior year unpaid obligations:			
2A Actual			
2B Anticipated			
3 Budget authority:			
3A Appropriation:			
3A1 Actual			
3A2 Anticipated			
3B Borrowing authority			
3C Contract authority			
Spending authority from offsetting collections (gross):			
Earned:			
***			
4 Nonexpenditure transfers, net:			
4A Actual transfers, budget authority (+ or −)			
***			
6 Permanently not available:			
6A Cancellations of expired or no-year accounts (−)			
***			
7 TOTAL BUDGETARY RESOURCES			
APPLICATION OF BUDGETARY RESOURCES			
8 Apportioned:			
Category A:			
8A1 First quarter			
8A2 Second quarter			
8A3 Third quarter			
8A4 Fourth quarter			
***			
9 Withheld pending rescission			
10 Deferred			
11 Unapportioned balance of revolving fund			
12 TOTAL BUDGETARY RESOURCES			

Source: Office of Management and Budget, *Circular A-11*, June 2006, Standard Form 132.

(a) Standard Form 132 shows the amount requested for apportionment by the agency and OMB's decision. A single apportionment is made for each appropriation or fund account.

(b) The top part of this form (lines 1–7) itemizes all the resources available for apportionment; the bottom part (lines 8–12) shows apportionments by quarter or project and amounts withheld from apportionment. The total on line 12 must equal the total on line 7.

some appropriations subcommittees have insisted that agencies within their jurisdiction spend funds according to the detailed justification schedules prepared for the appropriation hearings.

Agencies generally have accurate and timely information on the status of obligations. They know that overobligation violates the Antideficiency Act and that underobligation may cause them to lose resources. As the fiscal year winds down, agencies closely monitor obligations to ensure that virtually all remaining funds are used.

Guarding against overobligation depends not only on timely information but also on prudent financial management. At the start of a fiscal year, agency staff compare the resources on hand with the amounts projected for salaries, supplies, and other operating expenses to determine how they should manage their finances so that resources last through the year. Many guard against overexpenditure by making conservative assumptions, such as low turnover, and set aside money for unbudgeted contingencies. They often slow spending on contracts, equipment, and other discretionary items to ensure that they are not caught short before the year is over. As the fiscal year nears a close, many agencies find that they have been overly cautious and risk losing unspent funds. At this point, they typically accelerate spending on matters treated more conservatively earlier, leading them to obligate a large proportion of contract and procurement money during the last months of the fiscal year. Although the resulting year-end bulge in spending may appear to be wasteful, it is often the result of prudent financial management.

Outlays

Once the goods or services for which funds were obligated have been provided, the oblig-ation is paid off and the amount is recorded as an outlay on agency accounts. Outlays are normally processed through administrative routines that are handled by disbursement offices, not by program managers. Payments are made pursuant to vouchers or invoices that indicate the account from which the funds are drawn, the payee, amount to be paid, and other relevant information. Before payment, the spending agency preaudits vouchers to determine that the amount is correct, the goods and services have been provided according to specification, and the account or fund from which the payment is to be made is available for that purpose. Nowadays most payments are made in electronic form through disbursing offices operated by the Treasury.

Agencies prepare monthly budget execution reports, detailing the volume of obligations and outlays during the latest month and cumulatively during the fiscal year. In addition to these reports, each agency maintains its own accounts, which are much more detailed than those recorded on a governmentwide basis.

Although outlays come too late in the expenditure process to be an effective instrument of financial control, they cannot be ignored in managing federal expenditures. The timing and rate of outlays are important to the Treasury for managing the government's cash and debt. Also, the difference between outlays and receipts determines the size of the budget surplus or deficit. As long as the federal budget is accounted for on a cash basis, outlays will exert a strong influence on budget actions.

Closing Accounts

The final step in the spending process is the closing of appropriations accounts. When an account is closed, all remaining balances are canceled and are no longer available for expenditure. Fixed accounts (those whose

► **EXHIBIT 10-2**
Comptroller General Opinion on Propriety of Expenditure

The Principal Deputy General Counsel of the Central Intelligence Agency (CIA) requests our opinion on the propriety of using appropriated funds to purchase refrigerators for placement in the workplace. For the reasons stated below, should the CIA administratively determine that equipping the workplace with the refrigerators is reasonably related to the efficient performance of agency activities, we would not object to the CIA using appropriated funds to purchase refrigerators for the workplace. . . .

The issue here is whether the purchase of refrigerators may be considered a "necessary expense" of operating the facility. The general rule is that where an appropriation is not specifically available for a particular item, its purchase may be authorized as a "necessary expense" if there is a reasonable relationship between the object of the expenditure and the general purposes for which the funds were appropriated and the expenditure is not otherwise prohibited. B-210433, April 15, 1983. This rule of reason recognizes an agency's discretion in using its appropriation to fulfill its purpose.

We have addressed situations analogous to the one presented here. In 47 Comp. Gen. 657 (1968), we objected to the purchase of a coffee maker and related items because a purpose of the purchase was to enable the agency to provide coffee at meetings to its employees and others. We reached a different result where the agency determined that the purchase was necessary to compensate for a lack of available eating facilities. . . .

Accordingly, we would not object to the purchase of refrigerators should CIA administratively determine that equipping the headquarters facility with refrigerators is reasonably related to the efficient performance of agency activities, and not just for the personal convenience of individual employees.

Source: Government Accountability Office, *Central Intelligence Agency—Availability of Appropriations to Purchase Refrigerators for Placement in the Workplace,* B-276601, 158619, June 26, 1997, available on the GAO website under "Comptroller General Decisions and Opinions" at www.gao.gov/legal.htm.

(a) In most cases, spending agencies make their own decisions, based on accumulated precedents on the legality and propriety of expenditures.

(b) In the opinion excerpted here, the issue was referred by the CIA to the comptroller general, who made an authoritative decision, which then may serve as precedent for future expenditures.

(c) A key issue in this and many other rulings is whether the expenditure would benefit the government or only its employees. If only the latter benefit, the expenditure might be disallowed as not being a "necessary expense" that is reasonably related to the performance of agency activities. In this case, the comptroller general held that the purchase of refrigerators is a permissible public expense because it would enhance employee performance.

budget resources are available for obligation for a limited period) are closed according to a preset schedule. No-year funds that are available without a time limit remain open until all budget resources have been depleted or canceled.

The procedures for closing fixed accounts stretch over six or more fiscal years. The account is open during the period that funds are available for obligation—one year in the case of most appropriations. When this period ends, the account is in *expired* status for five years, during which no new obligations may be incurred but old ones are paid off as they become due. At the end of the five years, the account is *closed,* and any remaining balance is canceled.

DEVIATIONS FROM SPENDING PLANS

The sequence of steps from apportionment through the closing of accounts sometimes occurs as provided for in annual appropriations. Often, however, these plans are altered during implementation of the budget, and resources are augmented, diminished, or shifted from one purpose to another. Some of these actions are taken by Congress, others by spending agencies. Some of the variances are intended to change policy; most are means of coping with needs and opportunities that arise during the year.

Transfers and Reprogrammings

Nowadays agencies frequently finance unbudgeted needs by shifting funds from one use to another. These shifts are *transfers* when budget resources move from one account to another and *reprogrammings* when resources are switched from one activity to another within the same account.

Inasmuch as an appropriation is a legal limit on expenditure, funds may be transferred only pursuant to statutory authorization. Congress sometimes authorizes designated entities, such as the Defense Department, to transfer up to a certain amount or percentage of their appropriations among their accounts. An entity granted general transfer authority is usually required to notify relevant congressional committees when it moves funds from one account to another. In other instances, Congress directs certain agencies to transfer a portion of their appropriation to other agencies. When funds are transferred, the receiving account (whose resources are augmented) must abide by any restrictions or conditions pertaining to the original appropriation. For example, when one-year money is transferred to an account that has no-year funds, the transferred money retains its one-year status.

Transfers are easy to monitor because some accounts lose resources and others gain. Transfer inflows and outflows are recorded in the program and financing schedules (see exhibit 5-4) published in the president's budget and in the apportionment schedule shown in exhibit 10-1. Reprogrammings, however, may be difficult to identify because they do not change the volume of resources in the affected account. Reprogramming practices depend on the definition of programs and on guidelines provided in appropriations bills or in the committee reports accompanying these bills. There are no governmentwide reprogramming rules (the rules vary considerably among the appropriations subcommittees), nor is there a comprehensive register of these actions. Some rules only require that the relevant subcommittees be given advance notice of reprogrammings; others require advance approval by the subcommittees (and in some cases by the associated authorizing committees as well). In still other instances, the reprogramming takes effect unless the relevant committees or sub-committees disapprove it during a waiting period. Exhibit 10-3 shows some appropriations subcommittees' reprogramming rules and practices.

For more than two decades, there has been a marked tightening of reprogramming rules. Matters that once were handled informally now have prescribed procedures and reporting requirements; matters that once required only notification now require advance approval. Reprogramming thresholds—the amount of money above which the reprogramming rules are triggered—have been set very low for some agencies. Box 10-1 highlights a reprogramming conflict between the Department of Veterans Affairs and the Senate VA-HUD Appropriations Subcommittee. The subcommittee specified a very low threshold, only $250,000. The department maintained that it did not violate reprogramming rules when it shifted funds without notifying Congress, but a GAO investigation concluded otherwise—that the shift in funds should have been reported to the subcommittee.

In a typical year, federal agencies report a total of fewer than 1,000 reprogrammings. Most of these are concentrated in a few areas, such as defense and foreign assistance. Some departments do not report any reprogrammings, even when they are constantly moving funds from one use to another, juggling resources in response to pressures or opportunities encountered during the year. If all such adjustments were reported, the number of reprogrammings would add up to many thousands.

Why are there so few formal reprogrammings? Part of the answer lies in the broad scope of appropriations. At one time appropriations were extremely detailed; everything from authorized positions to supplies and travel were itemized. Itemized appropriations narrowed agency discretion and restricted agencies' freedom in shifting funds. But as the size and scope of government grew, appropriations were progressively consolidated into broad accounts so that many agencies now receive a lump sum for all salaries and operating expenses. Although the appropriations committees earmark or direct the use of funds in their reports, agencies have considerable flexibility in using appropriations, and they exercise this discretion routinely without calling formal reprogramming procedures into play. But when the appropriations committees demand that a particular shift be classified as a reprogramming, agencies must behave accordingly. As a general rule, reprogramming is taking funds from a "program, project, or activity" (these usually are specified annually in appropriations committee reports) or from a "congressional interest" item—an expenditure mentioned in the text of the appropriations act or the appropriations committee reports.

Reprogramming operates in a murky area of executive-legislative relations. Many are undertaken under an arrangement that permits the appropriations committees to review and block the proposed shift of funds. This "committee veto" is exercised despite the 1983 Supreme Court ruling in *INS* v. *Chadha* that all legislative vetoes violate the Constitution. A legislative veto gives the House, the Senate, or both the power to disapprove a pending executive action. Arguably, if vetoes by the House or Senate are unconstitutional, then vetoes by congressional committees should be as well. Nevertheless, committee review of reprogramming and of many other types of executive action has become common during the years since the *Chadha* decision.

Committee vetoes flourish because they are part of a quid pro quo in which Congress gives agencies discretion in exchange for retaining authority to review and disapprove proposed actions (such as reprogramming). If Congress

▶ EXHIBIT 10-3
Reprogramming Rules and Practice

RULES: DEFENSE APPROPRIATIONS ACT

No part of the funds in this Act shall be available to prepare or present a request to the Committees on Appropriations for reprogramming of funds, unless for higher priority items, based on the unforeseen military requirements, than those for which originally appropriated and in no case where the item for which reprogramming is requested has been denied by the Congress.

PRACTICE: HOUSE APPROPRIATIONS COMMITTEE REPORT

The Committee's perspective is one of ensuring that the funds made available in appropriations acts are in fact put to the use intended by the elected members of Congress, under the terms and conditions the Congress and the House and Senate Appropriations Committees place on the funding in question. . . . Regrettably, in recent years the Committee has observed a steady erosion of [Defense Department] compliance with these standards. . . .

In its fiscal year 2000 budget the Air Force acquisition community continues to blithely ignore specific Committee direction and law intended to ensure that funds appropriated for one purpose—for example, weapons procurement—are in fact used for that purpose and not for other efforts, such as research and development by:

> 1) Requesting hundreds of millions of dollars in various procurement programs, when in fact the intended use is to support operation and maintenance funding needs (in violation of DoD policy). . . .

Sources: *Department of Defense Appropriations Act for Fiscal Year 2000*, P.L. 106-79, 106th Cong., 1st sess., October 25, 1999; and House Appropriations Committee, *Department of Defense Appropriations Bill, 2000*, H. Rept. 244, 106th Cong., 1st sess., July 20, 1999, pp. 8–9.

(a) There are no governmentwide reprogramming rules; each set of appropriations subcommittees provides guidelines for the agencies in their jurisdiction. Sometimes (as in the first entry above) the guidelines are in the appropriations act; at other times, they are in the appropriations committee report. Pursuant to these directives, each agency has procedures for initiating reprogrammings and (when required) submitting them for congressional review.

(b) The rule exhibited here reflects a trend to more restrictive reprogramming procedures. Typical restrictions pertain to using programs to start or eliminate other programs or to finance an activity for which Congress denied an appropriations request.

(c) The report excerpted here sharply criticizes the Defense Department for violating reprogramming rules by starting new activities, using funds to continue programs terminated by Congress, and asking more than needed for one purpose in order to shift money to another purpose.

(d) Pursuant to these findings, the appropriations committees tightened the reprogramming rules for the Defense Department.

▼

BOX 10-1
Reprogramming Wars: Who Controls the Details of Federal Spending

For two centuries Congress and federal agencies have vied for control of the details of expenditure. Claiming the constitutionally prescribed power of the purse, Congress often insists that agencies spend money according to the fine print in appropriations acts and committee reports. But claiming that they need flexibility in carrying out authorized activities, agencies often deviate from the precise spending plan approved by Congress. Who wins this battle tells us a great deal about legislative-executive relations at different points in history.

The reprogramming rules prescribed by the VA-HUD Appropriations Subcommittees reflect congressional insistence that it control the details. The following report language was inserted in Senate Appropriations reports during the 1990s:

> "The Committee continues to have a particular interest in being informed of reprogrammings which, although they may not change either the total amount available in an account or any of the purposes for which the appropriation is legally available, represent a significant departure from budget plans presented to the Committee in an agency's budget justifications. Consequently, the Committee directs the Departments of Veterans' Affairs and Housing and Urban Development, and the agencies funded through this bill, to notify the chairman of the Committee prior to each reprogramming of funds in excess of $250,000 between programs, activities, or elements unless an alternative amount for the agency or department in question is specified elsewhere in this report. The Committee desires to be notified of reprogramming actions which involve less than the above-mentioned amounts if such actions would have the effect of changing an agency's funding requirements in future years or if programs or projects specifically cited in the Committee's reports are affected."

This language is extraordinarily restrictive in a number of ways. First, it has a very low threshold—$250,000—for notifying the appropriations committee of reprogramming. Second, it defines reprogramming to include actions that do not change the purpose of appropriations. Third, it requires that the committee be informed of reprogramming below this amount that would change future funding requirements.

continued

were barred from exercising this veto, it would probably withhold discretion from agencies and give them less flexibility in managing their budgets.

Impoundment

In addition to limiting the amounts that may be spent, appropriations establish the strong expectation that the funds Congress provides will be spent on planned activities. When an agency impounds—refuses to use all or part of an appropriation—it violates congressional intent. For example, if Congress were to appropriate $5 billion for education grants to states, but the government spent only $4 billion, education programs would have less money than Congress provided.

▼

BOX 10-1
Continued

Despite these rules, the Department of Veterans Affairs (VA) shifted funds among line items without going through reprogramming procedures. A 1999 investigation by the General Accounting Office (GAO) found that during fiscal years 1993 through 1998, VA used $61 million of travel funds on other operating expenses, such as salaries and equipment. According to the GAO report, VA systematically overestimated travel costs in preparing its annual budget and then switched the excess funds to other object classes (see exhibit 5-5 for a list of object classes). GAO took the position that these reprogrammings should have been reported to the appropriations committees; VA argued that the reprogramming rules refer to shifts between "programs, activities, or elements," not to shifts between object classes. In a letter to the GAO disagreeing with its conclusions, VA wrote that it

> "maintains an open dialogue with the Appropriations Committee staff. Over the years we have agreed that reprogramming requirements would apply to the major program activity components listed in the Program and Financing Schedule contained in the Appendix to the President's budget. . . . At no time was VA's interpretation of congressional expectations regarding reprogrammings challenged. . . . Redefining reprogramming requirements to apply to an object class level is inconsistent with the objectives of the Government Performance and Results Act and reinvention efforts, which encourage a focus on the performance not the categories of expenses."

Despite its view that the VA action constituted a reprogramming, GAO noted that the report language "does not have the force and effect of law and is not legally binding on an agency." If the same language were in the text of an appropriations act (as in exhibit 10-3), it would have a stronger legal basis. Why then do appropriations committees use report language rather than law? Possibly because they want to give affected agencies more flexibility. Why then do they criticize agencies for exercising their flexibility, as VA did? Possibly because they still want agencies to know that Congress controls the purse. Having it both ways generates friction between spending agencies and the committees, but it also establishes conditions under which they coexist, not always in peace, but with enough mutual accommodation that each can get on with its work until the next battle.

Impoundment is not a new practice. Over the years, most presidents impounded some appropriated funds, but their actions were limited to particular projects. Impoundment became a full-scale political battleground in the early 1970s, when Richard Nixon refused to spend billions of dollars Congress had added to his budget. Nixon claimed an inherent power to impound, but many in Congress insisted that the president must spend appropriated money—even when doing so would mean higher total spending (or a bigger deficit) than he wanted. To resolve this conflict, the Impoundment Control Act of 1974 (enacted in the same measure as the Congressional Budget Act) prescribed rules and procedures for dealing with cases in which the president or an executive official withholds budget resources.

Due to its abraded relationship with Nixon, Congress defined impoundment in exceedingly broad terms as any "action or inaction" that delays or withholds funds. This language could be read to include routine financial operations, such as a delay in awarding a contract to check the vendor's reliability. In practice, however, impoundment is narrowly applied to actions whose purpose is to curtail spending; actions that only incidentally affect the amount spent are not treated as impoundments. The line between routine financial management and impoundment is not always clear, and disputes sometimes arise as to how particular actions should be handled. One area of controversy is known as *de facto impoundment*—a situation in which the federal agency does not directly slow the rate of spending but takes indirect action that has the same effect. Suppose, for example, that an agency drags its feet in hiring examiners to process disability claims. The effect will be to reduce the amount spent on these claims. Should this tactic be treated as an impoundment? Program advocates typically argue that it should, but OMB rarely reports it as an impoundment.

The 1974 act divides impoundment into two categories and prescribes distinct procedures for each. A *deferral* delays the use of funds; a rescission cancels budget authority. Every impoundment is either a deferral or a *rescission;* it cannot be both or something else.

When the president defers funds, he submits a message to Congress setting forth the amount, the program and account affected, the estimated fiscal and program impact, and the length of time the funds are to be deferred. The president may not defer funds beyond the end of the fiscal year nor for a duration that would cause the budget authority to lapse or prevent the agency from spending the money prudently. The original Impoundment Control Act permitted the president to defer funds for policy reasons—for example, because he opposes a particular program or wants to spend less than Congress appropriated. In exchange for giving the president this broad authority, Congress reserved for itself the power to disapprove any deferral by vote of the House or Senate. Under current rules, the president may defer spending only for the specific reasons permitted by the Antideficiency Act: to provide for contingencies or to achieve savings made possible through changes in requirements or efficiency in operations. The president may not use the deferral power to change budget or program policies. The comptroller general reviews each deferral message and notifies Congress concerning the accuracy of the information, the legal status of the impoundment, and the probable impacts.

The deferral rules demonstrate reciprocity in executive-legislative relations. When Congress retained the capacity to uphold its position by reviewing executive policies, it granted the president power to defer. But when Congress was denied that capacity, it curtailed presidential power. Both branches were weakened: the president had less control of federal finances; Congress had less ability to influence executive actions.

Rescission

The relationship between the president and Congress is different in rescissions, and so too are the rules. The president may propose a rescission by submitting a message to Congress specifying the amount to be rescinded, the reasons, the accounts and programs involved, and the estimated budgetary and program impacts (exhibit 10-4). After receiving the message, Congress has 45 days of continuous session (usually a larger number of calendar days) during which it may consider a bill rescinding all, part, or none of the funds.

▶ **EXHIBIT 10-4**
Presidential Rescissions Message

Rescission Proposal No. R98-10
PROPOSED RESCISSION OF BUDGET AUTHORITY
Report Pursuant to Section 1012 of P.L. 93-344

Agency: Department of Agriculture	New budget authority $1,348,377,000 (P.L. 105-83) Other budgetary resources $270,000,000 Total budgetary resources $1,618,377,000
Bureau: Forest Service	
Appropriations title and symbol: National forest system 12X1106	Amount proposed for rescission $1,094,000
	Legal authority (in addition to sec. 1012):
OMB identification code: 12-1106-0-1-302	___X___ Antideficiency Act _____ Other
Grant program: _____ Yes ___X___ No	*Type of budget authority:*
Type of account or fund:	___X___ Appropriation _____ Contract authority _____ Other _____
_____ Annual _____ Multi-year _____ ___X___ No-Year (expiration date)	

Justification: The national forest system (NFS) provides for the delivery of goods and services associated with the principal NFS programs of land management planning, inventory, and monitoring; recreation use; wildlife and fisheries habitat management; rangeland management; forestland management; soil, water, and air management; minerals and geology; landownership; infrastructure. The proposed rescission is based on the affected program's FTE level and an estimate of its impact on the Department's civil rights resources, and is intended to offset supplemental appropriations for the Department's Civil Rights initiative. This action is taken pursuant to the Antideficiency Act (31 U.S.C. 1512).

Outlay Effect (in thousands of dollars)

1998 Outlay Estimate		Outlay Changes					
Without Rescission	With Rescission	FY 1998	FY 1999	FY 2000	FY 2001	FY 2002	FY 2003
1,400,000	1,399,070	−930	−164	. . .	. . .	. . .	. . .

Source: *Proposed Rescission of Budgetary Resources*, H. Doc. 215, 105th Cong., 2d sess., February 24, 1998.

(a) The president notifies Congress of every proposed rescission or deferral in a message that sets forth the reasons for the action and the estimated program and financial effects. The message exhibited here deals with rescissions; a similar one is used for deferrals. If the president fails to report an impoundment, the comp-

troller general may notify Congress. This notification has the same legal status as a presidential message.

(b) Every proposed rescission and deferral is assigned an alphanumeric identification. Rescissions are prefaced with the letter "R" and deferrals with the letter "D." The proposed rescission here, R98-10, was the tenth reported for fiscal 1998.

TABLE 10-1
Rescissions by Presidential and Congressional Initiative, 1974–2005

Millions of dollars unless otherwise specified

President	Fiscal years	Presidential initiative			Congressional initiative	
		Amount proposed for rescission	Amount rescinded	Percent rescinded	Amount rescinded	Percent rescinded
Ford	1974–77	7,935	1,252	16	1,405	53
Carter	1977–81	5,751	2,116	46	3,526	62
Reagan	1981–89	43,437	15,657	36	33,400	68
Bush	1989–93	13,293	2,354	18	26,821	92
Clinton	1993–2001	6,749	3,628	54	53,730	94
G.W. Bush	2002–05	0[a]	0	0	24,611	100
Total	1974–2005	76,022	25,007	33	143,493	85

Source: Government Accountability Office, *Updated Rescission Statistics, Fiscal Years 1974–2005*, B-306473, November 4, 2005.

a. President George W. Bush proposed billions of dollars in cancellations. By proposing them as cancellations instead of rescissions, he did not have to comply with the requirements of the Impoundment Control Act, but he was not able to withhold the funds from obligation for 45 days of continuous session, as the act provides. Congress approved many of his proposed cancellations as rescissions.

If Congress does not rescind the budget resources by the end of the 45 days, the president must release the funds and make them available for obligation. The comptroller general, who reviews all proposed rescissions and deferrals, may bring suit to compel the release of the impounded funds, but this has been a rare occurrence.

The president's record on rescissions is a measure of his budgetary influence and of his standing with Congress. The high-water mark for president-initiated rescissions came in fiscal 1981 and 1982, when Ronald Reagan proposed more than $23 billion in cancellations shortly after he became president, and Congress rescinded more than 65 percent of his request. Table 10-1 indicates that Reagan's rescissions amounted to nearly two-thirds of the total rescinded pursuant to presidential request since the impoundment process was initiated in 1974. Over the years, Congress has enacted only one-third of the rescissions proposed by the president. With fiscal 1981 and 1982 excluded, the rescission approval rate drops below 20 percent.

Rescissions stir conflict between the president and Congress. Every rescission the White House requests is a demand that Congress cancel resources it previously appropriated. By implication, and sometimes by press release as well, proposed rescissions make the point that Congress erred when it appropriated the money. This is not a message that appeals to legislators, especially when it comes from a president who has different budget priorities. In this contest, Congress has the advantage because the president must release the money if it refuses to pass a rescission bill. Over the past 30 years, presidents have been compelled to spend more than $50 billion of the $76 billion they wanted rescinded.

Table 10-1 also suggests that Congress has

another advantage in these budget wars. It can rescind funds on its own initiative—without waiting for a presidential request—simply by passing a bill canceling previous appropriations. In fact, for every dollar Congress has rescinded pursuant to the president's impoundment request, it has rescinded more than five dollars by enacting legislation on its own initiative. At first glance, this behavior may seem puzzling. Why would Congress take the initiative in rescinding funds it had appropriated? Why, if it does not like rescissions requested by the president, has it been so active on its own? The puzzle evaporates when it is recognized that Congress initiates rescissions either to thwart the president or to make room in the budget for other expenditures. When Congress refuses to approve a president's rescission, he can portray it as a cabal of spendthrift politicians who think nothing of wasting taxpayer money. To buffer itself against this charge, Congress sometimes rescinds items other than those the president proposed. It may even rescind more than the president requested, taking care to cancel spending on his priorities. In 1992, for example, George Bush proposed almost $8 billion in rescissions, indicating that he would demand additional rescissions as the year progressed and the presidential election neared. Congress rescinded about $2 billion of the amount requested, but it then added another $22 billion of rescissions, taking money from his priorities rather than from areas he wanted cut. Bush got the message and refrained from proposing additional rescissions.

Congress may also generate rescissions when the budget is tight and it wants to make room for additional spending. In some years, Congress has rescinded funds to pay for supplemental spending without exceeding the discretionary caps; in others it has used rescissions as "earnest money" to show that even

though it is spending more than the president wants, the additional amount has been offset by canceling old appropriations. Many congressionally initiated rescissions are of dormant or inactive funds, such as for weapons systems that have been delayed by technical problems or housing funds that have been reserved for future use.

Because they were devised during the Vietnam/Watergate era, when Congress was determined to rein in presidential power, the current rescission rules favor Congress. Some have suggested that the president's hand should be strengthened by forcing Congress to vote up or down on every requested rescission. This "expedited rescission authority" would still give Congress the last word, but it would no longer be able to win by inaction. However, inasmuch as the prevailing arrangements let Congress win by doing nothing, it has been unwilling to change the rescission rules.

MANAGING AGENCY FINANCES

Implementing the budget not only entails spending the money; it also means using resources efficiently and having timely and accurate information on the financial status and performance of programs and accounts. Implementing the budget brings into play financial accounting and reporting, management and internal control systems, performance measurement, and audit and evaluation. OMB has defined financial management to include systems that collect, analyze, and report data for financial decisionmaking, that control and account for financial transactions and resources, and that generate financial information in support of agency missions. Financial management goes beyond budget formulation and execution; it also includes property and inventory control, management of grants and contracts, debt and cash management, personnel and payroll systems, and procurement practices. Only those elements of financial management closely linked to budgeting are discussed here.

Fragmentation in Financial Management

It would be misleading to speak of a single financial management system for the federal government. Instead, there are many systems and even more subsystems within them—some operating independently, some coupled together. During the 1990s, emphasis was placed on integrating financial management systems, and significant progress has been made in most federal departments. Table 10-2 sets forth the responsibilities of major federal entities in financial management. The picture that emerges is of many participants, both at the center of government and in federal agencies, each with its own niche and ways of going about its work. In contrast to the many countries that entrust a broad range of financial responsibilities to the treasury or finance ministry, the United States splinters key functions among several entities. OMB has the lead role in compiling the budget and overseeing federal expenditures, the Treasury reports on the financial operations and condition of government, and the Government Accountability Office reviews agency accounting systems and financial statements. Over the years these entities have cooperated through the Joint Financial Management Improvement Program (JFMIP), a small unit that disseminates information on developments in financial management.

Fragmentation is built into the structure of the federal government. GAO works mostly for Congress, though it also has an array of quasi-judicial and administrative responsibilities. OMB serves the president and uses its budget powers to advance his policies and objectives. The Treasury is responsible for collecting taxes, managing the government's vast portfolio of debt, and preparing an annual financial report. Each has a distinctive perspective on the critical features of financial management. The budget is at the center of OMB's universe, with management ancillary to this core activity. GAO focuses on the review and evaluation of federal programs, and it views management as a tool for upholding legality and efficiency in the use of public money. The Treasury handles cash flows and maintains governmentwide accounting systems, for which it needs consistent and reliable data.

Accounting and Budgeting

For decades fragmentation resulted in weak coordination of budgeting and accounting, with each operating in its own sphere and having its own way of counting money. It was not supposed to be this way, for the Budget and Accounting Act of 1921 conceived of budgeting and accounting as interdependent processes. The budget would provide the basis for the accounting structure, and the accounting system would provide data for budget decisions. Over the years, however, budgeting and accounting drifted apart: the former was oriented toward obligations, the latter to cash and resources consumed. Budgeting is forward looking, a means of planning the programs and objectives of government. Accounting is backward looking, a means of recording transactions that have already occurred. The two were usually lodged in separate organizational units, and their data often were incompatible.

Moreover, accounting itself fragmented into numerous specialized systems. Beginning with budget and accounting legislation enacted in 1950 and 1956 and continuing into the 1980s, agencies were encouraged to devise accounting systems that served their particular needs. Within large departments,

TABLE 10-2
Major Financial Management Roles and Responsibilities, by Entity

Entity	Budget execution	Audit and evaluation	Financial management systems
Congress	Acts on supplementals, impoundments, and reprogrammings; sometimes monitors activities or expenditures	Imposes reporting requirements; conducts oversight; requests audits and evaluations from GAO and others	Establishes accounting structure; legislates policy on financial management systems and practices
Office of Management and Budget	Apportions budget resources; maintains full-time equivalent controls; monitors agency performance	Reviews agency spending and programs; focuses on high-risk areas; promotes performance measurement	Issues directives on management control, financial management systems, and other management practices; oversees CFO and GPRA implementation
Treasury	Manages cash and debt; matches spending against resources	None	Maintains governmentwide accounting system
Agencies	Spend resources and carry out activities; report to Congress, OMB, and others	Conduct internal audits and evaluations; respond to congressional and executive requests; compare planned and actual performance	Design and use financial management systems; maintain management controls; report on material weaknesses
Agency chief financial officer	Monitors financial execution of budget	Prepares financial statements, including data on performance	Promotes integration of accounting and budgeting systems
Government Accountability Office	Reviews and reports on impoundments; monitors Antideficiency Act violations; settles certain claims	Reviews programs and operations; audits financial statements of government corporations	Certifies agency accounting systems; advises Congress on material weaknesses in internal control systems
Inspector General	None	Audits financial statements; investigates spending and other actions; evaluates programs	Recommends changes to improve systems and performance
Federal Accounting Standards Advisory Board	None	None	Formulates accounting standards and principles

▼

BOX 10-2
Functions of Chief Financial Officers

Functions of CFO
- Oversees all financial management activities relating to the agency's programs and operations.
- Develops and maintains an integrated accounting and financial management system that complies with accounting and internal control principles, standards, and requirements.
- Ensures that the agency's system provides complete, reliable, consistent, and timely information, including cost information and information that facilitates the systematic measurement of performance.
- Monitors the financial execution of the budget.

Reporting Elements
- Agency five-year plans setting forth the agency's financial management strategy, including planned accomplishments and target dates.
- A governmentwide five-year plan submitted by OMB describing steps to be taken in improving federal financial management.
- Annual reports by agencies analyzing the status of financial management and including required financial statements and a summary of reports on internal accounting and administrative control systems.
- Annual financial statements, supported by relevant financial and program performance data, audited by the agency inspector general (or an outside auditor).

Source: *Chief Financial Officers Act of 1990*, P.L. 101-576, November 15, 1990.

---

individual bureaus and operating units were permitted to customize their accounting systems. This decentralized framework resulted in the federal government operating hundreds of separate systems that were unable to communicate with one another. It was not uncommon for the various systems to record transactions inconsistently and for the accounts maintained by bureaus to be incompatible with those maintained by their departments.

Since the 1990s, major efforts have been made to integrate accounting and budgeting as part of a broad move toward improving financial management in the federal government. A key development has been the

appointment of a chief financial officer (CFO) in all federal departments and major agencies. As prescribed by the Chief Financial Officers Act of 1990, the CFO is responsible for developing and maintaining an integrated accounting and financial management system, overseeing all financial operations relating to the agency's programs and activities, and monitoring the financial execution of the budget (box 10-2). The act does not expressly give the CFO a role in formulating agency budgets, but many have become involved. The law established the position of deputy director for management within OMB to serve as the CFO of the federal government.

Another important development in 1990 was the establishment of the Federal Accounting Standards Advisory Board (FASAB) by GAO, OMB, and the Treasury—the three agencies that claim lead authority over accounting standards. When FASAB recommends a standard, each of the three agencies promulgates it, thereby assuring conformity while allowing each agency to uphold its own role. Over the years, FASAB has issued a series of statements on financial accounting standards relating to the treatment of assets and liabilities; cost accounting concepts; accounting for inventory, property and equipment; and other matters. In 1996 FASAB issued a report that identified four principal objectives of federal finance reporting (box 10-3).

Standardization has enabled federal agencies to prepare audited financial statements and for the Treasury to develop a consolidated statement for the federal government. Prodded by various legislative initiatives, such as the Government Management and Reform Act of 1994 (which requires the audit of agency financial statements and the preparation of a consolidated financial statement for the federal government) and the Federal Financial Management and Improvement Act of 1996 (which directs auditors to report on whether agency financial statements comply with federal standards), agencies have improved financial reporting, and many now earn a clean audit.

As budgeting and accounting have become more closely linked, federal authorities face the question of whether accounting standards, which pertain to financial statements, should also be applied to the budget and related documents. The traditional rule has been that financial information prepared for use by outside parties (such as bondholders or shareholders) must comply with standards, but an entity may maintain internal records in any form it prefers. In business firms, the budget is an internal document that is not bound by accounting rules. In government, however, it is one of the principal means of communicating with citizens. At present, the federal budget does not comply with accounting principles, but there will likely be greater correspondence in the future. An increasing number of state and local governments present their budgets on the basis of generally accepted accounting principles, as do a number of national governments. The U.S. government has not yet moved in this direction, but under the impetus of recent financial management reforms, it may do so.

Traditionally, financial reporting has served such external requirements as assuring legality in expenditure. For this limited purpose, it sufficed to account for transactions in terms of obligations authorized or incurred and cash received or paid out. Accounting for obligations is essential to ensure that funds are spent in accordance with applicable law and that the agencies adhere to Congress's intent in making appropriations. Accounting for cash is essential for the Treasury's management of the government's debt.

In addition to these external requirements, agencies need timely and accurate financial data to manage their own operations. In particular, they need information on the cost of the goods and services they are providing. In cost-based (or accrual) accounting, income is recorded when it is earned, not when it is received, and costs are recorded when goods and services are consumed, not when money is disbursed. Cost-based budgets are useful in measuring the resources used in carrying out activities, controlling expenses, and improving efficiency in operations. They also provide useful data for preparing performance-based budgets, which show the outputs resulting from government expenditures.

▼

BOX 10-3
Objectives of Federal Financial Reporting

Budget Integrity

Federal financial reporting should assist in fulfilling the government's duty to be publicly accountable for monies raised through taxes and other means, and for their expenditure in accordance with the appropriations laws that establish the government's budget for a particular fiscal year and related laws and regulations. Federal financial reporting should provide information that helps the reader to determine

- how budgetary resources have been obtained and used and whether their acquisition and use were in accordance with the legal authorization
- what the status of budgetary resources is and
- how information on the use of budgetary resources relates to information on the costs of program operations and whether information on the status of budgetary resources is consistent with other accounting information on assets and liabilities.

Operating Performance

Federal financial reporting should assist report users in evaluating the service efforts, costs, and accomplishments of the reporting entity, the manner in which these efforts and accomplishments have been financed, and the management of the entity's assets and liabilities. Federal financial reporting should provide information that helps the reader to determine the

- costs of providing specific activities and programs and the composition of and changes in these costs
- efforts and accomplishments associated with federal programs and the changes over time and in relation to costs and
- the efficiency and effectiveness of the government's management of its assets and liabilities.

Stewardship

Federal financial reporting should assist report users in assessing the impact on the nation of the government's operations and investments, and how, as a result, the government's and the nation's financial conditions have changed and may change in the future.

Systems and Controls

Federal financial reporting should assist users in understanding whether financial management systems, internal accounting, and administrative controls are adequate to ensure that

- transactions are executed in accordance with budgetary and financial laws and other requirements, consistent with the purposes authorized, and recorded in accordance with federal accounting standards
- assets are properly safeguarded to deter fraud, waste, and abuse and
- performance measurement information is adequately supported.

Source: Federal Accounting Standards Advisory Board, *Overview of Federal Accounting Concepts and Standards*, Report 1, December 31, 1996, pp. 8–9.

The Federal Balance Sheet

It is common practice for businesses to report their financial condition on a balance sheet, which lists assets, liabilities, and net worth. The balance sheet is constructed on the basis of generally accepted accounting principles, which provide rules for evaluating assets and liabilities, setting aside reserves for financial risks such as bad debts, and recognizing income and payments. Because of inadequate accounting practices and critical differences between it and business, the federal government did not prepare a balance sheet until the late 1990s. However, accounting improvements and pressure on the government to provide a true picture of its financial condition have induced OMB, GAO, and the Treasury to draft a balance sheet for the government.

OMB's exercise indicated that the government's liabilities exceeded its assets by about $6 trillion at the end of fiscal year 2005. The Treasury reported net liabilities of $8.5 trillion for the same year. Various entries on one agency's balance sheet did not have corresponding entries on the other's. Thus while both agencies produced a balance sheet for the federal government, they did not treat entries consistently.

Care must be taken in interpreting the entries on a federal balance sheet. If a commercial entity had a negative net worth running into trillions of dollars, it would be insolvent. But the federal government has sovereign assets that do not appear on its balance sheet; foremost is the power to tax. If the present value of future revenue that would be generated by the tax laws now on the books were shown as an asset, the government would show a more favorable financial position. In other words, the balance sheet does a better job recognizing certain incurred liabilities than the future value of government's biggest financial assets.

Internal Control

Federal financial management is guided by the doctrine of internal control (sometimes referred to as management control). Under this doctrine, program managers have primary responsibility for ensuring that resources are used properly and efficiently and that financial and other matters are reported accurately.

At one time (generally before the 1950s), federal agencies had to obtain external approval before spending funds. Nowadays, each agency generally authorizes transactions on its own, determining the amount of money available for a purpose and whether management rules (concerning personnel, travel, purchases, and other administrative actions) have been complied with. Each agency keeps its own books, preaudits its operations, and reports on its financial performance and condition. The Federal Financial Integrity Act of 1982 requires every agency to establish systems of internal control that are in accordance with standards prescribed by the comptroller general. The systems must provide "reasonable assurance" that obligations and costs are in compliance with applicable law; that funds, property, and other assets are safeguarded against waste, loss, or abuse; and that revenues and expenditures are properly recorded.

OMB and GAO share oversight responsibility for internal control. OMB Circular A-123, which was significantly revised in 2005 to emphasize top management's responsibility for internal control, requires agencies and managers "to (i) develop and implement appropriate cost-effective internal control for results-oriented management; (ii) assess the adequacy of internal control in Federal programs and operations; (iii) separately assess and document internal control over financial reporting . . . ; (iv) identify needed improvements; (v) take corresponding corrective action; and, (vi) report annually on internal control through management assurance statements." The last requirement parallels a procedure that is required of all public companies. It mandates that agency managers sign an annual assurance statement relating to internal control over financial reporting. This statement should represent the agency head's informed judgment as to the overall adequacy and effectiveness of internal control within the agency. The statement must be an unqualified assurance (no material weaknesses), qualified assurance (some material weaknesses), or no assurance (the agency lacks adequate processes or has pervasive material weaknesses). In attesting to the reliability of financing reporting, management must be in a position to make the following eight assertions:

• *Occurrence and existence.* All reported transactions actually occurred during the reporting period, and all assets and liabilities exist as of the reporting date.

• *Completeness.* All assets, liabilities, and transactions are included, and no unauthorized transactions or balances are included.

• *Rights and obligations.* All assets are legally owned, and all liabilities are legal obligations.

• *Valuation.* All assets and liabilities have been properly valued, and costs have been properly allocated.

• *Presentation and disclosure.* The financial report is in the proper form and includes required disclosures.

• *Compliance.* Transactions are in compliance with applicable laws and regulations.

• *Safeguards.* All assets are safeguarded against fraud and abuse.

• *Documentation.* Documentation of all transactions and other significant events is readily available for examination.

The net effect of these new requirements is to greatly increase management's attentiveness to internal control. Senior managers can no longer regard internal control as a technical matter delegated to subordinates. They are responsible for assurance statements and for material weaknesses.

As required by law, GAO reviews internal control systems and reports on material weaknesses. In assessing whether a deficiency constitutes a material weakness, GAO advises agencies to consider the magnitude and sensitivity of the resources involved, conflicts of interest, violations of statutory requirements, and adverse publicity that would harm an agency's credibility. GAO's reports on management control typically find considerable waste and mismanagement in federal agencies.

Performance-Based Management

Since the late 1970s Congress has enacted nine laws affecting financial management (box 10-4). The earliest of these laws, the Inspector General Act and the Federal Managers' Financial Integrity Act, focused on wrongdoing and mismanagement by federal officials. The second pair of laws, beginning with the Chief Financial Officers Act, aimed to establish sturdy management systems. The last set has concentrated on spurring agencies to improve their performance and effectiveness.

A potentially important step in using the budget and related management processes to improve performance was taken in the Government Performance and Results Act of 1993. GPRA (or the Results Act, as it is sometimes called) prescribes a sequence of actions beginning with the development of performance measures, progressing to multiyear strategic plans, and concluding with agency and governmentwide plans linked to budget decisions (box 10-5). Once these instruments are in place, agencies are to report annually on performance and to periodically revise their strategic plans to reflect changes in objectives and priorities. GPRA also calls for the pilot testing

BOX 10-4
Laws Affecting Financial Management

Inspector General Act of 1978 (P.L. 95-452)
- Establishes independent inspector general offices in all federal departments and major agencies
- Conducts audits and investigations
- Recommends policies to promote economy, efficiency, and effectiveness
- Detects and prevents fraud and abuse
- Informs the agency head and Congress on problems and deficiencies

Federal Managers' Financial Integrity Act of 1982 (P.L. 97-255)
- Requires agencies to maintain internal accounting and administrative controls in compliance with standards prescribed by the comptroller general, to evaluate their management accountability and control systems, and to report yearly to Congress and the president on plans to correct material weaknesses

Chief Financial Officers Act of 1990 (P.L. 101-576)
- Requires 24 federal agencies to have a chief financial officer (CFO) responsible for overseeing all financial management activities relating to the agency's programs and operations and to prepare five-year plans, including milestones, for improving financial management
- CFO council, headed by OMB deputy director for management, reviews and recommends improvements in financial management

Government Performance and Results Act of 1993 (P.L. 103-62)
- Mandates that agencies submit initial strategic plans, with updates every three years, and performance plans covering each program activity
- On the basis of these plans, OMB includes a performance plan for the federal government in the president's budget
- Beginning in 2000, agencies report each year on the previous year's performance

Government Management Reform Act of 1994 (P.L. 103-356)
- Requires the audit of agency financial statements and the preparation and audit of a consolidated financial statement for the federal government

Federal Financial Management Improvement Act of 1996 (P.L. 104-208)
- Directs auditors to report on whether agency financial statements comply with federal financial management systems' requirements, federal accounting standards, and the U.S. government's Standard General Ledger

Accountability of Tax Dollars Act of 2002 (P.L. 107-289)
- Extends requirement that agencies prepare annual audited financial statements to nearly all executive branch agencies

Improper Payments Information Act of 2002 (P.L. 107-300)
- Requires agencies to monitor programs susceptible to improper payments and to report to Congress on actions to reduce such payments

Federal Funding Accountability and Transparency Act of 2006 (P.L. 109-282)
- Requires OMB to establish (by January 1, 2008) a database on the recipients of federal grants, loans, and contracts, available publicly online (see www.federalspending.gov)

▼

BOX 10-5
Major Features of the Government Performance and Results Act of 1993

Purpose
To improve program effectiveness and public accountability by focusing on results, service quality, and customer satisfaction; to help managers improve service delivery by planning for program objectives and providing them with information on program results and service quality; and to improve congressional decisionmaking by providing objective information on the relative effectiveness and efficiency of federal programs and expenditures.

Pilot Projects
Three sets of pilots: performance measures and reports (1994–96), managerial accountability and flexibility (1995–96), and performance-based budgeting (1998–99). (Some of the pilots were not conducted, and agencies moved directly to implementation.)

Strategic Plans
Agencies submit five-year strategic plans updated at least every three years. Plans are prepared in consultation with Congress and are to include a comprehensive mission statement, goals and objectives, how goals and objectives are to be achieved, relationship of annual performance goals to strategic objectives, external factors affecting achievement of goals, and program evaluation.

Performance Plans
Annual performance plans, consistent with the strategic plan, specify the performance to be achieved by each program activity, express goals in measurable form, describe processes and resources needed to meet performance goals, specify performance indicators, and provide a basis of comparing actual and planned performance.

Performance Reports
Annual program performance reports review whether goals for the previous year were achieved, and if they were not, explaining why they were not met.

Performance Budgeting
Following pilot tests of performance-based budgeting, the OMB director issues a report (by March 31, 2001) assessing the feasibility and advisability of including a performance-based budget (which shows the varying levels of performance that would result from different budgeted amounts) in the president's budget.

Source: *Government Performance Results Act of 1993*, P.L. 103-62.

of performance-based budgeting—an arrangement in which the money appropriated or spent is directly linked to the outputs or results the agency produces.

GPRA specifies six critical components for the strategic plans (see box 10-5). GPRA provides for agencies to consult with Congress during preparation of strategic plans and in subsequent updates or revisions. At the behest of various congressional committees, GAO assessed the initial round of strategic plans and found that many did not sufficiently define a strategic path for agencies to take in setting goals and measuring performance. In GAO's view, the strategic plans should be viewed as only the starting points in the broad transformation needed to implement performance-based management.

The next step in the GPRA process has been the submission of annual performance plans (that are consistent with each agency's strategic objectives) in tandem with its annual budget request to OMB. Guidance by OMB provides for each agency to revise its performance plan on the basis of financial and program decisions made in the president's budget. Agency plans must specify performance goals and indicators for the fiscal year, describe the operational processes and resources that will be needed to meet performance goals, and describe the means that will be used to verify measured results. OMB also requires that each program activity in an agency's program and financing schedules (described in exhibit 5-4) be covered by at least one performance goal or indicator. It also expresses the expectation that in time the annual performance plan will become an integral part of agency budget requests and budget justification submitted to Congress, and that agencies will restructure their appropriation accounts to provide a more systematic or functional presentation of budget and performance information. GPRA stipulates that on the basis of agency plans, OMB is to include a governmentwide performance plan in the president's budget.

The culmination of the GPRA process is implementation of performance-based budgets in which the level of resources is expressly linked to the level of outputs. This form of budgeting was tried in the 1950s and 1960s with little success, but in view of the overall emphasis on financial management reform, its prospects may be better this time. Much depends on the inroads GPRA makes in implanting a culture of performance in federal agencies and in orienting congressional committees to outputs and results. Some believe that GRPA has followed the path of previous reforms—a big investment by agencies at the outset leading to the generation of vast amounts of paperwork that satisfy formal requirements but provide little evidence that the innovations have made a dent in behavior or decisions. The one big difference this time is that Congress is involved and GPRA is anchored in law rather than just administrative practice. Some appropriations subcommittees have prodded agencies to highlight information on objectives and performance in their budget justifications. Yet it is one thing for Congress to request information on performance and results and quite another for it to appropriate money on this basis and to give federal managers sufficient freedom and incentive to improve operations. When Congress earmarks money to projects or activities and writes detailed operating rules into legislation and committee reports, it undermines the performance ethic that GPRA promotes.

The Program Assessment Rating Tool (PART)

Early in George W. Bush's presidency, OMB launched the President's Management Agenda to assess federal departments and agencies on five dimensions, one of which was the integration of the budget and performance. Agencies that meet all of the standards are given a green rating, those that demonstrate moderate success earn a yellow rating, and those judged to have unsatisfactory performance are given a red rating. Over time OMB adjusted the "traffic lights" scorecard to separately assess progress toward meeting OMB's budget and performance integration criteria. At the outset, most agencies earned red ratings. In fact, OMB, which produces the ratings, gave itself red ratings on all management dimensions. By 2006, however, OMB reported significant improvements in federal management, as measured by its budget and performance integration scorecard.

Because they focus on management processes, the traffic lights emphasize compliance with OMB-prescribed procedures rather than with substantive results. For example, one success indicator is whether agencies have developed strategic plans that contain outcome-oriented goals; another is that senior managers meet periodically to review performance information. In 2003 OMB moved to establish a parallel process—the Program Assessment Rating Tool (PART)—to assess all federal programs over a five-year period. PART is a menu-driven questionnaire consisting of 25 questions organized into four categories, as shown in box 10-6. Additional questions are addressed to each of seven types of federal programs (direct federal spending, competitive grants, block/formula grants, research and development, capital assets, credit programs, and regulatory programs). The answers to the questions are worded to elicit a "yes" or "no" answer. Every "yes" answer must be supported with the evidence prescribed in OMB's guidelines. OMB permits a "results not demonstrated" answer for programs that lack accept-

able performance measures. OMB publishes aggregate PART scores in the president's budget and on its website, but it does not break down the scores by question or category.

Although OMB has the final say in scoring the answers, agencies actively participate in the process, producing documents and other evidence that they hope will earn them a "yes." There is much negotiation between OMB and agency staff, and their overall relationship may influence the grade. Agencies receiving unsatisfactory scores can petition OMB to regrade their programs. Typically this involves producing additional evidence and often leads to a higher score. Sometimes the amount of documentation compiled for each program is truly voluminous, leading some to conclude that PART has become another paper exercise. A balanced assessment is that PART has generated greater attention to program results during OMB review of budget requests. The questions asked are relevant to agency and program performance, and the evidence demanded by OMB does provide insights into how well the program is managed and the results flowing from it.

OMB insists that there is no automatic linkage of PART scores and budget decisions. However, it also takes the view that federal dollars should be targeted to programs that can prove they have achieved measurable results. In fact, independent researchers have found that PART scores are correlated with presidential budget decisions. Programs with effective ratings are much more likely to be budgeted for increases than those rated ineffective. But PART scores are a weak influence on congressional decisions, especially when OMB seeks to eliminate programs rated ineffective. Thus far, PART has not uprooted the incremental tendencies of the appropriations committees.

▼

BOX 10-6
Program Assessment Rating Tool (PART)

How Programs Are Rated

Program Purpose and Design (20 percent)

Examines the clarity of program purpose and soundness of program design. Relevant source documents and evidence may include authorizing legislation, agency strategic plans, annual performance plans, and other agency reports.

Strategic Planning (10 percent)

Focuses on program planning, priority setting, and resource allocation. Includes an assessment of whether the program has performance measures with ambitious but achievable targets. Relevant evidence includes performance plans and reports, evaluation plans, budget submissions, and other program documents.

Program Management (20 percent)

Considers whether the program is effectively managed to meet performance goals. Relevant evidence includes financial statements, GAO and inspector general (IG) reports, budget execution data, and independent program evaluations.

Program Results (50 percent)

Considers whether the program is meeting long-term and annual performance goals. It also assesses how well the program compares to similar programs. Relevant documents and evidence may include annual performance reports, GAO and IG reports, and evaluations. In contrast to questions in the other sections, which are rated "yes," "no," or "not applicable," program results may be graded "yes," "large extent," "small extent," and "no."

Aggregate Rating

Score	Rating
85–100	Effective
70–84	Moderately effective
50–69	Adequate
0–49	Ineffective

Source: Prepared from various Office of Management and Budget documents available at these two OMB websites: www.whitehouse.gov/omb/part and www.expectmore.gov.

CONCLUSION

Managing expenditures involves a tug of war between the executive branch and Congress. Spenders want flexibility; Congress wants control. During the nineteenth century and the early decades of the twentieth century, Congress generally dominated the relationship, as it leveraged its power of the purse to enact detailed appropriations that restricted executive discretion. The balance tilted in favor of the executive branch from the New Deal through the Great Society—a period in which laws accorded broad operating freedom to federal agencies and appropriation accounts were broadened. But the tide turned again in the Vietnam/Watergate era, as Congress imposed numerous restrictions on administrative action, enacted the first formal limits on presidential impoundments, and issued numerous directives in laws and committee reports. Congress was spurred by real or perceived abuses of executive power and by prolonged conflict between it and the president. As legislative controls and restrictions multiplied, Congress was accused of micromanaging the executive branch and of meddling in the details of administration.

During the 1990s, there was a burst of initiatives to improve federal management. As well-intentioned as these initiatives may have been, they have not addressed the basic relationship between federal managers and congressional paymasters. Congress wants more by way of performance, but it has been reluctant to surrender controls and habits that stand in the way of improved performance. It hogties managers and then bashes them for not producing. This arrangement gives Congress the best of both worlds: it gets control and passes the blame on to bureaucrats. It passes laws, such as GPRA, that instruct agencies to file voluminous reports, but then it goes about its old ways in parceling out money and legislating restrictions. Sometimes the formula works, and managers perform despite the restrictions on their operating discretion. Yet, when they fall short of the mark, it reinforces the legislative belief that even more restraints are needed.

The National Performance Review, the centerpiece of Vice President Al Gore's campaign to "reinvent government," produced anecdotal evidence that federal managers dutifully follow the rules and spend just about every dollar provided to them. They have little flexibility and take few risks. Even when they see opportunities to spend money more wisely, they have little discretion to do so. This probably is an overstated picture of federal management, but it has more than a kernel of truth: managers often value compliance more than performance. Paradoxically, GPRA itself has become a vast compliance machine. Agencies produce strategic plans, not because they seek to transform themselves but because the GPRA calendar dictates that they do so. They generate performance measures because the law tells them to; whether the measures make a difference in their performance is another matter.

One of the great conceits of GPRA is that having more or different information changes behavior. But a reading of past reforms—performance budgeting in the 1950s, program budgeting and planning-programming-budgeting systems in the 1960s, zero-based budgeting in the 1970s—tells us that information by itself does not change anything. At the core, change is a matter of will and incentives—the drive to transform organizations and the inducement to do so. GPRA does not offer enough of either, so it may end up as a legislated substitute for change.

OMB has now completed a full PART cycle, in which almost all federal programs have been rated according to the methods prescribed in its Program Assessment Rating Tool.

Compared to past initiatives, OMB has successfully integrated consideration of performance into its internal budget processes. OMB examiners take PART seriously and use it in recommending spending levels; agency officials invest resources to improve their PART scores because they know that a low score might lead to recommended cuts in the president's budget. Over a short period, PART has become an integral feature of federal budgeting, but its future is still uncertain. One problem is that Congress generally has not been persuaded by PART in appropriating funds; another is that PART risks becoming a paper exercise unless it is reinvigorated by new ideas and interest. Ultimately, the fate of PART will depend on the path taken by President George W. Bush's successor. If the next president launches his or her own initiative, PART will fade away, just as many once-promising innovations have. But if the new president and OMB leaders embrace PART, then it may have the staying power to have long-term impacts on government performance and budget decisions.

11

Budgeting for the Long Term

This book has demonstrated that federal budgeting operates with many rules, procedures, and constraints. It is not the case that anything goes in budgeting, that spenders and tax cutters get whatever they want regardless of the budget's condition, and that vote-seeking politicians have no means of rebuffing powerful demands. Budgeting is a regulated process, with checkpoints and controls at various stages of presidential and congressional action. But budgeting also is a political process that is highly sensitive to the preferences of voters and interest groups and to the strong inclination of elected leaders to satisfy constituents. Thus budgeting is a contest between rules that block demands and political tendencies that open it to demands. Sometimes in the course of this contest the budget is thrown out of kilter, and large imbalances between revenues and outlays emerge. When this occurs, proposals are made for a constitutional amendment or legislative action to restore balance. The history of budgeting shows that rebalancing is as dependent on shifts in political sentiments as it is on new rules. However, rebalancing is more difficult when dealing with the long-term budget outlook, for today's politicians and voters have only a weak incentive to deal with tomorrow's problems.

Short of imposing constitutional handcuffs, can the machinery of budgeting be calibrated to facilitate budget adjustment, make it more expeditious and fluid as well as more attentive to the long-term interests

TABLE 11-1
Sequence of Discretionary Spending Control

Limitation or action	Control
Discretionary spending limits	Adjustable caps on total discretionary budget authority and outlays set in statute (which expired at the end of fiscal year 2002, but the president and some members of Congress have proposed their reinstatement).
Budget resolution aggregates	Ceilings on total budget authority and outlays (covering both discretionary and direct spending). Separate limits on total discretionary budget authority and outlays (enforced in the Senate but not in the House).
Section 302(a) allocations	Total budget authority and outlays in the budget resolution are allocated to committees with spending jurisdiction. All discretionary spending is allocated to the appropriations committees.
Section 302(b) subdivisions	Each appropriations committee subdivides its allocation of budget authority and outlays among its 13 subcommittees. The total allocated to these subcommittees may not exceed the amount allocated to the full committee.
Appropriations	The budget authority provided and outlays deriving from each appropriations bill are compared with the relevant subcommittees' 302(b) allocation. A point of order may be raised in the House or Senate against an appropriations bill that would cause the relevant 302(b) allocation to be exceeded.
Apportionment	Appropriations and other available budgetary resources are apportioned by OMB to each account, either by projects or by quarters of the fiscal year. The total apportioned may not exceed available resources.
Allotment	Each department or agency allots apportioned resources to its subunits. The total allotted may not exceed the amount apportioned.
Obligation	Obligations by agencies that commit the government to future payments. Agencies may not (with few exceptions) obligate in excess of available budget resources.
Outlay	Payment by the Treasury to liquidate obligations incurred by agencies.

of Americans, and do less damage to presidential-congressional relations and to legislative order and budget routines? This concluding chapter seeks answers by assessing existing budgetary institutions in the light of impending demographic pressures on the budget and the long-term outlook.

THE ADEQUACY OF BUDGET CONTROLS

At its core, budgeting is a process for deciding how much should be raised and spent. In budgeting for revenues, there is widespread agreement that it is unwise to reconsider the tax code annually. Businesses and households make decisions in light of their tax situation; neither should be subject to the vagaries of revenue legislation. It is on the spending side of the ledger that the adequacy of budget control is often called into question.

Table 11-1 indicates that the budget can effectively control discretionary spending through a sequence of actions linking the totals to individual transactions. This chain of control is designed to ensure that the sum of the many millions of obligations and outlays made each year does not exceed approved discretionary totals. Although there are some exceptions and breaches, each step in this table is governed by the rule that it may not exceed the amount the previous step allows. For example, the amount apportioned for an account may not exceed the amount available for obligation from appropriations and other budgetary sources. The controls are not quite as airtight as this example implies, but the sequence has kept discretionary spending within or close to preset totals. Because it is decided annually, discretionary spending is highly sensitive to the condition of the budget. Congress and the president have allocated more to discretionary programs when surpluses emerge, and smaller increases (after a lag of a few years) when deficits reappear.

This is not the case for mandatory programs. Past legislative actions, rather than current budget decisions, almost entirely determine the amounts spent each year on entitlements. In mandatory programs, the chain of control is inverted—rather than the totals constraining individual programs, the amounts spent on programs determine the total. This inversion impedes, but does not prevent, self-correction in budgeting. As discussed below, concern about the long-term fiscal health of the United States arises entirely out of the claim of entitlements on future budgets.

Simply because the budget does not constrain entitlements to the same degree as it does discretionary appropriations does not mean that spending is out of control. In establishing entitlements, the government accords priority to values other than budget control. Spending control is not the sole objective of budget decisions; Congress and the president have other political concerns, which sometimes override fiscal considerations. Social Security assures workers that they will have a financial safety net in retirement, Medicare and Medicaid give elderly and low-income

Americans access to health care, and unemployment insurance restores a portion of discharged workers' lost income. The government finances food stamps and other assistance programs that enable low-income families to maintain an acceptable standard of living. Through prescribed cost-of-living adjustments, the government protects recipients of various benefit programs against inflation. The common element in these programs is that their objectives are fulfilled by entitling beneficiaries to federal payments. Making these payments discretionary would bolster short-term budget control but diminish the financial protections afforded Americans.

Americans widely share the values underlying most entitlements. Public opinion polls show overwhelming support for Social Security, Medicare, and other major entitlements. While Americans do not like "welfare" programs, they endorse the view that government should assist low-income people in meeting basic needs. Americans may not favor every entitlement program, but the more people a program serves, and the more it costs, the more support it is likely to have. Americans are concerned about the cost of government but show little inclination to sacrifice income stability, health care, and other objectives on the altar of budget control.

For the government to have perfect fiscal control, each year's budget would be made anew, unencumbered by past commitments. Congress would annually decide how much to spend on pensions, medical assistance, food stamps, disability aid, unemployment insurance, and so on. The old days would be back; just about all spending would be discretionary.

However, a world of perfect budget control would not be a perfect world. Social insecurity would be widespread, with workers, employers, the aged, and others facing an uncertain and in many cases bleak future. Retired workers would have to go through the annual budget gyrations before knowing what the next year's Social Security payments or health services would be.

A strong case can be made that the country is better off because of the wide net cast by entitlements. Of course, not all such programs are equally meritorious, but their combined effect is to cushion households against the cyclical shocks of recession and temporary disability, and against the secular shocks of old age and infirmity. Entitlements ease anxieties about inflation, unemployment, illness, and disability. Entitlements dominate the budget because the biggest of these programs distribute benefits to a broad swath of Americans. In other words, the biggest programs do the most damage to budget control but the most good to society.

In principle, entitlements are incompatible with budget control; in practice, the two must be reconciled. The president and Congress must deal with annual budgets that include entitlements. They do so principally through reconciliation, which enables them to make marginal adjustments in entitlements while retaining the core benefits that affected programs provide. Congress occasionally makes big changes in entitlements through reconciliation, as it did in the 1996 overhaul of the welfare program, but the typical use of reconciliation is to prune a little here and there to meet the savings targets laid out in reconciliation instructions. After 30 years of cutting hundreds of billions of dollars from Medicare in this fashion, the hospital and medical benefits provided by Medicare are remarkably similar to those provided decades ago. Arguably, reconciliation has survived because it has not dismantled popular entitlements. It saves both money and programs by trimming expenditures at the margins and shifting some costs to beneficiaries and service providers.

Congress can continue to use reconciliation to whittle programs, but long-term projections of the imbalance between revenues and expenditures suggest that this tactic will not suffice when Medicare and Social Security spending surges in the future. It is highly unlikely that Congress will roll back entitlements to the point that they claim no greater a share of the budget two decades from now than they did at the start of the twenty-first century. The entitlement state is here to stay, but lively debate and frequent budget action on the role and obligations of the government in transferring money to American households will continue.

BUDGETING FOR THE FUTURE

The federal government faces two very different budget futures—a 10-year horizon of manageable deficits, and then a period 20 to 40 years out, during which the balances built up in Social Security will vanish, Medicare will have recurring financial crises, and Washington will have to make far-reaching changes in payments to the elderly or extract far more revenue from taxpayers. The two futures are joined in several ways. First, U.S. fiscal performance during the period immediately ahead will directly affect the ease with which the nation transitions to budgets beholden to aging baby boomers. It makes a big difference whether fiscal prudence or profligacy characterizes the period immediately preceding the retirement surge. The former would lessen the inevitable future shocks to the budget; the latter would add to them. Second, decisions on shoring up the long-term viability of Social Security and Medicare likely will be taken during the next decade, before the baby boom generation fully affects the budget's bottom line. If political leaders delay action on the grounds that the budget is in good shape, they will have a much more difficult time making needed adjustments later on when the budget is in bad shape.

The surplus years (1998–2001) offered the best opportunity for dealing with the demographic time bomb, but this opportunity was squandered by policy missteps and quashed by escalating national defense expenditures. At the start of the twenty-first century, both OMB and CBO issued rosy budget scenarios for the next decade. CBO projected that the budget would accumulate $5.6 trillion in surpluses, more than enough to pay off all the public debt, with money to spare for bolstering the financial position of the Social Security and Medicare trust funds. Budgetary history warns us, however, that all such projections are likely to be wrong, and that there is a huge difference between projecting a surplus and actually earning one.

Although CBO's projection was based on prudent assumptions—modest growth rates and a slower rise in tax collections than had occurred during the previous decade—force majeure (usually war or economic weakness) or just the political impulse to spend more and tax less derails even reasonable forecasts. As recounted in chapter 2, this is exactly what happened during the first years of the new century. The self-correction hypothesis predicts that changes in budgetary behavior will absorb the projected surplus before it is fully earned. On both the revenue and spending sides of the budget, opportunistic politicians depleted the coveted surplus.

In view of the bleak long-term budgetary outlook, rapid liquidation of the surplus was the wrong policy path. It left the country unprepared for the inevitable spending surge in the second decade of the new century and beyond, and took away the government's capacity to finance the transition to a new Social Security system or to replenish the existing system. A few statistics tell us that budget

discipline disappeared when surpluses arrived. In 2000 federal debt (including amounts owed to Social Security and other trust funds) totaled $5.6 trillion; by 2012, just a dozen years later, it is projected to be more than twice as much, $11.5 trillion. During the same dozen years, debt held by the public is projected to rise from $3.4 trillion to $5.7 trillion. Fiscal year 2012 will be an important marker in federal budgeting, for it will be the first year that a sizeable number of pensioners turn 65 and begin to receive Medicare benefits.

In sum, medium-term budget policy has left the federal government ill-prepared to handle the long-term fiscal problem. Nevertheless, the government will have to cope. It does not have a viable option of defaulting on pension and health care obligations, nor is it likely to produce sufficient savings by restraining discretionary appropriations or trimming entitlement benefits. Even if it does these things, it will have to borrow more or tax more. At this writing (in 2007), it is realistic to expect that the government will do both.

Social Security and Medicare

Even if the budget imbalances that emerged during George W. Bush's presidency were corrected, it is a sure bet that if current Social Security and Medicare policies continue without change, big deficits will emerge in the second decade of this century and will grow even larger in subsequent decades. The budget predicament can be summed up in a few trends (shown in table 11-2 and figures 11-1 and 11-2). First, the number of Americans age 65 and older is expected to double from 35 million (12.4 percent of the population) in 2000 to 70 million (19.6 percent of the population) by 2030. By 2050, the Census Bureau has estimated, more than 85 million Americans will be 65 or older. More important, the ranks of the very old (85 or older) are projected to escalate from only 4 million in 2000 to 10 million in 2030 and 21 million in 2080. This trend will adversely impact Medicare because seniors consume more health services as they age.

Second, the number of covered workers (those paying Social Security taxes) per Social Security recipient will decline from 3.4 in 2000 to 2.0 by 2050. As a consequence, more money will flow out of the Social Security and Medicare trust funds at a time when relatively less will be flowing in.

Third, CBO has projected that Social Security expenditures will rise from 4.2 percent of GDP in 2005 to more than 6 percent by 2030, and remain at approximately this level for at least another generation. Medicare and Medicaid also totaled 4.2 percent of GDP in 2005, but (using intermediate assumptions regarding future spending trends) will soar to over 9 percent by 2030, and to almost 13 percent by 2050.

Obviously, these trends are not sustainable. Normal self-correction will not suffice to deal with future Social Security and Medicare demands on the budget. But before yelling "crisis," it is appropriate to put the problem in perspective. First, Stein's Law (by economist Herbert Stein) predicts that trends that cannot continue will not. That is, there is no possibility of worst-case scenarios, or anything close to them, materializing. The federal budget will not be swallowed up by Social Security and Medicare. Long before it is, significant adjustments will be made in these programs. Second, as the population ages, the composition of spending will change; more public and private money will be spent on the elderly. In the same way that individuals change their consumption patterns as they go through different life stages, so too does a government faced with a changing age structure. There is noth-

TABLE 11-2
Projected Insolvency of the Social Security and Medicare Hospital Insurance Trust Funds

	Year	
Scenario	Social Security	Medicare Hospital Insurance
First year outgo exceeds income (excluding interest)	2017	2006
First year outgo exceeds income (including interest)	2027	2010
Year trust fund assets are exhausted	2040	2018

Source: *2006 Annual Report of the Board of Trustees of the Federal Old-Age and Survivors Insurance and Disability Insurance Trust Funds,* May 1, 2006, p. 9, available on the Social Security Administration's website at www.socialsecurity.gov/OACT/TRSUM/tr06summary.pdf.

ing amiss in spending a rising share of national income on the elderly when there are more elderly to spend it on. Third, because spending on the elderly cannot be permitted to crowd out other budgetary (and private) needs, significant changes will be made in Social Security and Medicare, though perhaps not as expeditiously or efficiently as some want. Social Security and Medicare will survive; both will be restructured long before they bankrupt the Treasury.

Although they are often lumped together, Social Security and Medicare face different financial situations and are treated differently in the budget. Social Security is off-budget; Medicare is included in the budget. Social Security is changed infrequently and never in reconciliation bills; Medicare is adjusted frequently, usually through the reconciliation process. Adjustments to Social Security are made only to shore up its financial condition; Medicare changes have often been made to improve the overall budget condition.

Financial difficulties will come earlier to

FIGURE 11-1

U.S. Population 65 Years and 85 Years and Older and Covered Workers per OASDI Beneficiary, Five-Year Intervals, 1960–2050ᵃ

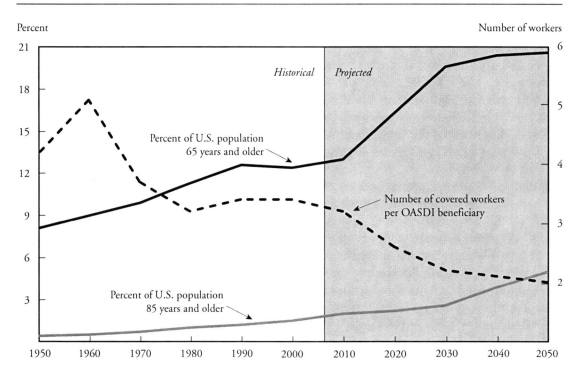

Sources: (1) *2006 Annual Report of the Board of Trustees of the Old-Age and Survivors Insurance and Disability Trust Funds,* May 1, 2006, table IV-B2, available on the Social Security Administration's website at www.socialsecurity.gov/OACT/TR/TR06/trLOT.html; and (2) U.S. Census Bureau.
   a. OASDI, Old Age, Survivors, and Disability Insurance, the official name for Social Security.

Medicare than to Social Security. Medicare's hospital insurance trust fund is expected to be depleted by 2018, while Social Security is projected to remain solvent until 2040 (figure 11-3). Future increases in Social Security payments will be due almost entirely to wage and price changes and increases in the number of recipients. In addition to being affected by these factors, Medicare spending is sensitive to the diffusion of medical technology, utilization rates for medical services, and inflation in the health care sector. These variables are less predictable than those driving up Social Security expenditures.

Both Social Security and Medicare have attracted a slew of proposals to resolve their financial difficulties. For both programs, some advocate higher taxes, while others favor benefit cuts. Some promote privatization of all or a portion of these programs as a means of offloading the financial problems; others vigorously insist on public funding and operation. Some endorse an injection of general revenue; others fear that this remedy would shift much of the burden to taxpayers. The key issue is who should pay for keeping the programs solvent: active workers or beneficiaries, young or older Americans?

FIGURE 11-2
Social Security, Medicare, and Medicaid Expenditures as Percent of GDP, 1970–2050

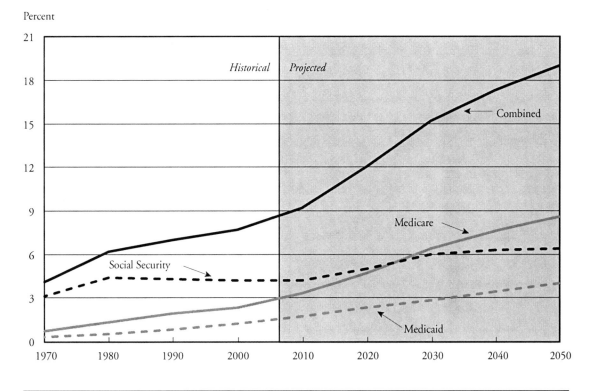

Percent

Historical | *Projected*

Combined

Medicare

Social Security

Medicaid

1970 1980 1990 2000 2010 2020 2030 2040 2050

Source: Congressional Budget Office, "Intermediate Long-Term Spending Projections," spreadsheet, December 2006; and *Budget of the United States, Historical Tables, Fiscal Year 2001,* table 1.2, table 13.1, and *2000 Annual Report of the Trustees of OASDI,* table III.C1, p. 189.

The political lineup in Washington will go a long way toward influencing the answers to these questions. Whole or partial privatization may advance if Republicans were to control both the White House and Congress but would be impeded if Democrats had control. Divided government might induce the two parties to craft a reform package that retains basic Social Security and Medicare benefits, trims future costs, and adds a layer of privatized pensions or medical insurance. On the other hand, continued economic growth may further delay action as additional revenue extends the solvency of these programs.

Social Security

The future capacity of Social Security to pay promised benefits will depend more on the fiscal position of the federal government than on the balances in the trust funds. Although these balances are projected to reach $6 trillion by 2025, the Social Security system will not have this cash on hand. Instead, if current practices are continued, it will hold notes attesting to the amounts owed to it by the government. According to projections, the government will have to repay this debt by 2040, after which it will be liable for Social Security benefits, even though it no longer owes anything to the trust

FIGURE 11-3

Projected Actuarial Balances of Social Security (OASDI) and Medicare Hospital Insurance (HI) Trust Funds, 10-Year Intervals, 2000–80[a]

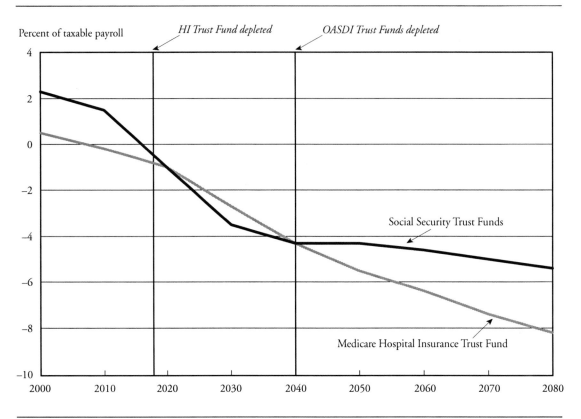

Sources: *2006 Annual Report of the Board of Trustees of the Old-Age and Survivors Insurance and Disability Trust Funds,* May 1, 2006, table IV-B1, available on the Social Security Administration's website at www.socialsecurity.gov/OACT/TR/TR06/trLOT.html; and *2006 Annual Report of the Boards of* Trustees *of the Federal Hospital Insurance and Federal Supplementary Medical Insurance Trust Funds,* May 1, 2006, table III.B7, available on the Centers for Medicare and Medicaid Services website at www.cms.hhs.gov/ReportsTrustFunds/downloads/tr2006.pdf.

a. The balance is the annual difference between cost and income rates as percentages of payroll. Amounts are based on intermediate assumptions.

funds. If the government were to lack the ability to finance these payments, Social Security would be unable to meet its obligations. This scenario strongly indicates that it is at least as important to strengthen the fiscal condition of the government as it is to build up balances in the Social Security trust funds. A financially strong federal government will be able to pay benefits even if the Social Security trust funds were depleted; a Social Security system with huge balances will have to forfeit on its

promises if the federal government were financially weak.

Financing Social Security certainly will be easier than assuring the future fiscal viability of Medicare. The actuarial shortfall in Social Security receipts over the period from 2005 to 2080 has been estimated at less than 2 percent of covered payrolls, the portion of wage income that is subject to Social Security taxes. The gap is smaller early in this 75-year timeframe and much greater in the latter part. This means that any policy change that reduced Social Security spending or increased revenues by 2 percent would eliminate the entire gap for approximately the next 30 years, though not for the full period covered by actuarial projections. Any combination of policy changes (such as raising the age at which retirees obtain full benefits, adding on a percentage point each to the payroll tax paid by employers and employees, or reducing the annual adjustment of Social Security payments for inflation) that adds up to 2 percentage points would put Social Security on a sound financial basis for an extended period.

If resolution of the Social Security problem is so readily at hand, why hasn't it been adopted? The main reason is that while there is a surfeit of proposals for Social Security, none has sufficient support. Despite overwhelming political support, Social Security splits politicians along party lines and Americans along generational lines. Many Republicans, led by President George W. Bush, favor substituting private retirement accounts for a portion of Social Security. This switch would significantly reduce the government's future financial exposure because it would no longer guarantee a fixed benefit (indexed annually to price changes) for the privatized accounts. In promoting this approach, President Bush has argued that Americans would earn higher benefits by investing their own savings than they would receive from traditional Social Security payments. Most Democrats, however, insist that Social Security remain a mandatory, federally funded program and that shortfalls in the trust funds be dealt with either by trimming benefits for some recipients or by boosting government support.

Agreement on Social Security is not likely to be forthcoming until the two parties compromise on their differences. Because almost all Americans have a stake, significant changes in Social Security taxes or benefits require bipartisan cooperation. Going it alone will not suffice, even if one party has a majority in both houses of Congress and holds the White House.

Any attempt to fix Social Security also will have to reckon with the different perspectives and interests of young and older Americans. Retired Americans and those nearing retirement take Social Security for granted and rely on monthly payments. Many younger citizens, however, lack confidence that Social Security will be available when they retire 30 or more years from now. They have been fed a drumbeat of doomsday forecasts of Social Security's inevitable insolvency. Although they may not want to cut benefits for current recipients, many do not want their Social Security taxes increased.

Although it is hard to foresee exactly how the political and intergenerational schisms will be resolved, it is a near certainty that steps will be taken to restore Social Security long before the trust funds are depleted. It is also highly probable that the traditional Social Security system will be retained for retired workers and those approaching retirement. One may also expect that reforming Social Security will combine some tax increases and benefit cuts, as well as new voluntary accounts alongside the mandatory accounts that have defined Social Security since its inception. Within these broad parameters, politicians will patch together a package that draws widespread support.

Medicare

Fixing Medicare will be much more difficult, both because the financial deficits will be vastly larger and emerge much earlier, and because Americans favor expansion, not contraction, of the health care benefits available from the government. The addition of prescription drug benefits in 2003 attests to ongoing support for expanding Medicare. Yet, it is also true that Congress and the president have sought repeatedly to trim Medicare expenditures, usually by reducing payments to providers. With few exceptions, these cutbacks have made a negligible dent in Medicare's long-term imbalances. Using similar tactics in the future would not even come close to keeping Medicare solvent. Although all components of the vast Medicare program are in financial jeopardy, the biggest problem is in the Hospital Insurance (HI) trust fund, which pays for hospital care and is funded by a payroll tax. Under current law, the imbalances of this fund alone will exceed $20 trillion by 2080. The trustees of the HI trust fund have estimated that it would require a 120 percent increase in income, or a 50 percent reduction in outlays, to bring this fund into actuarial balance. The longer these adjustments are delayed, the greater they will have to be.

Some of the solutions that have been proposed for Social Security would not work for Medicare. Raising the eligibility age for Medicare—it is now 65—would add millions of seniors to the ranks of Americans lacking health insurance. Another proposal authorizing Americans to establish their own medical savings accounts (MSAs) has been actively promoted by President George W. Bush, and is being applied on a limited basis. Conflict over MSAs resembles the clash over Social Security, with Republicans taking the view that the accounts will give citizens strong incentives to be efficient consumers of health services, and Democrats arguing that affluent and healthier people will opt for MSAs and Medicare will be burdened with caring for the sick and poor.

Because Medicare finances services furnished by hospitals and other providers, it is subject to the same trends and pressures that have beset the overall cost of health care in the United States. For an extended period, the cost of these services has increased more rapidly than overall prices. At present, health care claims approximately 16 percent of GDP, a proportion that is far greater than in any other country. Medicare cannot be restructured without fundamental changes in the provision and pricing of private health services. Ultimately, therefore, the fate of Medicare is intertwined with the structure and delivery of health services.

As with Social Security, fundamental change in Medicare will have to await bipartisan cooperation. Until then, political leaders will try to muddle through with marginal modifications that postpone the day of reckoning and enable Medicare to stay afloat a bit longer. Some adjustments will curtail payments to providers, others will boost premiums and other charges, especially for upper-income participants.

If the past is a guide, Medicare will continue to be a heavily legislated program, with numerous adjustments made every few years (or more frequently). Politicians will strive to avoid explicit rationing of health services, but they will devise forms of implicit rationing that dampen the use of various services, and they will impose higher charges on some Medicare recipients. Arguably, however, these adjustments will not suffice to avert more fundamental changes in both the provision and financing of health care.

The long-term viability of Social Security and Medicare will depend not only on policy adjustments but also on the performance of the economy over the next 30 years and beyond. A robust economy may make these programs sustainable over an extended period; a weak economy will make it difficult for the government to meet these expenses even if it were to trim Social Security and Medicare benefits. The effect of the economy can be quite dramatic, as shown by projections forecasting the depletion of Social Security trust funds (see figure 11-3). In 1999 the Social Security trustees estimated that Social Security would be able to make payments until 2034, while Medicare would run out of money in 2015. By 2006 the projected viability of Social Security was extended by six years, while three years were added to the estimated life of Medicare. The revised projections for Social Security were due to the economy's strong performance, and the Medicare revisions were attributable to both general economic conditions and a projected slowdown in inflation in the health care sector.

Even a seemingly small variation in economic conditions can make a substantial difference in the future affordability of Social Security and Medicare. For example, if the economy were to grow 2.7 percent a year between 2006 and 2036, GDP would grow (in 2006 dollars) from $14 trillion to approximately $31 trillion. But if growth were slightly higher, 3.0 percent a year, GDP would be about $34 trillion. This additional money would greatly ease the burden of financing Social Security and Medicare payments.

Although many factors go into determining economic performance, it is highly probable that the economy will be markedly larger in 2035 if the federal government runs a budget surplus by saving the money built up in the Social Security trust fund. These surpluses would provide a pool of money for investments and over time lead to a more productive workforce and a bigger economy.

Looking 30 to 50 years ahead, one can envision successful self-correction in Social Security and Medicare. Government will spend much less on these programs than it would under current law but much more (as a share of GDP and of budget outlays) than it now does. To repeat what was said earlier: it is inevitable that when the elderly are a higher proportion of the population, government will spend correspondingly more on them. Any other outcome would be politically untenable.

LENGTHENING THE TIME HORIZON OF BUDGETING

Because it is an annual process, budgeting inevitably truncates the time perspectives of decisionmakers. It induces politicians to look for short-term fixes that enable them to muddle through from one year to the next while ignoring the long-term implications of government commitments and citizen expectations. In the annual format, what matters most is getting the decisions made, even if this means deferring hard choices to another day. There are means, of course, for taking a longer view, but these generally are outside the time frame of budgeting. In fact, this is the rationale for the annual report issued by the trustees of the Social Security and Medicare trust funds. It looks ahead 75 years to estimate the actuarial deficit in these funds under different economic and demographic assumptions.

Although the president and Congress deal with the budget each year, both have taken steps to inject a longer-term focus into the annual debate over revenue and spending policies. CBO's baseline budget projections have a 10-year horizon, and congressional budget resolutions, which must cover at least 5 fiscal years, sometimes cover the same 10-year period as the CBO projections. Moreover, several Senate rules require legislative action to consider the longer term: (1) the PAYGO rule requires that revenue and direct spending legislation be deficit neutral within three different time frames covering 10 years; (2) the Byrd rule bars reconciliation legislation that would cause or increase a deficit beyond the time frame of the reconciliation instructions; and (3) a limitation on long-term spending proposals prohibits the consideration of legislation that would increase direct spending by more than $5 billion in any of 4 consecutive 10-year periods extending through fiscal year 2055. Furthermore, in order to enforce budget rules, pending and enacted legislation is scored by CBO and the Joint Committee on Taxation against 10-year budget baselines and other time periods, as appropriate.

During the Clinton presidency, OMB extended the time horizon of its budget estimates to 10 years, but the Bush administration has shortened it to 5 years, claiming that the future is too uncertain to produce reliable estimates. Some have argued, however, that the true motive is to veil the long-term implications of tax cuts and spending increases. But OMB does publish both a balance sheet of federal assets and liabilities and a long-run outlook in the "Stewardship" chapter of the *Analytical Perspectives* volume of the president's budget. These presentations take a hard look at the government's financial condition and obligations; they are not intended to cast the administration's budget policies in a favorable light. The balance sheet estimates that the federal government's net liabilities escalated from $16.6 trillion when George W. Bush became president in 2001 to $20.6 trillion in 2006. Because of accounting rules, this estimate does not include the present value of future Social Security and Medicare liabilities. OMB provides a fuller picture of the government's dismal fiscal future through projections that estimate debt held by the public soaring from 35 percent of GDP in 2000 to as much as 260 percent in 2080. Although it cautions that the long-run budget outlook is highly uncertain, OMB unequivocally asserts that "the budget is on an unsustainable path."

OMB does argue that future liabilities would be lower if Congress were to adopt the spending cutbacks proposed by the president. Overall, however, the outlook is adverse, even if adjustments were made in Medicare and some other entitlements.

From time to time, CBO has produced long-term budget projections through 2050. The projections show six different possible scenarios, ranging from low revenue and high expenditure growth, to high revenue and low expenditure growth. The main purpose of the CBO report is to demonstrate that the government's fiscal future is heavily dependent on policy choices. Under all scenarios, the government faces growing deficits, but there are enormous variances between the most and least favorable scenarios.

Building Sustainability Analyses Into the Budget

The United States lags behind some advanced countries in incorporating long-run analyses into ongoing budget work. Australia produces an intergenerational report every five years, while the United Kingdom publishes long-term projections each year. The European Commission assesses the long-term fiscal implications of the budget policies of member countries, emphasizing year-to-year improvement or deterioration. The methodologies of these and other studies vary. Some estimate the gap between the present value of future spending obligations and the yield from the existing tax system, or estimate the amount of tax increase that would be required to close the gap; some construct various scenarios to show the sensitivity of future budget conditions to changes in underlying assumptions.

Sustainability analyses address three related questions about the future financial condition of government:

—*Solvency.* Will government be able to pay future obligations if it continues on its present budget course? The United States is one of the few industrialized countries in which future financial solvency is in question. The threat of insolvency is likely to impel significant changes in revenue and spending policy long before the federal government defaults on its obligations.

—*Stability.* Can the government stay on its budget course for an extended period? In particular, will government have to increase the tax burden in order to finance its obligations? Some national governments have taken significant steps to stabilize budget policy by funding pension liabilities as they are incurred, not when they are paid out. This typically entails shifting all or a portion of a social security program from a defined benefit plan, which guarantees future payments, to a defined contribution system, which guarantees only the amount paid into the fund, not the level of benefits. The proposed shift to private Social Security accounts would have a similar effect. Stabilizing Medicare expenditures depends on constraining the rise in health costs to correspond with the trend in GDP. As argued earlier, reining in Medicare expenditures cannot be achieved in isolation from far-reaching changes in delivering and financing health care.

—*Fairness.* Will tomorrow's citizens have to bear a higher tax burden or receive lesser benefits than today's? Has government shifted the cost of benefits for today's recipients to future taxpayers? Using a technique known as "intergenerational accounting," economists have concluded that Americans above the age of 70 have very low, or even negative, tax rates, while those in their teens or younger face tax rates above 70 percent. Assuring intergenerational fairness is an explicit element of government budget policy in some countries but not in the United States.

Constraining Future Liabilities

Sustainability analyses provide information on the budget outlook over an extended time horizon. They do not, however, compel political leaders to change budget course, nor do they even compel them to consider the long-run fiscal implications of their actions. In the time-compressed environment of annual budgeting, it usually is more expedient for politicians to broker deals by shifting costs or problems to the future than by exercising self-restraint.

Taking proper account of the future might be abetted by establishing rules that restrict the capacity of politicians to adopt policy changes that would adversely affect the government's long-run fiscal position. One version of such a rule would bar Congress from passing legislation that would cause the net present value of future deficits to increase. This rule would be enforced by constructing a long-term baseline similar to the 10-year projections produced each year by CBO, scoring proposed or enacted legislation against that baseline, and discounting policy changes to present value. This approach would require resolution of some difficult technical issues, including the assumptions to be used, dealing with uncertainty, and selecting the discount rate.

This type of rule would constrain policy initiatives that affect future budgets but would not diminish the long-term burden of existing entitlements. Some have called for government to conduct mandatory reviews of all entitlement programs, possibly through sunset rules that automatically terminate these programs at fixed intervals (such as every 5 or 10 years) unless they are renewed by Congress. There is little reason to expect sunsets to curtail universal benefits, such as Social Security and Medicare. Judging from experience in governments that have adopted sunset procedures, they might facilitate the elimination of some small programs but would not impact the costly entitlements that benefit a broad swath of Americans.

Biennial Budgeting and Appropriations

Although long-term budgeting is not yet within reach, lengthening the budget process to a biennial cycle has been a recurring goal of reformers. Such a cycle would set a two-year minimum for authorizing legislation and provide for the president to submit a full budget every other year. Congress would switch to a biennial schedule for the budget resolution and regular appropriations bills. However, the president and Congress would have the option of making supplemental budget decisions in the off year. Inasmuch as the appropriations process is the main sticking point in biennial proposals, it is the focus of the present discussion.

Advocates in both the executive and legislative branches have advanced a barrage of arguments in favor of a two-year process. Most address the internal operations of Congress or federal agencies and seek to ease congestion of legislative calendars and agency budget schedules. Some view biennial budgeting as a means of liberating the process from the details of expenditure and orienting it to larger policy issues. Freed from the tight deadlines of an annual cycle, the argument runs, agencies would have more time for strategic planning and program review.

Legislative supporters of a biennial budget complain about the amount of time the annual appropriations bills take, their tendency to crowd out other legislative business, and the conflicts generated by the need to settle the same matters every year. They blame the appropriations process for the decline in authorizing activity and view appropriations as a grinding process that is often completed behind schedule long after the fiscal year has started. According to critics, the appropriations committees hold on to the annual time frame because it enables them to earmark money to favored projects.

Congressional reformers envision a two-year schedule in which substantive legislation would be considered the first year and spending bills the second. They believe this arrangement would encourage more active congressional oversight of government agencies and performance, and more attention to long-term issues.

In terms of budget control, the argument for a biennial budget rests on expected changes in the focus of appropriations. A one-year appropriations process inevitably concentrates on year-to-year changes in spending items at the expense of considering the long-term direction of federal programs. A lengthier cycle might be less incremental and more change oriented, less locked onto inputs and details and more focused on outputs and results, less interested in micromanaging agencies and more concerned about strategy and priorities, and less focused on the year immediately ahead and more on long-term fiscal conditions.

Are these expectations realistic? Not if past reforms, such as the planning-programming-budgeting system (PPBS) introduced in the 1960s and zero-based budgeting tried in the 1970s, are a guide. Both reforms sought to break budgeting away from incremental routines and to frame financial decisions more strategically. Neither succeeded, and their failure was most pronounced in the appropriations arena. Reformers counter with the argument that past budget innovations would have retained annual appropriations; the current one would do away with them. Moreover, they insist that the results would be more favorable this time because changes would be made in congressional operations, not just in executive branch budget formulation.

If the federal government were to shift to biennial appropriations, the United States would be among the first to take this step, though not the first to establish a multiyear budget cycle. Many countries have adopted a medium-term expenditure framework, which enables them to make annual budget policy within a multiyear context. Governments in some countries have given agencies discretion to carry over unused operational money from one year to the next, and a few even allow agencies to prespend a small portion of the next year's appropriation. Some have multiyear budgets that specify the operating resources agencies will receive for each of the next several years and the programs they will carry out during that period. Significantly, however, interyear flexibility and multiyear arrangements have not preempted annual appropriations. The lesson from other countries is that it is feasible to lengthen the policy horizon while continuing to make appropriations every year.

In fact, Congress has moved substantially away from annual spending control. For one thing, discretionary appropriations control only one-third of federal spending. For another, a sizable portion of these appropriations are made on a no-year basis, and the funds remain available for obligation indefinitely. Moreover, when it sets discretionary caps, Congress makes multiyear spending decisions.

It seems odd that for much of the budget, the only options are the short leash of annual appropriations or the freedom of permanent entitlements. Biennial appropriations would provide an additional option that would be sensible for many programs, such as capital expenditures and military procurement, that have long planning cycles.

Despite the strong arguments for lengthening the budget process, any changes to this critical process that has operated on an annual basis since the start of American democracy must take into account the broader implications for the political system. Shifting to a biennial cycle would ripple beyond the appropriations process to the operation of Congress and its relationships with executive institutions. Congress would still have the power of the purse, but it would hold the strings more loosely. How loosely would depend on the extent to which two-year appropriations bring about the behavioral changes its advocates expect. The behavioral response would provide answers to a number of questions. Will a biennial cycle enhance or impair the government's capacity for self-correction when changes in political or economic conditions warrant adjustments in budget policy? Will agencies regard the second year of a biennial appropriation as a floor from which to campaign for supplemental funds? Will the president and Congress make such substantial use of supplemental appropriations in the off year that the process would be biennial in name only? What changes have to be made in congressional operations and committee work to assure vigilant oversight of federal programs and agencies? Ideally, biennial budgeting should be viewed as a step toward a longer perspective.

CONCLUSION

Unless it changes course, the federal government will pay a heavy price for ignoring the long-term consequences of budget policy. One need not subscribe to doomsday scenarios to anticipate that tax burdens will be higher and certain benefits lower in the future than they are today. This adverse trend will be driven not only by the changing age structure of the

United States but by neglect, over an extended period, of long-term budget issues. The problem is not a lack of data—the country is awash in projections of future strains on the budget and the gap between expected revenues and expenditures—but a lack of political will.

All democracies have a political incentive to shift costs from today's voters to tomorrow's taxpayers. Some governments are constrained by accounting rules that require them to recognize a portion of future liabilities as current expenses; others have adopted policies that protect their fiscal future against the inevitable surge in the number of elderly citizens eligible for public benefits. The federal government has done relatively little thus far. It, too, will be compelled by demographic changes to address the huge fiscal imbalances that await the country.

By acting later, the government will face a much more arduous task than if it had already faced up to the problem. Although the precise terms are unknown, one may anticipate that improving long-run budget stability will entail a combination of political, policy, and procedural elements. The most important political ingredient will be cooperation (or, at least, consultation) between Democrats and Republicans. Neither party can nor should try to go it alone in restructuring Social Security and Medicare. The policy changes made by government will significantly affect almost all Americans. Neither party can shoulder the political risk alone. It may be appropriate to devise special political arrangements, such as a nonpartisan commission, to recommend policy changes to Congress. This device was used successfully in 1983 when Congress made significant changes in Social Security. It was not the path taken by Bill Clinton when he proposed to restructure health care nor the one taken by George W. Bush when he sought major changes in Social Security. In both cases, unilateral action failed.

The policy changes will almost certainly combine tax increases and spending cuts. But how these are apportioned among various groups of taxpayers and beneficiaries is highly uncertain. Future presidential and congressional elections may significantly influence the magnitude and distribution of the changes that will be made. Regardless of election outcomes, however, upper-income citizens are likely to face higher taxes and lower benefits in the future. Benefits will be means-tested, and tax rates will be boosted on relatively affluent Americans. It remains to be seen whether these changes will undermine political support for major entitlements.

Finally, the federal government will inch toward procedures that impel budget makers to give due regard to the long-run fiscal consequences of their actions. Information on future impacts will be more fully integrated into budgetary practice, and some restrictions will be placed on actions that would adversely affect the long-term fiscal health of the United States. But even strict rules will not put an end to budgetary opportunism, as politicians maneuver to increase benefits and hide costs. Budgeting in the future will still be familiar to those who practiced it in the past.

Federal Budget–Related Internet Sites

OFFICE OF MANAGEMENT AND BUDGET

Internet address: www.whitehouse.gov/OMB

Agencies' communications to Congress

Appropriations reports within seven days of enactment

Circulars, bulletins, press releases, and testimony

Executive budget and supporting documents

Financial management policies

Midsession Review

PAYGO reports and estimates of PAYGO balances

Governmentwide performance plan

Management reform/GPRA

Sequester Update Report

Statements of administration policy (SAPs)

CONGRESSIONAL BUDGET OFFICE

Internet address: www.cbo.gov

Analysis of budgetary topics and the president's budget

Cost estimates, studies and reports, and testimony

Economic and Budget Outlook

Economic and budget projections

Current status of discretionary appropriations

Emergency spending under the Budget Enforcement Act

Monthly budget review

Options for changing and spending revenue

Projected federal tax revenues and the effect of changes in tax law

Unauthorized appropriations and expiring authorizations

LIBRARY OF CONGRESS

Internet address: thomas.loc.gov
Congressional bill summary since 1973
Congressional bill text since 1989
Congressional directory and committee
    membership
Congressional Record since 1989
Committee reports since 1995
House committees' hearings transcripts
Roll call votes since 1990
Public laws since 1973

GOVERNMENT ACCOUNTING OFFICE

Internet address: www.gao.gov
Comptroller general decisions and opinions
Performance and accountability
Policy and guidance material
Reports on federal agencies' rules
Testimony

HOUSE APPROPRIATIONS COMMITTEE

Internet address: www.house.gov/
    appropriations
302(b) allocations
Committee and subcommittee membership
Committee letters to the administration
News releases
Program terminations since fiscal 1996
Schedule of markups and hearings
Status and summary of current
    appropriations bills

HOUSE BUDGET COMMITTEE

Internet address: www.house.gov/budget
Budget resolution
Committee membership
Hearings transcripts
Issue papers
Press releases
Schedule

GOVERNMENT PRINTING OFFICE

Internet address: www.access.gpo.gov
Committee prints since 1997
Committee hearings since 1997
Congressional bills since 1993
Congressional Record since 1994
Congressional reports since 1995
Economic Report of the President since 1995
Executive budget since 1995
Public laws since 1995
United States Code

TREASURY DEPARTMENT

Internet address: www.treas.gov
Annual report
Daily and monthly Treasury statements
Press releases and speeches
Treasury Bulletin

SENATE APPROPRIATIONS COMMITTEE

Internet address: www.senate.gov/
    ~appropriations
302(b) allocations
Committee and subcommittee membership
Hearings, markup, and conference schedule
Press releases
Status and summary of current
    appropriations bills

SENATE BUDGET COMMITTEE

Internet address: www.senate.gov/~budget
Analysis of president's budget
Budget Bulletin
Chairman's mark
Economic Bulletin
Hearings transcripts
Press releases
Schedule

Glossary

ACCRUAL BASIS—the basis of accounting that records revenues when they are earned and expenditures when costs are incurred, regardless of the period in which money is received or payments made.

ACCRUED EXPENDITURES—charges that reflect liabilities incurred for services received, goods or other property received, or amounts becoming owed under programs for which no current service or performance is required. Expenditures accrue regardless of when cash payments are made.

ADVANCE APPROPRIATIONS—budget authority provided in an appropriations act to become available in a fiscal year beyond the one for which the act is enacted. The amount is included in the budget totals for the fiscal year in which the amount will become available for obligation. *Also see* Forward funding.

ADVANCE FUNDING—budget authority that may be obligated or spent during the current fis-

cal year from the next year's appropriation. When obligated in advance, budget authority is increased for the current fiscal year and decreased for the next fiscal year.

ALLOCATION—in executive budgeting, allocations are budget authorities or other resources transferred to another account to carry out the purposes of the parent account. For use in congressional budgeting, *see* Committee allocation.

ALLOTMENT—a distribution by an agency to officials or administrative units authorizing them to incur obligations within a specified amount and period. The total amount allotted by an agency cannot exceed the amount apportioned by the Office of Management and Budget.

ALLOWANCE LETTER—a letter sent to each agency by the Office of Management and Budget after the president's budget has been submitted to Congress. The letter advises the agency of budget decisions and multiyear planning estimates, employment ceilings, and other significant policy and administrative matters.

ALLOWANCES—amounts included in the budget to cover possible additional expenditures for statutory pay increases, contingencies, and other requirements.

ANNUAL AUTHORIZATION—an authorization of appropriations for a single fiscal year, usually for a definite amount of money. Ongoing programs with annual authorizations are supposed to be reauthorized each year. If they are not reauthorized, Congress often enables them to continue by appropriating money for them.

APPORTIONMENT—a distribution made by the Office of Management and Budget of amounts available for obligation. Apportionments divide these amounts by periods (usually quarters) or projects. The apportionment limits the amount that may be obligated. When an account is apportioned, some resources may be reserved pursuant to the Antideficiency Act or may be proposed for rescission pursuant to the Impoundment Control Act.

APPROPRIATED ENTITLEMENT—an entitlement whose budget authority is provided in annual appropriations acts instead of in substantive law. These entitlements are classified as direct spending by the Budget Enforcement Act.

APPROPRIATION—a provision of law providing budget authority that enables an agency to incur obligations and to make payments out of the Treasury for specified purposes. Appropriations are the most common means of providing budget authority. Annual appropriations are provided in appropriations acts; most permanent appropriations are enacted in substantive law.

APPROPRIATION LIMITATION—a provision in an appropriations act that limits the amount that may be obligated or spent for specified purposes. The limitation may be applied to direct loan obligations, guaranteed loan commitments, administrative expenses financed out of trust funds, or other purposes.

APPROPRIATIONS ACT—a law making annual appropriations. The law may be a regular, supplemental, or continuing appropriation.

AUTHORIZATION ACT—a law that establishes or continues one or more federal programs or agencies, establishes the terms and conditions under which they operate, sets other policy requirements or restrictions, authorizes the enactment of appropriations, and specifies how apportioned funds are to be used.

BACKDOOR SPENDING—*see* Direct Spending and Spending Authority.

BALANCED BUDGET—a budget in which receipts equal or exceed outlays.

BALANCES OF BUDGET AUTHORITY—budget authority provided in previous years that has not been spent. Obligated balances are amounts that have not been liquidated; unobligated balances are amounts that remain available for obligation.

BASELINE—a projection of revenues, expenditures, and other budget amounts under assumed economic conditions and participation rates, and assuming no change in current policy. The baseline is usually projected annually by the Congressional Budget Office for each of the next 10 (or fewer) years. It is used in preparing the congressional budget resolution, scoring the budgetary impact of legislation under pay-as-you-go rules, and estimating the budgetary impact of provisions in reconciliation bills.

BIENNIAL BUDGET—a budget for a period of two years. The federal government has an annual budget, but proposals have been made that it adopt a biennial budget.

BORROWING AUTHORITY—a type of spending authority that permits a federal agency to incur obligations and to make payments for specified purposes out of funds borrowed from the Treasury or the public. Except for trust funds and certain other entities, borrowing authority is effective only to the extent provided in appropriations acts.

BUDGET AMENDMENT—a revision to a pending budget request submitted by the president before Congress has completed action on the original request.

BUDGET RESOURCES—the amounts available (regardless of source) for obligation in a fund or account. These resources include new budget authority, recoveries or restoration of budget authority provided in previous years, transfers from other accounts, fees and other collections deposited in the account, and unobligated balances.

BUDGET AUTHORITY—authority provided by law to enter into obligations that normally result in outlays. The main forms of budget authority are appropriations, borrowing authority, and contract authority. Budget authority also includes the subsidy cost of direct and guaranteed loans but not the unsubsidized portion. Budget authority may be classified by the period of availability (one year, multiyear, or no year), by the timing of congressional action (current or permanent), or by the specificity of the amount available (definite or indefinite).

BUDGET ENFORCEMENT ACT OF 1990—an act of Congress that established limits on discretionary spending and pay-as-you-go rules for revenue and direct spending.

BUDGET RESOLUTION—a concurrent resolution passed by both houses of Congress that presents the congressional budget for each of the succeeding 10 (or fewer) fiscal years. The budget resolution sets forth budget totals and functional allocations and may include reconciliation instructions to designated House or Senate committees. *Also see* Reconciliation instruction.

BUDGET SURPLUS OR DEFICIT—the arithmetic difference between budget receipts and outlays. The deficit is the excess of outlays over receipts; the surplus is the excess of receipts over outlays.

BUDGETARY RESERVES—funds withheld from apportionment by the Office of Management and Budget, as authorized by the Antideficiency Act. Unless expressly authorized by other laws, such reserves may be set aside only because of savings due to changes in requirements or efficiency of operations. Reserves are reported to Congress, as required by the Impoundment Control Act.

BUSINESS-TYPE STATEMENTS—financial statements (published in the budget) for government corporations, certain revolving funds, and government-sponsored enterprises. These statements differ from budget schedules in that they principally focus on assets and liabilities rather than on budgetary resources.

CAPITAL BUDGET—a budget that segregates capital investments from operating expenditures. Investment in capital assets is excluded from calculation of the surplus or deficit, but the operating budget is charged for depreciation and/or debt service. The federal government does not have a capital budget, but investment expenditures are shown in supplementary budget schedules.

CASH BASIS—the accounting method in which revenues are recorded when received and expenditures are recorded when paid, without regard to the accounting period in which the revenues were earned or the costs incurred.

CHIEF FINANCIAL OFFICER—an official appointed pursuant to the Chief Financial Officers Act of 1990 to oversee financial management activities relating to the programs and operations of an agency, develop and maintain an integrated accounting and financial management system, and monitor the financial execution of the agency's budget.

CLOSED ACCOUNT—an account whose balance is canceled and is no longer available for obligation or expenditure. An account (such as a one-year appropriation) that is available for obligation for a limited period is closed five years after obligations may no longer be drawn against it. *Also see* Expired account.

COMMITTEE ALLOCATION—the distribution, pursuant to section 302 of the Congressional Budget Act, of new budget authority, entitlement authority, and outlays to House and Senate committees. The allocation, which may not exceed the relevant amounts in the budget resolution, usually is made in the joint explanatory statement that accompanies the conference report on the budget resolution.

COMPARATIVE STATEMENT OF NEW BUDGET AUTHORITY—a table, in the report of the House or Senate appropriations committee on an appropriations bill, that compares the amount recommended for each account with the amount appropriated for the previous fiscal year and the amount requested by the president.

CONCURRENT RESOLUTION ON THE BUDGET—*see* Budget Resolution.

CONSTANT DOLLARS—the dollar value of goods and services, adjusted for changes in prices. Constant dollar series are used to compute the inflation-adjusted level of budget receipts and outlays.

CONTINGENT LIABILITY—a conditional obligation that may become an actual liability if certain events occur or fail to occur. Contingent liabilities include loan guarantees, bank deposit insurance, and price guarantees.

CONTINUING RESOLUTION (CONTINUING APPROPRIATION)—a joint resolution that provides budget authority for programs or agencies whose regular appropriation was not enacted by the start of the fiscal year. A continuing resolution is usually a temporary measure that expires at a specified date or is superseded by enactment of the regular appropriations act. Some continuing resolutions, however, are in effect for the entire fiscal year and serve as the means of enacting regular appropriations.

CONTRACT AUTHORITY—legislation that permits obligations to be incurred in advance of appropriations. With certain exceptions, contract authority is effective only to the extent provided in appropriations acts. When contract authority is provided, Congress appropriates funds to pay off obligations incurred pursuant to it.

COST-BASED BUDGET—a budget whose expenditures are based on the goods and services consumed rather than on the amounts obligated or outlayed.

COST ESTIMATE—an estimate prepared by the Congressional Budget Office of the outlays that would ensue from reported legislation over a five-year period. The cost estimate, which is required by the Congressional Budget Act, is usually published in the report accompanying the legislation.

CREDIT PROGRAM ACCOUNT—the budget account into which an appropriation is made to cover the subsidy cost and/or administrative expenses of a direct or guaranteed loan. The appropriated funds are then disbursed to a financing account.

CREDIT SUBSIDY COST—the estimated cost, over the duration of a direct or guaranteed loan and calculated on the basis of the net present value, of the projected cash flows of the loan or guarantee, excluding administrative expenses. For direct loans, the subsidy cost is the net present value of the following cash flows: disbursements, payments of interest and principal, recoveries, fees, and other payments. For loan guarantees, the subsidy cost is the net present value of government payments for defaults, interest subsidies, and other payments less the estimated payments to the government for fees, other charges, and recoveries.

CURRENT DOLLARS—the dollar value of a good or service in terms of prices paid at the time the good or service is sold. *Also see* Constant Dollars.

CURRENT LEVEL—classification used by the House Budget Committee in making section 302 allocations to committees. It refers to new budget authority and outlays resulting from existing law, in contrast to discretionary action—the new budget authority and outlays resulting from new legislation.

CURRENT SERVICE ESTIMATE—estimates in the president's budget of the levels of budget authority and outlays that would be required in the next and subsequent fiscal years to continue existing services. These estimates reflect the projected cost of continuing federal programs if there are no policy changes. *Also see* Baseline.

DEFERRAL—an action or inaction that temporarily withholds, delays, or precludes the obligation or expenditure of budget authority. Deferrals may be made only for the purposes authorized by the Antideficiency Act (or another law), not for policy reasons.

DEFICIENCY APPORTIONMENT—an apportionment (by the Office of Management and Budget) of available budgetary resources in an amount that may compel the enactment of supplemental budget authority. Such apportionments may be made only under the conditions allowed by the Antideficiency Act.

DIRECT LOAN—a disbursement of funds (not in exchange for goods or services) that is contracted to be repaid. An appropriation is made to cover the subsidy cost and administrative expenses of each direct loan program.

DIRECT SPENDING—budget authority and ensuing outlays provided in laws other than appropriations acts, including annually appropriated entitlements. Direct spending is distinguished by the Budget Enforcement Act from discretionary spending and is subject to pay-as-you-go rules.

DISCRETIONARY SPENDING—budget authority, other than appropriated entitlements, and ensuing outlays provided in annual appropriations acts. The Budget Enforcement Act limits discretionary budget authority and outlays.

DISCRETIONARY SPENDING LIMITS—ceilings set by the Budget Enforcement Act on budget authority and outlays for discretionary programs. Appropriations causing budget authority or outlays to exceed the limit may compel a sequestration.

EARMARKING—earmarked revenues are dedicated by law to a specific purpose or program. The revenues include trust funds, special funds, and offsetting collections credited to appropriations accounts. Earmarked expenditures are dedicated by an appropriations act or the accompanying committee report to a particular project or activity.

EMERGENCY SPENDING—an appropriation that the president and Congress have designated as an emergency. Under BEA, an emergency appropriation causes an increase in the relevant discretionary spending limits to accommodate the additional spending.

ENTITLEMENT AUTHORITY—a provision of law that obligates the federal government to make payments to eligible recipients. Entitlement authority may be funded in either an annual or permanent appropriation.

EXPIRED ACCOUNT—an appropriation or fund account whose balances are no longer available for incurring new obligations because the time available for incurring such obligations has expired. Outlays may be made from expired accounts to liquidate previously made obligations. *Also see* Closed Account.

FEDERAL DEBT—the total amount of Treasury debt and agency debt, consisting of debt held by the public and debt held by trust or special funds.

FEDERAL FUNDS—all monies collected and spent by the federal government, other than those designated as trust funds. Federal funds include general, special, public enterprise, and intergovernmental funds.

FINANCIAL STATEMENTS—statements reporting on the financial condition of agencies or other federal entities, including statements of financial condition, results of operations, cash flows, and a reconciliation to the budget.

FINANCING ACCOUNT—an account established pursuant to the Federal Credit Reform Act of 1990 that receives disbursements from a credit program account and handles all other cash flows to or from the government resulting from direct or guaranteed loans. Financing accounts are not included in the budget totals.

FISCAL POLICY—federal policies concerning revenues, spending, and the deficit intended to promote the nation's macroeconomic goals with respect to employment, output, prices, and the balance of payments.

FISCAL YEAR—the accounting period for the budget. The fiscal year for the federal government begins on October 1 and ends the next September 30. The fiscal year is designated by the calendar year in which it ends; for example, fiscal year 2000 began October 1, 1999, and ended September 30, 2000.

FIXED ACCOUNT—an account whose funds are available for a definite period, in contrast

to accounts that have no-year funds. Unobligated balances in fixed accounts expire (are no longer available for obligation) at the end of the period for which they are available.

FORWARD FUNDING—budget authority that becomes available for obligation during one fiscal year and continues to be available through the next fiscal year. The budget authority is counted in the fiscal year for which the appropriation is made.

FULL FUNDING—the provision of budget authority to finance the full estimated cost of a project or activity, such as ship construction, that will be completed in subsequent years. Full funding also refers to the appropriation of the full amount authorized in authorizing legislation.

FUNCTION OR FUNCTIONAL CLASSIFICATION—a classification of budgetary resources in terms of the principal purposes they serve. A function may be divided into two or more subfunctions. The last three digits of an account's identification code represent the subfunction into which the account has been classified.

GOVERNMENT-SPONSORED ENTERPRISE—an enterprise established by the federal government but privately owned and operated. These enterprises are excluded from the budget totals because they are private entities. However, financial information concerning them is included in the budget.

GRAMM-RUDMAN-HOLLINGS PROCESS—the process established by the Balanced Budget and Emergency Deficit Control Act of 1985 (commonly known as the Gramm-Rudman-Hollings Act), which included fixed deficit targets and the sequestration of budgetary resources if the projected deficit was greater than the target. The Budget Enforcement Act of 1990 superseded these procedures.

GROSS DOMESTIC PRODUCT (GDP)—the market value of all final goods and services produced within the borders of a country in a given period. GDP can be expressed in current or constant dollars.

IDENTIFICATION CODE—the eleven-digit code assigned to each appropriation or fund account that identifies the agency, account, timing of the transmittal to Congress, type of fund, and account's functional classification.

IMPOUNDMENT—an action or inaction by a government officer or employee that precludes or delays the obligation or expenditure of budget authority. *Also see* Deferral, Rescission.

INTERNAL CONTROL—the systems and practices of an agency to safeguard its assets, ensure the accuracy and reliability of accounts, and foster compliance with prescribed financial management policies. Sometimes referred to as management control.

JUSTIFICATION MATERIAL—the documents and schedules submitted by an agency to the appropriations committees in support of its budget request. The material typically explains changes between the current appropriation and the amounts requested for the next fiscal year.

LINE-ITEM VETO—the power of the president to veto part of a bill passed by Congress. The Line Item Veto Act of 1996 authorized the president to cancel parts of legislation containing discretionary budget authority, new direct spending, or limited tax benefits. This act was ruled unconstitutional by the Supreme Court in 1998. At present, therefore, the president must veto or sign the entire measure.

LIQUIDATING ACCOUNT—an account (established pursuant to the Federal Credit Reform Act) to handle all cash flows resulting from direct or guaranteed loans made before fiscal 1992.

LIQUIDATING APPROPRIATION—an appropriation to pay obligations incurred pursuant to substantive legislation, usually contract authority. A liquidating appropriation is not recorded as budget authority.

LOAN GUARANTEE—a commitment by the federal government to pay part or all of the loan principal or interest to the lender in the event of default by the borrower. The subsidy cost of new loan guarantees is included in the computation of budget authority and outlays.

MANAGEMENT FUND—an account authorized by law to receive budgetary resources from two or more appropriations to carry out a common purpose or activity not involving a continuing cycle of operations.

MEANS OF FINANCING—certain financial flows to the federal government that are not included in budget receipts or outlays. These include funds borrowed from the public, seigniorage, and credit-financing accounts.

MIDSESSION REVIEW OF THE BUDGET—an updated summary of the president's budget containing revised estimates of revenues, budget authority, and outlays, as well as other information. The midsession review is supposed to be issued by July 15.

MONTHLY TREASURY STATEMENT—a summary statement issued each month by the Treasury presenting data on receipts, outlays, and the surplus or deficit for the latest completed month and for the fiscal year to date, with comparisons to the same period in the previous year.

MULTIYEAR APPROPRIATION—budget authority provided in an appropriations act for a period in excess of one fiscal year. Multiyear appropriations may cover periods that do not coincide with the start or end of a fiscal year.

MULTIYEAR AUTHORIZATION—an authorization of appropriations for a period in excess of one fiscal year. Programs with multiyear authorizations must be reauthorized periodically.

NATIONAL INCOME AND PRODUCT ACCOUNTS— quarterly and annual accounts providing data on aggregate economic activity. Federal revenues and outlays in these accounts differ in some details from those reported in the budget.

NO-YEAR APPROPRIATION— budget authority provided in an appropriations act that remains available for obligation for an indefinite period. These funds do not lapse if they are not obligated by the end of the fiscal year.

OBJECT CLASSIFICATION— a classification identifying expenditures by the goods or services purchased (such as personnel, supplies, and equipment). An object classification schedule is included in the budget for each appropriation account.

OBLIGATED BALANCE— the amount of obligations incurred for which payment has not yet been made. This balance usually is carried forward until the obligations are paid.

OBLIGATION— binding agreement (such as a contract awarded, service received, or similar transaction) that will require payment.

OFF-BUDGET— budget authority, outlays, or receipts of federal entities that are excluded by law from the budget. These entities currently include the Social Security trust funds and the Postal Service.

OFFSETTING COLLECTIONS— receipts from the public that result from business-type activities and collections from other government accounts. These collections are not counted as receipts but are netted against budget authority and outlays.

ONE-YEAR APPROPRIATION— budget authority provided in an appropriations act that is available for obligation only during a single fiscal year, usually the fiscal year specified in the enacting clause of the appropriations act.

OUTLAYS— payments made (usually through the issuance of checks, disbursement of cash, or electronic transfer) to liquidate obligations. Outlays during a fiscal year may be for payment of obligations incurred in previous years or in the same year.

PAYGO (pay-as-you-go)— the procedure established by the Budget Enforcement Act to ensure that direct spending and revenue legislation does not cause an increase in the deficit or reduce the surplus. PAYGO requires that an increase in the deficit or reduction in the surplus due to new legislation be offset by other legislation or sequestration.

PERFORMANCE BUDGETING— a form of budgeting that relates resources provided in the budget to measurable results.

PERFORMANCE PLANS— annual plans, prescribed by the Government Performance and Results Act of 1993, to inform Congress and the public of each agency's major programs and activities, the measures used to gauge performance, the strategies and resources required to achieve goals, and the procedures used to verify performance information.

PERMANENT APPROPRIATION— budget authority that becomes available without any current action by Congress. Budget authority is deemed to be permanent if it derives from legislation enacted in previous sessions of Congress.

PROGRAM ACCOUNT— *See* Credit Program Account.

PROGRAM AND FINANCING SCHEDULE— a schedule published in the president's budget that presents data on each account. The schedule consists of several sections that provide data on obligations (by program), gross budgetary resources, new budget authority, outlays, and offsets.

PROGRAM, PROJECT, OR ACTIVITY (PPA)— an element within a budget account. For annually appropriated accounts, PPAs are defined by appropriations acts or accompanying reports. For accounts not funded by annual appropriations, PPAs are defined by the program listing in program and financing schedules.

PUBLIC DEBT—funds borrowed by the Treasury from the public or from a fund or account. The public debt, which is subject to a statutory limit, does not include agency debt (funds borrowed by other federal agencies).

PUBLIC ENTERPRISE FUND—a revolving account for business-type activities that is financed by offsetting collections credited to the account.

REAPPROPRIATION—congressional action that continues the availability of all or part of the unobligated portion of budget authority that has expired or would otherwise expire. Reappropriations are counted as new budget authority in the fiscal year for which the availability is extended.

RECEIPTS (or BUDGET RECEIPTS)—collections from the public, including tax receipts and social insurance premiums. Budget receipts do not include various offsetting collections, which are accounted for as negative outlays.

RECONCILIATION BILL—a bill containing changes in law recommended by House or Senate committees pursuant to reconciliation instructions in a budget resolution.

RECONCILIATION INSTRUCTION—a provision in a budget resolution directing one or more House or Senate committees to recommend legislation changing existing law to bring spending, revenues, or the debt limit into conformity with the budget resolution. The instructions specify the committees to which they are directed, the dollar changes to be achieved, and usually a deadline by which the legislation is to be reported.

RECONCILIATION PROCESS—procedures established in the Congressional Budget Act by which Congress changes existing laws to conform revenues and spending to the levels set in a budget resolution.

REPROGRAMMING—the shift of funds from one purpose to another within the same appropriations account. Reprogramming often entails formal notification and the opportunity for congressional committees to disapprove the shift.

RESCISSION—the cancellation of budget authority previously provided by Congress. The Impoundment Control Act prescribes procedures for presidential notification and congressional action on rescission proposals.

RESCISSION BILL—a bill reported pursuant to a president's rescission message that cancels budget authority previously provided by Congress.

RESERVES—*See* Budgetary Reserves.

REVOLVING FUND—an account or fund in which the income derived from its operations is available to finance the fund's continuing operations without fiscal year limitations.

SCOREKEEPING—procedures for tracking and reporting on the status of congressional budget actions affecting receipts, budget authority, outlays, the surplus or deficit, and the public debt.

SCORING—procedures and rules for measuring the budget impact of legislation for purposes of the Budget Enforcement Act. The Office of Management and Budget is responsible for scoring enacted legislation to determine whether a sequester is required.

SECTION 302—*See* Committee Allocation.

SEQUESTER—the cancellation of budgetary resources pursuant to the Budget Enforcement Act, in response to a violation of the discretionary spending limits or the pay-as-you-go rules.

SPECIAL FUND—funds earmarked by law for special purposes. There sometimes is little practical difference between a special fund and a trust fund, but special funds are classified as federal funds.

SPENDING AUTHORITY—the term designated by the Congressional Budget Act for borrowing authority, contract authority, entitlement authority, and authority to forgo offsetting collections (the borrowing authority for which is not provided in advance by appropriations acts). *Also see* Direct Spending.

SPENDOUT RATE—the rate at which new budget authority provided by Congress is spent by federal agencies, hence the rate at which outlays occur. Sometimes referred to as the outlay rate.

STATUTORY DEBT LIMIT—the maximum amount, established by law, of public debt that may be outstanding. The limit covers virtually all debt issued by the federal government, including borrowing from trust funds, but excludes some debt incurred by agencies.

STRATEGIC PLANS—multiyear plans required by the Government Performance and Results Act, containing a mission statement, general goals and objectives, strategies for achieving the goals, the relationship between the strategic goals and annual performance goals, key external factors, and program evaluations.

SUBSIDY COST—*See* Credit Subsidy Cost.

SUPPLEMENTAL APPROPRIATION—an act appropriating funds in addition to those provided in an annual or continuing appropriations act.

TAX EXPENDITURE—revenue losses attributable to provisions of federal law that allow a special exclusion or deduction from income, or that provide a special credit, preferential tax rate, or deferral of tax liability.

Tax expenditures entail no payment from the government. Rather, the Treasury forgoes some of the revenue it would otherwise have collected, and affected taxpayers pay lower taxes than they otherwise would have had to pay.

TRANSFER—the shift of budgetary resources from one appropriations account or fund to another—in contrast to reprogramming, which shifts resources within the same account. Funds may be transferred only as authorized by law.

TRANSFER PAYMENTS—payments the government makes to individuals for which no current or future goods or services are provided in return. These payments include Social Security, unemployment insurance, veterans' benefits, and various welfare payments.

TRUST FUNDS—accounts designated by law as trust funds for receipts and expenditures earmarked for specified purposes.

UNDISTRIBUTED OFFSETTING RECEIPTS—receipts that are recorded as offsets against total spending rather than against particular accounts or functions. These include income from the sale of major assets and from offshore oil leases.

UNIFIED BUDGET—a comprehensive budget that includes all receipts and outlays from federal funds and trust funds. Off-budget entities (the Postal Service and Social Security) are excluded from the unified budget, but data relating to them are presented in the budget.

UNOBLIGATED BALANCE—the portion of budget authority that has not been obligated. Unobligated balances are carried forward until the period for which they are available ends.

USER FEES—fees charged to users for goods or services provided by the government. In levying or authorizing these fees, Congress determines whether the revenue should revert to the Treasury or should be available to the agency providing the goods or services.

VIEWS AND ESTIMATES—a report issued each year within six weeks after submission of the president's budget by each House or Senate committee with jurisdiction over federal programs. Each views and estimates report contains committees' comments or recommendations on budgetary matters in their jurisdictions.

WORKING FUND ACCOUNTS—funds established to receive advance payments from other agencies or accounts. Consolidated working funds do not finance the work directly; they reimburse the appropriation or fund account that finances the work performed.

Index

Breinigsville, PA USA
14 December 2010
251188BV00008B/1/P